Revolutionary Emotions in Cold War Egypt

History of Emotions

Series Editors:
Peter N. Stearns, University Professor in the Department of History at George Mason University, USA and Susan J. Matt, Presidential Distinguished Professor of History at Weber State University, USA.

Editorial Board:
Rob Boddice, Senior Research Fellow, Academy of Finland Centre of Excellence in the History of Experiences, Tampere University, Finland
Charles Zika, University of Melbourne & Chief Investigator for the Australian Research Council's Centre for the History of Emotions, Australia
Pia Campeggiani, University of Bologna, Italy
Angelika Messner, Kiel University, Germany
Javier Moscoso, Centro de Ciencias Humanas y Sociales, Madrid, Spain

The History of Emotions offers a new and vital approach to the study of the past. The field is predicated on the idea that human feelings change over time and they are the product of culture as well as of biology. Bloomsbury's History of Emotions series seeks to publish state-of-the-art scholarship on the history of human feelings and emotional experience from antiquity to the present day, and across all seven continents. With a commitment to a greater thematic, geographical and chronological breadth, and a deep commitment to interdisciplinary approaches, it will offer new and innovative titles which convey the rich diversity of emotional cultures.

Published:

Fear in the German Speaking World, 1600–2000, edited by Thomas Kehoe and Michael Pickering
Feelings and Work in Modern History, edited by Agnes Arnold-Forster and Alison Moulds
Feeling Dis-Ease in Modern History, edited by Rob Boddice and Bettina Hitzer
Emotional Histories in the Fight to End Prostitution, by Michele Renee Greer
Emotions and Migration in Argentina at the Turn of the 20th Century, by María Bjerg
Emotions in the Ottoman Empire, by Nil Tekgül
The Business of Emotion in Modern History, edited by Andrew Popp and Mandy Cooper
The Renaissance of Feeling, by Kirk Essary

Forthcoming:

Emotions and the Letter, edited by Katie Barclay and Diana G. Barnes
The Fear of Robachicos in Mexico, by Susana Sosenki

Revolutionary Emotions in Cold War Egypt

Islam, Communism, and Anti-Colonial Protest

Christiane-Marie Abu Sarah

BLOOMSBURY ACADEMIC
LONDON • NEW YORK • OXFORD • NEW DELHI • SYDNEY

BLOOMSBURY ACADEMIC
Bloomsbury Publishing Plc, 50 Bedford Square, London, WC1B 3DP, UK
Bloomsbury Publishing Inc, 1359 Broadway, New York, NY 10018, USA
Bloomsbury Publishing Ireland, 29 Earlsfort Terrace, Dublin 2, D02 AY28, Ireland

BLOOMSBURY, BLOOMSBURY ACADEMIC and the Diana logo
are trademarks of Bloomsbury Publishing Plc

First published in Great Britain 2024
This paperback edition published in 2025

A catalogue record for this book is available from the British Library.

A catalog record for this book is available from the Library of Congress.

ISBN: HB: 978-1-3503-8376-0
PB: 978-1-3503-8379-1
ePDF: 978-1-3503-8377-7
eBook: 978-1-3503-8378-4

Series: History of Emotions

Typeset by Integra Software Services Pvt. Ltd.

For product safety related questions contact productsafety@bloomsbury.com.

To find out more about our authors and books visit www.bloomsbury.com
and sign up for our newsletters.

Contents

List of Figures vi
Acknowledgments vii
Note on Translation and Transliteration ix

1 Over-Emotional Students?: Reconceptualizing "Arab Emotions" in Cold War Egypt 1
2 Virtue and Vice in Twentieth-Century Egypt: Emotions and the Moral Marketplace 17
3 The Ballad of King Faruq: Egyptian Experiences of the Second World War 31
4 The Muslim Brotherhood and Young Egypt on Trial: Conversion, Competition, and Compromise 45
5 "Allahu Akhbar, Long Live the Workers!": Communist Clubs and the Islam Question 75
6 "Shaykh in a Dance Club!" and Other Shocking Tales 95
7 Paul Revere's Ride through the Suez Canal: The 1951 Revolution 117
8 "Those Who Jest in a Time of Gravity": Emotional Appeals and the Cairo Fire 139
9 Conclusion: Emotions and Protest in the Cold War Middle East 159

Notes 175
Bibliography 226
Index 248

Figures

2.1	Ridicule as a Type of "Moral Talk"	18
2.2	Enrollment in Egyptian Higher Education, 1930–52	21
2.3	Using Hand Gestures, Facial Expressions, and Vocalizations to Express Value Judgments in Egypt	25
2.4	The Arabophone Moral Imaginary: Terms of Negative Valuation	27
4.1	Making Men in Muslim Brotherhood Newspapers	58
4.2	The Egyptian Anti-colonial Demonstrations of Spring 1946	65
4.3	Jeep Case Defendants Following the Verdict	71
5.1	Egyptian Communist Clubs, 1939–51	78
5.2	The Egyptian Marxist Myth and the Revolutionary Script	82
5.3	Communist Pasha	88
6.1	Moral Metaphors in Egypt: The Wolf in Pasha's Clothing	103
6.2	Considerations for Analyzing Morality Tales	113
7.1	Egyptians Celebrate the Treaty Abrogation	121
7.2	"Red Dinshaway" Takes the Stage	130
7.3	The Asinine English	133
7.4	Muslims and Christians Send a Message about Religious Unity	135
8.1	"Operation Flatten" or the Construction of Pegasus Avenue	143
8.2	The Razing of Kafr ʿAbduh	144
8.3	Commando Training on Campus	145
8.4	The Cairo Fire of 26 January 1952	151
9.1	Egyptian Perspectives of the Cold War	172

Acknowledgments

Writing a book incurs countless debts which can never be fully repaid. Nevertheless, I count it my privilege to be indebted to the following individuals.

At the University of Maryland, I remain grateful to Peter Wien, who with wisdom and patience guided the project when it was still inchoate and helped draw form out of chaos. With abiding appreciation I also recognize the work of Antoine Borrut, whose skill in source critique spurred the climb to higher levels of academic rigor—but whose mentorship and scholarly *joie de vivre* brought the insurmountable down to the horizon. Piotr Kosicki, Richard Price, and Madeleine Zilfi each deserve credit as well for drawing attention to global connections.

Were it not for the scholarship of Peter Stearns, the inkling to explore Arab emotions would never have crossed my desk. Thank you for your years of counsel and instruction while I was at George Mason University. Cemil Aydin also deserves high recognition for his early research guidance and formative conversations on Islamism and identity. In addition, I am grateful to Elizabeth Thompson, Mona Russell, Jamie Whidden, and Mustafa Aksakal for their comments and feedback on the later chapters of this manuscript. Other contributors are too many to list, but include the scholars at George Mason University's Center for Global Islamic Studies, as well as the faculty and staff at the Center for World Religions, Diplomacy, and Conflict Resolution in Arlington, Virginia. Through many years of conversations, you shaped and honed the ideas that flowed into this book.

Overflowing praise and enthusiastic obeisance must be made to those who keep the Library of Congress, the International Institute for Social History (Amsterdam), Dar al-Kutub, the Bibliotheca Alexandrina, and the National Archives. Similarly, I am grateful to the staff at the University of Maryland's McKeldin Library, the University of Michigan's Hatcher Graduate Library, the University of Washington's Suzzallo and Allen Libraries, the American University in Cairo's Rare Books and Special Collections Library, the University of Washington Libraries, and the Cornell University Library. Thank you for finding the forgotten, securing the impossible, and helping the past speak.

To the faculty, students, and staff of Erskine College, thank you for providing a healthy harbor for scholarly study. In the Department of History and Political Science, I am indebted to Dr. John Harris for helping navigate the publication process. Much tribute also belongs to Dr. Alessandra Brivio, whose adept leadership, friendship, and steadfast support steered us through first-year teaching, a pandemic, and many other storms. In the Department of Psychology, Dr. Briana Van Scoy deserves recognition for her counsel, mixed with rousing conversations on cults, emotions, and group behavior that enrich my afternoons. And to everyone in the Erskine Building, thank you for the days bursting with joy and laughter: you are my academic haven.

To the women of the Abu Sarah family, thank you for your fortitude and your fidelity. I will always remain humbled by Habiba, whose dignity and virtue are a crown of honor. It was your hospitality that shattered all preconceptions, and you will always remain an exemplar to us all. Acknowledgments are also due to Zakiyya for her research assistance and deep conversations on what it means to feel. Many thanks to Myrna as well for her humor and help in navigating Cairo streets and dodging bureaucratic barriers.

In the Arnold family, I owe much to my father and grandfather. You modeled a sincere faith, strong work ethic, tireless service, and the eternal satisfaction of disassembling, reassembling, and exploring the mechanics of life. My buoyant sister, it was your grit that encouraged me to endure, survive, fight, and have fun. And there would be no words, no poetry, no beauty without my mother, who encouraged the short stories of youth, proofread every paper, and fashioned my love for writing. You taught empathy to an analyst and inspired me to see the spark of the divine in all mankind.

Finally, to the one who anchors the heart while making ideas soar:

To Aziz:
Your honor and strength
Your patience and support
Your humor and enduring spirit
Made graduate school possible.
Without you, this book would have never been written.

Note on Translation and Transliteration

Transliteration of Arabic text in this book follows the style guidelines established by the *International Journal of Middle East Studies (IJMES)*. Accordingly, the Arabic letters ʿayn and hamza have been preserved in all cases, the nisba ending is transliterated as -iyya when not in iḍāfa, and tāʾ marbūṭa is transliterated as "a" not "ah" (hence *Ākhir Sāʿa* rather than *Ākhir Sāʿah*).

Arabic terms found on the *IJMES* Word List—including words such as effendi, jihad, hadith, and fatwa—are rendered according to English usage, without diacritics, and without italics. Similarly, Muhammad Naguib [Muḥammad al-Najīb], Gamal Abdel Nasser [Gamāl ʿAbd al-Nāṣir], Sohag [Sūhāj], Giza [Jīza], and other proper nouns follow their standard English spellings.

In concordance with *IJMES* style, personal names, place names, book and journal names, and political parties appear without diacritics for accessibility and ease of reading. Only technical terms appear in text with diacritics. For reference purposes, full diacritics for all names and titles appear in endnotes and bibliography entries.

All translations are my own except where otherwise noted. I have tried to honor both the spirit and the letter of the original texts, but brackets indicate places where the difference between literal and figurative language is significant. Translations of political tracts, news articles, and editorials adhere as much as possible to literal meaning; more liberty has been taken in translating poetic verse, in hopes of capturing some of the cadence and color of the original.

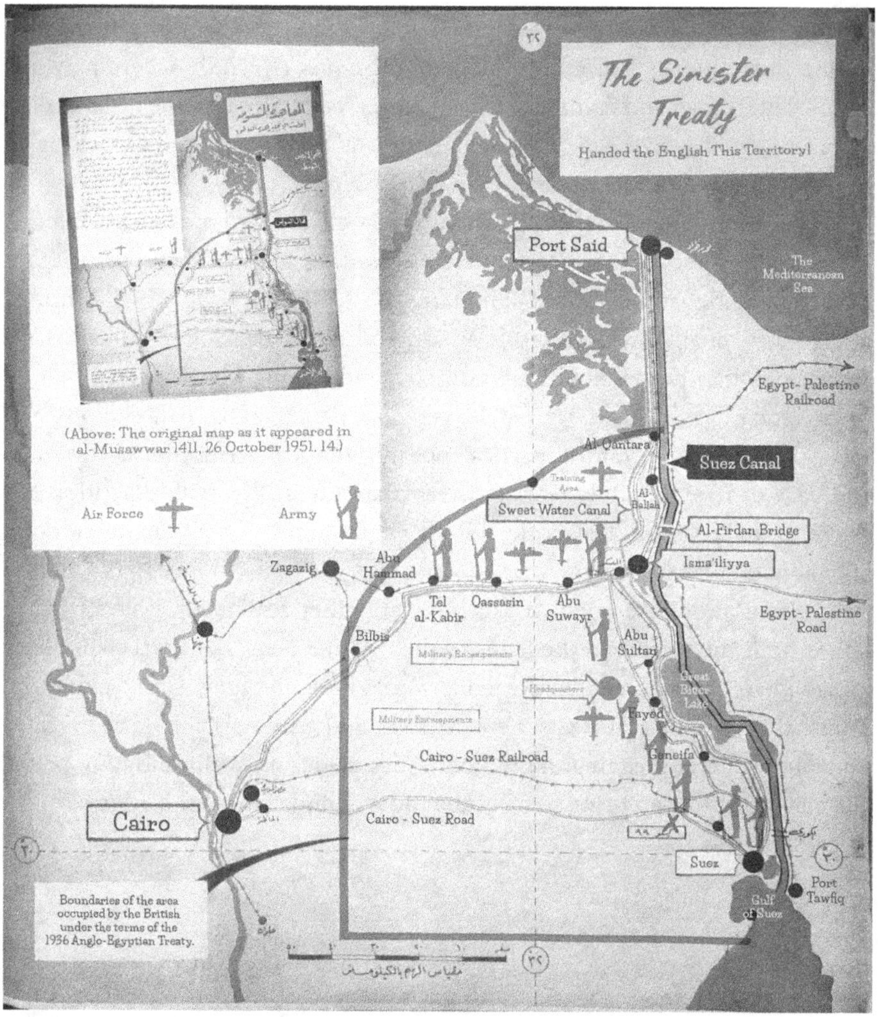

Map of the Suez Canal Zone, occupied by the British under the terms of the 1936 Anglo-Egyptian Treaty. The original map (in the inset) was printed during the 1951 Suez Crisis; the map shows both how close the occupation zone came to Cairo and how large the British loomed in the Egyptian imagination.

1

Over-Emotional Students?

Reconceptualizing "Arab Emotions" in Cold War Egypt

What emotions drive men to sacrifice themselves for a cause? Egyptian doctor Muhammad Wilaya reflected on this question in June 1942 as the Second World War battered North Africa. It was unclear what prompted his musings—but the British were euphemistically calling the tumultuous events of prior weeks "the Flap." Cairo had been rocked by pro-German/anti-British demonstrations, Field Marshal Erwin Rommel's Panzer Army was storming toward the Egyptian-Libyan border, the Egyptian police had arrested communists distributing anti-fascist literature, and locals were seized by both fear and hope that a German invasion might bring Britain's sixty-year occupation of Egypt to an end.[1]

As this political tempest raged, the doctor pondered. The article he penned for the prominent Arabic journal *Majallat al-Risala* finally concluded that men who joined underground cells were simply "hysterics." Volatile and radical [*mutaṭarrif*], men driven by emotions, such individuals seized on any passing ideology then cast themselves on the pyre of self-sacrifice. "If we review historical events, we find that the first supporters [of a cause] and the most zealous fighters in reaching miraculous goals are they, the hysterics," Dr. Wilaya explained. "How the hysteric loves suffering, if only to gain special importance in the eyes of men."[2]

Yet as the weeks passed, the doctor's diagnosis did not seem to sit well with a reader named Mustafa Jabir. Composing his letter to the editor, Jabir asked Dr. Wilaya to clarify his comments. What was the doctor's opinion of *fidāʾīyīn* ["self-sacrificers"; guerrillas, commandos, and bombers sent on deadly missions]? Were such men driven by "lofty principles?" "There have been many opinions and conflicting accounts about these groups," Jabir acknowledged.[3]

A few weeks later, the journal published Dr. Wilaya's unequivocal response: *fidāʾīyīn* were moved by mental illness, not lofty ideals. "The tendency toward self-sacrifice is motivated by psychological complexes"—namely, masochism, Dr. Wilaya insisted. "Self-sacrifice is the cousin of suicide."[4]

Despite the doctor's answer, Jabir was unsatisfied. He wrote back one last time to *al-Risala*, complaining that nobody bothered to consider what the *fidāʾīyīn* themselves believed. "To the good Doctor [Wilaya], and to the broader group of researchers and writers, I hope one of them will write about the *fidāʾīyīn* as a group and their principles."[5]

Emotions history has long been a topic of study among scholars of medieval Islam—and recently, the study of emotions has ballooned in European and American history. However, scholars of the modern Middle East have been slower to take the "emotional turn."[6] This caution reflects an important awareness: as an imagined geography where racial and religious others dwell, the Middle East has long occupied space in the Western imagination as a vague zone of emotional radicalism, prone to violent storms of sentiment.[7]

In the nineteenth century, this emotional cartography was integral to both the British imperial sense of self and the civilizing mission. Visiting Egypt in 1854, nurse Florence Nightingale contrasted her own feelings of love and sympathy with the debased state of Egyptian emotions, which she described as mired in misery, contempt, and sensualism. Finding local populations as repulsive as reptiles (and placing Arabs in the evolutionary rank "somewhere between the monkey and the man"), she likened Egyptians to an agitated herd of "angry cows."[8] Early histories of emotions echoed these ideas: *The Progress of Nations* (1861) recounted how throughout history superior races had conquered and civilized the subject races, allowing "the bright rays of reason" to dawn over their base emotions and "spread that respect for authority, that readiness to believe, that empire of emotions."[9]

Opinions about Egyptian emotions multiplied following the inauguration of the Suez Canal in 1869 and the British occupation of Egypt in 1882. British politicians justified their conquest as a reluctant intervention to secure Suez against the "emotional," "irrational" Egyptian masses running amok "under the influence of ephemeral passion."[10] When Britain's colonial subjects founded the National Party in 1907 to seek independence, the sincerity of Egyptian national sentiment raised further skepticism. British journalist Hamilton Fyfe wrote that Arabic newspapers like *al-Liwaʾ* and *al-Ahram* had taken advantage of the fact that Egyptian "emotions are easily played upon." With their "furious ravings," the press had created a generation of young middle-class men "intoxicated by silly nationalism."[11]

In 1918 as the First World War neared an end, Egyptian demands for self-determination in the spirit of Woodrow Wilson's Fourteen Points were again rebuffed by the British high commissioner, and that "silly nationalism" developed into the 1919 Revolution.[12] Colonial administrators were once more quick to dismiss the movement and its emotions. As Egyptians protested the arrest of nationalist leaders and demanded Egypt's full independence from colonial rule, the British police chief in Cairo, Thomas Russell, denounced demonstrators as a "dangerous mob." In his estimation "Anyone who understands the Orient knows how inflammable the crowd is and how mass hysteria can seize upon it within a few minutes."[13] His sensational account caricatured the Egyptian protesters as "shrieking and yelling … heads back and their mouths wide open … beards and chests white with dried saliva," adding that "I saw several fall spinning to the ground in fits of mad hysteria." The famous Ladies' Demonstrations that March he denounced as "a mob of Muhammadan ladies." Even the positive emotions of the 1919 Revolution he impeached as "frenzied demonstrations of joy."[14]

Yet if one gives a closer reading to colonial accounts of Middle Eastern emotions, discordant details emerge. The British police chief recalled that the shaykhs of al-Azhar sought his permission to hold their demonstrations in March 1919. A few sentences before calling them a "dangerous mob," Russell also admitted that during their demonstration al-Azhar unit leaders approached him to ask the police chief if he "was satisfied with the discipline they were keeping in the rear."[15]

British self-fashioning as "always keeping calm" merits its own scrutiny. Russell worried about the "constant danger" of "irritated" and "infuriated" Commonwealth troops roaming downtown Cairo in gangs searching for civilian victims. The police chief's account of the March demonstrations described how he blocked a group of Australian soldiers with hockey sticks looking to "make a mess," and how he seized the gun of an English soldier who had lost control, hell-bent on shooting an Egyptian civilian. Russell admitted that he "pacified [the Australian and English soldiers] for depriving them of their sport by telling them to meet me later on in the Ezbekiya gardens … when I would promise them some useful street fighting."[16]

Despite the discrepancies, the 1919 Revolution would hardly be the last Arab protest movement to be characterized as a violent mob. In response to Egyptian independence in 1922, British administrators shifted to "empire by treaty": Egypt's new Parliament received sovereignty in name, but the British retained control of many commercial interests, infrastructure contracts, and banking networks. Most importantly, the British continued to command the Suez Canal Company, along with its related shipping firms, oil refinery, industrial zone, and military base.[17]

The Suez Canal had long been important as Britain's artery to India. It was the transit point for cotton crops and other imperial goods, and a staging ground for Commonwealth troops when war or uprisings in the colonies threatened imperial order. With the First World War, the Canal additionally became the empire's fuel line, bringing petroleum from Abadan, Iran, to the Royal Navy's Mediterranean fleet. The Second World War expanded the importance of Suez even more. The base became the main staging ground for the entire Middle Eastern theater, swelling to become the largest military base in the world: a sprawling, 120-mile-long complex of thirty-eight army camps, ten airfields, power stations, ammunition depots, hospitals, repair workshops, and more.[18]

The deterioration of British-Soviet relations in 1946 further increased Suez's standing. From 1946 to 1951, British and American military planners drafted strategies to use Egypt as the command center for an invasion of the Soviet Union in the event of a third world war. Embracing the Goldilocks principle, they reasoned that the UK, India, and Kenya were too far from the USSR for staging an attack, and Iraq and Germany too close. But Egypt was just right: it provided the best platform for naval, air, and ground attacks on the USSR. From the highly defensible and well-developed Suez base, British and American bombers could reach 94 percent of Soviet oil refineries.[19]

Suez was important in other ways. By the 1950s, Suez was the transit point for 50 million tons of British goods. The Canal Zone was also entangled in Egypt's local economy, directly employing 71,000 workers and floating many local industries dedicated to provisioning Canal Zone company towns. Finally, the Canal Zone was a choke point for both British and Egyptian oil supplies. Nearly 70 percent of British crude oil passed through the Canal, and some two-thirds of Egyptian gasoline (as well as motor, cooking, and heating oil) flowed from the Anglo-Egyptian refinery in Suez.[20]

Egyptian calls for complete independence thus continued to be rebuffed through the Second World War and into the early Cold War. When anti-colonial demonstrations rocked Cairo in spring 1946, British pundits refused to recognize the validity of the discontent: a speaker in the British House of Commons stood on the floor and scorned the protests as "riots of over-emotional, nationalistically-minded students."[21] When Egyptian students again protested British occupation in summer 1947, *The Times* of London disparaged the demonstrations as rage-driven outbursts. That same year, British Arabist H.A.R. Gibb maligned Muslim Brotherhood marches as the "product of primitive Islamic romanticism, with an emotional reason of its own. It is not a rational assertion that one type of political organization is more desirable than another, but a revolt."[22] By dismissing Egyptian sentiments as irrational, pundits neatly foreclosed discussion about the legitimacy of claims over territorial sovereignty.

Finally in autumn 1951, a broad anti-colonial struggle against the British occupation of the Suez Canal Zone coalesced in Egypt. The struggle rallied a diverse array of parties and organizations across the political spectrum: the Muslim Brotherhood, Muhammad's Youth, Daughters of the Nile, Young Egypt, and communist clubs like the Worker's Vanguard and Democratic Movement for National Liberation all joined the movement. Western journalists anxiously described the uprising as the "Suez Emergency" and spoke of emotional hysteria, with *The Economist* describing protestors in the Canal as "hysterical crowds" caught up in "the violent nationalist fever that has spread over the Middle East."[23] But Egyptians celebrated the moment as the "1951 Revolution."

As an early Cold War revolution, the Suez Canal struggle that autumn was part of a global wave of anti-colonial movements that came to characterize the 1950s. The revolution also helped trigger what Jack Goldstone has identified as a wave of regional "Arab Nationalist revolutions" lasting from 1952 to 1969.[24] Despite its importance, however, Egypt's 1951 Revolution has remained relatively unstudied.[25] This is because the revolution came to a crashing halt with the Cairo Fire of Saturday, January 26, 1952. "Black Saturday" gave the government casus belli to launch a counterrevolutionary crackdown in the name of public safety, and six months later Egypt's Free Officers launched a successful military coup that toppled the monarchy and ushered in six decades of military rule. The new regime under General Muhammad Naguib and General Gamal ʿAbdel Nasser swiftly paved over memories of the failed 1951 Revolution. In its place, they constructed their own myth of the "1952 Revolution."

In his 1992 book *Nasser's Blessed Movement*, Joel Gordon deconstructed long-standing myths about the coup that July. As Gordon explained, once in power the Free Officers wove tales of how their glorious "1952 Revolution" had channeled the will of the people in vanquishing a depraved monarchy. Gordon pointed out this "history of the victors" exaggerated the degree to which the military takeover was by popular demand. He also noted that not everyone bought in to the military's myth: political dissidents (including old-guard Marxists and Muslim Brotherhood members) published revisionist scholarship in Arabic, which argued the military had "usurped true revolutionary momentum" by seizing power.[26] These revisionist histories were also flawed; they overstated the extent to which a people's revolution was imminent and interrupted by the military coup. That said, since Gordon's focus was the Nasser regime, it was beyond the scope of his book to recover stories of the tumultuous Canal Struggle that preceded the coup.[27]

As a result, until today English-language scholarship on the 1951 Suez Canal struggle has remained scarce, and the history of early Cold War Egypt still centers on familiar narratives: the 1952 Revolution, General Nasser, the Free Officers, the nationalization of the Suez Canal in 1956, and Nasser's particular brand of Third-Worldism. Only one book covers the Canal Struggle—and the book relies on British and American diplomatic records. Unsurprisingly, it describes the "Suez Emergency" of 1951 as an extremist revolt launched by Arab fanatics espousing "militant Islam."[28]

By accessing Arabic primary sources and Egyptian narratives, this book offers an important reappraisal of this struggle. With the aid of testimonies recovered from Muslim, Christian, and Jewish activists involved in the struggle, the book challenges colonial accounts of the conflict. The study also fills in important details about the early Cold War Middle East. Already in the late 1940s, for instance, Muslim Brotherhood members beat Nasser to the punch, advancing Islamism as a Third-Way doctrine and the perfect middle between communism and capitalism. Egyptians further connected their struggle to other anti-colonial movements, with activists parading Mohammed Mossadegh triumphantly through Cairo following Iran's nationalization of the Abadan oil refinery in March 1951. A moment of possibilities, the Canal Struggle would moreover prove a turning point in the developing Cold War. In a moment when the United States' star was rising and US foreign policy doctrines toward the Middle East were in flux, American diplomats decided how to respond to Egypt's appeals to liberty, democracy, and a shared legacy of struggle against British tyranny. The British too faced important decisions, as Coptic Christian and Muslim leaders joined hands to demand the English relinquish their military base colony.[29]

In an important return, this book recovers the leadup to that failed and forgotten "1951 Revolution." Taking the perspective of Egyptian activists and journalists on the ground, the book recovers a lost revolution of the early Cold War, and the stories, poetry, images, and emotions that accompanied the Egyptian anti-colonial struggle. In doing so, the book bridges a major gap in Middle Eastern history and explores a forgotten feature of the struggle for decolonization: battles on the emotional front.

Emotions in the Modern Middle East

At first glance it may seem strange to study emotions at the end of empire. However, in recent years scholars have pointed out that conquest and liberation, colonization and decolonization—all require not only political and economic realignments, but also shifts in culture, values, and sentiments.[30] Ruth Craggs and Claire Wintle, for instance, argue that music, clothing, and other cultural objects were "gauges, microcosms and agents of decolonization."[31] In the same way, emotions too reflected and disrupted the colonial order.

Still, studying sentiments in Middle Eastern protest movements is questionable, considering British and American authors have long overdetermined the role of emotions in Arab politics—and used "Eastern emotionalism" as a foil for "Western rationality." J.H. Denison's *Emotion as the Basis of Civilization* (1928) made this link explicit by contrasting the "emotional culture" of Greece, Rome, and Christian Europe with that of Islam. Locating "Mohammedan Civilization" as frozen in an intermediary phase of affective evolution, he extolled Islam for ushering savage Arab tribes out of anarchy and into a rudimentary form of brotherly unity—albeit "by means of warlike emotions" and "wild enthusiasm."[32]

Similar discourses still permeate modern media landscapes. Studying American talk about the Middle East, scholar Sara Ahmed finds emotion words like "hate-filled" and "fanatic" applied liberally to those who "look Muslim." She argues that these conversations construct the Middle East as a homogeneous region of hostility; this alien land can then be contrasted with (and in fact helps constitute) "our nation" as loving, civilized, and rational. The division also allows for emotional disengagement: if "they" are foaming fanatics, then we only need concern ourselves with (as one post 9-11 pundit described) "the importance of the lives of *rational* people."[33]

However, rather than drive Middle Eastern historians away from the subject of emotions history, such challenges make it imperative that Arabophone scholars engage with the emotional turn. For as the long history of British dismissals of Egyptian emotions indicates, emotions were important for both maintaining imperial power relations and challenging that same affective order. Describing the dynamics of affective politics, Sara Ahmed explains that this is not unusual: those in power often impress ideas about emotional difference onto racialized, gendered, classed, or political others as a form of affective dominance.[34]

This emotional boundary-work can serve important social functions, but digging into emotions and imagined geographies one quicky unearths a methodological problem: scholars take a leading role when it comes to drawing emotional borders. Sociologist James Jasper warns that especially when writing about social movements, even scholars tend to "fail the common humanity test" when describing the emotions of others. Be the subject communist activists, far-right identity movements, pro-life protestors, Islamist groups, or any other political movement, we feel *with* activists we support but read the emotions of political "others" as disingenuous, dangerous, and irrational. In part, this emotional bifocalism occurs because emotions are a form of claims-making: activists assert the right to grieve or the right to feel angry, and supporters attuned to the narrative allow themselves to empathize with that "righteous anger." If the claim is perceived as threatening, however, audiences affectively protect themselves through apathy or scorn, and retreat behind scripted condemnations of "their aggressive rage."[35]

This social psychology of emotional consent makes the feelings of protesters highly polarizing. As Rob Boddice reflects, it also means:

> Humans are involved in a never-ending process of bearing witness to pain or of choosing *not to bear witness*. … [T]he pain of racial others, dubbed "inferiors", the pain of the poor or uneducated, dubbed "degenerate" … each in its own way has been othered, sidelined, reduced, justified, condoned, condemned and mythologized.[36]

Boddice's observation certainly rings true when reading Middle Eastern emotions: Western audiences rarely *feel with* Arabs and Muslims; however, condemnations of their anger, justifications of their pain, and myths about their emotional lives—such as the myth that "love" is not in the Qur'an—can be found in abundance. A thoughtful engagement with emotions history is thus vital for understanding the modern Middle East. For if dismissing someone's emotions is an act that constitutes them as "others," then bearing witness to those emotions is an important corrective. Reading firsthand what Egyptians said about their own sentiments is the first step in this process, and can contribute to deconstructing persistent stereotypes about Arab emotions.

With these challenges in mind, this study set out on a transnational search for sources on the emotional worlds of Egyptian protesters. Visiting archives such as Dar al-Kutub (Cairo), the Bibliotheca Alexandrina (Alexandria), the Internationaal Instituut voor Sociale Geschiedenis/IISG (Amsterdam), and the Library of Congress (Washington, DC), the study collected traces of human lives: court cases and club newspapers, poetry and personal diaries, photographs and news clippings. The study also drew on the rich Arabic periodical repositories at the University of Michigan, the University of Washington, and Cornell University.

The search specifically focused on collecting documents from members of five associations active in Egyptian anti-colonial protests of the late 1940s:

- The Muslim Brotherhood (Jamaʿat al-Ikhwan al-Muslimin),
- The Society of Our Master Muhammad's Youth (Jamaʿat Shabab Sayyidna Muhammad),
- Young Egypt (Misr al-Fatah),
- The Workers' Vanguard (Taliʿat al-ʿUmmal), and
- The Egyptian Movement for National Liberation/EMNL (al-Haraka al-Misriyya l-al-Taharrur).

This combination (which included two Islamist and two communist groups) ensured a diverse sample of individuals of different faiths, ethnic backgrounds, and political outlooks.

A few books have surveyed the long history of these organizations, tracing political, intellectual, and economic developments across the 1920s–70s. James Jankowski documents the history of Young Egypt; both Richard Mitchell and Brynjar Lia have written excellent political and intellectual histories on the foundation and growth of the Muslim Brotherhood.[37] Meanwhile, Selma Botman, Rami Ginat, Tareq Ismael, and Rifaʿat El-Saʿid chronicle Egyptian communism, focusing on intellectual currents and trends.[38]

This book builds on these studies and shifts the lens, crafting a cultural history of storytelling and protest movements in early Cold War Egypt. Uniquely, the study also adds Muhammad's Youth to the discussion. An important group that broke away from the Muslim Brotherhood in the late 1930s, Muhammad's Youth prided itself on being more conservative and committed than their ex-Brothers—and the association's stories accentuate both the spectrum of political options available in early Cold War Egypt and the violent turn the Muslim Brotherhood took.

The study further undertakes an unconventional comparison, juxtaposing communist and Islamist groups like the Workers' Vanguard and Muslim Brotherhood. This represents an important intervention. Existing studies of Arab protest politics overwhelmingly focus on Islam, taking "Islamic activism" and "Muslim revolt" as objects of analysis.[39] However, focusing solely on Islam and protest is problematic. First, Islamist groups never operated in a vacuum: the Muslim Brotherhood competed with the myths and moral content of organizations like Young Egypt and the Workers' Vanguard. Second, the scholarly fixation on Islam isolates Muslim protest groups as historically unique—and in doing so, misses how ideas about Islamic morality changed over time and were exchanged and negotiated across political and confessional borders. By decentering Islam, returning these groups to their Cold War context, and comparing stories told by Muslim, Christian, Jewish, and Marxist activists, this book demystifies Islamic protest and humanize Muslim activists as individuals navigating diverse spectrums of practice in a particular historical context. The approach also highlights congruences in how communist and Islamist clubs navigated feelings and made arguments about moral behavior.

Overall, from publications like *Akhir Saʿa, al-Ithnayn, Majallat al-Risala, al-Ikhwan al-Muslimin, al-Daʿwa,* and *Shabab Sayyidna Muhammad,* new stories emerge of Egyptian efforts to mobilize feelings against the British. These stories speak to both the diversities of different emotional communities and similarities of human experience. The exchange between Dr. Wilaya and Mustafa Jabir illustrates one meaningful similarity: like their American and British counterparts, Egyptians also argued about the emotions of activists who took to the streets. The conversation in *al-Risala* would prove to be one debate among many, as Egyptians in the 1940s and 1950s discussed the morality of feelings in protest politics. Underscoring these conversations were fundamental disagreements about which sentiments and what protest measures were morally justified, as well as a very human fascination with activists and their emotions. Who were these young men and women who turned out to join demonstrations? What sentiments fueled their commitments?

Theorizing Emotions in Revolution and Protest

Entering the world of activist emotions means first stepping through the door of human attachments. And as James Jasper writes, "To understand emotions, we must examine human attachments *in all their diversity*: [attachments] to our own bodies, to the physical world, to concrete and abstract others, taken singly and collectively, *to ideas and moral principles, to places and things, and to our own self-images.*" Our emotions, he adds, "tell us how we are doing in relation to what we value."[40]

By this measure, Egypt's late monarchial period, lasting roughly 1946–52, reads as a pivotal moment for shifts in Egyptian attachments. In these years, students formed paramilitary brigades (including mixed Muslim-Christian brigades and an all-female battalion) to fight the British. Their Cold War revolution failed spectacularly. But the exercise in reading Arab emotions speaks to deeper questions of how (and why) protests mobilize feeling, and the revolutionary potential of emotions.

Before accompanying activists on campaign, it is worth noting how fields like emotions history and social movement theory can contribute to mapping protest movements. Starting with "emohistory" or "history from the inside out," the history of emotions explores how emotional experiences and taxonomies vary across time, between cultures, and among subcultures.[41] Since Kathleen Vongsathorn notes that the history of emotions still orbits around American and European case studies,[42] the pages that follow explore less familiar emotional constellations. Only one history book currently explores emotions in the modern Middle East (Joseph Ben Prestel's *Emotional Cities: Debates on Urban Change in Berlin and Cairo*); two books investigate emotions in the early modern Ottoman Empire.[43] Still missing from Middle East history is a theoretical framework for emotions concepts in the Arabic language, a book that spotlights individual experiences, and a historicization of Middle Eastern emotions vis-à-vis twentieth-century debates in psychology and psychiatry. These are a few of the gaps this book addresses.

For anyone who has experienced the emotional charge of a political demonstration, music concert, or religious service, emotions history can speak to certain commonalities of human experience. Medieval historian Barbara H. Rosenwein, for instance, studies the formation of *emotional communities* (groups in which "people adhere to the same norms of emotional expression and value").[44] Her concept resonates for understanding how activists forged communities of sentiment, convincing others to share emotions like faith, hope, joy, and outrage.

Since unruly emotions can disrupt day-to-day tasks, William Reddy considers how societies organize emotions into *affective regimes.* These systems of emotional practice assign emotions to appropriate spaces, objects, genders, and modes of expression.[45] Expanding on Reddy's concept, this study tracks how activists challenged these regimes by staging emotional "outbursts,"[46] violating affective rules and hierarchies, and directing anger upward toward the powerful. Jasper argues such strategies "transform feeling rules": by seizing the ability to freely "display the emotions associated with political agency—anger, indignation, pride, and so on," actors emotionally liberate themselves from affective (and political) regimes. His observation is important for discussions of decolonization. Anti-colonial protestors faced emotional constraints, and had to negotiate the strategic trade-offs involved in expressing emotions like anger. However, as we shall see, some political groups rejected these constraints entirely and asserted their right to be angry.[47]

Scholars also point out that emotions are a form of appraisal or stance-taking. Emotional red flags like anger and shame are often termed *moral emotions*, because they help us evaluate whether a behavior is right or wrong, good or bad.[48] Such sentiments serve as a "moral barometer," providing "immediate and salient feedback on … social and moral acceptability."[49] Since politicians and protestors work to persuade others what should and shouldn't be, one can thus predict that much of their time will be spent voicing value judgments through the performance of moral emotions.[50] This proved true when watching Egyptians wage political campaigns.

One final concept from emotions history proves important for the study of social movements.[51] Stephanie Downes has asked how people "feel *things*" (or assign feelings to objects).[52] This study asks the related question of how people feel *moved* (or assign feelings to action tendencies). As social organizers fought to move supporters out of their seats and into the streets, successful campaigns hinged on the link between emotions and motion.

This connection is important to explore because Egyptians clearly shared the idea that feelings and actions were intertwined. Popular Arabic terms used to describe feelings, for instance, referenced movements of the body. Egyptian writers spoke of:

- *ʿĀṭifa* – A passion-feeling; an emotion (from *ʿaṭafa*, a verb meaning "to incline, lean toward, or feel something")
- *Shuʿūr* – A perception-feeling; a sentiment, affect, or instinctively felt knowledge (related to Arabic terms for poetry, hair, hackles, and the sensation of goosebumps moving up the arm or along the back of the neck)
- *Iḥsās* – A sensation-feeling; a touch, sensation, or sensitivity in the body (from *ḥasa*, the sensation of running a brush or hand over the skin)
- *Infiʿāl* – An action-feeling; an emotional agitation, excitation, or state of being affected by something[53]

That said, these terms varied from author to author: a book by Muhammad Nasir written in 1900 defined *shuʿūr* as a perception-feeling related to an object, and described *iḥsās* as an inclination toward an object.[54]

To account for both similarities and differences in emotional experiences, this study broadly defines emotions as complex "multicomponent phenomena," or socialized responses that coordinate "changes across physiology, subjective experience, and behavior."[55] This definition reflects twentieth-century Arabic concepts of emotions as *doing something* to the body, or translating environmental feedback and linking judgments to motivated movements.[56]

One final methodological note regarding Egyptian emotions: eagle-eyed observers will note that as this book documents activist emotions, some paragraphs depart from the affect-free, "scholarly mode" of discourse, switching to familiar names, shorter sentences, and sensory details (all taken from activist memoirs and political tracts). This is purposeful. In code-switching, I hope to draw attention to our own unspoken emotional production rules: how we as scholars reproduce, negotiate, and violate the emotional regimes of "rational," "professional" scholarly writing.

This code switching also represents an attempt to faithfully convey the spirit of the Arabic source material. By reproducing some of the code-switching and prosody found in Egyptian stories, I have tried to translate texts in a way that highlights how emotional production worked. Susanne Stadlbauer, for instance, notes that Arabic-speakers linguistically *code-switch* to elicit emotions: they change to either conversational, familiar *ʿāmmīyya* (dialectical Arabic) or poetic *fuṣḥá* (literary Arabic) to communicate feelings.[57] This book's study of Egyptian media confirms and expands her observations, exploring the strategies Arabic speakers used to try and elicit emotion.

A last pattern that deserves special note is the prominent role of storytelling in emotional production and social activism.[58] Emotions have a storied structure: our ideas about "what love looks like" are attached to prototypical stories, and to be considered "rational" an emotion must be justified by a reasonable narrative. If we want to understand a person's emotions, we thus must listen to the stories they tell.[59]

Storytelling, emotions, and activism intertwine in other ways. Social scientists have found that narratives help us empathize and understand the emotions of others. Stories further aid in persuasion, social coordination, and the preparation of motor responses.[60] Each of these functions is vital for the construction of social movements. Within stories, for instance, we find *scripts* or learned "rules of procedure" for how to behave in certain situations.[61] Readers will be familiar, for example, with the script for attending a university lecture. The script features established *roles* (professor and student), standard *actions* (sitting at a desk, responding to questions), and prescribed *emotions* or moods (rapt attention). Because such scripts help produce and maintain social order, activists could strategically violate scripts to attract attention and overthrow regimes.[62]

To trace how storytelling and emotions propel social movements, this book thus catalogs activist *morality tales*: didactic narratives used to transmit norms and values, teach emotions, communicate counsel, and impel action.[63] By taking narratives about morality (*akhlāq*)[64] as a broad category of analysis, the study illuminates a rich history of hybridity in activist storytelling, as activists blended American, French, and Egyptian history with stories from Islamic, Jewish, and Christian lore. The resulting journey moves through personal biographies, news stories, and fables, and follows these colorful stories through twists and turns: Islamic parables about sailing ships, communist tragedies ripped from Greek myth, and popular folktales about Juha's Nail and Paul Revere's Ride through the Suez Canal. By wandering this path, the book thus captures an expansive picture of how anti-colonial campaigns negotiated Egypt's "collective treasury of legends"[65] to fight occupation on the emotional front.

Conclusion: Revolutionary Sentiments

Building up from these foundations, the following chapters explore how activists negotiated morality tales and moral emotions during the leadup to Free Officer's "revolution" of July 1952. Chapter 2 travels back to Cairo to tour the colorful world of "moral talk": the hand gestures, vocabularies, facial expressions, images, and emotions that Egyptians used to express value judgments and negotiate norms. Chapter 3 moves into the Second World War as a moment of rupture, recounting how the conflict rocked the foundations of the colonial order and triggered a sea change in public sentiments.

The next two chapters introduce Egyptian anti-colonial associations and their members. Chapter 4 compares the conversion narratives and affective environments of Muslim Brotherhood and Young Egypt. The chapter culminates with the Brotherhood's 1946 civil war and the capital murder cases that ensued—a dramatic period that begat charges of misinformation and fake news and fierce battles over whom to trust. Chapter 5 shifts the lens to members of the Workers' Vanguard and Egyptian Movement for National Liberation. Beginning with communist conversion stories, the chapter follows activists as they attempted to convert followers, avoid arrest, and market Marxist ideas about morality.

Chapter 6 takes a deep dive into the pages of Egyptian magazines and club newsletters, to recite the lost parables of communist and Islamist societies. In an original contribution, the chapter explores moral watchdog articles penned by Sayyid Qutb, as well as "gender mixing and murder" morality tales from *Shabab Sayyidina Muhammad* (the newspaper of Muhammad's Youth). A useful study for students and scholars, the chapter maps outrage politics and emotional appeals in Egyptian media, and offers an outline for how to read and interpret morality tales.

Finally, Chapter 7 steps into the heady and hopeful revolutionary moment of autumn 1951, immersing readers in the moral emotions and morality tales of the Canal Struggle. With political societies damaged and regrouping, the developing "1951 Revolution" rekindled hope for change, with Egyptians printing humorous anti-British cartoons, calling on compatriots to take up righteous and rational anger, and disciplining emotions to undercut British charges of fanaticism. Despite these struggles, the 1951 Revolution ended with a series of dramatic events: Operation Eagle on January 25 (a colonial massacre of 50 Egyptian policemen), the Cairo Fire of January 26, and the government suppression of Egyptian activist associations. These events are covered in Chapter 8. Then, Chapter 9 summarizes the lasting effects of 1951 as the revolution that failed, and trace the path to Nasser's nationalization of the Canal and the 1956 Suez Crisis.

Overall, these stories speak beyond their immediate context of Cold War Egypt. For students and scholars of human behavior, the chapters shed light on how we participate in local emotional and moral "economies" by investing in, producing, marketing, negotiating, and contesting emotional and moral regimes.[66] For activists and idealists, the book provides a strategy manual for how storytelling and emotional performances launch movements and forge revolutions. For critical curmudgeons, this study catalogs why emotions fall on deaf ears and why social change is so difficult to realize; it also conveys a cautionary tale against the weaponization of passion.

Finally, for curious observers of contemporary politics, this book explains why social media thrives on outrage, and why protest movements seem to ride a wave of sentiment. These questions are of paramount importance, as recent years have seen conflicts rage over the tears of Greta Thunberg (2019) and Kyle Rittenhouse (2021) (with the latter's tearful breakdown viewed over 2.3 million times in a span of 24 hours). Supporters celebrated the emotional outbursts as sympathetic and heroic, while adversaries derided the displays as irrational and absurd.[67] The tearful displays and angry outbursts of Egyptians likewise met with divergent reactions: sympathy, annoyance, alarm, and fury. Activists' emotions thus once were and still remain sites of intense controversy, absorbing and polarizing audiences. This study dives into the rift—and explores the whirlwind of dissent over the activist's emotions.

2

Virtue and Vice in Twentieth-Century Egypt

Emotions and the Moral Marketplace

What words or images come to mind when imagining morality in the modern Middle East?

While many might associate morality with vague images of bearded men and veiled women, mosques and prayer beads, paging through Egyptian magazines of the 1940s, a more diverse world unfolds. To take one example, in August 1948 the magazine *Akhir Sa ʿa* cut the heads off photographs of Egyptian politicians and transported them onto the bodies of zoo animals. Doubling down on its prank, the magazine in November pasted the politicians' heads atop the bodies of scantily clad cabaret girls and belly dancers (see Figure 2.1).

Readers might not immediately think of ridicule as a form of moral messaging. However, the colorful collages provide a snapshot of a diverse and flourishing Egyptian moral imaginary (underpinned by a rich sense of humor). Working to puzzle out the relationship between morality and humor, Immanuel Kant theorized that jokes can have a moralizing effect and impart moral messages: we use comedy to "satirize vice and portray folly as worthy of ridicule."[1] Read in this way, the images in *Akhir Sa ʿa* certainly imparted a moral message: they revoked the dignity of Egypt's political elite, criticized their character flaws, and portrayed them as easy women selling themselves to please an audience.

Images like these invite us to dive deeper into the moral ecosystem of mid-century Cairo. The city boasted a lively moral marketplace—a place where Egyptians produced, marketed, negotiated, and contested emotions and ideas about morality. Entering this arena of controversy, the chapter begins by historically situating the changing moral universe of early-twentieth-century Egypt. Touring sites where Egyptian youth learned about morality, the chapter catalogs the vibrant vocabularies, gestures, and images that Egyptians used to communicate value judgments. As the chapter argues, these vocabularies were

السياسة في حديقة الحيوان
الرقص في لاظوغلي

Figure 2.1 Ridicule as a Type of "Moral Talk."

Akhir Sa'a mocks Egyptian politicians of the Wafd Party, Sa'dist Party, and People's Party by pasting their heads on the bodies of zoo animals and dancers.

Source: (Top) "Al-Siyāsa fī ḥadīqat al-ḥayawān," *Ākhir Sā'a* 719, August 4, 1948, 22–3. (Bottom) "Al-Raqṣ fī Lāẓūghlī," *Ākhir Sā'a* 735, November 24, 1948, 26–7. Hatcher Graduate Library, University of Michigan.

the building blocks of *moral regimes*: value systems that organize and assign relative worth to people, spaces, objects, genders, and forms of labor.

Overall, the history herein invites reflection: what do we recognize as "moral talk"? Religious discourses are often the easiest to identify—however, not all moral evaluations of things (and people) are attached to scripture. Rather, moral assessments more often involve swift and implicit judgments about what is good, normal, and valuable. For scholars and students, this poses a challenge: how do we learn to recognize moral vocabularies and narratives about right and wrong? How can learning to analyze "moral talk" and "moralpolitik" contribute to our understanding of the past and make us more savvy navigators of today's media spaces? With an eye toward recognizing moral chatter (and especially non-religious forms of moral talk) in the political arena, the following pages lay a foundation for answering those questions.

The Moral Economy of Twentieth-Century Egypt

In early-twentieth-century Egypt, making moral citizens and teaching moral regimes was an uneven and contested process, with production spread across many different workshops. For instance, Egyptians learned about morality in the home, the classroom, and religious institutions. Moral socialization was also negotiated in parliaments and courtrooms, workplaces, marketplaces, and media spaces.

For Egyptian activists who came of age in the 1940s, however, moral norms had changed dramatically from the world their fathers had known. Egyptian religious culture was changing: encounters with Western missionaries—and competition with those missionaries—fueled the development of lay movements in the Egyptian Muslim and Christian communities. Egyptians increasingly read and interpreted scripture for themselves, worked to modernize religious practice, reflected on religion's relationship to new scientific knowledge, contributed their time to charitable associations, and blended religious practice with political activism. In this way, lay movements both brought religion further into the political sphere and challenged the "monopoly of religious knowledge" held by Muslim ʿulamaʾ and Coptic priests.[2]

State organization and the state's role in moral production were also shifting. Since 1882 Egypt had been under British occupation; but the First World War empowered an Egyptian national movement. As part of this movement, Egyptian industrialists, merchants, and a growing middle class of professionals demanded a broader space for political participation. Nationalist activists organized themselves as the Wafd Party, held meetings in mosques and churches, and turned new social spaces like cafés into "revolutionary hubs."[3]

The 1919 Revolution that grew from this nationalist movement achieved Egyptian independence in 1922, the establishment of a parliament, the formation of political parties, and universal suffrage for Egyptian men. Women also asserted rights in these new political spaces: in 1923, the Egyptian Feminist Union was established, and over the next decade Egyptian women's societies demanded suffrage and engaged in exegesis of Islamic scripture, arguing veiling was not a requirement in Islam.[4] In terms of Egypt's moral marketplace, this democratization meant that more and more people were contributing to debates and policymaking on moral matters.

Following the 1919 Revolution, the Wafd Party claimed political and moral leadership over the nation, and Wafd leaders (men like Saʿd Zaghlul and Mustafa al-Nahhas) were enshrined into the canon of Egyptian heroes. The Wafd Party also built an Egyptian national myth around the 1919 Revolution. This narrative posited a grand rupture between the "shame" and "dishonor" of the 1906 Dinshaway massacre (a British colonial massacre of Egyptian villagers), and the 1919 Revolution, which restored Egypt's national honor.[5] But despite the Wafd's nationalist myth and the granting of nominal Egyptian independence, the British remained entrenched in Egypt.

As part of the compromise of partial independence, Egypt's new constitutional monarchy (*c.*1923–52) charged the government with protecting "public morality" and guarding public order. The 1923 Constitution broadly described the state's moral duties as preventing behaviors inciting discord [*fitna*], "disturbing the public peace," "damaging the public interest," or violating "the sanctity of morals [and] good character."[6] The new Egyptian Penal Code of 1937 added clarification, criminalizing and giving the state the power to punish behaviors leading to the "corruption of morals"—a category that included prostitution, adultery, corrupting the youth, and debauchery.[7] This revised legal system was a complex hybrid of local custom, Islamic Ḥanafī *fiqh* [jurisprudence], Ottoman *kanun*, and French legal traditions. For instance, Egyptian statutes were drafted using the French Penal Code of 1810 and Law of July 19–22, 1791 as models; these French codes similarly prohibited offenses "contre les bonnes mœurs" [against good morals] and "outrage[s] public à la pudeur" [public outrages to decency], such as corrupting the youth and outraging feminine modesty.[8]

As part of this changing moral order, the modern Egyptian state increasingly subsumed religion under the broader heading of public morality. Article 13 of the Egyptian Constitution of 1923, for instance, declared it the state's duty to "protect the freedom to perform religious rites and beliefs," but only so long as those beliefs were "in accordance with common customs in Egypt, [and] provided these [rites] do not disturb public order or contradict morals [*al-ādāb*]."[9] The 1937 Penal Code also contained statutes criminalizing blasphemy and other "misdemeanors pertaining to the religions." The code defined such misdemeanors as public perversions of sacred scripture, public ridicule of religious ceremonies, and the desecration of spaces, objects, or symbols venerated by any "religious community [*milla*] or group of people."[10]

The context of these laws revealed the legal reasoning at work. Blasphemy laws appeared in the Penal Code just before crimes against "public objects," and were prosecuted in conjunction with anti-incitement laws (§§ 171, 172, 174, 176). Like European penal codes, blasphemy in Egypt was thus seen as constituting an endangerment to public order and public objects. In short, Egyptian law treated religion and public morality as "public goods"—an integral part of the social order in need of government protection.[11]

This attempt to subsume religion under other legal categories—as well as the effort to reconcile religious traditions with modern formulas (like the idea of the "sanctity of morals and good character")—reflected a broader shift underway in Egyptian epistemologies. This shift was visible in educational trends: from 1930 to 1950, the number of Egyptians enrolled in Western-style universities expanded rapidly, while enrollment at the Islamic institute of al-Azhar grew at a slower pace. In fact, the 1945 school year marked the first time that more Egyptians enrolled at secular universities than al-Azhar (see Figure 2.2).

These shifts in schooling contributed the refashioning of space, gender norms, and epistemologies in Egypt. From the 1890s to 1920s, Egyptians celebrated cultural awakening (*nahḍa*), crowding coffeehouses for lively debates about new art forms and scientific discoveries. A literary revival saw a renewed interest in Greek literature, with thinkers like Ahmad Luṭfī Sayyid,

	Universities*	al-Azhar**
1930/1931	2,266	9,116
1936/1937	8,312	12,274
1939/1940	8,803	13,666
1942/1943	9,513	13,200
1945/1946	15,360	14,748
1948/1949	20,088	18,694
1950/1951	31,744	---
1951/1952	53,338	19,227

Figure 2.2 Enrollment in Egyptian Higher Education, 1930–52.

* Combined figures for Egyptian University/King Fu'ad University, 'Ayn Shams University, and Alexandria University. Data for Dar al-'Ulūm, the teacher's training college, is unavailable.

** Al-Azhar had three internal colleges but was not designated a university until 1961.

Source: James Jankowski, *Egypt's Young Rebels: Young Egypt, 1933–1952* (Stanford: Hoover Institution Press, 1975), 2; Kirk J. Beattie, *Egypt During the Nasser Years: Ideology, Politics and Civil Society* (Boulder: Westview Press, 1994), 22.

Taha Husayn, and Tawfiq al-Hakim publishing translations and adaptations of Aristotle, Sophocles, Ovid, and other Greek and Roman works in Arabic. By the 1920s, Egyptian nationalism thus mixed ideas of modernism, rationalism, and civilizational progress with the concept of Egypt as a cosmopolitan nation that had assimilated and Egyptianized the Arab, Greek, Roman, and Islamic empires that had passed through. Egypt, the argument went, was the inheritor of Greco-Roman culture and the classical tradition—a bridge between East and West.[12]

These twentieth-century creative encounters introduced to Egypt new moral lexicons. Greek and Islamic concepts of selfhood mixed with Durkheimian sociology and Freudian psychoanalysis, and Egyptians increasingly spoke of "deviance" [*inḥirāf*], "abnormality" [*shudhūdh*], "hysteria" [*histīryā*], and the "psyche" [*nafs*]. By the 1940s, psychology was entrenched in the scholarly community and had expanded to fill the pages of popular magazines. Egyptian doctors launched psychology journals such as *Majallat ʿIlm al-Nafs* (est. 1945); court trials used the new vocabulary to explain criminal behavior; popular magazines like *Akhir Saʿa* and *al-Ithnayn* freely analyzed the psyches of husbands, wives, and children; thinkers like Sayyid Qutb referenced Sigmund Freud and avidly read *Majallat ʿIlm al-Nafs*; and authors like Tawfiq al-Hakim, ʿAli Ahmad Bakathir, and Naguib Mahfouz rewrote Oedipus Rex with the Oedipus complex in mind. In short, lay psychology was "drowning the marketplace." These changes represented an earthquake in the "moral topography of modern selfhood,"[13] altering popular concepts about sexuality, morality, emotions, and the brain.

New fields like psychology also altered the culture of emotions in Egypt. Already by the turn of the century Egyptian philosophical and literary journals were saturated with discussions about the importance of rationality (*ʿaql*), debates about the relationship between anatomy and emotions, and descriptions of how to cultivate moral emotions (*al-iḥsāsāt al-adābīyya*) like conjugal love and "family feelings."[14] By the 1940s, it was common to see articles about emotions framed by eclectic quotes and ideas adapted from classical Greek philosophy (Aristotle, Plato), medieval Islamic philosophy (al-Farabi, al-Ghazali), early modern philosophy (René Descartes, Nicolas Malebranche, François-René de Chateaubriand), modern psychiatry and psychology (Josef Breuer, Emile Kraepelin, Sigmund Freud), and modern Egyptian philosophy (ʿAbbas Mahmud al-ʿAqqad).[15]

Taking part in this process of emotional production, Arab writers discussed how to best discipline the passions through the cultivation and education of emotions [*tarbīyya al-ʿawāṭif*]. They described which emotions should be stirred by ideas like "God" and "the homeland" (pride and affection). Authors also shared opinions about the appropriate affects for different roles (i.e., soldiers, citizens, husbands, and wives), and debated how emotions should be gendered—puzzling out whether men and women had unique emotional experiences, and whether these experiences were inborn or the result of environment. "Modern women" who worked, for instance, were speculated to be evolving: moving from emotionalism to reason, and replacing feminine affects (like modesty/*ḥishma*) with masculine fearlessness and daring.[16]

Notably, these debates included specific understandings of how emotions stirred the body. Egyptians described emotions as generating physical movement and stimulating physiological sensations (like blushing and fluctuations in heartbeat). A 1940 article by Siddiq Shaybub summarized some of these modern concepts of what emotions "did" and how they intersected with biology: borrowing from the work of Sigmund Freud and Josef Breuer, Shaybub described emotions as "barbaric" passions brewing in man's subconscious like a storm or "violent force." These passions must be civilized, Shaybub explained—lest the continuous clash between "our moral, civilized emotions and the instinct of barbaric pleasure buried in us" boil to the surface as "hysteria" or inappropriate emotional displays.[17]

To prevent such pathological displays, Shaybub called on Egyptians to civilize their sentiments. In other words, emotions should be assigned to appropriate times, spaces, and modes of expression. For instance, Shaybub explained, passions should either be channeled through poetry and music or expressed to a psychiatrist—for "just as internal inflammation produces fever" if given no outlet, so too would repressed fears, furies, and desires lead to psychological disorders if not channeled properly.[18]

In the 1930s, this moral marketplace underwent another shift. Economically, the Great Depression rocked the cotton market, causing economic crisis: whereas the average daily wage in Egypt in 1929 could buy 8 kg of rice, by 1933 Egyptians could only afford 3.5 kg with their pay. Politically, the imposition of the British and French Mandate system, violent suppression of Arab independence movements, suspension of the Egyptian constitution by a Palace-aligned government in 1923, rise of fascism in Europe, and rigged Parliamentary election of 1938 triggered a shift to more radical populist politics. Writers now denounced the Pharaohs as having been "out of touch with the broad sectors of Egyptian society," and Egyptians shifted toward Arab-Islamic nationalism, which argued for Arab solidarity in the face of colonial violence and advanced Islam as the remedy to the Western materialism that had caused economic and moral crisis.[19]

One of the premier platforms for interwar debates about Arab-Islamic revival was the cultural and literary organ *Majallat al-Risala*, established in January 1933. Dubbed "a 'revolution' in Egyptian publishing" (on account of the sway it held in terms of circulation numbers, the prominence of its contributors, and the foundational place it occupied in popular dialogue), *al-Risala* circulated some 20–40,000 copies of each issue. As a magazine dedicated to *adab* [literature, etiquette, and comportment], contributors both critiqued and built on the cosmopolitan writings of Arab Renaissance writers like Taha Husayn and Tawfiq al-Hakim. *Al-Risala* also evidenced another trend in the Egyptian moral economy: rising literacy rates and new technologies (like film, radio, and Roneo machines) were opening up new media spaces for moral production. Ziad Fahmy records over 163 new periodicals established in the 1890s, 278 in the 1900s, and 442 new periodicals established in the 1920s, and male literacy rising from around 9 percent in the 1890s to just under 20 percent by the end of the 1920s.[20] In the final years of the Egyptian monarchy (1946–52), male literacy climbed to 40 percent, and political associations rapidly proliferated and produced their own journals.[21]

Transformations underway in Egyptian urban space were a last change worth noting in these years. Cairo's population topped 1 million in 1927, with urbanization bringing more Egyptians from the provinces to the city.[22] In the 1910s and 1920s, imperial commerce and trans-Mediterranean exchange also brought European-style restaurants, clothing, and department stores to downtown Cairo. Besides bringing different moral communities into contact, these spaces added to an increased visibility of European culture and visibility of women.[23] By the late 1930s and 1940s, unveiling became the fashion among middle- and upper-class women in the city, and elite Egyptian women drove cars and mixed with men in new entertainment spaces like cinemas, casinos, and dance halls.[24]

The Language of Virtue and Vice: Normative Discourses in 1940s Egypt

Considering these shifting moral maps, how did Egyptians communicate normative concepts in the 1940s? As Phil Hopkins has warned, answering this question is not a straightforward proposition—because "Moralistic narratives need not, and usually will not explicitly refer to 'morality' or 'ethics' in terms we would readily recognize as such." Often learned at a young age and taken for granted, moral discourses tended to pass unnoticed, being communicated implicitly rather than explicitly.[25]

Surveying Egyptian magazines and club newsletters of the 1940s—publications like *Akhir Sa'a, al-Ithnayn, Majallat al-Risala, al-Ikhwan al-Muslimin, al-Da'wa, Shabab Sayyidna Muhammad, al-Fajr al-Jadid, Kifah al-Sha'b*, etc.—it becomes clear that Hopkins' word of caution is worth heeding. Arabic "moral talk" was not always easy to recognize. For instance, normative signaling often combined emotional displays, linguistic cues, gestures (i.e., crossing one's arms, shaking the head), vocalizations (i.e., sighs, teeth sucking, tongue clicking, "tsk tsk" sounds), and facial expressions (i.e., frowning, bearing the teeth, or tilting back the head and lifting the eyebrows) (see Figure 2.3).[26]

A review of the "moral vocabulary" of 1940s and 1950s Egyptian magazines introduces us to the Arabophone moral imaginary of the time. Terms frequently appearing in moral debates included words like *akhlāq* [pl., morals, morality], from a triliteral root meaning "to be created, shaped, molded, fit, or suitable." The term *ṣāliḥ* [pious, righteous]—from the root "to be good, in order, useful, fit, or suitable"—was also commonly used.

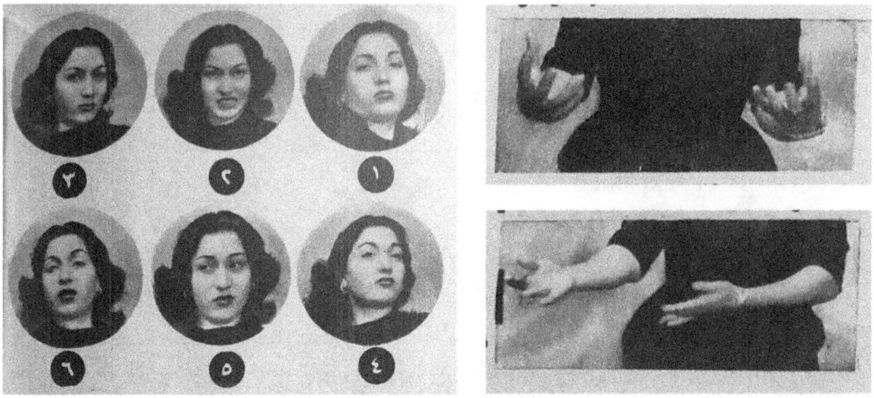

Figure 2.3 Using Hand Gestures, Facial Expressions, and Vocalizations to Express Value Judgments in Egypt.

A magazine article in *al-Ithnayn* challenged readers to match the facial expression with the appropriate sayings and hand gestures. Expression No. 2 (top center) was matched with both the claw-like hand gesture at the top right and the popular expression of anger "'āwza āshrab min dammak" [lit: "I want to drink your blood"; fig: "I want to kill you"]. Expression No. 5 (bottom center) was matched with the exasperated open palm gesture (bottom right), and the saying "āyh dah kulhu?" [lit: "what's all that?"; fig: "what the hell is that?"].

Source: "Hadhā al-wajh li-ayy yadayn?" *al-Ithnayn* 877, April 2, 1951, 36. Courtesy of Cornell University Library.

Other vocabularies of virtue included terms of purity like *ṭāhir* [clean, pure] and *ikhlāṣ* [purity, fidelity]—the latter coming from a root meaning "to be unmixed." Egyptians also used terms of increase and elevation to express moral uprightness: words like *faḍīl* [good, virtuous] hailed from a root meaning "to be in surplus, overflow." Similarly, the term *zakiy* [pure, blameless] derived from the root "to grow or increase," and *sharīf* [honorable] came from the root "to be well-bred, noble, raised or exalted."

The most frequently used term for morality, *ādāb*, was polysemous. In its singular form *adab*, the word denoted etiquette and good manners, as well as a mode of Arabic literature that combined literary style with the promotion of cultural values. In its plural form *ādāb*, the term meant "morals" or "morality." The polysemy of *adab* (pl. *ādāb*) was important, because it reflected the fact that in the Arab moral imagination, language and morality were linked: as an Arabic proverb explained, "he who knows the language finds his morals refined."[27] *Al-Risala* described the link between morality and language in similar terms: a man upright in morality (*ādāb*) was a man who was filling himself with the correct literature (*adab*).[28]

Notably, these concepts of virtue were all metaphors: man is a container (who needs to be filled with good things); virtue is cleanliness; virtue is a direction (forward, up); virtue is like language (everything in its proper place). Such metaphors were not unique to Egyptian magazines: similar conceptual metaphors exist in other languages, including Persian, French, and English, and are often used to explain both moral concepts and emotional experiences (i.e., "love burns," "anger ignites").[29]

Conceptual metaphor theory provides an explanation for these patterns. The theory argues that humans take "clearly delineated and concrete experiences" (like the experience of being sick or dirty), and use these concrete experiences to conceptualize more "abstract and elaborate concepts" (like moral judgments and emotional experiences).[30] As Paul Ricœur phrased it, metaphors thus serve a "picturing function," allowing men to "set before the eyes" the abstract concept being described.[31] The Arabic terms for metaphor—*majāz* [metaphor; lit. "a passage, corridor"] and *istiʿāra* [metaphor; lit. "a borrowing"]—further allude to the fact that metaphors made ideas more accessible, connecting concepts and borrowing meaning (transferring ideas from a source domain to a target domain).[32]

Arabic terms from 1940s magazines used to describe vice (summarized in Figure 2.4) reflect this use of metaphors to concretize or "embody" abstract moral concepts. The depraved man, for instance, was described as *munḥarif*

Cluster I – Terms of Contamination and Decay			
Arabic	*Transliteration*	*Definition*	*Root*
فاسد	*fāsid (n. fasād)*	bad, rotten, corrupt, immoral	"to decay or rot"
قبيح	*qabīḥ*	disgusting, repugnant, ugly, shameful, foul	"I. to be repulsive, disgusting, shameful; (II) to disfigure"
قذر	*qadhir*	dirty, filthy	"to become dirty, unclean"
دنس	*danis*	unclean, dirty, soiled, polluted	"to be soiled, defiled, dirty"
مريض	*marīḍ*	sick, ill	"to be ill"
رجس	*rajis (n. rijs)*	filthy, dirty	"to be dirty; to commit a shameful act"
خبيث	*khabīth*	evil, wicked, harmful, malignant, nauseating disgusting	"to be wicked" (related to *khabath*: slag/waste from metal refining, refuse)
Cluster II – Terms of Deviation, Excess, and Breaking (Going Beyond the Limits)			
فاجر	*fājir (n. fujūr)*	licentious, obscene, shameless	"to break apart or burst out"
انحلال	--- *(n. inḥilāl)*	dissolution, decay	"to decompose or break apart"
فاسق	*fāsiq (n. fisq)*	sinful, godless, immoral	"to stray or deviate"
فاحش	*fāḥish*	disgusting, immoderate, dirty, obscene	"to be monstrous, excessive, exorbitant"
مضل/مضلل	*muḍil/muḍallil*	deceptive, misleading	"to stray, lose one's way, go astray"
منحرف	*munḥarif (n. inḥirāf)*	depraved, perverted, deviant	"to veer off or depart from [a path or line]"
مخل	*mukhill (n. ikhlāl)*	disgraceful, shameful, immoral	"(IV) to pierce [a veil], transgress, or violate"
Cluster III – Terms of Exposure			
اباحي	*ibāḥī*	licentious, over-permissive	"to reveal, become known, open"
فاضح	*fāḍiḥ (n. faḍīḥa)*	shameful, disgraceful, scandalous	"to expose faults"
خليع	*khalīʿ*	morally depraved, dissolute	"to take off [i.e., a hat, clothes], remove, throw off"
متهتك	*mutahattik*	insolent, shameless, dishonorable	"to expose, tear off, dishonor, rape"
Cluster IV – Terms of Lowness and Decrease			
خسيس	*khasīs*	despicable, vile	"to become less, diminish"
سافل	*sāfil*	low, base, despicable	"to be low, base"
نذل	*nadhil*	low, vile, debased	"to be low, base, depraved"
Cluster V – Terms of Aversion			
مكروه/كاره	*makrūh/karīh*	hated, odious, repulsive	"to hate, to be disgusted"
مقرف	*muqrif*	disgusting, loathsome, repulsive, nauseating	"to peel back [a rind, bark, skin, crust, scab], to feel disgusted"
مخجل	*mukhjil (n. khajal)*	shameful	"to be ashamed, embarrassed"
مخزي	*mukhzī*	shameful, disgraceful, vile	"to be vile, base, despicable"
شنيع	*shanīʿ*	atrocious, hideous, heinous	"to be hideously ugly, repugnant"

Figure 2.4 The Arabophone Moral Imaginary: Terms of Negative Valuation.

* Unless otherwise noted, all terms listed are in adjective (*ṣifa*) form. Terms commonly used as nouns are included in parentheses.

(having veered off a path), and the corrupt politician described as *fāsid* (decayed and rotten). In fact, Arabic terms of negative moral valuation could be broadly grouped into five categories: "Cluster I: Terms of Contamination and Decay," "Cluster II: Terms of Deviation, Excess, and Breaking," "Cluster III: Terms of Exposure," "Cluster IV: Terms of Lowness and Decrease," and "Cluster V: Terms of Aversion."

These clusters were not hard-and-fast categories: clusters overlapped, and terms could express more than one idea at the same time. (For instance, terms of contamination often communicated aversion as well.) Nevertheless, placing terms in conceptual clusters highlights how normative expressions in Egypt were linked to a few foundational metaphors. Cluster I, for instance, suggested Egyptians conceptualized morality as preventing disease and contamination. Cluster II, meanwhile, indicated the Egyptian moral universe was built around divisions of labor and role socialization—being "in place," "molded," or "fit for" certain tasks and roles.

That unusual Arabic term *adab/ādāb* further illustrated how morality was role and place-dependent. As Arab moral philosophers explained, language and morality were linked because knowing *the proper place of words* meant understanding *the proper place of humans* in society and *the proper times and places for different behaviors and emotions*.[33] In an 1883 text used as an Egyptian school manual, for instance, Muhammad ʿUmar al-Bagouri argued that each room of the house had its own morality, with different rooms requiring different behaviors. (For instance, a well-mannered man would never eat in the bathroom!)

A morality manual by Sayyid Muhammad used in Egyptian primary schools (which activist Sayyid Qutb counted among his cherished possessions) similarly described rules for conduct according to one's role and station: children, students, men, and women were assigned distinct behavioral expectations. Finally, an oft-cited Muhammad Masʿud text from 1913 delineated an *adab* for different situations (such as walking, sleeping, and eating). At first glance, moral rules for things like "walking" might seem foreign—but if one considers unspoken rules about personal space and stepping on the back of someone's shoe, such moral concepts come sharply into focus (and make us consider how our own society creates and polices norms for different actions, spaces, jobs, genders, etc.). For Masʿud's part, his morality of walking instructed readers not to stomp the ground like a horse, and to clean one's feet to avoid smells (lest companions flee from your presence).[34]

Magazines thus revealed that in the Egyptian moral imaginary, different roles, spaces, and situations called for distinct behaviors and emotions. Immoral behaviors were things which broke, burst out of, transgressed, or strayed from their "container" or "place" (as conveyed through Cluster II terms like *fājir*, *fāsiq*, *mukhill*, and *munḥarif*).[35] Alternately, Egyptians conceptualized immorality as that which contaminated society (Cluster I), broke boundaries or exceeded the limits (Cluster II), laid bare shameful things (Cluster III), brought one low (Cluster IV), or triggered a gag or disgust reflex (Cluster V).

Conclusion: Mapping the Egyptian Moral Marketplace

The late Egyptian monarchy coincided with major changes in the urban moral economy. In twentieth-century Egypt, urbanization and colonization brought different communities and their moral regimes into contact. The state's role in moral production and policing expanded, and Egypt experienced a boom in political participation. Educational practices shifted. Rising literacy rates and religious lay movements democratized moral production processes. Equally controversial were shifts in gender norms, foodways, sartorial habits, and entertainment practices. Overall, the generation that came of age in the 1930s and 1940s had thus witnessed colossal changes in the Egyptian moral marketplace—transformations that were still underway, still new, and still unfamiliar (especially to young villagers freshly arriving in Cairo to find work or attend university).

The burgeoning media environment of early-twentieth-century Egypt also made newspapers and magazines a rapidly growing theater for moral production. As a result, lifestyle journals overflowed with debates about dress habits and consumption behaviors.[36] Editorialists discussed the morality of different leisure activities (music and dance shows, erotic novels and prostitution, alcohol and drug use).[37] Pundits argued about the proper comportments for men and women, and debated the manners of minorities.[38] The behavior of merchants, politicians, and religious leaders was put under a magnifying glass; there were critiques of the unique moral failings of the rich and the poor, and discussions about the behavior of urban versus rural denizens.[39] The home—as the primary site for the production of moral citizens—received the most scrutiny from Egyptian social commentators, who debated the best way to discipline domestic spaces.[40]

These shifts show that it is impossible to reduce moral production in Egypt to simply "Islam" or the question of "religion and state." Moral norms were diffusely produced and policed in homes, schools, neighborhoods, workplaces, marketplaces, religious communities [*milāl*], public media spaces (magazines, films, advertising), state institutions (the palace, parliament, courts), and interactions with foreigners and foreign institutions. Moreover, not all moral judgments were expressed in a religious idiom. Egyptians were moral bricoleurs, eclectically referencing ideas from divine scripture, morality manuals, scientific texts, and popular media.[41] Similarly, "moral talk" came in many forms, ranging from jokes and gossip to shared vocabularies, hand gestures, and facial expressions.

Holding a magnifying glass up to this world of "moral talk" reveals a hybrid moral ecosystem, in which Muslims, Copts, Jews, and atheists co-produced and shared many common value vocabularies. Often, these shared moral vocabularies could be recognized by watching out for certain metaphors and emotions. For Egyptians, this included shared metaphors about contamination, lowness, excess, and boundary breaking. Emotions were also a hybrid terrain, with Egyptians conceptualizing emotions through a mix of classical Greek philosophy, medieval Islamic philosophy, modern psychiatry, and more.

This fluid mixing produced broad similarities (or some level of isomorphy) between moral imaginaries and emotions concepts in English and Arabic. But despite these broad similarities, I would caution against interpreting isomorphy as evidence of biologically fixed "basic emotions." As shall be seen, the Egyptians and the English did share similar concepts about anger and pride, shock and shame. However, emotional and moral learning was heterogeneous across different individuals, families, and communities, and Egyptians creatively interpreted emotional cues from their bodies and their environments. Thus, to paraphrase Lisa Feldman Barrett: when dealing with Egyptian emotions, variation was the norm.[42]

3

The Ballad of King Faruq

Egyptian Experiences of the Second World War

It was June 1942, and the city of Cairo buzzed with tense speculation. In Libya, Allied troops fought to hold the Gazala Line against German and Italian forces. By the end of the month, the situation looked dire: the Axis had broken through, pushed across the border, and charged 250 miles into Egyptian territory. Now with the German army camped a mere 160 miles from the Egyptian capital, British Commonwealth infantry from India, South Africa, and New Zealand were entrenched at El Alamein in a last effort to keep Cairo from falling.[1]

In Cairo's wealthy European quarter, Diane Rossano passed most of her summer evenings that year at home. Scion of Egyptian-Italian Jews and daughter of the director of the Egyptian National Bank, Diane spoke French and Italian at home. During the daytime she counted bills at the bank, and in the evenings she listened to her mother humming passages from *Rigoletto, Il Trovatore*, or *La Traviata* along with the gramophone.[2]

Their parlor gradually filled with talk of European politics. The Jewish family had been watching the rise of the Mussolini regime with concern. By summer 1942, concern transformed into fear. As the First Battle of El Alamein raged to the west and air raid sirens disrupted life in the city, many of Diane's relatives and friends evacuated Cairo for the Sudan or British Palestine. Finally Diane's father called the family together, and in a meeting that stretched late into the night, the household discussed whether to leave Egypt.

It was Diane's boyfriend who convinced the Rossano family to stay. A handsome blonde Egyptian military officer (whose mother was English and father Turco-Circassian), Osman had met Diane at a formal ball. The two began dating after Diane convinced the young Muslim officer to join her Marxist salon, where she gathered with friends to discuss European literature. Now, Osman reassured the family that he could use his military contacts to evacuate them if the time came. As a result, Diane stayed in Cairo—and a month and a half before the Second Battle of El Alamein, she and Osman created a scandal in both their respective social circles by wedding across religious lines.[3]

That summer unfolded differently for another Egyptian teenager. Despite the drama unfolding in the Western Desert, back in Cairo school had just let out for the summer—and a new class of high school students was celebrating a successful graduation. Ahmad ʿAdil Kamal was among the celebrants; he had just turned sixteen and was scheduled to start classes at Fuʾad University in the fall. After graduation, he recalled spending his summer nights at home with family: a private boy with only a few friends, Ahmad loved to collect stamps and play chess with his parents.[4]

The self-described introvert did not realize it, but his life was about to be upended. He lived in Hadaʾiq al-Qubba, a busy urban neighborhood known for its proximity to the royal palace. The neighborhood was also near the British War College and the army barracks, and hosted multiple social clubs for officers, government officials, and petroleum employees. Since Egypt was in the throes of the Second World War, Ahmad encountered many British, Indian, and Australian soldiers coming and going that summer.[5] However, the trigger that changed his life was innocuous: one evening, three boys from the neighborhood stopped and invited the shy Ahmad to the cinema. They had a *loge* [box seats] that seated four, but Tahir, ʿAli, and Muhammad were one man short. Ahmad agreed to be their fourth, and the boys set off for the show.

Ahmad remembered the trip vividly because he never made it to the cinema. On the way to the theater, the call to prayer [*adhān*] sounded from a nearby recreation center. ʿAli, the pious boy of the bunch, asked the friends to stop so he could go inside and perform the *maghrib* prayer. Ahmad, Tahir, and Muhammad agreed—but since they were not particularly pious, they waited for their friend outside.

The minutes dragged by: ʿAli did not return. Frustrated, the boys trudged inside, only to discover the house was a Muslim Brotherhood center. Cornered by a very enthusiastic and persistent host, they were cajoled into signing a membership roster and staying for a lecture. Sixteen at the time, Ahmad was not impressed: he spent the entire time sourly thinking "I didn't leave my house to hear hadith. … What do these people want? … What do they want from me?"[6]

The lecture went so long, the boys missed the show. As a result, the journey home was uncomfortable. Upset, the young men mocked the sermon, and Ahmad ended the night with nothing but bitter feelings toward the Muslim Brotherhood. He never planned to return.

A week or so later, however, Ahmad received an unexpected visitor: a Muslim Brotherhood member showed up at Ahmad's home. As the recruiter explained, it was his job to follow up with "absentee members." Not considering himself a member (he had signed the roster to hasten the end of their harassment), Ahmad remembered being furious about this *iftiqād*[7] or follow-up visit. But the indefatigable Brother still managed to coax the teenager into attending a second lecture.

At this second meeting, Ahmad found himself liking the sermon despite his misgivings. He found the speaker (Muhammad al-Khudari) and his lecture about hope engaging; Ahmad also discovered that one of his neighbors—a young man his age named Husayn ʿAbd al-Samiʿ—was attending. The two began walking to the club together to hear al-Khudari speak, chatting and joking along the way. Some of Ahmad's friends, including skeptical Tahir from the ill-fated theater trip, also joined them. And slowly, Ahmad said, "In this way I emerged from my solitude into a spirit of community."[8]

Two individuals from two very different backgrounds, both Ahmad and Diane would join anti-colonial societies on the eve of the popular struggle for British evacuation. Both would make huge personal sacrifices in the name of a cause. Some of their choices were unexpected, even counterintuitive. Despite his rancor against the group, Ahmad Kamal would whole-heartedly join the Muslim Brotherhood and be arrested for building and planting bombs. Diane Rossano would abandon her husband and children to continue the communist revolution from exile abroad. For their decisions, both activists would be vilified as "radicals," "terrorists," and "fanatics." But what tales did they tell about their activism, emotions, and struggles in early Cold War Egypt?

Cairo under Occupation

The Second World War put pressure on the moral order the 1919 generation had built and disrupted almost every aspect of Egyptian life. The war brought to Egypt a flood of hundreds of thousands of refugees, along with a wave of foreign troops: a mix of English, Polish, Australian, New Zealander, South African, Indian, Canadian, French, and Greek servicemen. By November 1941, the Commonwealth garrison Cairo swelled to 140,000 men.[9]

Young and untrained and housed at Qasr al-Nil barracks in the Cairo city center, the influx of soldiers added to visibility of foreigners and disrupted the city's social life. Drunk soldiers caroused through the downtown, groping women, robbing passersby, and commandeering Egyptian cars and taxis. The foreign soldiers also played the "tarbush game"—competing to see who could knock the most red hats off local pedestrians.[10] They may have picked up the game watching Egyptian schoolchildren: kids in Cairo reveled in toppling the red hats from their peers' heads.[11] However, the wartime context, the power dimension of the occupying soldiers, and the fact the tarbush was a symbol of Egyptian national pride (akin to an American flag pin) meant that Egyptian adults read the hat-attacks as something less than friendly.

Commonwealth troops further offended Egyptians by belting out verses to a British army ballad called "The Ballad of King Faruk [Faruq]." The song started in Cairo cinemas: it was tradition that at the end of every film a photo of the king would appear and an instrumental version of the Egyptian national anthem (*al-Salām al-Malakī al-Miṣrī*, by Verdi) would play. Around 1941, Australian soldiers in the audience began inventing their own lyrics to the song. As the esteemed anthem played, the Australians began singing: "King Faruk, King Faruk, hang your bollocks on a hook …" In 1942, Scottish soldier and poet Hamish Henderson added multiple ribald verses to the esteemed anthem; his version swept the barracks and became an instant classic. Now, Commonwealth soldiers sang the following:

> O we're all black bastards / But we *do* love our king /
> Every night at the flicks / You can hear us fuckin' sing: /
> *Quais ketir* [Very good] King Faruk, /
> *Quais ketir* [Very good] King Faruk, /
> O You can't fuck Farida[12] if you don't pay Farouk.
> ….
> If her boudoir you pass 'tween the hours of ten and two
> You will see all the Wafd[13] standing waiting in a queue.
> Though Nahhas[14] ain't an ass, / Though Nahhas is a crook,
> Still he can't fuck Farida if he ain't got *filoos* [money].
> ….
> O this song that you've heard is the song the Gippos[15] sing, /
> And they'd sing just the same if they'd Nahhas for a king.
> *Kwise kateer* [Very good], Nahhas Pash',
> *Kwise kateer* [Very good], Nahhas Pash',
> O we won't mind your morals if you hand out the cash.[16]

Historically, the ballad can be read as a cathartic outlet for cultural dislocation and the frustrations of wartime. To the British men, the song served as a show of masculine camaraderie and virility, with verses describing masturbation (enjoining listeners to "pull your wire" and "pull your pud"), anal intercourse, prostitution in the Clot Bey district of Cairo, and vulgar catcalling (with one line shouting in hackneyed Arabic "Show me pussy!"). The tune also served as protest against higher-ups: commanding officers tried to squelch the ditty, but the rank-and-file merely added the British ambassador to the song, singing if "Ole Sir Miles with his wiles / In advance tries to book / But he can't fuck Farida if he don't pay Faruk."[17]

Egyptians, however, experienced the song as profoundly humiliating. The ribaldry highlighted the indignity of British occupation, and piled on defamation of the Queen, insults to female modesty, disrespect for honored Egyptian national symbols, and mockery of the subservient comportment of ordinary Egyptians in the face of insult (with lines parroting "Very good, King Faruk" / "Very good, Nahhas Pasha"). The song also brimmed with racism and bigotry (with Egyptians called "damn [n–word]," "wogs," "black bastards," "Gippos," and "buggers" in the song). Finally, the ballad underscored the Egyptian government's failures in policing public morality: lyrics mocked moral problems that Egyptians themselves considered sources of national shame, such as prostitution in Clot Bey, government corruption, and the king's womanizing.[18]

Overall, Egyptian activists cited the soldiers' behavior as one factor that inspired them to anti-colonial activism after the war. Free Officer General Muhammad Naguib remembered, "Their troops marched through the streets of Cairo singing obscene songs about our King, a man whom few of us admired, but who, nevertheless, was as much of a national symbol as our flag." He recalled getting in a fight on a bus with an intoxicated British soldier, and being assaulted by three drunken South Africans who hit him over the head with a beer bottle and stole his wallet.[19] As late as 1954, communist EMNL activist Diane Rossano said she was "still furious at the memory of these colossal drunks" groping women. She remembered being assaulted, then rescued by her brother.[20] Muslim Brotherhood activist Ahmad ʿAdil Kamal and communist activist Mubarak ʿAbdu Fadl similarly listed the disturbances caused by soldiers "rampaging" through the downtown as motivating their anti-colonial activism in postwar Cairo.[21]

The Second World War opened the door for anti-colonial activism in Egypt in other ways. The war effort required almost a million Egyptian workers, who in grueling conditions built military barracks, dug trenches and defense lines, operated repair workshops and depots, ran shipping and warehouse services, paved roads, and manufactured industrial materials and army issue items for arriving troops. Egyptian medical staff fumigated and immunized soldiers, transported the wounded, and treated the ill. War furthermore forced a wholescale shift of Egyptian agricultural production. When American import protections in 1942 led to the crash of Egypt's main industry (cotton), the British pressured landlords and farmers to convert acreage to wartime food crops. There was a scramble to reallocate land, and ultimately Egypt would provide Allied forces with 60,000 tons of wheat and maize in 1943, another 30,000 tons of wheat, maize, and barley in 1944, and thousands of tons of potatoes a year at the reduced rate of 9 Egyptian pounds per ton (instead of the market price of 23–5 Egyptian pounds per ton).[22]

While Egyptian civilians suffered shortages from the requisitions (shortages exacerbated by an Italian blockade of Mediterranean shipping), most vital consumer goods went to the war effort. Egypt contributed 395,522 spools of thread and 80,000 thousand pounds of sugar (1943–5) to the Allies (and sold more sugar at extremely reduced rates). Moreover, 70 percent of Egyptian cement went to the Allies during the war, along with vegetables and vaccines. A particularly painful gift was a loan to Britain of 400 million pounds sterling, which would become a sore spot after the war: British refusal to service or repay the loan would cause diplomatic tension and public protest (as the lack of sterling exacerbated Egyptian economic troubles).[23] Egypt's conversion of the workforce would also have lasting effects, triggering a postwar unemployment and urban poverty crisis (which likely gave a push to the recruitment efforts of labor unionists and social service-based societies like the Muslim Brotherhood).

Political disruptions were also rampant. Egyptian prison cells opened to provide additional workers to the war effort, while thousands of political prisoners flowed in. The German march through North Africa inspired Egyptian plots to partner with the Germans to end the British occupation. By 1941, pamphlets calling for revolution and the assassination of British officials were commonplace, and in summer the Egyptian general ʿAziz al-Misri infamously attempted to defect (allegedly to join either Rommel or the anti-colonial uprising underway in Iraq). The British Administration arrested Young Egypt members and communists, and shipped Muslim Brotherhood leader Hasan al-Banna out to the provinces for safe keeping.[24]

The worst political crisis, however, was the February 4 Incident. The crisis began when a series of political maneuvers in January 1942 forced the resignation of the Egyptian prime minister. However, with German forces advancing in the Western Desert and a pro-Axis politician (ʿAli Mahir Pasha) vying for the empty prime minister's seat by organizing street demonstrations, British ambassador Sir Miles Lampson decided to intervene. He believed the best formula for political stability was a "three-legged stool" approach to diplomacy—a tripartite balance of power between the British Residency, the Egyptian King, and the Wafd (Egypt's most respected political party). As a result, Lampson gave King Faruq an ultimatum: appoint the head of the Wafd Party, Mustafa al-Nahhas, to form a government by February 4 or accept the consequences.

King Faruq balked. Nahhas in office would weaken the palace's position, while an ʿAli Mahir premiership would strengthen the monarchy. So Faruq stalled, the deadline for the ultimatum passed, and Lampson's patience evaporated. On February 4, the ambassador ordered the British military to surround ʿAbdin Palace with tanks and armored trucks. Then, he stormed inside and presented the king with an abdication proclamation. The move humiliated the king and forced his cooperation: Faruq agreed to appoint a Wafdist cabinet, and Nahhas assumed office.[25]

Although aimed at imposing stability, the act of British bayonet diplomacy permanently overturned Lampson's "three-legged stool" strategy. News of the February 4 Incident circulated first by word of mouth—then following the end of the war, *Akhbar al-Yawm* published the full story in November 1945. Egyptian politicians in the opposition rushed to spread news of the "outrage" and "humiliation" of February 4, comparing the incident to the 1906 Dinshaway massacre. Since Dinshaway was the founding trauma that legitimized the 1919 Revolution, this comparison was revolutionary.

Sayyid Qutb was one activist who helped spin February 4 into a new revolutionary myth. In December 1945, he wrote the "shame of 4 February" echoed the "shame of Dinshaway." As he proclaimed, February 4 should thus be "engraved in letters of fire" on the hearts of Egyptians; it should make blood boil, agitate every nerve in the body, and make the heart beat with anger and vengeful rancor [*naqma*] against the British.[26] Other nationalist activists took up the call of February 4. Khalid Muhyi al-Din later wrote that "After 4 February, the feeling of patriotism turned to gushing rage, and a feeling of the need to do something."[27] Naguib called February 4 "my explosion point" that pushed him to revolt; he could no longer stand debasement at the hands of the British.[28] The foundations for a new revolutionary myth were being laid.

"Leader of the Monkeys": The Collapse of the Wafd's Moral Credibility

When news leaked to the press that the Wafd had been ushered into office by British tanks, political aspirants challenged the Wafd's moral leadership and symbolic status as representatives of the Egyptian national struggle. The opposition condemned Nahhas as a traitor and accused the Wafd of being British pawns.[29] Egyptian politician Makram ʿUbayd (known as Egypt's human "political barometer"[30]) was one of the first to capitalize on the moment. In the aftermath of February 4, ʿUbayd published a scathing exposé of Wafd corruption called *The Black Book in the Black Era* [*al-Kitāb al-Aswad fī al-ʿAhd al-Aswad*]. Released in spring 1943, the book provided a lurid and detailed catalog of misdeeds perpetrated by members of the Wafd: graft, election-fixing, nepotism, bribery, war profiteering, contracting schemes, and more.[31]

Taken together, the February 4 Incident, *Black Book* scandal, and opposition campaigns undermined an important political sentiment: feelings of trust, admiration, and loyalty toward Wafd leaders. Describing the experience, Free Officer Muhammad Anwar al-Sadat wrote: "Nothing is more painful for young men than to be disillusioned in a leader who was once their idol. When we were schoolboys we had gone out twice a day to have a look at Nahhas (cheering and applauding) … he had been a mythical hero—a peerless symbol of patriotism, self-sacrifice, and devotion." But as Sadat explained, Egyptians no longer associated these feelings with Nahhas after February 4. "[H]e lost everything, and we came to regard him as a traitor."[32]

As historian Rifʿat Saʿid has pointed out, in the 1930s the popularity of Mustafa al-Nahhas and the Wafd had been a cap, limiting membership in organizations like the Muslim Brotherhood and Misr al-Fatah.[33] Now the two scandals—February 4 and *The Black Book*—created a rush of disaffiliations from the Wafd, as activists went in search of new vehicles for their political hopes. Activists remembered the sea change well: Mustafa Haykal related that February 4 destroyed any thoughts he had of joining the Wafd and gave him the push he needed to become a Marxist.[34] Latifa al-Zayyat similarly explained that in 1943 (her second year of university), she faced a decision of affiliation—and only two options seemed viable. As she recalled, "Any real nationalist had to make a choice, a decision, to become a communist or a member of the Muslim Brotherhood …. This was especially true after the failure of the established parties."[35] Both the Egyptian editorialist Sayyid Qutb and military officer ʿAbd al-Munʿim ʿAbd al-Raʾuf left the Wafd for the Muslim Brotherhood after the scandals (although Qutb would not officially declare his membership until 1953).[36] The Wafd—once champions of the Egyptian national movement—was morally bankrupt, and Nahhas lampooned in the press as the "Leader of the Monkeys."[37]

King Faruq's Watermelon

King Faruq was among the first to attempt to step into the moral vacuum created by the fall of the Wafd. Since the late 1930s, the young king had morally competed with the Wafd for influence by emphasizing his personal piety and cultivating ties to al-Azhar.[38] In summer 1937, palace advisors had even tried to advance Faruq as a candidate for the defunct caliphate. To this end, in June 1937 Faruq and his advisors proposed adding a religious element to the new king's coronation ceremony at the Citadel of Muhammad ʿAli Pasha. They argued the coronation should involve a religious oath of allegiance [*bayʾa*] on Thursday, in which al-Azhar Shaykh Muhammad al-Maraghi would present Faruq with the crown and sword of Muhammad ʿAli. This would be followed by a Friday prayer at the al-Azhar Mosque.

These attempts at marrying monarchial power with religio-moral leadership, however, vexed Faruq's political rivals. Prime Minister Mustafa al-Nahhas (known at the time as a pious Muslim) led Parliament in objecting vigorously to the religious investiture idea, complaining that coronation "was a purely constitutional matter and religion had nothing to do with it." Negotiations dragged into July, with Prime Minister Nahhas so "determined that there should be no element of religion" that he threatened resignation.[39] Nahhas won his case, and the *bayʾa* and religious investiture were removed from the order of ceremonies.

However, it was more difficult to refuse the king's attendance at Friday prayers—so the argument over the coronation ceremony shifted to *where* King Faruq would pray. Faruq submitted al-Azhar, the Citadel Mosque, and al-Husayn Mosque as prestigious candidates; eventually, he was forced to settle for the Rifaʿi Mosque (the resting place of his father King Fuʾad, next to the Citadel).[40] In this way, Parliament continued to emphasize that the king's authority was hereditary and constitutional, rather than derived from religious institutions (as a prayer at al-Azhar mosque might suggest) or a popular mandate (as al-Husayn Mosque might communicate).

While the Wafd won these battles in the 1930s, troubles after February 4, 1942 reignited the struggle for moral hegemony. By early 1943, the king was redoubling his displays of public piety. In January, Faruq began growing a beard and appeared on the cover of *al-Musawwar*, head bowed and holding prayer beads [*misbaḥa*] at the side of the Shaykh al-Azhar. This pious posture gained momentum after *The Black Book* controversy and Faruq's hospitalization from a car accident that November. Looking to convert sympathy from the car accident into a public relations boon, the palace launched a campaign to portray Faruq as a paragon of piety, scheduling the young monarch for mosque visits and charitable events.[41]

It did not take long for this campaign to flounder ignominiously, however. First, the Palace overstepped when it convinced the minister of Waqfs [Islamic Endowments] to issue a fatwa concerning the "discovery" that King Faruq was *sharīf* (a descendant of the Prophet Muhammad) through his mother Nazli Sabri. This was a problem: the Prophet Muhammad was from Arabia, whereas it was well-known that Faruq and his mother were of Turkish and French ancestry. As a result, the fatwa was widely ridiculed. As Nahhas vividly recalled upon hearing the news of Faruq's "discovery": "Glory! … I laughed as I have never laughed in my life!"[42]

A larger problem hindering Faruq's bid for moral hegemony was his reputation as a womanizer and gambler. Unlike criticisms of the Wafd, however, criticisms of the king could not be found on the pages of most magazines and newspapers: the monarch was legally protected from insult by lèse-majesté [*al-ʿayb fī al-dhāt al-malakiyya*] laws. Nevertheless, moral criticism circulated in underground newspapers, diplomatic communiques, popular slogans, and court cases. Four months after the February 4 Incident, for instance, a lèse-majesté case revealed that shaykh Husayn Muhammad al-Najjar had given a Friday sermon in which he said the king "keeps company with fornicators and wine drinkers." Another activist was arrested after Friday prayers in al-Khazindar Mosque for publicly denouncing Faruq's corruption and gambling.[43]

Jokes were another important form of moral judgment—so important that they were legally policed. For instance, actor and comedian Ismaʿil Yassin was a repeat offender in lèse-majesté trials, landing in jail three times for insulting the king; the first time was for a joke called "His Majesty's Watermelon." The joke was based on wordplay: the term *qarʿa,* which means "bald," is also an Egyptian colloquialism meaning "useless" (often used in the marketplace to suggest a person has been scammed). According to Yassin's joke, a watermelon vendor was selling melons by shouting "The King's Watermelon! The King's Watermelon! [*Baṭṭīkh al-malik! Baṭṭīkh al-malik!*]" However, when a customer called on the seller to open one of the melons, they discovered that it was *qarʿa* [useless, bald]. Not missing a beat, the savvy seller shouted "King Faruq's Watermelon! King Faruq's Watermelon!"[44]

Gossip was another channel through which moral opinions circulated. Some speculation about royal scandals was the standard chatter typically exchanged about celebrities and high-status figures. However, rumors could also function as an important mode of moral judgment, and as a social performance of boundary maintenance.[45]

Gossip as a form of moral policing was thus rife in 1940s Egypt. As Minister of Interior Murtada al-Maraghi recalled from those years, Faruq caroused openly, sitting with dancers at the Automobile Club and the Auberge nightclub. "Rumors spread about [Faruq] that his bed was not a night without a beautiful woman, whether a dancer or non-dancer." As Maraghi explained, "A man may be tolerated if he is a murderer, thief, or drug dealer—but he cannot be forgiven if he is a womanizer."[46] Scandalously, Faruq brought his women to official functions rather than enjoying his dalliances in private. In 1946, the king offended both British and Egyptian moral sensibilities by imposing one of his mistresses on a diplomatic dinner party. The woman's presence caused such a stir, Lord Killearn upbraided Major-General Charles Allfrey for having "badly let British moral standards down" by allowing the woman to dinner. When Husayn Sirri Pasha confronted Faruq on the debacle, the king protested that Edward VIII, Prince of Wales, had behaved in a similar fashion—to which Sirri retorted that the abdicated King Edward was hardly an example worth citing.[47]

Rumors also swirled around the widowed Queen Mother Nazli and her romance with Ahmad Hasanayn. This liaison ended with Hasanayn's untimely (and to many, suspicious) death in a car accident in 1946. That same year, the Queen Mother Nazli further upset moral norms by fleeing Egypt with her daughters Faʾiqa and Fathia [Fathiyya] (Faruq's sisters). By 1948, the royal women had settled in Beverly Hills and were enjoying the nightlife and social scene there, generating gossip about the state of the Palace. The situation worsened with Princess Fawzia's [Fawziyya's] divorce from the Shah of Iran in November 1948; seeding gossip, the Wafdist paper *al-Nida*ʾ published an article on January 20, 1948, on the newly single Fawzia's comings and goings to the flat of a young man in Zamalek. Most shocking was King Faruq's divorce from the beloved Queen Farida in November 1948. Rumor had it that Queen Farida's parting blow in the divorce was a message to Faruq, asking him to "take good care of [our] daughters, so that they do not become prostitutes like their aunts [Faʾiqa, Fathia, and Fawzia]."[48]

By 1949–51, the press began launching more direct assaults on the throne. Ahmad Husayn and Young Egypt constituted the king's most outspoken critics. In June 1950, the association launched a campaign to broadcast the monarch's improprieties. One article asked "How has the name of Samia Gamal [a famous belly-dancer] become associated with the name of the king?"; other headlines criticized the king's gambling habit (with two articles entitled "Gambling, Gambling, and Gambling Clubs!!" and "The [French] Newspaper *Le Figaro* Asks 'Is Gambling Part of the Religion of Islam?'"). The campaign was successful: by fall the paper's circulation had doubled.[49]

In 1949, the king's advisors were further implicated in the Palestine arms scandal, involving government ministers selling army rifles on the black market. This money-making scheme doomed Egyptian soldiers to carry outdated First World War service weapons into the 1948 War with the State of Israel. Egyptians denounced the arms scandal as sordid betrayal of the nation's military servicemen, and called it the nail in the coffin of the monarchy. As Free Officer Khalid Muhyi al-Din remembered it, the king "had truly fallen. All the credibility he had accumulated between 1936 and 1942 … had been lost and destroyed by the shell-fire in Palestine."[50]

Slogans chanted in demonstrations summarized the king's moral standing by the end of the decade. Slogans derided Faruq's womanizing, with protesters chanting phrases such as "Where is the food and clothing, Oh King of Women?" and "King of Egypt, Sudan, and Samia Gamal." Protestors also mocked Faruq's inability to manage his own household, shouting "Where is your mother, Oh Faruq?" and repeating the proverb "[He] who can't rule his mother can't rule [a nation]!" Other slogans called "Down with the son of the whore [Nazli]!" Finally, after the king's divorce, protestors cheered Queen Farida for having left the Palace, chanting "From the whorehouse to the house of purity, Oh Farida!"[51]

Overall, the slogans highlighted the close link in the Egyptian moral imagination between the household and the nation—a connection first noted by scholars Beth Baron and Lisa Pollard. The editor of *al-Risala*, Ahmad Hasan al-Zayyat, confirmed this link in 1942 by quoting a proverb about the connection between the health of the home and the health of the state: "the nation is the family repeated, and the homeland is the house magnified."[52] As Zaki Mubarak warned, "[T]he palace is the moral symbol of this country's spirituality."[53] Criticism of King Faruq's moral failings and family scandals were therefore not idle chatter—they represented a potent challenge to the monarchy.

Conclusion: *Moralpolitik* in "The House of Egypt"

In a study of the "moralpolitik" of late-nineteenth-century Egypt, Lisa Pollard notes that the British justified their occupation of Egypt by highlighting the country's moral and emotional failures. "The contract that was established between the British and the Egyptians between 1882 and the 1919 Revolution was based on an understanding that the British would leave after Egyptians matured and demonstrated a new assortment of virtues, morals, and behaviors." In the 1919 Revolution, the Wafd similarly based its leadership claims and national demands on the idea that Egypt had become modern and civilized, and its new "moral and material condition" made the nation ready for independence. Wafd leaders argued that their political party embodied the modern family values of the middle class—the Wafd was thus the best candidate to "father" the nation.[54]

Now under the late constitutional monarchy, the "domestic-nationalist" discourse remerged—but this time to cry moral crisis. Existing dissatisfaction developed into open fractures with the Second World War, the occupation of Cairo, and the British besiegement of ʿAbidin Palace on February 4, 1942. The end of the war, lifting of censorship, and a series of political scandals then opened opportunities for social entrepreneurs to advance new worldviews.

Seizing the moment, Egyptian politicians and activists sounded the alarm about moral crisis. Opposition parties and activists argued that the Wafd and the king were morally bankrupt, along with their claims of leadership over the "house of Egypt." As evidence of the failure, magazines and newspapers pointed to the dissolution of Egyptian family life: wives abandoned the home for cafes and theaters, husbands dallied with dancers, and divorce rates soared.[55] Makram ʿUbayd's *Black Book* was one of the many manifestos that cried moral panic: ʿUbayd argued the nation was passing through an "age of 'pornography' in the full meaning of the term." Integrity had deteriorated, and the scales of justice overturned. Egyptians must thus restore "national and personal dignity, dutifulness to the *al-ḥudūd* [boundaries; divine statutes or limits], the preservation of honor, and protecting *al-ḥurumāt* [things sacred and inviolable]."[56]

But who would restore the moral order and become the new guardian of the national family? According to the moral metaphors circulating, the Wafd was a zoo and the king as disappointing as buying a bad watermelon. The wilting credibility of the main political players thus triggered a fierce struggle to claim the mantle of moral leadership. A month after the February 4 Incident, the leader of the Muslim Brotherhood Hasan al-Banna tossed his hat in the ring and announced for the first time his candidature for the Ismaʿiliyya House of Representatives seat. That same year, the communist associations Iskra and al-Qalʿa were established, to be joined in 1943 by the Egyptian Movement for National Liberation and in 1945 by *al-Fajr al-Jadid* (the magazine that would form the base for the communist group the Workers' Vanguard). The race to market new moralities to Egyptians thus took off running. By 1947, Egypt could count at least 20 communist factions and some 135 Muslim religious societies (most of which were charitable, but many of which engaged in politics).[57] As communist recruiter Yusuf Hazan described the post-1946 environment: "Recruit? The word doesn't fit. You only had to strike a match, and everything went up in flames!"[58]

4

The Muslim Brotherhood and Young Egypt on Trial

Conversion, Competition, and Compromise

With the scandals in the Wafd Party in spring 1943, many Cairo political societies stepped in to fill the void. Two prominent associations competing to fill the gap were Young Egypt (Misr al-Fatah) and the Society of the Muslim Brothers (Jamaʿat al-Ikhwan al-Muslimin)—better known as the Muslim Brotherhood or simply the Brothers (Ikhwan). The two groups quickly found that recruitment was not easy: like chess-playing introvert Ahmad ʿAdil Kamal, many Egyptians were suspicious of the political associations and their claims. When Abu al-Futuh ʿAfifi first saw Brotherhood slogans on the street, for instance, he assumed it was just another self-serving political party using Islam to get votes. So, he disregarded the advertisements. When a friend later asked him to join the group, he said "I completely refused … I retorted that this is just their way to reach government office!" (He eventually conceded and became a dedicated member.)[1]

Considering this mistrust, how did the Muslim Brotherhood and Young Egypt draw in members and compete in the Egyptian political marketplace? What kind of affective environment did the groups foster? As this chapter explores, to attract and retain members, Egyptian political societies produced emotional goods and services and worked to build and maintain trust. Myths as narratives of collective significance were a potent way Young Egypt and the Muslim Brotherhood achieved this. They claimed Egyptians and Muslims had been humiliated and brought low, but the faithful (through their strivings) would restore the community to greatness.[2]

Political societies also differentiated themselves by adapting popular currents of the era. In the 1930s, Misr al-Fatah and the Ikhwan fluidly borrowed from European fascism, integral nationalism, Pharaonism, Islamic modernism, Sufism, Salafism, Protestant revivalism, and democratic liberalism. And by the

1940s, the two organizations increasingly adapted elements from communism. However, neither group engaged in "high fidelity imitation" of any particular tradition—instead, the associations were bricoleurs, testing and modifying ideas.[3]

This flexibility was necessary for group survival—but such practices also posed a conundrum. Political associations had to remain competitive, so they made moral compromises, borrowed from unorthodox sources, and colluded and compromised with the British, the Wafd Party, and other political actors—all while denouncing competitors for these same moral compromises. However, when making "deals with the devil," groups had to maintain enough behavioral and ideological consistency to maintain trust and avoid disrupting the narratives of virtue and heroism that sustained member commitments. The result of this conundrum was a colorful history of moral contortionism, alongside public reassurances that the societies remained pure to their principles.

As the 1940s wore on, some Egyptians became disillusioned, interpreted double-dealing as hypocrisy, and abandoned the clubs. However, even as purity narratives became more and more unbelievable, some members (like Ahmad and Tahir) intensified their commitments and embraced violence rather than abandon their investments, the affective community they had built, and their narrative identities as saviors of society.

Young Egypt responded to scandals and membership flight by doubling down and instructing members to participate in violent virtue signaling—a decision that landed the group's leader in prison. The Muslim Brotherhood, meanwhile, devolved into a civil war, a series of violent attacks, and the government dissolution of the society. Caught in the middle of the tempest, one of Ahmad's closest friends entered the Ministry of Interior on December 28, 1948, approached the Egyptian prime minister, and shot him in the back. The doomed decision ended with the reciprocal assassination of Muslim Brotherhood leader Hasan al-Banna and two court cases that put activist stories about "doing wrong and feeling moral"[4] on trial. Arrested and arraigned as part of the "Jeep Case," Ahmad and Tahir stood accused of capital murder, bombings, and plotting to overthrow the government as part of a terrorist organization. The trial became a high-stakes drama, in which Egyptians debated the defendants' motives and morals. Meanwhile, Ahmad and his friends were thrust into a life-or-death struggle to convince the court of their good faith.

Through the pages of society newsletters and the eyes of group members, this chapter reconstructs this history of how Young Egypt and the Muslim Brotherhood competed through the 1940s. The first part of the chapter briefly explores the collective myth and conversion stories of Young Egypt members, alongside the group's history of moral compromises. The second part of the chapter then looks at Muslim Brotherhood members, focusing on the society's affective environment and decision to embrace violence. The result is a very human history of two controversial organizations, which polarized Egyptian opinion in the 1940s (and in the case of the Muslim Brotherhood, continues to polarize opinion today).

"Necessity Knows No Law": Misr al-Fatah

In 1940s Cairo, one of the primary players among conservative clubs was the group Young Egypt. Established in 1933 by energetic law students Ahmad Husayn and Fathi Radwan, the association began its career by declaring itself the champion of Egyptian masculinity and traditional family values: its early platforms emphasized abolishing "immorality, alcoholic beverages, and effeminacy" from Egyptian society.[5] The group also distinguished itself in the 1930s by embracing Pharaonism, a secular nationalist doctrine which called for a revival of modern Egypt based on the recovery of the nation's ancient Egyptian past. The 1922 discovery of Tutankhamun's tomb—coming on the heels of the 1919 Revolution—had sparked a fashion for pharaohs and hieroglyphs and ancient Egyptian archaeology; seizing on the fad, Egyptian leaders talked of restoring the greatness of Pharaonic Egypt and made "pilgrimages" to the Valley of the Kings and Karnak to visit the ancient ruins.[6]

In this climate, Young Egypt leader Ahmad Husayn adapted Pharaonism into a myth about personal and national rebirth. Husayn outlined this narrative in an early manifesto entitled *Imānī* [My Faith], in which he described how a scouting trip to Luxor in December 1928 sparked a personal "rebirth." In a day "chiseled in my memory," Husayn said he stood at attention with his scouting troop as they lowered the Egyptian flag for the evening. The bugle called; dusk rolled across the desert ruins. "For the first time in my life, I stood in front of the flag, as if I were in prayer," Husayn wrote. In this moment of intense national pride, Husayn watched his fellow scouts, "their eyes shining with this holy flame that eyes reflect when men are in spiritual ecstasy," and he felt his spirit soar over Egypt. That evening, he said, "I felt rebirth growing in my soul and in my mind … it was the beginning of my development—my entrance into a new world."[7]

Husayn's concept of rebirth in those years was spiritual, but not necessarily religious. As Husayn clarified in *Imānī*, while visiting Karnak he asked the heavens what would bring life to the ruins. He received no answer; but drawing his finger through the sand, he found himself tracing out one word: faith. As Husayn narrated, he thus left Karnak convinced of "the need for faith *in our greatness*, in order to resurrect the glory of ancient Egypt."[8]

In his quest to restore Egypt greatness, Husayn first instructed group members to perform rebirth by changing their names. As Husayn wrote, "Since that night [at Karnak], I devoted my life to the *revival of the glory* of Pharaonic Egypt … appealing to people to take Pharaonic names—starting with myself. I took the name Aḥmas … a shortening of my name, Ahmad Husayn."[9] This rebirth and name change inducted members into a lived morality tale.

Known to scholars as a "biographical reconstruction" (and more popularly known as a conversion story), these self-narratives were extremely important for social activism. Biographical narratives helped individuals produce personal transformation, perform new identities, and integrate themselves into the group.[10] Like many conversion stories, Husayn's narrative also organized time into a clear chronotrope or temporal schema, creating a grand rupture between "the old life and the new." Egyptian history was re-mapped to fit this revival narrative: ancient Egypt had once been great, it had fallen, now Young Egypt would make Egyptian great again.[11] This narrative provided a shared story about who Egyptians were and where they were headed; the "moral of the story" was a process of collective becoming, or a transformation to greatness. As compared to the progress myths of communist clubs (explored in the next chapter), revival myths were a common narrative mode for conservative political movements, and typically followed a high–low–high pattern (describing a magnificent past, decline, and return to glory).

In addition to unifying members around a group narrative, Young Egypt creatively borrowed from modernist movements like scouting and Romantic nationalism. The society emphasized that Egypt could only become great through masculinity, and an active "martial spirit," British evacuation, the eradication of foreign influence from Egypt, and spiritualism (as opposed to Islamic piety). The association also borrowed the organizational modes, patriotic displays, and nativism of European fascist movements. That said, the association adapted fascist modes selectively: it vocally condemned Nazi racism—along with other foreign doctrines like capitalism, communism, and imperialism.[12]

Echoing worldwide trends, in 1933 the Egyptian Watani Party created a paramilitary group called the Blue Shirts. The precedent inspired Young Egypt to launch its own paramilitary corps, the Green Shirts, in 1934. The following year, Britain increased its troop strength in Egypt, pouring fuel on political tensions, and in January 1936 the Wafd Party decided to establish its own Blue Shirts. That same month, palace politician ʿAli Mahir became prime minister and gave Young Egypt a huge boon: he cultivated ties with the association, in order to use it in street battles against the Wafd Blue Shirts. With this political patronage, Misr al-Fatah and their Green Shirts experienced a membership boom in 1935–6 that would position the society as a major political player for the rest of the decade.[13]

That said, Young Egypt's fasco-Pharaonic phase did not last. By the late 1930s, the association was facing financial troubles and competition from a new player on the market—the Muslim Brotherhood. As a result, shortly on the heels of the Muslim Brotherhood's decision in February 1939 to declare itself a political organization, Young Egypt rebranded itself with religious colors. In January 1940, Husayn performed the pilgrimage to Mecca, and in March he officially changed the party name to the "Islamic National Party." As Egyptian historian ʿAli Shalabi has argued, however, the change was not motivated by any sudden piety on Husayn's part, but rather a desire to bolster flagging membership and compete with the more popular Muslim Brotherhood.[14]

As part of his religious rebranding, Husayn went on a second pilgrimage to Mecca in January 1941 and drafted a new party program that included a call for the foundation of an Islamic University. However, Misr al-Fatah's publications validate Shalabi's argument that the shift in orientation was superficial: despite the name change, articles in the organization's newspaper remained largely consistent with earlier runs of the journal. There were vague overtures to Egyptian and Islamic identity—but little or no interest in theological discussion, Islamic ritual, or quoting scripture.[15]

At the same time Young Egypt was rebranding itself as religious, in spring 1940 club leader Ahmad Husayn approached the British Residency with professions of friendship—a blatant betrayal of the association's anti-colonial platform. To keep the association loyal and in line, the British took the olive branch and agreed to provide Young Egypt with funding. But the agreement only lasted six weeks before crumbling: an unknown agent leaked news of the deal, and Misr al-Fatah was so discredited by charges of British collaboration the society almost collapsed. As a result, over the next year Young Egypt swung to the opposite extreme: it tried to regain credibility through fiery anti-British speeches and religious rhetoric. The campaign ended in disaster: with the Second World War raging in North Africa, the British had little patience for wartime radicalism and ordered Husayn's arrest.[16]

By 1943, Young Egypt was back on the streets, thanks to a partnership with the Palace. In spring, the association switched sides again. The ailing Wafd Party (weakened by the *Black Book* scandal) tried to reinforce its ranks by releasing Young Egypt members from prison in exchange for votes in the upcoming election. The Wafd sweetened the deal by promising the organization's leaders government posts and providing financial assistance and facilities.

As part of this budding Wafd–Young Egypt alliance, between June and August 1944 Ahmad Husayn and his deputy Muhammad Subih again approached the British to make a deal. Their overtures prompted the British official overseeing the agreement to wryly remark that the society "reminded me of the Devil, who when ill was ready to be a saint."[17] Despite misgivings, the British agreed to another entente: they would supply Young Egypt with paper for printing tracts at the reduced military rate of 55 pounds per ton (as opposed to the black-market price of 450 pounds per ton).[18]

Misr al-Fatah took the paper. As Ahmad Husayn put it, "Necessity knows no law."[19] Less than two months later, however, Young Egypt was facing another self-made crisis. Members accused Husayn of becoming a propagandist for the Wafd, colluding with the British and Americans to import paper, and selling that paper on the black market for personal profit. The controversy resulted in a wave of defections, with Young Egypt members switching to other organizations. Similar to the membership flight of 1940, the defections prompted another spate of radical virtue displays: Young Egypt activists attacked bars and participated in grenade assaults to prove their mettle as an honest and patriotic association serious about British evacuation.[20]

By 1948, the Palestine War put the group back on the road to recovery. The dissolution of the Muslim Brotherhood that year also produced a membership boom, as a wave of ex-Muslim Brothers looked for new societies to join. But with Islamic activism now risky and communist associations becoming more popular, in 1949 Misr al-Fatah rebranded itself again: this time, the organization changed its name from the Islamic National Party to the Socialist Party. As before, the change was "little more than emotional sloganeering," as James Jankowski has pointed out. The society's "socialism" was limited to calls for land reform and workers' rights.[21]

Overall, Young Egypt's flexible approach was visible in the party's statements for the elections of January 1950. The party paper called for an Islamic–socialist synthesis, declaring that their socialism was "distinguished from Western socialism, in that we believe in God, religion, and morals." Articles in the issue appealed to Copt voters (praising Christ's message of peace and love and describing a joint Muslim–Christian struggle against European atheism and immorality). Other articles praised the Muslim Brotherhood and courted former members of the Islamic association.[22] A day later, Young Egypt scored its first major electoral victory: Young Egypt's vice president was elected to the Chamber of Deputies.

Despite the victory, Young Egypt's shifting strategies through the 1940s proved costly. The organization's frequent rebranding and attempts to "play all sides" hurt its reputation, triggered multiple waves of membership flight, and prompted radical (and costly) credibility-enhancing displays. The society also earned a dubious reputation for moral compromises, rebrandings, and ideological acrobatics. The "devil when ill" could very well put on the trappings of sainthood (and self-professed saints could make deals with the devil)—but too many ideological switches and interest-based violations of principle were bad for business. Husayn might argue that "necessity allows the forbidden," but members could (and did) leave if they felt the organization was out for its own benefit. After all, Egyptians had a name for disingenuous men who professed virtue: those who put on piety like a turban [*ḥāmil ʿimāmat al-taqī wa-l-waraʿ*].[23]

"Our Islam": The Muslim Brotherhood

At the same time Young Egypt competed for influence, another extra-parliamentary association was building a more formidable following: the Society of the Muslim Brothers (or the Ikhwan/Brothers). Better known as the Muslim Brotherhood, the club was the initiative of Hasan al-Banna, the eldest son of a village shaykh. Hasan had started formal education at a *madrasa* at age nine—but since he started school late, he did not memorize the Qurʾan in time to meet the entrance requirements for al-Azhar's Islamic seminary system. As a result, he entered Egypt's government-run, Western-style secondary schools.

As an adolescent, the young man became involved in lay activism: he joined an association of teachers and classmates called the Society for Morality and Ethics (Jamaʿat al-Akhlaq al-Adabiyya) and helped established a group called the Society for the Prevention of the Forbidden (Jamaʿat Manaʿ al-Muharramat). Around the same time, Hasan became a member of the Hassafiyya Sufi order, and in 1923 he and his best friend Ahmad al-Sukkari established the Hassafiyya Society for Charity. The society's goal was simple: compete with the American Presbyterian mission, which had arrived in town earlier that year.[24]

After Hasan completed his secondary schooling, his family relocated to Cairo so Hasan could attend the teacher's training college Dar al-ʿUlum. The transition to city life was difficult: the family moved over a dozen times between August 1924 and January 1926 (moves that continued into the early 1930s). During the day Hasan studied Western literature and Islamic modernism at the college, and in his spare time he worked with his father repairing watches and taking odd jobs.[25]

Upon graduation in 1927, Hasan took a teaching job in Ismaʿiliyya along the Suez Canal—the heart of the British presence in Egypt. There, he continued affiliating with different societies. He joined the Association for the Prevention of Narcotics and an unidentified "worker's club" associated with one of the Canal Zone cooperative societies. He also became one of the first members of the newly established Young Men's Muslim Association (YMMA) (opened in response to the establishment of the YMCA). Within a year, Hasan began writing articles for the YMMA's paper, *al-Fath*.[26]

In late spring 1929, Hasan al-Banna and his friends Ahmad al-Sukkari and Hamid ʿAskariyya decided to begin holding their own YMMA-style meetings in Ismaʿiliyya; they named the group the Muslim Brotherhood. The society started modestly, with members painting advertisements on walls in the middle of the night and recruiting through kinship networks. The group focused on Sufi piety, charitable work, and education, working to respond to English and American missionaries proselytizing in the Canal Zone. In response to the opening of Egypt General Mission schools in Ismaʿiliyya, for instance, the young club opened the Islamic Freedom Institute (est. 1931) and the School for Mothers of the Believers (est. 1932). As it expanded, the Brotherhood further launched summer camps to compete with the American Presbyterian Mission's Vacation Bible Schools and preached sermons in cafés (like American and British missionaries). This focus on missionary competition was reflected in the Ikhwan's first conference in May 1933, which discussed the Christian missionary problem.[27]

This engagement with Western missionaries proved vital for the group's takeoff. In summer 1933, a public scandal called the Turkiyya Hasan affair erupted. European missionaries stood accused of beating a Muslim student to make her convert. In response, the YMMA, National Party, and Ikhwan formed a coalition called the League for the Defense of Islam. The campaign was a turning point for the Ikhwan: the Brothers convinced one of the YMMA founders to help them underwrite a weekly journal (*al-Ikhwan al-Muslimin*, est. June 1933), and by year's end the Brotherhood doubled its branches.[28]

The Arab Revolt in Palestine (1936–9) gave the Brotherhood another boost. The Ikhwan and YMMA ran a campaign promoting a unified pan-Islamic front against British imperialism in Egypt and Palestine. The front also ran a fundraising drive that gave the Ikhwan a windfall of capital. Membership in the society swelled: by autumn 1937, an independent surveyor estimated Brotherhood membership to be about 20,000, and in 1938 the association founded its first weekly publication, *al-Nadhir*. By 1940, the Brothers were offering regular Tuesday lectures, scouting activities, public speaking classes, study groups, and small libraries.[29]

The Affective and Moral World of the Muslim Brotherhood

As the Brotherhood developed, it increasingly distinguished itself through its club myth and the affective environment it fostered. Emphasizing Islamic lay activism, the association appealed to the new generation of Egyptians who had received hybrid educations (attended primary school at a Qur'anic school/*kuttāb*, then enrolled in Western-style, government-run secondary schools).[30] In line with this hybrid epistemological outlook, al-Banna marketed himself as a modern lay scholar, quoting a mix of Islamic hadith and Western authors like George Bernard Shaw, Isaac Newton, and Herbert Spencer. Rather than wearing a turban and robe [*ʿimma* and *kākūlā*] like a traditional Islamic scholar [*ʿālim*], al-Banna frequently wore a Western suit and nationalist fez, a sartorial signaling of what Gudrun Krämer calls the "Islamic modern." These visual markers distinguished him as a modern middle-class professional and "fezzed shaykh" (lay activist).[31]

The association adopted modern recruitment strategies, attracting members through sports, scouting, drama clubs, and charitable activities. Nearly every branch had a theater troupe where local kids could take acting lessons and stage passion plays.[32] Sports teams formed a cornerstone of the association's affective environment, and were particularly "fundamental to [the Brotherhood's] ability to recruit and integrate young men in the organization." By the end of the 1940s, the society counted ninety-nine football teams, thirty-two basketball teams, twenty-seven ping pong teams, nineteen weightlifting teams, and sixteen wrestling teams.[33] Jabir Qumayhah, for instance, remembered being first attracted to the Brotherhood out of a love of ping-pong: "The thing that drew me to the Brotherhood branch was the presence of a ping-pong table," he explained.[34] Mahmud ʿAssaf similarly joined the Muslim Brotherhood in 1941 through a soccer scrimmage in his town of al-Qatawiyya.[35]

Understanding that many Egyptians were suspicious of political associations, the Ikhwan introduced potential members to doctrinal positions gradually. First, potential recruits were invited to join a sports match or attend an event, where they built relationships with current club members. No conversion to a life of piety or ideological commitment was required to attend the group's social events; instead, there were four levels of membership: assistant/helper [*musāʿid*], member/affiliate [*muntasib*], worker [*ʿāmil*], and fighter [*mujāhid*]. Only those in more advanced ranks of the organization (workers and fighters) committed to studying the Qurʾan.[36] These strategies helped lower entry costs, making it easy to affiliate with the group.

As the group's leader, Hasan al-Banna also played an essential role in attracting new members. Followers and detractors alike recognized him as charismatic, and described his charisma as a function of his relational gifts and ability to produce emotions in listeners. Ahmad Kamal, for instance, recalled that al-Banna sprinkled colloquial Arabic and humor into his sermons, which were so intimate that Ahmad felt the leader was having a conversation with him.[37] Al-Banna also used rhetoric and inflection in a way that inspired listeners to trust his sincerity. The leader could connect with others, even in throngs of people, and would pause during speeches to greet visitors from the provinces by name and ask about their families.[38] Jabir Qumayhah, who saw al-Banna speak at a tent meeting in Upper Egypt in the late 1930s, said the sermon was like nothing he had heard before in mosque. It was colorful, simple, and living: al-Banna used concrete stories and analogies (comparing the nation to a sailing ship), which Qumayhah understood as a boy and remembered years later. "But even more importantly than this, I had the powerful feeling … that he was directing his gaze and his words to me, and no one else." Qumayhah said he felt al-Banna could stir and awaken "invisible 'connections' in listeners."[39]

Outsiders also noted al-Banna's relational abilities: as American visitor Robert Jackson described after meeting the leader in 1946, al-Banna "didn't incite or stir up sentiment through shouting and agitation," and he was not a demagogue. Instead, Jackson explained, he was a relational networker who made everyone feel they had a special friendship with him. In this way, he convinced individual after individual, and linked them together with an unbreakable bond.[40] In short, al-Banna had an emotional and social intelligence that even outsiders recognized.

Under al-Banna's leadership, the Brotherhood developed a powerful group narrative of bringing men from darkness to light. But whereas Young Egypt's Pharaonism hinged on a romanticized reading of ancient Egyptian history, the

Muslim Brotherhood's narrative pivoted on a romanticized reading of Islamic history. Young Egypt called men to restore the glory of ancient Egypt; the Muslim Brotherhood called followers to restore "true Islam" [*al-islām al-ḥanīf*], and preached the need for a deliverance [*inqādh*] and renaissance [*baʿth*] of the Muslim community.

In constructing the society's myth, al-Banna transformed the story of early Islam into a morality tale of covenant, dissolution, and revival. This mythic timeline began with the foundation and expansion of the early Islamic state under the Prophet Muhammad; but the Islamic nation forsook this ideal order, falling into factionalism and allowing non-Arabs (Persians, Turks, and Mamluks) to have authority in the Islamic state. Their depravity allowed the Mongols to sack Baghdad, ending the Abbasid caliphate in 1258 CE. As a result, Christianity gathered its troops, launched nine crusades, and established a Crusader state in Jerusalem [*sic!*].[41]

In al-Banna's chronotrope, this caliphate–dissolution–revival cycle then repeated itself. God empowered Egypt to restore Jerusalem under the leadership of Salah al-Din, and under Baybars the Egyptians defeated the Mongols at ʿAyn Jalut and reestablished the Abbasid caliphate in Cairo. This new Islamic caliphate expanded and conquered Constantinople [*sic*]. Over time, however, the Ottomans succumbed to weakness, allowing Europe to occupy Ottoman territories and crush the Ottoman caliphate in 1924. Al-Banna's mythic cycle then ended with a message of hopeful expectation: anti-colonial revolts in Egypt, Iraq, and Palestine portended a coming "return of the Islamic nation."[42]

Historically speaking, the myth was an odd arrangement of anachronisms (the Sack of Baghdad in 1258 CE described as preceding the Siege of Jerusalem in 1099 CE), elisions (the long leap from the Prophet Muhammad to the Abbasids, and the leap from Baybars to the Sack of Constantinople), silences (the "forgetting" of the Shiʿi Fatimid caliphate in Cairo and the Umayyad caliphate in Córdoba), conflations (the merging of the Mamluk's "Islamic caliphate" with the Ottoman caliphate to force continuity), and inconsistencies (the blaming of Turks and Mamluks for the collapse of the Abbasid caliphate, but the "Egyptianization" of the Turkic-Mamluk Baybars in order to celebrate an "Egyptian" restoration of the caliphate). That said, the cyclical nature of the Ikhwanid founding myth so closely resembled the Qurʾanic "Covenant–Betrayal–Redemption myth" identified by R. Stephen Humphreys, it can be considered a subtype of the genre.[43]

More generally, the myth echoed the high–low–high pattern common in revival myths. And notably, this revival myth came fully equipped with a prescribed set of emotions that should guide the transition from humiliation back to greatness. As Hasan al-Banna exhorted followers, the struggle to restore Islam was a jihad of the heart. In a message entitled "To What Do We Summon the People?" he defined jihad as "an active and powerful emotion: an overflowing of longing for the honor [ʿ*izz*] and glory of Islam, and a yearning desire for her dominion and power; [this emotion] sorrowfully weeps over how weak the Muslims have become and how far they've fallen into humiliation."[44] Another statement by al-Banna described the society's purpose as to "revive the feeling of national dignity and liberate souls from weakness."[45]

This myth also gave group members a prescribed set of roles, based on a vision of chivalry and masculinity. Members were to be "monks by night, knights by day" and "soldiers of god," with the leader instructing activists to "always consider yourselves soldiers in the barracks awaiting orders."[46] Such terms sought to bestow members with agency and potency, and called them to take up heroic roles in a developing battle saga.

Revival myth in hand, the Muslim Brotherhood constructed and promoted an Islamic ethic for the *effendiyya*. Citing a part of Qurʾan 13:11 the society argued that Egypt's social and political conditions would only improve through industrious self-improvement.[47] The program was practical and straightforward: Egypt's problems had been caused by blindly imitating foreign systems; the solution was thus a return to Islam—an endogenous system that "guarantees to supply the rising nation with its needs."[48] Al-Banna was careful to define what he meant by "Islam," however. The Islam that would bring well-being was not traditional Islam, "confined to conscience and temple."[49] Nor was their Islam the Islam of the religious establishment, which had clambered in bed with corrupt politicians and was contributing to Islamic decline by focusing on boring philosophical theories rather than action. (Islamic education should be practical, interesting, and not boring, the club's newspaper argued.)[50] Instead, only an active, universal Islam would bring revival—an Islam that refused the distinction between religion and state. Al-Banna distinguished this type of Islam by dubbing it "our Islam" and declaring the Brotherhood had "inherited this pure Islam."[51]

To support this reading of Qurʾanic scripture, al-Banna located modern nationalist and internationalist ideas in religious text. (As al-Banna explained, "the Brotherhood has *found* the correct program in God's Book."[52]) As part of these eisegetical interpretive labors, al-Banna read Qurʾan 8:39 ("And fight them until there is no *fitna*, and the religion is all for God")[53] as an injunction to create an Islamic nation and expand it to encompass the entire world. He interpreted a fragment of Qurʾan 49:13 ("O mankind, indeed We have created you … and made you peoples and tribes that you may know one another") as a call for the creation of a common nationality.[54] Acknowledging that such scriptural interpretations were not exactly orthodox al-Banna warned followers that "some members of the official religious establishment [*al-ʿulamāʾ al-rasmiyīn*] will deem your understanding of Islam preposterous!"[55]

Equally controversial, the society called for a sweeping revision of the existing social divisions of labor: an expansion of the religious field into education, governance, security, and economy.[56] For instance, the organization proposed annexing state elementary schools to mosques, "the employment of Azharites in military and administrative posts," and "the surveillance of [government] employees' personal behavior."[57] The society also demanded clerical control over moral policing and campaigned against popular religious practices, including traditional wedding customs, funerals, births, holidays, and the *zār* (exorcism, generally performed by a female medium).[58]

Such policy ideas might not sound attractive to everyone—but one thing that made the Brotherhood's message compelling was the performances of cooperation and selflessness that accompanied the ideas. Brothers were expected to be model moral citizens: men should be literate and educated, avoid coffee, tea, and other stimulants, refrain from smoking, drinking, and gambling, wear and eat locally produced goods (instead of foreign products), and keep a clean house (for "religion is built on cleanliness," al-Banna explained).[59] Brothers were taught to embody virtues like honesty, bravery, fairness, faithfulness, forgiveness, humility, and service to others. Men were further told to be manly, maintain good physical health, be industrious, and excel at their jobs (see Figure 4.1). (Notably, al-Banna's main corpus of *rasāʾil* [messages] did not address women, and the society's newspapers were overwhelmingly aimed at male readers.)[60]

To enact these behavioral changes, the club embedded members in a strong social environment: it encouraged extensive social contact (building in time for both teaching and fun), had members check on one another, used kinship terms like "brother" and "sister," and created high-commitment cells called "families." Ahmad ʿAdil Kamal described the profound effect of this social environment. He gradually began to attend the club every day, until eventually he was placed in a family. His "family" saw one another constantly, learned everything about one another, and grew to love one another more than themselves.[61]

Another member, Jabir Qumayhah, described the social environment as full of fun and laughter. He remembered going on hikes and competing in soccer matches. The trips strengthened "the bonds of love and brotherhood," he explained.[62] As Taha Saʿd ʿUthman remembered, "We would go on Thursdays at night, pray, and then enter our room. Everybody from the family would take

Figure 4.1 Making Men in Muslim Brotherhood Newspapers.

While content addressing women did appear in Muslim Brotherhood magazines, most of the club's publications targeted male readers. Advertisements promoted men's underwear and herbal health drinks (left), calisthenics articles described the "exercise of the week" (right), and articles featured pictures of young men enjoying club social events.

Source: (Left) *Majalat al-Mabāḥith* 29, 27 Shaʿbān 1369/June 13, 1950; (Right) *al-Daʿwa* 3, 7 Jumādá al-ʾŪlá 1370/February 13, 1951, 14 in IISH COLL00329. Egyptian Religious Movements Periodical Collection, International Institute of Social History, Amsterdam.

all his money out of his pocket and put it together on a handkerchief. Some had a lot, some had a little—some did not have anything." The money was then split equally between the family members.[63]

Activists described how these relationships provided many socio-affective benefits: the group gave them a sense of self-esteem, certainty, and purpose. Hasan Dawh, for instance, had recently moved from a rural town to the bustling capital city of Cairo. He initially felt out of place in the city: urban elites mocked his simple speaking style and Saʿidi accent. But the Brotherhood valued his humble comportment and plainspoken style, and gave him an important role traveling out to the villages to preach. This made him feel valued; he felt that in the Ikhwan, he was making a meaningful contribution to a shared goal.[64] A new member echoed Dawh's sentiments during a speech in 1942, testifying that "A year ago, I was roaming through life aimlessly, I didn't have a purpose"—but after meeting Brothers at the Qena Division, he felt his soul rise, "and from that moment I became a soldier among soldiers marching toward the goal!"[65]

Other Ikhwan members similarly felt alienated and looked down upon by urban denizens. Muhammad Anwar al-Sadat (who would later become Egyptian prime minister) moved to Cairo in 1925. Feeling self-conscious of his poverty in the midst of urban affluence, he said he took solace in a sense of non-material superiority. "The set of values on which I was brought up in the village, and which city life so lacked, supported me," Sadat wrote:

> It deepened my feeling of inner superiority, a feeling which has never left me and which, I came to realize in time, is an inner power independent of all material resources. Indeed, that feeling [of inner superiority] perhaps gains strength as material resources diminish.[66]

For his part, al-Banna actively encouraged Egyptians to cultivate this sense of self-esteem based on superior moral virtues. As he acknowledged, the West belittled the East for lacking "the material power [that comes] from money and equipment and war machines … but even more important and necessary is spiritual power."[67] After joining the Brotherhood, Sayyid Qutb similarly argued that Egyptians should take pride in their moral values, rather than worry about their lack of material resources and struggle to keep up with the West. "Should not spiritual capital [*raṣīd al-rūḥ*; spiritual balance/credit], intellectual resources, and the heritage of heart and soul be treated the same as goods and money in human life?" he reasoned.[68]

Rituals and meditative exercises were another important way club members co-produced emotions. Members memorized aphorisms and sang Sufi hymns; more committed ranks attended all-night prayer and *dhikr* sessions.[69] By participating in these services, members engaged in the joint production of what Julia Clancy-Smith has called "sociospiritual services."[70] Speaking in layman's terms, Ahmad ʿAdil Kamal described what this looked like on the ground: the young men participated in Tuesday services and learned to recite scripture. Sermons worked to instill certain sentiments in attendees, calling members to particular emotional postures and indirectly advertising the emotional benefits of belonging. The nomenclature al-Banna used for his sermons reflected the importance of emotional production: as Ahmad remembered, "[al-Banna] hated calling it a 'lecture.' He would say 'It's not a lecture, it's an *ʿāṭifa* [feeling, passion]; so say 'Passion Tuesday'—not 'Lecture Tuesday' or 'Lesson Tuesday.'"[71] Al-Banna himself described his religious mission as unifying and "awakening feelings" in a population whose sentiments were divided.[72]

Published sermons primarily focused on affirming positive feelings like hope and brotherhood. Nations, al-Banna reasoned, could not advance without "a true awakening of spirits, souls, and feelings"—and particularly feelings of faith, hope, and pride. "Everything around us heralds hope!" al-Banna would say.[73] In a passage from "Our Call in a New Phase," the leader exhorted members about the importance of emotion:

> We want souls that are young and active and strong! Hearts that are new and beating! Feelings that are fervent and kindled and ablaze! Spirits that are vigorous and visionary and aspire to the heights … It's necessary to hone these goals and ideas, restrain these emotions and feelings, and focus—until they become a creed that does not accept debate, and does not allow for doubts or misgivings.

He added that before calling men to prayer and fasting, call them to three feelings: "faith in the greatness of The Message, pride in embracing it, and hope God will support it. *Do you believe?*"[74] For his part, Ahmad felt these affective labors were successful: he said being in the Brotherhood gave him a boundless hope and confidence he could accomplish anything.[75]

That said, the society's strong socio-affective environment had a coercive side. Brothers surveilled one another's behavior. By proposing a ban on popular religious practices like the *zār* and *mawlid* celebrations, and by calling for moral policing and an "Islamic government whose members are *practicing* Muslims,"[76] the Ikhwan's program also sought to invest the association with a monopoly on Islamic religious practice. Al-Banna, for instance, argued that two types of Muslims existed: the vast majority, who "perform prayer in a mechanical way inherited from their parents," and the select few who understood "the secrets of prayer" (secrets understood and taught by the society).[77] In short, the Brotherhood sought broad powers over religious boundary-creation and policing, *including the ability to define who constituted a true Muslim.*

A communist anti-Brotherhood tract published in 1946 suggests this strategy created a powerful barrier to exit for Ikhwan members. The tract tried to reassure Brothers thinking of leaving the society that resigning from the Muslim Brotherhood did not mean that one had left Islam.[78] The comment was significant: the Brotherhood, it seemed, had convinced at least some that membership was commensurate with being a "real Muslim." This conflated club membership with membership in the Muslim community—and salvation itself.

From the "Fezzed Shaykh" to "Shaykh Rasputin"

In his sermons, al-Banna prayed that outsiders would recognize that Brotherhood members loved others more than they loved themselves, were working for God not their own interests, and were offering themselves as sacrifices to restore Egypt's honor [*ʿizz*], religion, and hope. And indeed, as the Brotherhood grew, it tried to differentiate itself from the Wafd and Young Egypt by claiming the Brotherhood was honest and authentic (as one tract declared, "the invitation of the Brotherhood is a pure white call").[79] These appeals to morality had traction: as other parties become entangled in corruption scandals, the Brotherhood appeared an attractive alternative.

Ikhwan member Ahmad ʿAbd al-Majid recalled that this reputation for clean dealing won over many young activists. As he wrote, "the broad masses that followed the Brotherhood's movement did not follow it from an Islamic orientation or Islamic ideology, but because of their confidence in the Brotherhood's capabilities and its *naẓāfa* [lit.: cleanliness, fig.: lack of corruption] as a political course for achieving the demands of the masses."[80] ʿAbd al-Majid's discounting of the importance of religious ideology was probably an overstatement. However, his sentiments about the organization's reputation for clean-dealing revealed that in a climate of corruption, the Brotherhood's purity claims were compelling.

That said, as the society grew it confronted difficult decisions about how to answer competitors and adapt to shifts in the political landscape. Tracts from the mid- and late-1930s focused on competing with Young Egypt. A 1934 tract reflected the interwar passion for scouting and masculinity, describing how the nation must impress its "sons with a proper masculine disposition."[81] Responding to Young Egypt's formation of the Green Shirts and the Wafd's Blue Shirts, the Brothers added their own paramilitary group—the "Battalions" [*katāʾib*] around 1937.[82] Despite forming this paramilitary wing, the Ikhwan's Fifth Conference (1939) denounced Young Egypt as an example of narrow chauvinism and rejected the club's violent bar-sacking as too radical.[83]

By 1938 the Brotherhood was not only competitive—it had become a leader in extra-parliamentary politics. With increased success, however, came increased temptation. The first storm arrived in autumn 1939 and began with a disagreement over money: members expressed dissatisfaction that al-Banna was using donations for the Arab Revolt in Palestine for internal administrative purposes. Tied up in the money dispute was a disagreement about the role of Brotherhood deputy Ahmad al-Sukkari, who had accepted Prime Minister ʿAli Mahir Pasha's offer of patronage. This placed the Brotherhood in the orbit of the Palace (much like Young Egypt). The dissenting faction also raised questions about praxis: younger members demanded armed resistance against the British—but al-Banna (wanting to placate political allies and keep club members out of prison) preached gradualism and reformism.

As the split widened, Young Egypt began a wave of bar-sacking initiatives—and widely publicized these activities at Fuʾad University, denouncing the

Brotherhood for its inaction. Muslim Brotherhood activist Mahmud ʿAbd al-Ḥalim was a student leader on campus and understood "this action and this challenge was directed at the Ikhwan." Young Egypt sought to "surpass [the Brotherhood] in the field of action, and [knew] action will draw attention." In response, ʿAbd al-Halim wrote an article for the Brotherhood's magazine *al-Nadhir*, denouncing the bar sackings as foolish, futile, and contrary to the Prophet Muhammad's example of peace.[84]

Despite the article, "formidable pressure for revolutionary action was building up" in the Brotherhood. In early 1940, a group of disaffected Brothers split off to form a new club: the Society of Our Master Muhammad's Youth (Jamaʿat Shabab Sayyidna Muhammad).[85] The Muhammad's Youth faction did not command the same numbers as the Ikhwan, but it was an active and dynamic club, on account of its stricter approach to membership and high-commitment cells.[86] Muhammad's Youth became important for the pressure it exerted on the Brotherhood: Shabab activists denounced the Ikhwan for crooked leadership, moral permissiveness, and a lack of commitment to the armed struggle. This radical posture succeeded in attracting disgruntled Muslim Brotherhood and Young Egypt members. In a major blow in 1940, both Husayn Yusuf (one of the Ikhwan's youth leaders) and Mahmud Abu Zayd (editor of the Brotherhood magazine *al-Nadhir*) left to join Muhammad's Youth, with Zayd taking the Brotherhood's publishing license with him.[87] As a result, that year al-Banna moved the Ikhwan toward a greater emphasis on "struggle and action," approving the establishment of a militant "Special Section" [*Niẓām al-Khāṣṣ*].[88]

The discrediting of the Wafd Party following the February 4 Incident revived the Ikhwan's flagging fortunes, offering the club opportunity for political expansion. In March 1942, Hasan al-Banna seized this opportunity, announcing his candidature for the Ismaʿiliyya House of Representatives seat. Concerned, Prime Minister Nahhas pressured al-Banna to withdraw from the race, in exchange for a government publication license for *al-Ikhwan al-Muslimin*. Al-Banna took the deal and withdrew his candidature. Outraged, a wave of members left the club.[89] Muhammad's Youth capitalized on the moment by poaching Muslim Brotherhood members and denouncing the Ikhwan's "ignominious capitulation."[90]

In the years after the Second World War, the Brotherhood flourished. But as scandals in the Wafd gave a push to the expansion of extra-parliamentary associations, the Brotherhood soon faced a new competitor: communist clubs. To respond, the Brotherhood retooled its platform and creatively repositioned its Islamic system as a middle ground between the capitalist and communist blocs.

One of the earliest "Third Way" doctrines of the Cold War, the Brotherhood's "third bloc" concept was articulated in a 1947 book by Bahi al-Khuli, entitled *Islam, not Communism nor Capitalism*. A Brotherhood article the following year argued that Islam was an ideal synthesis, merging capitalism and communism into a spiritual, "reasonable socialism."[91]

In this early Cold War milieu, the Brotherhood received another windfall when one of Cairo's war profiteers, press barons, and paper suppliers, Muhammad Hilmi al-Minyawi, joined the association. He helped the society establish multiple periodicals and journals for young anti-establishment writers. The talented Sayyid Qutb was hired as the editor of *al-Fikr al-Jadid* (est. 1948), which although independent of the Ikhwan was bankrolled by Minyawi and fostered a community of revolutionary intellectuals, including Naguib Mahfouz.[92] As a result of his work at the journal, in the next two years Sayyid Qutb moved into the Brotherhood orbit, intellectually transitioned to Islamism, and began expanding on the Ikhwan's "third way" doctrine, publishing *Social Justice in Islam* (1949), *The Battle of Islam and Capitalism* (1951), and multiple articles on Islam as a "third bloc."[93] *Social Justice in Islam*, for instance, called for "absolute emotional emancipation" from materialism and the quest for power, and placed Islam as a harmonious middle between communism and Christianity.[94]

Just as the Muslim Brotherhood had adapted strategies from Christian missionaries and Young Egypt in the 1930s, in the early Cold War the Ikhwan also undertook to learn from communism. In the late 1940s, the Brothers sent members to observe communist cells in order to copy Marxist organizational strategies.[95] Taking a page from socialism, the Ikhwan also began calling for land redistribution, an end to "oppression by monopolistic companies," and the nationalization of Egyptian industries.[96] The Brothers further worked to address Marxist complaints about Egypt's "three ills" (poverty, ignorance, and disease), by opening medical clinics, insurance providers, and commercial startups; by the late 1940s, the society thus added to its portfolio a factory, a mine, and shipping interests.[97]

This competition with communist clubs came to a head in spring 1946. Buoyed by the end of wartime censorship in early 1946 a broad coalition of students (Wafdists, communists, and Muslim Brotherhood members) organized anti-colonial demonstrations in Cairo demanding British evacuation. On February 9, the students began a march from Fu'ad University to the Palace. Prime Minister Mahmud al-Nuqrashi (of the Sa'dist Party) ordered a police cordon to stop the procession, so police met the students as they crossed the 'Abbas Bridge. There was a tense standoff—then police commander Salim Zaki Pasha gave the order to turn back the students with billy clubs. When that failed, the police opened fire. Twenty students died: some from gunfire, others falling to their deaths and swallowed by the Nile River.[98]

The deaths of their peers infuriated the students. Determined to ensure their friends had not died in vain, over the next three weeks the protest movement escalated. On February 17, the Nuqrashi government was forced to resign. The resignation empowered rather than quenched the movement, and on February 21 a massive protest was held outside the British Qasr al-Nil Barracks in downtown Cairo (see Figure 4.2). When British military trucks tried to force their way through the crowd (ramming protestors), students swarmed the vehicles. In a chaotic and unclear sequence of events, British troops were called in and used live fire on the crowd, and students and workers burned military vehicles, ransacked the Royal Air Force Personnel Office and Officers' Club, and attacked foreign establishments. To restore calm, the British government announced on March 8 it would partially evacuate Egypt, leaving military personnel only in the Canal Zone. However, the demonstrations continued, demanding full evacuation.[99]

It was in this climate that Ahmad ʿAdil Kamal—now a senior in the Business School at Fuʾad University (and still furious from being hit with a police billy club in the ʿAbbas Bridge demonstration)—was invited to visit the home of Brother Husayn ʿAbd al-Samiʿ. At the house, he was extended a special invitation to join the Special Section, the Ikhwan's elite paramilitary branch. Ahmad was allowed to invite two others, so he chose two friends: Tahir ʿImad al-Din (his friend from that ill-starred theater trip) and ʿAbd al-Majid Hasan (a veterinary student). Together with his band of brothers, the boys trained to fight for British evacuation, going out to the desert to practice with Beretta pistols and Tommy guns.[100]

Meanwhile, the new People's Party government headed by Ismaʿil Sidqi worried the student demonstrations would usher the Wafd back to power. Determined to prevent his rivals from retaking the prime minister's seat, Sidqi offered the Muslim Brotherhood a deal: help disband the demonstrations, and the government would give the association paper and a publishing license to make *al-Ikhwan al-Muslimun* into a daily. Al-Banna accepted, purportedly providing the government with lists: the names and addresses of student activists on the left. The Brotherhood then deployed teams to break up protests and urge workers to return to their posts (and when that failed, they reportedly intimidated workers with sticks and pistols). As a result, the Sidqi government was able to close down leftist magazines and arrest hundreds of activists in "The Great Communist Plot" that summer.[101]

Figure 4.2 The Egyptian Anti-colonial Demonstrations of Spring 1946. Students and workers protest in Cairo on 21 February 1946, demanding British evacuation.

Source: "Anti-British Riots in Cairo: Scenes of the Disorders Which Have Threatened Anglo-Egyptian Relations," *Illustrated London News*, March 9, 1946, 261. © Illustrated London News Ltd/Mary Evans.

Ultimately, the crackdown proved counterproductive. The Sidqi government was forced to release most of the leftist activists for lack of evidence—and the communists emerged looking like the heroes of the national cause. Meanwhile, the Brotherhood beat back accusations the society had sold out. As members disaffiliated in droves, the Brotherhood approached the cusp of civil war. Free Officer and Brotherhood member Khalid Muhyi al-Din was one activist who left the group around that time. As he recalled, activists felt that in allying with Prime Minister Sidqi, the Ikhwan had "revealed its political face, behaved as a political group, and abandoned pretensions of religious purity .... We started to feel that they were just like other politicians: they preferred their own interests over what they claim are principles."[102] Taha Sa'd 'Uthman and Ahmad al-Gibali also left the Brotherhood after the 1946 incident.[103]

A series of violent attacks on cinemas, British ministries, churches, the YMCA, and foreign-owned shops accompanied the disaffiliations. The Muslim Brothers were suspected—but they were allied with the Sidqi government, so no arrests were made.[104] Meanwhile, the Wafd and leftist associations declared war on the Ikhwan–Sidqi bloc. Articles levied a long list of accusations at the Brotherhood, including lying, immorality, hypocrisy, sedition, lining their pockets, and misleading Muslims in the name of religion.[105] On National Struggle Day in November 1946, university students began chanting "No Fascism—No Brotherhood—No Trafficking in Religion!" The chants caused the gathering to devolve into a brawl between student clubs.[106]

That winter, violent attacks multiplied. Still suffering fallout from the Sidqi alliance, the Brotherhood had entered into a *fitna* (internal civil war). "The most serious crisis in the movement since its foundation," the *fitna* resulted in mass disaffiliations, investigations against club leaders, resignations, and leadership struggles.[107] To stop the hemorrhage of members, the Ikhwan focused on credibility-enhancing displays and virtue signaling, in the form of violent anti-colonial attacks.

In December 1946, Ahmad thus sat with his cell in a member's home. They prepared fuses, connected them to detonators and blasting gelatin, and wrapped the packages in craft paper. The cell then executed a series of Christmas Eve attacks on British soldiers and Egyptians suspected of collaborating with the British. They attacked bar patrons, hurled hand grenades at the Anglo-Egyptian Union (a British club), and attacked Egyptian police stations.[108]

The civil war unabated, in early 1947 al-Banna's best friend and group co-founder Ahmad al-Sukkari was expelled from the organization. Al-Sukkari had been advocating an alliance with the Wafd and seems to have challenged al-Banna's leadership. Now a free agent, al-Sukkari joined the Wafd and began writing articles against the Brotherhood; Salih 'Ashmawi, head of the society's militant Special Section, replaced al-Sukkari as al-Banna's deputy.[109] With 'Ashmawi's accession, the civil war deepened, and another cluster of attacks came in summer 1947 against the Metro Cinema, Cosmo Cinema, and Cinema Metropole; a group called Rabitat al-Shabab (a combination of Wafdists and disaffected Brotherhood activists, perhaps on al-Sukkari's initiative) was blamed.

The Brotherhood's reputation was crumbling. The Coptic newspaper *al-Manara al-Misriyya* between May and October 1947 caricatured al-Banna as an ass—a "donkey for imperialists" and "clown for rent."[110] The 1948 Palestine War and competition between the Wafd and the Saʿdist Parties (using activist associations as muscle) accelerated the slide toward street war. As Brothers and Young Egypt members joined the burgeoning volunteer movement preparing to fight in Palestine, the new prime minister, the Saʿdist Party's Mahmud al-Nuqrashi, attempted to arrest the Brotherhood's armament by seizing an Ikhwan arms cache in the Muqattam hills in January 1948. Undeterred, when the British evacuated Palestine that May, Misr al-Fatah and the Ikhwan took the opportunity to push for British evacuation of Egypt by launching a string of bombings against British and Jewish targets (denouncing Jews as a "Fifth Column" plotting to colonize Egypt). In response, communist articles accused the Brothers of advocating Islamic imperialism and being American agents. *Al-Hawadith* wrote an article entitled "Deutsche Egypt, after Deutsche Rome," comparing al-Banna to Mussolini and Hitler, and *Sawt al-Umma* ran with the headline "Shaykh Rasputin … Losing his Mind and His Manners." Finally, an article condemned al-Banna as the "Shaykh of *Taḍlīl*" [misinformation].[111]

In this climate of polarization, the Muslim Brotherhood and other organizations warned members to ignore outside news, and only trust information sanctioned by the society. In multiple articles, the Muslim Brotherhood's newspaper *al-Daʿwa* described other news outlets as the "enemies of truth." The paper denounced the "flood of lies from the news" and told members "do not pay attention to what is written" in other news sources—members "must rely on news reported to them through representatives of the Center … or published in the newspaper *al-Daʿwa.*"[112]

Ironically, the Brotherhood was not alone in telling members to distrust outside news. The communist paper *al-Fajr al-Jadid* condemned "fake news" [*khabaran kādhabān*], while Muhammad's Youth articles denounced the "dirty press" [*al-ṣuḥuf al-qadhira*] and the "dissolute press" [*al-ṣuḥuf al-khalīʿa*]. For their part, Ahmad Husayn and Young Egypt dubbed themselves the "bold press" who represented the "free pens."[113]

In part, these claims reflected a real problem with government censorship and misinformation in 1940s Egypt. However, dissuading group members from believing outside information was also a coercive strategy. By discounting divergent opinions, organizations could exercise more sway over the beliefs and behaviors of members. People make decisions based on the information they trust—so bad information tended to produce bad decisions.

The Muslim Brotherhood on Trial

With political parties and associations drawing battle lines, as well as burgeoning civil unrest in response to the Palestine War, the Egyptian government declared martial law. In October 1948 the police confiscated another arms store at the estate of Brotherhood paramilitary commander Shaykh Muhammad Farghali. A worse blow came in November: Ahmad and Tahir were transporting explosives in a Jeep when the car had battery troubles. A suspicious neighbor noticed the Jeep had no plates and shouted for the police. Ahmad and Tahir were arrested, and the Jeep's contents led to the arrest of some twenty-nine other Ikhwan members suspected of involvement in bombings and anti-colonial paramilitary operations in Cairo. Their subsequent trial would be known as the "Jeep Case."[114]

On December 4, infamous Cairo police commander Salim Zaki was killed by a bomb while trying to put down anti-colonial university demonstrations. Suspecting the Brotherhood, the Nuqrashi government issued a decree dissolving the Ikhwan, seizing its assets, and ordering that any Brotherhood members who did not disaffiliate be expelled from universities and government offices. The Ministry of Interior justified the dissolution on the grounds that the society "provoked disorder" and was working on "revolutionizing political and social principles by force and terrorism" to overthrow the government.[115] One of those ejected from his university program because of the government order was Ahmad's friend and cell member, twenty-year-old veterinary student ʿAbd al-Majid Hasan.

Twenty days after the decree, ʿAbd al-Majid donned a police uniform and waited in a café outside the Ministry of Interior. Ahmad and ʿAbd al-Majid's cell had been monitoring the prime minister's comings and goings for days—so when the minister's motorcade left his home, the boys called ʿAbd al-Majid at the café and gave him the green light. ʿAbd al-Majid entered the Ministry of Interior lobby, and as Prime Minister Nuqrashi headed for the elevator, ʿAbd al-Majid approached him, pulled out a gun, and shot him three times in the back.[116] Two months later, the Saʿdist Party responded: on the evening of February 12, 1949, two men approached Muslim Brotherhood guide Hasan al-Banna on the street and gunned him down.[117]

Now in charge, Brotherhood paramilitary commander Salih ʿAshmawi tried to keep the organization from collapsing. He was greeted with a series of articles and interviews by respected al-Azhar Shaykh Ahmad Muhammad Shakir, who denounced the Muslim Brothers as Kharijites and apostates.[118] Meanwhile, that summer the murder trial against twenty-year-old ʿAbd al-Majid Hasan opened. Hastily organized, the proceedings began in August 1949.

In the courtroom, the attorney general and public prosecutor denounced the Brotherhood as a criminal "league of sacrilege" [*ʿaṣba min al-fijār*], made up of men "seduced by Satan" who "distort The Word [of God] from its contexts, and invent lies against God to justify their crimes."[119] In contrast, ʿAbd al-Majid's defense lawyer (Ahmad al-Sadah) described his client as a victim, and painted a picture of a sincere and deeply religious boy who had struggled with mental illness following the death of his father. Drafted into the Brotherhood at age fifteen, the high school student had been recruited by members of his local mosque, then led astray by teachers he thought were respectable, the lawyer argued. On the stand, ʿAbd al-Majid then testified how he had joined the family system, how the family members came to know everything about one another, and how a boy from school (Ahmad) had eventually invited him to join the elite and militant Special Section. In the Special Section, ʿAbd al-Majid said he was introduced to leaders of the Ikhwan in contact with al-Banna. "This had a great effect on me. I firmly believed it impossible that these individuals—people of great status—who are working for Islam, will order me at some point to do something incompatible with Islam."[120]

In closing statements, the defense attorney once again asked the court to see his client as a victim: the Brotherhood had exploited ʿAbd al-Majid's piety and respect for authority figures, and guided the boy to religious fanaticism. (ʿAbd al-Majid had been the youngest of the conspirators, and in police interrogations he had described feeling social pressure not to fail in his mission.) The attorney concluded the twenty-year-old had merely been a patriot following orders, who had fallen victim to "demagoguery" and coercion.

The trial rushed to close before elections—the government feared the Wafd might return to power for the first time since the 1943 *Black Book* scandal. As a result, the ruling was handed down on October 13, 1949, along with a judicial opinion on the case. The court rejected ʿAbd al-Majid's claims to good faith, and declared that the assassin was a young man of majority, fully aware of his actions, who knew murder was forbidden by Islam. Then, the court "sent ʿAbd al-Majid's papers to the Mufti."[121] The Egyptian Grand Mufti, Hasanayn Muhammad Makhluf, reviewed the papers and provided a fatwa [legal opinion] stating that Prime Minister Nuqrashi's killing had been a violation of Islamic law. Back in the courtroom, the judge then pronounced the court's verdict: in murdering Nuqrashi, Hasan had claimed a right that belonged solely to the law; he had committed an act forbidden by God. Then, the judge sentenced ʿAbd al-Majid to death. After the student's appeal for pardon failed, he was hung on April 25, 1950.[122]

In contrast, Ahmad's trial for the Jeep Case moved at a glacial pace, with the proceedings stretching from December 1949 to February 1951. Ahmad and his thirty-one co-defendants stood accused of murder, bombings, plotting to overthrow the government, criminal endangerment, theft and extortion, sabotage to public utilities, attacks on police and government facilities, conspiracy to rob the National Bank, poisoning police horses, radio operating without a license, and a host of other crimes.[123] Having learned from ʿAbd al-Majid's failed appeal, defendants denied all charges and claimed any confessions were extracted by torture, rather than describe themselves as victims. Nevertheless, their case looked grim.

In a twist of fate, however, partway through the case Egypt held elections. Hoping to court votes from Muslim Brotherhood members, the Wafd intervened in the Jeep Case to demand the Saʿdist government trying the case be investigated for its involvement in the al-Banna assassination. The strategy won the Wafd the needed votes: the party emerged victorious in elections and returned to power in January 1950.

For Ahmad and the other Jeep Case defendants, there was a burst of hope: the Wafd government moved the trial from military to civil court, and Wafdist lawyers joined the defense team for the Muslim Brothers. Now on the defensive, the prosecution condemned the Brothers as terrorists and charlatans; in reply, one of the defense lawyers passionately declared that the prosecution "alters the facts, distorts [their] pride, and transforms angels into devils!" The defense then argued that any militant pamphlets or seized weapons were leftovers from the Palestine War, and any new weapons were not for terrorist attacks or overthrowing the Egyptian government, but for fighting a foreign occupier. To strengthen these claims, the defense summoned two Egyptian generals and the Mufti of Palestine to testify on the Brothers' behalf.[124]

When the Jeep Case judgment was announced in March 1951, it sent shock waves through Cairo. The verdict represented an enormous departure from the Nuqrashi assassination ruling: the court dismissed the charges of attempting to overthrow the regime, and instead convicted Ahmad ʿAdil Kamal and the other Brothers on lesser charges like public endangerment. As the verdict explained, the group deserved clemency "since they had lofty purposes, which aimed first to achieve national goals."[125]

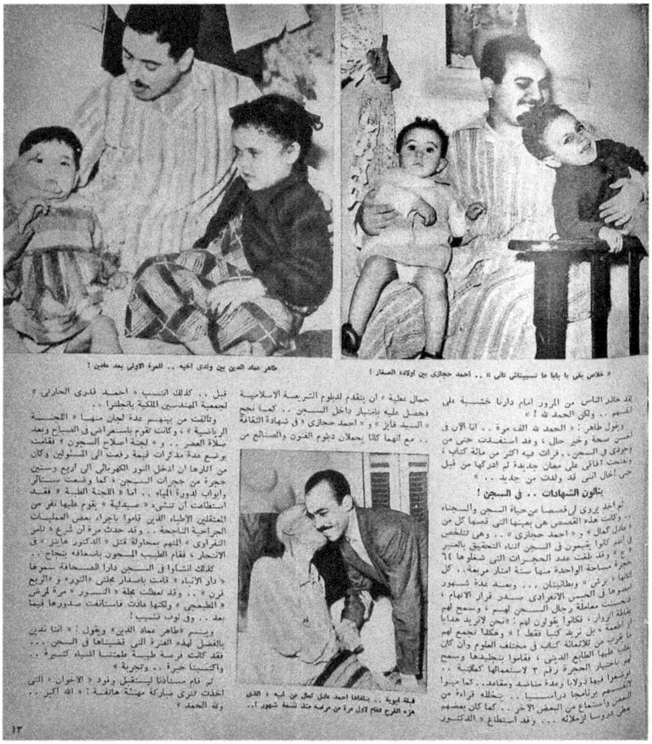

Figure 4.3 Jeep Case Defendants Following the Verdict.

Muslim Brotherhood activist Ahmad ʿAdil Kamal (bottom) receives a kiss from his infirm father, after receiving a reduced prison sentence of two years. In the upper photos, Tahir ʿImad al-Din (left) and Ahmad Hijazi (right) embrace their children. The photos communicated a clear moral message about the defendants, framing them as "family men." Overall, most news coverage of the verdict was sympathetic, with even the liberal journal *al-Musawwar* showing pictures of the men celebrating with their families and being greeted by a joyful crowd.

Source: "Al-Qaḍiyya allatī Shaghalat al-Raʾy al-ʿĀmm Ṭawīlan," *al-Muṣawwar* 1380, March 23, 1951, 13. University of Washington Libraries.

The court's clemency note echoed the association's myth: the court declared that in teaching the ideals of Islam, "raising morale," and stirring emotions, the Brotherhood had raised the souls of Egyptians from the submissiveness of an occupied people and done a service to Egyptian society. True, the arrested Brothers had "deviated from the right path" in pursuing violence. However, it was the court's duty to teach the young men a lesson and set them again on the straight path (see Figure 4.3).[126]

Conclusion: A "Brotherhood of Satan"?

Despite the moment of joy that accompanied the end of the Jeep Case, the Brotherhood's reputational rehabilitation did not last. Moreover, by summer there were already signs the Wafd–Ikhwan alliance was dead. A confrontation at al-ʿAdawi Mosque (a center of Wafdist support in downtown Cairo) highlighted the resumed rivalry.

The altercation occurred around midday at the time of Friday prayer. As the *khaṭīb* [mosque preacher] delivered the sermon, a Muslim Brotherhood member stood up and tried to hijack the service by preaching his own sermon to the assembled crowd. The Ikhwan member was not authorized to teach, however, so the *khaṭīb* interrupted him. In response, the Brother hurled an antisemitic slur common in the aftermath of the 1948 Palestine War: he called the *khaṭīb* a Jew.

The insult started a brawl. Angry mosque attendees rushed to deliver potent negative feedback to the Muslim Brotherhood member: they beat the would-be-preacher with shoes and drove him out of the mosque. Afterward, the *khaṭīb* reported the incident to the police, while youth from the Wafd worked to reclaim territory around the mosque. Roaming the streets in the neighborhood, the young Wafdist activists ripped down Ikhwan posters, and replaced them with new graffiti about the Ikhwan being a corrupt "Brotherhood of Satan."[127]

After his death, some would characterize Hasan al-Banna as a scheming, power-hungry fanatic—others would celebrate him as a saintly martyr wrongfully slain. Both narratives were their own type of morality tale: men are not born villains or saints, and neither caricature is capable of explaining al-Banna's successes, failures, and the turbulent evolution of the organization he built. The Muslim Brotherhood's popularity during the decade was only legible in light of the factional and corrupt political context of late monarchial Egypt, the strategic decisions the Ikhwan made to remain competitive, and how the society combined myths, day-to-day affective labors, social capital, and coercion to win converts.

In short, the Muslim Brotherhood and Young Egypt were popular because they provided good products. The groups can be credited with creating two of the most competitive organizational products on the market—societies well-adapted to the particularities of British-occupied Egypt in the late constitutional monarchy (with its characteristic competition between the Palace, political parties, and extra-parliamentary associations). The societies sampled a broad palette of ideological trends and learned organizational strategies from other associations. They advertised, differentiated themselves from competitors, and employed modern recruitment strategies.

Particularly successful, the Muslim Brotherhood advanced a simple, coherent, and comprehensive reform program, which interwove patriotic anti-colonialism and religious revivalism with an anti-corruption platform. The society performed the world it hoped to create. Forming families that cared for one another and performing an Islamic society that was both "religion and state," the association tried to create new realities on the ground as much as interpret things "as they really were." After all, despite Sayyid Qutb's claims that an Islamic bloc already existed (and this Cold War bloc was "a historical fact, a geographical fact, an economic fact, and an intellectual and emotional fact"), Muslim countries were not a unified front (geographically, economically, emotionally, or otherwise).[128] But by speaking of a "world Islam" united against imperialism the Brothers endeavored to make this transnational community a fact.

The Brothers' success further stemmed from how they embedded their program in a strong socio-affective environment featuring "families" and a fatherly figurehead. Members took part in service projects and worked to meet material and nonmaterial needs (helping members find employment; sponsoring sports activities; founding schools; and opening cooperative societies and health clinics). The club cultivated positive feelings of faith, pride, hope, strength, certainty, and camaraderie. The Brotherhood adeptly negotiated religious capital (shared texts and symbols). And they used their interpretive labors to craft these resources into a distinct interpretation of Islam: "our Islam."

Finally, the association inspired adherents with a revival myth. This myth gave members a meaningful role in a shared story; it further used emotional cues to describe how this present darkness of corruption and humiliation would transform into a proud dawn. Admittedly, there were darker shades to this uplifting tale: to remain competitive, groups embraced odd bedfellows and made "deals with the devil," and their opponents aired their affairs. The Brotherhood also established steep exit costs by conflating group membership with being a "true Muslim," and encouraging members to discount information that conflicted with the society's myth.

In modern public debate, this tendency to disregard and/or screen out non-consonant information is often called the "echo chamber," "filter bubble," or "information bubble" effect, and is blamed on new technology. However, Egypt's tumultuous postwar world shows that the phenomenon predates social media. Moreover, scholars have found the bubble metaphor is misplaced: individuals who disregard outside information tend to engage *more* intensely with exogenous media (in order to refute and discredit outside news). Any filtering thus happens internally, as individuals conform information to their myth and teach themselves that outside information cannot be trusted.[129] The history of Egyptian activism sustains these findings; narrative-based confirmation bias existed independent of algorithms and social media. Moreover, biases were not impenetrable: leaders told members to distrust the "dirty press," but whether individuals embraced distrust was negotiated, not deterministic.

What of the young men who did follow those directives? A few years after the 1951 Revolution in Egypt, an American psychologist reflected on why certain individuals intensify beliefs when confronted with contradictory information. In a passage that would become famous as the foundation of cognitive dissonance theory, Leon Festinger wrote:

> A man with a conviction is a hard man to change. Tell him you disagree and he turns away. Show him facts or figures and he questions your sources … We have all experienced the futility of trying to change a strong conviction …. Suppose an individual believes something with his whole heart; suppose further that he has a commitment to this belief, *that he has taken irrevocable actions because of it*; finally, suppose that he is presented with evidence … that his belief is wrong: what will happen? The individual will frequently emerge, not only unshaken, but even more convinced of the truth of his beliefs than ever before.[130]

Watching the most committed members of clubs like Young Egypt and the Muslim Brotherhood, these statements ring true—but there was also more to the mix than just the suppression of cognitive dissonance and the maintenance of the organization's myth. As activists described, there were sunk costs and identities involved, relationships and public images to uphold, emotional payouts to abandon, and much more.

Moreover, many members did leave, describing their exit as a moment of rupture when the organization's claims rang hollow and the morality tale collapsed. The Muslim Brotherhood had many of these moments: the 1939–40 financial scandal and schism, the spring 1942 deal with the Wafd, and the 1946–9 strikebreaking and civil war. By the end of the 1940s, the Brotherhood's appeals were therefore only proving a partial success. Of those Brothers who remained (like Ahmad, Tahir, and veterans of the Palestine War), it was often because they had invested too heavily to "change careers." As fate would have it, the Brothers thus found themselves weathering a cold front just as the fight against the British was heating up.

5

"Allahu Akhbar, Long Live the Workers!"

Communist Clubs and the Islam Question

While Egypt's political parties of the 1930s and 1940s formed paramilitary brigades and engaged in street battles, Cairo's upper crust formed societies of a different tenor. In the interwar period, two early anti-fascist societies were established in the salons of Cairo: the Union of Peace Partisans (est. 1934) and the Democratic Union (est. 1939). This interwar anti-fascist movement would provide fertile soil for Egypt's second-generation communist associations—groups which would become an important alternative for young activists not interested in joining Young Egypt, the Muslim Brotherhood, or Shabab Sayyidna Muhammad.

The anti-fascist leagues attracted a mélange of educated Egyptians and Europeans. Young men and women gathered to discuss European literature and world events (such as the Spanish Civil War, Adolf Hitler's accession to the German Chancellorship, and the Ioannis Metaxas regime in Greece). At this time, three friends—Yusuf Darwish, Raymond Duwayk, and Ahmad Sadiq Saʿd—joined the Union of Peace Partisans. All three were Egyptian Jews who had studied at French *lycées*; Darwish was freshly returned from France (having studied law at the University of Toulouse). Two other Egyptian Jews—Diane Rossano and her cousin Henri Curiel (both children of bankers)—joined the Democratic Union.

It was in this milieu that Diane and Henri became communists. Diane described her Marxist conversion as a rational coming-to-consciousness of exploitative class structures; Henri said he could not remember how he became a communist, only that it had been like a "new birth."[1] Notably, both stories conformed to a well-recognized mode of communist conversion narratives: communists activists tended to narrate their "communist awakenings" as a purely intellectual enlightenment, "presenting communist propositions as though they arose spontaneously from independent reflection" after Marxist literature drew their attention to the exploitative nature of capitalist economic structures.[2]

Such intellectualist myths had silences, however. They omitted recruitment processes, relationship-building, and other socio-affective factors. Henri's wife, for instance, later explained it was Henri's "brother Raoul who had led him to throw himself into the study of Marxism," and Diane offhandedly mentioned being introduced to historical materialism by an Italian boyfriend in 1941.[3]

While many of their friends fled to British Palestine in the summer of 1942 as the Germans advanced toward Cairo, Diane decided to stay to weather the war. That fall, she wed Osman, a Muslim officer and fellow activist from her literary salon. Meanwhile, Henri had no choice but to stay—he was rounded up in a police search for political dissidents and thrown in prison.

In the spring of 1943, the Battle of Stalingrad ended with a Soviet victory, and Egyptians became engrossed with the *Black Book* controversy. Recently released from prison, Henri the banker's son emerged to find the Democratic Union dissolved by the government. Distressed by the antisemitism and ethno-religious exclusivism of other societies, that autumn Henri recruited his friend David Nahum to help him start a new organization. David recruited Diane, and in turn she recruited her new husband Osman.[4] In October 1943, the group launched their first communist association, the Egyptian Movement for National Liberation/EMNL. They inaugurated the organization with a cadet training course at "the Palace" (the Curiel's country home): some six instructors and two dozen friends gathered to read Stalin, learn about dialectical materialism, and sing "La Marseillaise" and "The International."[5]

How would the EMNL and other Egyptian communist associations approach the question of building a moral society—and how would they try to make this vision competitive in the moral marketplace of 1940s Egypt? As this chapter explores, constructing a moral Marxist in postwar Cairo was not an easy commission for communist activists. Granted, Stalin's 1943 victory over Hitler had made him the hero of anti-fascism and anti-imperialism, just as the Wafd was suffering scandal after scandal. This historical conjuncture triggered a boom in Egyptian communist societies. However, the groups sprouted just as the Cold War began and the Muslim Brotherhood reached its apogee. The EMNL and Workers' Vanguard thus faced an uphill battle to assert moral mettle, even as British propaganda and Egyptian competitors worked to discredit the new societies as Soviet shills.

Being a Communist in Early Cold War Cairo

Egyptian communist clubs in the 1940s were active and tenacious—but since they were illegal under Egyptian law, they were difficult to track and map. Communist groups only existed underground, and frequently underwent name changes and reinventions linked to schisms, mergers, arrests, and the use of organizational fronts. Figure 5.1 sketches the main communist societies in these years (including group names and aliases, founders, dates of activity, and periodicals).

As the chart reflects, immediately prior to 1946 major communist organizations included

- People's Liberation [Tahrir al-Sha'b], est. 1939 by Marcel Israel;
- Iskra, est. 1942 by Hillel Schwartz;
- The Egyptian Movement for National Liberation/EMNL, est. 1943 by Henri Curiel;
- *Al-Fajr al-Jadid* [*The New Dawn*] publishing group, est. 1945 by Yusuf Darwish, Raymond Duwayk, Sadiq Sa'd, and Ahmad Rushdi Salih.

Besides Salih, the founders of all these associations were Jewish—a reflection of the clubs' origins and ancestry in the interwar anti-fascist leagues.

Among these organizations, two poles of activity would dominate the 1940s scene: the relatively stable New Dawn/Workers' Vanguard bloc (on the left side of the chart) and the mercurial EMNL–DMNL (on the right side of the chart). The Workers' Vanguard was anchored by its journal *al-Fajr al-Jadid* and its four founders (Darwish, Duwayk, Sa'd, and Salih); by 1946 the group had coalesced into the People's Liberation, before changing its name to the Workers' Vanguard (Tali'at al-'Ummal) in 1950. The EMNL, meanwhile, underwent many mergers and schisms.

Programmatically, Egyptian communist clubs emphasized British evacuation, national liberation, democracy, and social and economic reform. Performing the world they hoped to create, EMNL members worked to model these tenets through social service projects and educational programs; the group emphasized gender equality, and decreed that all members must work to increase their knowledge and establish democracy "by promotion being from the bottom to top."[6]

Communist clubs also vigorously opposed defining men based on race, gender, or creed—a platform that would attract many ethnic and religious minorities to their ranks. The black Nubian student Mubarak 'Abduh Fadl

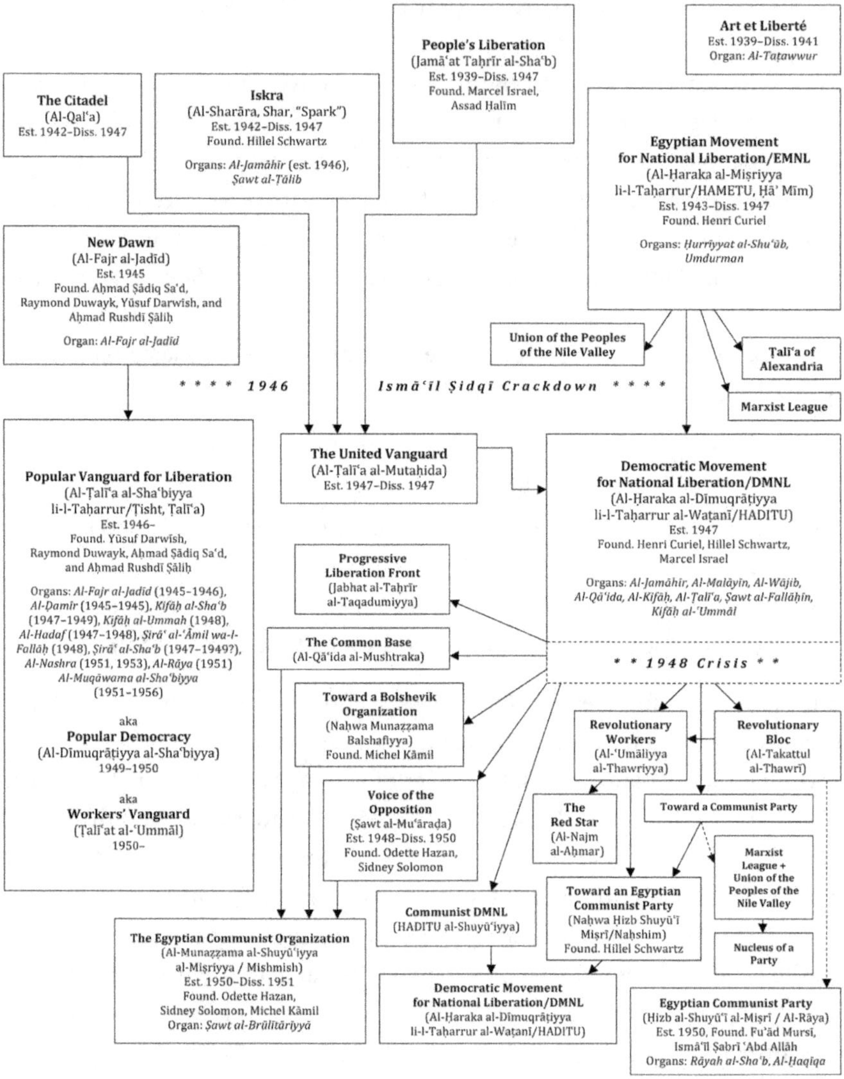

Figure 5.1 Egyptian Communist Clubs, 1939–51.

Source: The *Ṭalī'at al- 'Ummāl and Egyptian Communists in Exile* Collections at the IISH; Selma Botman, *The Rise of Egyptian Communism*, 33–113; Tareq Y. Ismael and Rifa'at el-Sa'id, *The Communist Movement in Egypt*, 32–81.

described being attracted to the EMNL because of its emphasis on care for the poor,[7] and Latifa al-Zayyat (who left the Wafd for a communist group around 1943) testified to the appeal of communist egalitarianism. "What appealed to me very much in Marxism … was the ethics … the absence of discrimination in religion, race, sex."[8]

Recruitment flowed through kinship and friendship networks in urban minority communities. Many Coptic activists (Fransis Kirilus, Fawzi Habbashi, and Widad Barsum, for instance) were introduced to communism through other Copts.[9] ʿAbduh Fadl was introduced to the EMNL through another Nubian student.[10] Diane Rossano and Yusuf Hazan (a French-Algerian Jew) similarly came to the EMNL through Jewish friends.

Since communist associations used a Western reading curriculum (and communist literature at the time was in French and English), communist groups primarily attracted individuals who had studied at missionary schools and/or French-speaking secondary schools [*lycées*]. For instance, Henri Curiel attended Jesuit school; Diane Rossano and many others (Inji Aflatun, Hillel Schwartz, Rifʿat al-Saʿid, Marcel Israel, Muhammad Sid Ahmad, Ahmad Sadiq Saʿd, and Anwar ʿAbd al-Malik) received their educations in *lycées*. Diane, for her part, remembered being sent off to school every morning wearing a French beret and a crisp white pinafore.[11]

These demographics reflected an important trend: Egyptians in the 1940s tended to select organizations that maximized (or at least conserved) existing social capital. Per this conservation of capital principle, individuals usually joined associations that leveraged social networks, epistemologies learned in *kuttāb* or *lycée*, and familiar rituals and forms of distinction (e.g., Qurʾanic recitation and food practices on the one hand, or Western etiquette, literature, and sartorial habits on the other hand). As communist texts emphasized Western epistemologies, they were most accessible to urban elites and minorities who had studied at missionary schools or *lycées*.

Sharif Hatata, for instance, pointed out that his social and ethnic position (as half-English/half-Egyptian) excluded him from entertaining the idea of Brotherhood membership. "Belonging to a modern [living situation], it was difficult for me to join traditional political movements." For him a political association "had to be something progressive, open, that wasn't traditional or fanatical. And it had to be something rational."[12] In Hatata's terminology, then, his educational upbringing made him seek an organization based in Western, post-Enlightenment epistemology (i.e., something "progressive" and "rational," not "traditional").

The tendency toward conservation of capital had importance consequences; it meant that class, confession, ethnicity, and education frequently guided affiliation decisions, and could create high barriers to entry for certain clubs. For instance, while Sharif Hatata said Iskra appealed to him because it stressed studying and reading, Thuraya Shakir had a different experience as a woman from upper Egypt. Introduced to Iskra through her husband, Shakir struggled to understand the curriculum, and complained that "Everybody was talking in French, all of them, there was nobody *not* speaking French. … Because Arabic was the language they used for talking to servants only."[13]

Sulayman al-Rifaʿi, who had attended an industrial school in Mansurah, also struggled. Despite being an avid reader, he went away from his second meeting with the communist society Bread and Freedom feeling depressed, having not understood a word the speaker said.[14] Nawal al-Saʿdawi, pressured by a classmate into reading the Iskra newsletter *al-Jamahir* around 1946, remembered similar frustrations. She would furtively read the underground paper in the girl's bathroom at school, but was exasperated at being "barely able to decipher … or to understand" the paper's opaque style—which she said was "more difficult than that of *al-Akkad*, or my uncle Shaykh Muhammad, or [the eighth century Arab scholar] Ibn al-Muqaffaʿ." The paper frustrated her so much that Nawal would tear it into pieces and angrily flush it down the toilet. But her friend "continued to thrust this newspaper on me" and use words Nawal could not understand: "The word dialectics made me feel depressed."[15]

Other factors raised membership costs in communist associations. The British Residency pressured the Egyptian government to repress communist groups; as a result, membership remained illegal, and being caught meant time in prison. Potential recruits had to consider this cost, as well as the high social costs of opposition from peers and family members. Mubarak ʿAbduh Fadl, for example, was a student of al-Azhar when he joined the EMNL. A half-blind Nubian, Mubarak felt marginalized at the venerated Islamic institution, and sought a route for nationalist engagement. When his father discovered Mubarak's communist commitment, however, there was shouting and tears. Confronting his son, Mubarak's father expressed concern his son's activism would endanger his ability to generate income for the family. "What you believe is to the benefit of the poor," his father admitted, "but whoever joins this kind of work must be rich!" ʿAbduh Fadl refused to quit the association, however, and was banished from home. In the end, his father's concerns about the costs of communism proved correct: ʿAbduh Fadl was arrested multiple times, and in 1948 was expelled from al-Azhar for his political activism. He shrugged off the expulsion. As he explained, he anyway did not want to spend his life reading Qurʾan at funerals—the expected fate for a low-level *ʿalim*.[16]

Overall, the costs of communism made Marxist associations most accessible to Egyptians who already had extensive resources (or who were not afraid of losing the resources they had). These costs affected membership and group structure. The illegal organizations had to organize as small, covert cells of

5–10 members each. Despite the illegal nature of their activities, the groups still managed to recruit: figures are sparse and unreliable, but at peak membership (*c.* 1947) the EMNL likely counted 600–700 members.[17] When the EMNL merged with People's Liberation, Iskra, and al-Qalʿa that year to form the DMNL, the association swelled to approximately 1600 members. The DMNL then reportedly grew to some 4000–5000 members before breaking into more than twenty splinter groups with the onset of the 1948 Palestine War. These figures were impressive for an underground movement, but still modest compared to the Brotherhood—which by the late 1940s claimed to command some 250,000 members.[18]

The Making of a Moral Marxist

Despite structural limitations, Egyptian communist activists articulated a coherent Marxist myth with well-defined moral scripts. Adapting the revolutionary scripts of the Enlightenment (and particularly the "universalist model of the French and Bolshevik revolutions"[19]), communist activists sought to awaken men to exploitative class structures, moving society from slavery to freedom and from darkness to light.[20]

A 1945 illustration appearing in *al-Fajr al-Jadid* provided the clearest articulation of the Egyptian communist myth (see Figure 5.2). The illustration was an adaptation of the French Revolution etching the "Réunion des trois ordres" from 1789. The top panel described the first act in the mythic narrative, showing a peasant carrying landowners and men of religion on his back (accompanied by the text "the peasant [*fallah*] before the revolution"). The bottom panel depicted the triumphant "after," in which the peasant carried meat and was carried by the ruling class. This bottom scene was labeled "the peasant [*fallah*] after the revolution."

In this way, the drawing divided time into two mythic eras: an unjust "before" and a triumphant "after." Notably, to achieve this bipartite dispensational scheme, the Egyptian version removed the central panel of the French original—there would be no unity in this myth. Instead, there was a moment of rupture: "the revolution" (an event that promised to bring an inversion of the ruling order). The Marxist myth thus outlined a dualistic chronoscape; it also presented well-defined roles (peasant, priest, landowner) and a clear path of action driven by a revolutionary script.

Figure 5.2 The Egyptian Marxist Myth and the Revolutionary Script.

An Arabic adaptation of the French Revolution etching "Réunion des trois ordres," as printed in the communist journal *al-Fajr al-Jadid*. (The original image in French can be found at "Réunion des trois ordres" Print, c. 1789, Library of Congress Prints and Photographs Division, CPH 3b41650.)

Source: "Al-Fallāḥ qabl al-Thawra… al-Fallāḥ baʿd al-Thawra," *al-Fajr al-Jadīd* 5, July 16, 1945, 24 in IISH ARCH02315/Folder 97. The Taliʿa al-ʿUmmal Collection, International Institute of Social History, Amsterdam.

In addition to this moral myth, Egyptian communists expressed many opinions about how a just society ought to operate. Moral critique in communist articles denounced a variety of bad behaviors; Workers' Vanguard publications like *al-Fajr al-Jadid* and *Kifah al-Shaʿb,* for instance, frequently condemned social cheating, exploitation, and racism. Communists also wrote articles on the negative effects of hashish smoking and gambling (condemned as a form of wasteful luxury spending).[21] Notably, articles tended to articulate a highly class-based vision of morality, condemning the behaviors of Egyptian aristocrats, capitalist elites (bosses and landlords), and middle-class intellectuals, while praising workers and peasants.[22]

Islam, the Opium of the People?

Despite their strong moralism, Egyptian communists were perpetually on the moral defensive. Several factors negatively affected communism's moral standing in the Egyptian public eye. Communism was reputed to be a foreign, atheistic doctrine; there was also a popular perception of communists as elite and Westernized. Consequently, these were the battlegrounds on which communist clubs would fight to signal moral probity.

The religious question was one of the first moral issues that Egyptian communist groups worked to untangle in the postwar milieu—and Marx's dictum "Religion … is the opium of the people" was one hurdle to clear. Opponents quoted the dictum to demonstrate that communism was atheistic and disrespectful of religious tradition. Egyptian communists thus worked to reinterpret and contextualize the phrase.[23]

To refute the idea that communism was hostile to religion, communist activists first declared they were opposed to religious exploitation—not religion itself. Communist activist ʿAbd al-Mughni Saʿid pointed out that Lenin stated that "each member [of the communist party] believes what he wants … communism does not interfere in his religious faith." He added that "socialism does not attack religion in and of itself, but rather attacks the capitalist *exploitation* of the idea of religion."[24]

In his 1940 course on Marxism, People's Liberation founder Marcel Israel similarly cited Lenin's stance on religion to demonstrate that communism was not hostile to religious faith.[25] An EMNL–DMNL tract pledged respect for religion in general, but denounced the exploitation of religion by "reactionaries."[26] Even Iskra, often denounced by EMNL activists as atheistic, was careful to condemn religious *fanaticism* and the *use of religion* by reactionaries to sow discord.[27]

Workers' Vanguard activists were perhaps the most meticulous about toeing this line, as their focus was on recruiting Egyptian workers and professionals rather than elites. *Kifah al-Shaʿb*, for instance, carried stories about how religion was being used to oppress workers and peasants. One article described how shaykhs in the provinces were helping the Ministry of Interior by collecting personal information and compiling intelligence reports on political activists. Another story described how a factory owner had fired a worker on the pretext that the worker ate during Ramadan; thus, the paper moralized, the factory owners "dishonestly feign religious devotion to satisfy their special interests."[28] The paper further denounced "reactionary religious bodies" like the conservative Coptic Union and decried the fact that "capitalists among the Jews and Copts (like Ḥaim Dura) support the Muslim Brotherhood."[29]

Kifah al-Umma, another Vanguard publication, took aim at both the Ikhwan and the Central Christian Union (al-Ittihad al-Masihi al-Markazi), describing these as fascist groups formed by the "ruling classes" in order to prevent the people from rising up. Such fascist religious associations "present themselves to the people as their savior from their weariness and dissatisfaction," the paper wrote, "[but] is the purpose of this call [*da'wa*] only religion?"[30]

Communists were also careful to attack groups like the Ikhwan for *exploiting* religion—not for being religious. *Al-Fajr al-Jadid* described the Ikhwan's platform as a racist theory encouraging world conquest and calling for "a spiritual and intellectual return to the Middle Ages."[31] Other articles accused the Brothers of advocating Islamic imperialism and fascism, and engaging in disingenuous, grasping, selfish politicking.[32] Many such critiques were grounded in the fact that the Brotherhood had agreed to serve as "muscle" for the Sidqi government in quashing student and worker protests in 1946.[33] A statement from an EMNL-led trade union, for instance, worked to dismantle the Muslim Brotherhood's altruistic image, arguing:

> Today the naked intentions of this Society have been exposed to the people: from calling for [religious] sectarianism aimed at splitting the ranks of the people for the benefit of imperialism, to fighting the Students' General Executive Committee with fascist methods … A worker who joins any of [the Muslim Brothers'] committees represents no one but himself.[34]

Perhaps the most extensive moral critique of the Ikhwan was a joint EMNL–Wafd tract released in 1946 (around the time of the Brotherhood–Sidqi strikebreaking incident), entitled *The Muslim Brotherhood in the Balance.* Ostensibly authored by one "Muhammad Hasan Ahmad," the name was a pseudonym for multiple contributors, including Marxist al-Azhar shaykh 'Abd al-Wahid Busaila and Wafdist-communist professor 'Abd al-Rahman al-Nasir. The recurrent theme of the tract was to show the Brotherhood as a fascist organization, which exploited religion and had forsaken all morals in allying itself with capitalism and colonialism. The tract particularly criticized the Brotherhood alliance with Isma'il Sidqi Pasha, and an Ikhwan article in *al-*

Daʿwa entitled "National Conquest [*Waṭaniyya al-Fatḥ*]," which had called the process of Islamic expansion a beneficent colonization.[35]

While Egyptian communists agreed that the manipulation of religion was contributing to Egypt's problems, they were divided as to whether religion could be part of any solution. The Union of the Peoples of the Nile Valley, a small club comprised of Egyptian bureaucrats (specifically, a group of friends from the tax office), answered this question in the affirmative, embracing religion and religious practice. This position matched their target demographic (Egyptian social servants).[36]

The Jewish founder of People's Liberation, meanwhile, argued that religious sentiment could contribute to solving the problem of British occupation. Specifically, the fact that the British were Christian and the Egyptians Muslim could be exploited: "religion in a colonized country takes on a progressive nationalist content—especially if the colonizer belongs to another religion."[37] Police-seized meeting notes from Workers' Vanguard leader Yusuf Darwish, however, suggested that their activists disagreed with this strategy: "The Resistance should not do religious propaganda … It's not our role to provoke religious sentiment."[38]

Curiel defined the EMNL's position as "religious neutrality." He acknowledged that reactionaries exploited religion and used it as a cudgel against communist groups. However, he argued that "the most stupid reply to such an attack would be to struggle not against reaction, but against religion." He added that fighting religion in Egypt would be a "truly suicidal enterprise." Moreover, he continued, it was wrong-headed, since many religious leaders and believers had joined the struggle for economic and social liberation. For instance, the EMNL had recruited members from the Islamic institute of al-Azhar, who were helping the EMNL make inroads into the countryside, at a time when the society only had footholds in urban areas. (Curiel concluded: "Long live the revolutionaries of al-Azhar!")[39]

Interested in building bridges between the communist movement and religious communities in Egypt—and determined to contribute to the creation of an Islamic progressive movement—the EMNL actively worked to establish student sections at al-Azhar and circulated tracts on campus.[40] As a report outlining the organization's program for al-Azhar argued:

> Men of religion in this country have always played an important part against Imperialism … The importance of [al-Azhar] is as follows: they are the religious body which assists reactionaries; their men represent the working classes; they

> enjoy spiritual confidence among the people; their roots go deep among many classes of Egyptians—teachers, preachers, Imams, etc.
>
> As they are so important, we must win them away from reactionarism and the Palace .... Reactionarism pretends to support religion, but the men of al-Azhar are the best people to understand religion truly.[41]

Overall, communist approaches to religion were thus heterogeneous; even within the same organization, activists often disagreed. The activists of *al-Tatawwur* provide one glimpse into these disputes. In 1940, the paper ran an article entitled "The Development of the Idea of God and Its Evolution," a critique of religion that was painstakingly worded. Despite its provocative title, the article denounced only idolatry, without directly arguing against the existence of God. Maintaining careful ambiguity through and through, it concluded that with the Bolshevik Revolution, mankind had turned to unbelief. However, the author declined to explain whether this represented a culmination of historical development or a setback. The article thus implied that the idea of God was a man-made invention—but phrased the idea vaguely enough to allow its author legal cover.[42]

Behind the scenes, however, members of *al-Tatawwur* became embroiled in a bitter dispute over the religious question. In one meeting, ʿAbd al-Mughni Saʿid defended religion by arguing that individuals who advocated materialist views were "tools of Zionism and promoters of immorality," expressing their own private opinions rather than those of the group. His statements sparked a conflict with other members of the staff (particularly with Italian member Marcelle Biagini, who accused him of being a fanatic and a fascist). As a result, Saʿid left the club to advocate for a synthesis of Islam and communism he called Islamic socialism. Saʿid was not the only one: Curiel's refusal to construct an Islamic–communist synthesis similarly led to the 1945 departure of ʿAbd al-Fattah al-Sharqawi from the EMNL.[43]

Whether or not they agreed on the place of religion in politics and society, many Egyptian communists still cited religious and/or ethical values as playing a role in their activism. Coptic communist Fransis Kirilus, for instance, recalled that his Christian education had instilled in him a compassion for the poor, which inspired his communist commitment. Taha Saʿd ʿUthman, meanwhile, was a devout Muslim; he found no contradiction between communism and Islam, explaining that Islam was a religion of the poor, which proclaimed equal rights and measured men by their devotion rather than their class position.[44] Mustafa Haykal was also a pious Muslim, liberal, and supportive of the separation between religion and state. His father was a member of the High Council of ʿUlamaʾ and a supporter of Shaykh ʿAli ʿAbd al-Raziq; Mustafa had thus been brought up according to ʿAbd al-Raziq's dictum that Islam was "a message, not a government—a religion, not a state." These religious credentials helped Haykal's communist group Tanzim al-Qalʿa attract devout Muslims and al-Azhar students.[45]

Regardless of their religious outlook, there was one thing Egyptian communist associations shared in common: an interest in making inroads into religious spaces. Workers' Vanguard activist Hilmi Yassin stood by the mosque after Friday prayers to invite attendees to literacy classes at their "youth group" (a communist front).[46] The EMNL established cells on the al-Azhar campus and sent their recruiter Ahmad Khidr to the YMCA and YMMA so he could meet and poach potential members. Finally, Mustafa Haykal's small Marxist group al-Qalʿa attended Ikhwan lectures and called Muslim Brotherhood members in the neighborhood to invite them to meetings—practices that eventually got them banned from Brotherhood services.[47] When it came to recruitment and politicking, the boundaries between "religious" and "secular" space were thus heavily blurred and openly crossed.

Combatting "Communist Pasha"

The religious front was not the only field on which communist activists had to assert moral legitimacy. The overrepresentation of foreigners and elites in the Egyptian communist movement, communism's origins as a European doctrine, and the foreign reading curriculum all made the movement seem immoral and un-Egyptian. Compounding the problem, many communists spoke French and English (rather than Arabic) and followed urban, elite habits. Iskra members in particular (as well as many members of the EMNL) were elite and thoroughly Westernized: they attended French schools and discussed French literature, wore European clothing (including shorts and bathing suits), danced, drank alcohol, and let men and women mingle in late night soirées. These habits gave Iskrans a reputation for being sexually licentious, elitist, and Western-oriented—a reputation opponents worked to project onto the communist movement as a whole. (A 1945 anti-communist article in *al-Ikhwan al-Muslimun*, for instance, alluded to popular rumors that communist associations were recruiting through libertine parties.)[48]

The moral dubiousness and Western habits of communist elites heaped on social costs for the average Egyptian. Coptic activist Geneviève Sidarus, for instance, initially refused to join the communist clubs on her university campus. After EMNL members worked to convince her that Marxist groups were not hostile toward religion, Sidarus joined—but the decision cost her dearly. She was arrested at a co-ed, Western-style party at a private apartment, and when her fellow students learned of the arrest, they harassed and shamed Sidarus. To salvage her reputation, she was forced to take out a newspaper notice defending her honor and claiming the arrest had occurred during the daytime (not at night).[49]

Egyptians from the provinces especially struggled to overcome the cultural and moral gap between "the values of the village" and the lifestyles of urban communists. Thuraya Shakir (a Muslim whose mother had converted to Catholicism) described feeling "shocked" by the behavior and dress habits of the Iskra girls. While rural Jewish, Christian, and Muslim women traditionally wore long gowns (*jilbāb*) and headscarves, the urban girls in Iskra were elite and Europeanized. As Shakir related:

> [Inji Aflatun] took me to clubs … Most of them were Jews, speaking French all the time and very westernized … wearing shorts and wearing I don't know what … I felt that I was a stranger …. And we come from Upper Egypt, very closed off, and I couldn't.[50]

Figure 5.3 Communist Pasha.

A stock character in *Akhir Sa'a*, the wealthy, overweight "Communist Pasha" typically appeared reading the newspaper, giving ridiculous policy suggestions, and making absurd comments about Russia. Left: "Communist Pasha—The best thing about communism is that it prevents people from becoming rich… [instead], it makes everyone equally poor!" Right: "Communist Pasha—In Russia, there's social justice. There's no 'full rich' and 'hungry poor'… all are poor and hungry!"

Source: (Left) *Ākhir Sā'a* 691, January 21, 1948, 13; (Right) *Ākhir Sā'a* 690, January 14, 1948, 16. Hatcher Graduate Library, University of Michigan.

This image of the elite Egyptian communist—an image fueled in part by the actual practices of Egyptian communist clubs—was so ingrained in the Egyptian popular imagination, *Akhir Saʿa* satirized it with a recurring cartoon character called "Communist Pasha." The name highlighted the contradiction between communist teaching and communist practice. Overweight and wealthy, "Communist Pasha" was an unflattering figure, always reading the news and making comments about Russia as a model nation (see Figure 5.3).

To counter these images, communist groups toiled to appear virtuous per Egyptian social norms. The EMNL and Taliʿat al-ʿUmmal worked to make members adhere to ideas of propriety appropriate to Egyptian life in the 1940s, dividing men and women into separate cells.[51] When the EMNL and Iskra merged in 1947 to create the DMNL, Curiel also successfully lobbied for women and foreigners to be secluded in their own cells—the foreigners (largely Iskra members) being segregated on the grounds they did not have the "proletarian" character the movement was trying to cultivate. The DMNL bylaws further tried to ensure the organization remained respectable, listing as a membership duty that "members must by their behavior set a good example. They must avoid everything which may touch their honor or reputation, [and] must be careful about the feelings of others and their opinions."[52]

Communists took other steps to assert their honorable character. The Jewish Curiel fasted Ramadan, justifying the decision by arguing that "When you're a communist, you must behave in an exemplary manner, and this conduct is a better way of serving our cause than the longest speech." He added that "we must respect the social customs of the environment."[53] Hilmi Yassin, meanwhile, reported that "Membership in [the Workers' Vanguard] resembled priesthood; moral stature was stressed … The member had to be responsible in his private life, and the organization had the right to interfere in a member's private life." To ensure propriety, the society also established a "corridor" separating Greek and Francophone members from the main membership (Egyptian workers)—and only those who mastered Arabic were admitted as full members.[54]

Female activists faced special challenges, and in some cases went to great lengths to fight sexual slander. For instance, Latifa al-Zayyat recounted:

> I fought against the Muslim fundamentalist groups which tried to defame my reputation—they called me a prostitute and other such things. I remember I went home and wept. But I said, "this is public work, this is not the last time I will be defamed." This turned me into a puritan. Really, because they said that … communists were immoral … communists became puritans, to maintain their image with the public, especially those who were working in close connection with the masses.[55]

Other activist tried alternate approaches. Some communist activists exchanged European names for Muslim names or used pseudonyms: Hillel Schwartz became Hilal Adham and Henri Curiel called himself Yunis. Diane Rossano also took the name Didar Fawzy (although she said it was her husband's grandmother who gave her the Arabized moniker). Inji Aflatun and Muhammad Sid Ahmad (an elite Muslim who had grown up speaking only French) worked to improve their Arabic. The men of the Workers' Vanguard went a step further: Ahmad Sadiq Saʿd, Raymond Duwayk, and Yusuf Darwish converted to Islam (and Curiel considered it).

As part of these demonstrations of moral probity and "Egyptianness," Egyptian communists also used light religious discourse in speeches and tracts, such as Arabic idioms referring to God and terms like "*shahīd*" and "jihad."[56] (This was not unusual: Christians, Jews, and Muslims in Egypt had been using the term "jihad" to describe the national independence struggle since the 1919 Revolution.) Communists further learned to use piety displays to signal propriety and counter Brotherhood campaigns. In one notable incident, Muslim Brotherhood members tried to derail the election campaign of communist candidate Yusuf al-Mudarrik in Shubra al-Khaymah. To discredit Mudarrik, the Brothers accused him of being an infidel. But Mudarrik countered the charges with a unique strategy: he rallied the workers in a piety display, with chants of "God is Great, Long Live the Workers!" [*Allāhu akhbar, wa yaḥyā al-ʿummāl!*].[57] In doing so, Mudarrik sent an important message: he would not let the Brotherhood claim hegemony over Islamic devotion (or factory space). Thus, despite being on the moral defensive, Egyptian communists found creative ways to signal moral probity.

These attempts to construct a "moral Marxist" would come crashing down with the 1947 United Nations resolution on Palestine. As the brewing conflict in Palestine developed into an active war between Egypt and the new state of Israel, the Egyptian press filled with anti-Zionist articles that often bled into antisemitism. Since Jews were demographically overrepresented in the communist movement, opposition parties like the Muslim Brotherhood and Young Egypt quickly collapsed Zionists, Jews, and communists into one category.

Young Egypt was one group who worked to paint communist competitors as Jews and Zionists. Ironically, Young Egypt defended the morality of these attacks, claiming its denunciation of Egyptian Jews was not an exercise in racism or intolerance, but an exercise in self-protection. As Young Egypt phrased it (in an article calling Egyptian Jews a "fifth column"), "The issue we have is not an issue of religion or race, but rather the interests of Egypt, which we put above everything—*above Zionism and Judaism and communism*—and all the associations in this world."[58] The statement was typical of the era, heuristically collapsing communism, Zionism, and Judaism.

Perhaps the largest blow to the movement, however, was a wave of investigations and arrests in 1948. DMNL members Henri Curiel, Raymond Stambouli, and Yusuf Hazan were among those detained and sent to the Huckstep internment camp. Media coverage of the arrests repeated and reinforced the moral criticisms that had plagued Egyptian communist clubs since their founding. An infamous photo taken at the time of Henri's 1946 arrest once again made the rounds in Egyptian newspapers. The photo showed the "Jewish, communist millionaire" wearing shorts! (Many Egyptians saw shorts as a sign of foreignness). Another article described how investigators uncovered letters between the arrested activists and communist organizations in Moscow—taken as proof "the communists in Egypt are connected to the outside [i.e., Russia]"![59]

Equally damning, activist Inji Aflatun was propped up as a straw (wo)man for the communist movement as a whole, taken to represent the moral depravity of the Marxists. Multiple articles characterized Inji as a foolish, sexually deviant aristocrat; a news report on her arrest described Inji unbuttoning her blouse in front of investigators and being remonstrated by her own mother (the owner of a Parisian haute couture boutique), who reportedly exclaimed "Oh child! You have forty dresses! What communism!? … What nonsense." As the quintessential "communist aristocrat," Inji (and her forty dresses) would become a refrain in the Egyptian press, alongside Henri's shorts and "Communist Pasha."[60]

More arrests came with the Egyptian government's declaration of martial law in May 1948. At the time, Diane's husband Osman had been posted to al-ʿArish (near the Egyptian-Palestinian border) on account of the developing Palestine War. As a result, when the political police came for Diane in Cairo, she was not there. The lucky miss gave the family time to burn their documents.[61]

In the end, some 1,300 political dissidents were incarcerated in the devastating 1948 roundups, which used the Palestine War as *casus belli* against the Jewish, Zionist communists. The arrests widened political fissures in the DMNL, which splintered into dozens of factions. Moreover, in the face of antisemitic attacks, arrests, and property seizures, some 16,500 Egyptian Jews left for Israel and another 6,000 departed for Europe and the Americas between 1948 and 1951.

It was a devastating blow to the communist movement. Stambouli called it "the end of a dream that had been coming true. We had thought of ourselves as Egyptians, even while admitting that Egyptians saw us as foreigners. It was all over. Now we weren't just foreigners, but Jews, [and] therefore the enemy."[62]

Conclusion: Marketing Marxist Morality to the "Man on the Street"

In postwar Cairo communist activists advanced a doctrine with popular economic reform proposals—but a doctrine laden with extremely unpopular cultural and moral connotations. Egyptian communist associations in the 1940s thus tried to blend Marxist egalitarianism with local sensibilities, using their interpersonal, rhetorical, and interpretive skills to try and build a competitive organizational product fit for the Egyptian moral market. In this process, activists relied heavily on European texts (Marx, Tolstoy, Lenin) as sources of authority—but tried to temper these with references to local thinkers (Salama Musa, ʿAli ʿAbd al-Raziq). As it had been with the Muslim Brotherhood's leveraging of Islamic texts, Egyptian communists used these texts as raw materials for interpretive labors: it was not always what a text said that mattered, so much as what it could be *made* to say. Thus, Lenin could be used to endorse private piety (just as the Brotherhood located nationalism and internationalism in the Qurʾan). As Pierre Bourdieu put it, "particularly elastic authors transfer so well. All great prophecies are polysemic. … Such elastic thinkers are manna from heaven when it comes to serving expansionist strategic uses."[63]

The ideological systems that resulted from the productive labors of the EMNL and Workers' Vanguard thus held a few things in common with the Ikhwanid platform. However, of the two systems, the Brotherhood's program was better adapted to the Egyptian market. Egyptian communists tried to position their ideology as minimally counterintuitive to their Egyptian audience—but activists struggled against a public perception that communists were dissimilar from the average Egyptian, and unable to speak the same language. To stay competitive, communist activists tried to bridge the gap—whether that meant learning Arabic, requesting name changes, converting to Islam, or encouraging activists to write articles "of interest to people," "connected with the lives of the masses" (rather than "dry and theoretical" articles using "words which the least educated of people cannot understand").[64]

But the gap remained. And with the especially high costs of communist membership, communist groups struggled to recruit Egyptians from non-elite backgrounds. Fakhri Labib, for instance, said he resorted to putting on old clothes and sitting in cafes in working-class neighborhoods (like Shubra and Imbaba), and pretending to be unemployed to strike up conversations with workers. Coptic communist Geneviève Sidarus was similarly asked to stand in front of factories to try and attract workers (she refused out of consideration for her reputation, as such behavior was unbecoming for a respectable woman of the time).[65]

Communist activist Fauzi Habbashi later explained the problem in stark terms when justifying why he had dismissed Coptic communist Abu Sayf Yusuf's bid for leadership of the Egyptian Communist Party. As Habbashi reasoned, as much as Yusuf might argue that "religion was something personal, and that politics was something public," Habbashi felt it was about appealing to "the man in the street." And despite being very much a mythical figure, in the Egyptian imagination the "man on the street" was Arabic-speaking, male, and Muslim.[66]

Communists thus struggled to gain a mass following and fought a losing battle against accusations that communism was foreign and immoral. And in the end, communist activists working in Arabic-speaking communities resorted to speaking of their platforms as "socialist," avoiding the term "communist" altogether. Advertising strategies reflected this: when police caught Jewish communist Bakhur Minahim Munshaf painting slogans on walls in the ʿAbdin district, the messaging was divided by linguistic audience. In French, he had been painting "Long Live Communism!"; but in Arabic, his graffiti read "Socialism Will Lead the World" and "Socialism Against Imperialism."[67] Egyptian communism would thus remain on the moral defensive—and like the Brotherhood, suffered a blow on the eve of nationalist revolution that dispersed many of the movement's most energetic activists.

6

"Shaykh in a Dance Club!" and Other Shocking Tales

In summer 1946, Shaykh ʿAli al-Tantawi wrote to the Egyptian journal *Majallat al-Risala* with a story. One day having gone to the mosque, Tantawi was surprised to encounter a well-known sinner, praying fervently. His interest piqued, Tantawi asked the young man what prompted his repentance. This was what the young man said:

> Have you not heard the story? A local shaykh named Salah al-Din saw that only the elderly were attending mosque; so he asked his followers "Where are the youth?" His followers answered, "The youth are in cinemas, casinos, and dance clubs." The shaykh was distraught but intent on doing something, so he approached the owner of the local club and asked to speak at intermission.
>
> The club owner thought the shaykh was insane—he must have escaped from a mental hospital! But the shaykh was offering good money to rent the club. Plus, the owner reasoned, a shaykh preaching at a dance club would make a big splash in the news! The theater owner thus agreed to let the shaykh speak, and began advertising a special "surprise."
>
> The night of the event, people came from far and wide to see the advertised "surprise." And the first act was a dancer so good, men would have traded their honor for her. But when the curtain rose a second time, the dancer had disappeared—and there stood the shaykh with his beard and robes.
>
> There was utter silence. Then, the audience grew angry. They whistled, mocked, and cursed the shaykh; they offered him wine, and asked him to take off his robes and show them his "talent." Eventually however, they grew tired of shouting and started listening.
>
> The shaykh began to preach. He preached in a way that moved hearts: he described how their love for the dancer was a low love, and called them to a higher love. He explained that illicit sexual desire was fleeting and unfulfilling, and he reproached them for lusting after the dancer. "Don't you have sisters? Don't you have daughters?" The shaykh beseeched the crowd to consider how

they would feel if one of their daughters were forced into such work.

At those words, the club patrons shed tears of mercy for the dancer, and "had compassion for her, and resolved to look at her as one looks at one's daughter, seeking to protect [*yastur-ha*; lit: cover her] and shelter her." So they rescued the dancer from "this mud," she married a pious man, "and now she is a housewife and mother of children." Even the club owner started visiting the shaykh and might soon close his club to find honorable work.

Tantawi ended his morality tale with this wish: "If only a shaykh would enter every dance club! If only a shaykh would enter the Ministry of Education!"[1]

The years leading up to the 1951 Revolution marked a boom in the Egyptian marketplace for morality tales. By summer 1951, newspaper production rates soared. The British ambassador reported to the foreign secretary that the Muslim Brotherhood, Young Egypt, and various communist clubs were circulating some 150,000 copies of newspapers and newsletters. The new Muslim Brotherhood paper *al-Da ʿwa* had sold 50,000 copies in its first week of publication in February, and in its second week circulated 80,000 copies.[2]

In these spaces, social reformers fought to advance their agendas in print and spun tales about how a new moral order might look. How did a communist morality tale read, and how did it compare with the parables of clubs like the Muslim Brotherhood and Muhammad's Youth? Considering their conflicting social views, did communist and Islamist stories share anything in common? Recovering the narrative ephemerata of Egyptian activism—stories told as part of campaigns then forgotten—helps answer these questions.

As the narratives reveal, groups like the Muslim Brotherhood and the Workers' Vanguard used distinct discourses to discuss morality. However, societies shared more in common than they might have liked to admit. Specifically, activists used moral emotions, metaphors, and maps as fundamental technologies for mobilizing change. A comparison of Egyptian activist tales (*c.* 1945–52) highlights how these moral codes operated, and equips us to better evaluate the political claims and emotions embedded in campaigns.

Moral Emotions: The Affective Gatekeepers of the Moral Order

In February 1942, the Egyptian writer Zaki Mubarak published an article entitled "The Worst of Enemies." The title was inspired by a Prophetic saying or hadith: "The worst enemy of your enemies is yourself—that which is between your sides" (paraphrased, "You are your own worst enemy").[3] Taking liberty with the proverb, Mubarak argued, "The importance of this hadith is that it alerts [us] to a danger that threatens our moral strength: the danger that comes to us from wives and children." Railing against the "tyranny of the feminist movement," Mubarak warned that wives and children were out of control. Women were participating in beauty pageants and flouncing about without headcoverings, and students were using their university studies as an excuse to remain dependent upon parents until age thirty.[4] The solution, Mubarak argued, was for men to reassert their dominance. "Man will not taste happiness or honor unless he is the first and last master at home," he wrote. Mubarak then doubled down on his statement: a woman could not live without a master because women had a "canine nature."[5]

Such comments might stir emotion, even today. In fact, the article was likely written for that very purpose. Mubarak was known for his lack of tact: one frequently found him on the pages of Egyptian newspapers and magazines, embroiled in editorial battles with other Egyptian thinkers (including Taha Husayn, Ahmad Amin, ʿAbbas Mahmud al-ʿAqqad, and even the *al-Risala* editor Ahmad Hasan al-Zayyat). Infamous for being irritating, Mubarak enticed others to outrage. It helped him attract attention: Egypt was a media-rich environment where writers competed for readers. Controversy cut through the noise, focusing eyes and emotions on the source of the disruption. As a result, although Mubarak's outrageous opinions saw him dismissed from two university teaching positions, he relished (and built his career on) controversy. He even declared his resolve to "terrorize" the men of Fuʾad University, al-Azhar, and the Ministry of Education.[6]

"The Worst of Enemies" was therefore not representative of Egyptian opinion at large so much as one of Mubarak's characteristic attempts at rabble-rousing. And predictably, a few weeks after the article appeared, *al-Risala* decided to publish one reply to Mubarak written by a woman from Sohag (in Upper Egypt). In a letter to the editor, the Muslim woman named Buthayna expressed her outrage at Mubarak's comments. "Dr. Zaki Mubarak, in what century do we even direct these disgraceful words to women, who gave birth to genius and helped establish civilization?"[7]

The exchange was revealing. Mubarak had expressed indignation [*ghaḍab*] at changing gender roles, fashion magazines, new dress habits, Egyptians dousing themselves in perfume, and men and women roaming about without hats and veils (important, he explained, because headcoverings separated humans from animals). But his comparison of women to dogs elicited outrage from Buthayna.

(No one seemed to express much anger at his comments about freeloading college students.) The exchange illustrated how individuals often expressed "moral emotions" to attract attention and send messages about right and wrong.

Moral emotions were sentiments involved in the production and policing of the moral order. Described by scholars as part of the "behavioral immune system," moral emotions (like shock, anger, guilt, and disgust) sent a swift signal that something was wrong, allowing for a speedy response to the perceived threat.[8] Functioning as a kind of "emotional moral barometer," moral emotions bridged cognitions and value judgments with facial expressions, hand gestures, physiological responses (nausea, adrenaline, arousal), and movements (distancing, cringing, attacking). Moral emotions thus proved useful for screening information and providing "immediate and salient feedback on … social and moral acceptability."[9]

In Egypt, moral emotions were learned as part of the uneven, ongoing, and contested process of moral and emotional socialization.[10] At a young age, Egyptians learned how different emotions like dignity [*karāma*], longing [*shawq*], and forms of shame [*dhull, ʿayb,* and *ʿār*] should stir or change one's body. Students learned which situations should elicit which emotions—for instance, how should a person feel and how should the body change when singing the national anthem? In childhood, Egyptians also learned role-specific emotions, gendered emotions, professional emotions, and status or class-based emotions—as well as emotional display rules (how and when to show or conceal emotion). Finally, Egyptians moved through different emotional spaces, with mosques and bars, homes and workplaces each having their "own guidelines, standards, and expectations for emotional expression."[11] These emotional regimes, or rules of emotional practice, were foundational to social life.[12]

Surveying Egyptian journals, commonly expressed emotions included the four affective gatekeepers of the moral order: anger, shock, shame, and disgust. Among these, provoked and indignant anger [*ghaḍab*] was perhaps the most common moral emotion in Egypt, as the exchange between Zaki Mubarak and Buthayna illustrated. Occasionally a writer expressed the storming, uncontrolled rage of *hayajān*, the frustrated fury of *ḥanaq*, or the galling, furious ire of *ghayẓ*. However, outraged *ghaḍab* was by far the most common way that Egyptians like Buthayna sent negative feedback, urged confrontation, and prescribed punitive action.[13]

Expressions of shock also abounded in Egyptian media. Individuals sometimes described feeling *sadma*, the violent shock of a sudden blow or collision; Egyptians typically used this term to describe social tragedies, family deaths, personal traumas, and diabetic shocks. The feeling was understood as painful, traumatic, and potentially deadly.[14] There was also unexpected, gasping surprise [*mufājā'a*]—sometimes good, sometimes bad—used to describe a plot twist in a story, an unexpected birthday party, or a military ambush.

The story "Shaykh in a Dance Club" expressed two other types of shock. The narrator voiced his positive, marveling wonder [*'ajab*] upon encountering the sinner praying at the mosque. Meanwhile, the club owner and the club audience were struck by confused, frozen astonishment [*dahsha*] at the shaykh in the dance club. The story linked this latter type of surprise with a concrete action: the audience fell immediately silent ("*dahsha* tied the tongues of the attendees").[15] As articles suggested, writers used to shock to focus attention on unexpected stimuli and underscore that something was unusual, unanticipated, or "out of place." Descriptions of shock also highlighted the fact that Egyptians imagined emotions moving the body: *emotion* produced *motion.*

One important sentiment Egyptian journals used to structure moral behavior was shame. Rather than constitute a single feeling, however, there were many shames in the Arabophone moral imaginary. There was demeaning *dhull*, a humiliation that forced a man to his knees and made him hang his head (or "bend the neck"). *'Ayb* was also common—this was the "shame on you!" feeling of having done something to metaphorically disfigure one's face. Less common but still significant was *faḍīḥa*, the "what will they think?" (other-oriented), mortifying shame of having a scandal exposed.[16]

But the strongest shame was *'ār*. To feel *'ār* was to know abject disgrace—the everlasting ignominy of having one's honor irreparably shattered. Understood as something that would drive a man to suicide, follow him to the grave, inspire honor killings, and mar the family name for generations, *'ār* was the term Egyptian activists used for collective political traumas like the "shame of Dinshaway" (a colonial massacre of Egyptian villagers) and the "shame of 4 February" (when the British surrounded the Palace with tanks). It was also the term activists used to describe cowardice, intentionally throwing away one's chastity, or betraying one's country.[17]

That said, shame was not always bad in Egypt—shame could also reflect good upbringing and high standards. For instance, certain situations called for *khajal* (a feeling tied to blushing); this feeling of respectful shyness should be felt in the presence of elders and in-laws. *Khajal* could also be experienced as personal embarrassment when failing to achieve a goal. Another feeling was *ḥayā'*, the guiding conscience emotion. *Ḥayā'* was an uncomfortable (but necessary) embarrassment and "shrinking of the soul from foul conduct." Finally, Egyptians expressed *ḥishma*, a modest impulse to cover out of a sense of decency and decorum (often felt when encountering outsiders and members of the opposite sex).[18]

Both conscience-guiding *ḥayāʾ* and modest *ḥishma* were understood to be positive emotions that prevented bad behavior. Meanwhile, modest *ḥishma* and respectful *khajal* contributed to reinforcing gender and age hierarchies. Women and children were expected to feel shy and deferential *khajal* more often and more intensely than men, and journals similarly described modest *ḥishma* as a strongly gendered "female emotion." (Two types of shame, *ḥishma* and *ʿār*, were also notable for being morphologically related to terms for genitals or "covered parts"—*maḥāshim* and *ʿawra.*)[19]

Each emotion corresponded to implied movements. *ʿAyb* and *khajal* made a person shrink and hide the face, the humiliation of *dhull* forced a man to his knees, and *ʿār* ground a man into the earth until he was dust. In contrast, proud sentiments like *sharaf*, *karāma*, and *ʿizza* did the opposite. The status-raising, elevated "I'm honored" feeling of noble *sharaf* made one stand straight and tall. Dignified *karāma* raised the head and face. And the man proud of his achievements, his country, or his family felt a sense of strong, masculine, mighty *ʿizza* [pride] in his muscles. Notably, Arabic sentiments were linked to body parts (and especially to the face): a man with *ʿizza* had a proud nose, a humiliated man was a man "without a nose," a furious man had a hot or swollen nose, and a man seized by prideful anger [*ikhrinṭām*] had a high and twisted nose.[20]

As a morality tale, "Shaykh in a Dance Club" was notable for putting pride and shame front and center. The story described a shaykh transgressing Egyptian norms by bringing religion into a dance club. The shaykh's sermon in the club thus constituted a breaching experiment: by transgressing established norms, the shaykh revealed how the social order was maintained.

The shaykh's disciples warn that the social pioneering attempt will be risky, and express concerns that the club patrons will "jeer at us and harm us" (both forms of social policing). And as predicted, the crowd at the nightclub demonstrates how entertainment space was policed in the 1940s: when the shaykh appears on stage the audience becomes angry and mocks him. Their anger sends a message that the shaykh has trespassed; in their social imagination, the shaykh is "out of place." The club patrons also provide specific feedback about what behaviors they feel are appropriate for the club: they offer the shaykh wine and tell him to strip, dance, and arouse them. In other words, the clubgoers demand the shaykh adhere to the social scripts for a nightclub and perform the behaviors suitable for that space (and his on-stage role). Despite this feedback, the shaykh refuses to shame. Instead, he stands tall and stages a pride display, working to transform social norms by refusing to cower for his violation. He then preaches a sermon to convince club patrons that *their* behavior, not his, is shameful. In the story, the shaykh succeeds; the audience is ashamed and changes their ways.

The story showed how emotional performances could be revolutionary. Pride and shame entailed arguments about what things should be respected and valued. Egyptian social norms dictated pride during national parades and deference to elders, with violations liable to attract punishments ranging from frowns and "tsk" noises to angry comments and corporal punishment. This was because showing pride or shame at the wrong time potently challenged the social order. Activists could thus affectively subvert the system by refusing to honor respected people, places, and objects—or by putting on pride displays and *refusing to shame* for acts others found wrong.

While scores of other emotions contributed to the maintenance of the moral order, one last emotion that Egyptians frequently expressed in editorials was shuddering, recoiling disgust [*ishmiʾzāz*]. Zaki Mubarak, for instance, expressed disgust at wives "contaminated" by feminism, and Hamid Badr similarly described female immodesty as "disgusting" [*qabīḥ*].[21] Conservative pundit Sayyid Qutb went a step further; in an article complaining about beachgoers, he argued that bikini-clad girls were nothing but stray animals, "disgusting, cheap meat"—filthy "cockroaches."[22] (This opinion was likely informed by Qutb's village upbringing and a broken romance after his move to the city, which shaped his outspoken views on urban women.)[23]

Disgust revealed how heavily the Arabic emotions lexicon relied on metaphors. Metaphors helped "set before the eyes" and physically embody abstract concepts like moral repulsion. By attempting to transfer the physical nausea of decaying meat to a value judgment about women's dress habits, for instance, Qutb worked to infuse "the feelings attached to the symbolizing situation" into the situation being described.[24] Phrased differently, Qutb's analogy sought to transfer the feeling of seeing a skittering cockroach to the experience of seeing a woman on the beach.

Importantly for social activism, metaphors also sketched a path for movement. More than just a linguistic flourish, calling women "disgusting, cheap meat" bridged a moral concept (promiscuous clothing) to a physiological response (the reflex to gag and spit out bad meat).[25] Ahmad Amin similarly used a chemistry metaphor to compare anger to the explosive reaction of volatile diatomic gases: anger's path indiscriminately moved outward (scorching anyone in the immediate vicinity). Creatively, he also described love as a solvent dissolving the soul, but sharpening sensory perception and feelings [*ḥass*].[26]

Egyptian activists typically used expressions of disgust to encourage distancing or "cleaning." An anonymous religious scholar, for instance, condemned corrupt Islamic scholars working with the government with a string of similes: "Like dung beetles they fear perfume, like bats they flee the light, like bacteria they die from purity, like demons they fear goodness." The anonymous scholar then added an explicit action script about what should be done: al-Azhar should be cleaned of these men as one sweeps away "mud on the road."[27]

Whether describing women as cockroaches or preachers in politician's pockets as dung beetles, moral metaphors were often dehumanizing, using the human–animal divide to devalue and revoke humanity. However, there was something more to bug metaphors: after all, if denying humanity was the only aim, then any animal (cat, rabbit, bird) would serve the purpose. Instead, activists strategically chose animal comparisons to create *actionable metaphors*. By depicting Isma'il Sidqi Pasha as a wolf (see Figure 6.1), the Workers' Vanguard warned Egyptians to be on their guard. Similarly, by calling bikini-wearing women stray animals and cockroaches, Qutb demanded the stray animal be brought back to its pen, the cockroach exterminated. Each comparison implicitly transferred action scripts from the source domain to the target domain.

Overall, it was these vivid metaphors that kindled emotion, made Qutb's moral watchdog articles evocative and engaging, and propelled him to the forefront of Cairo's literary scene. His success makes all the more sense considering Qutb had gotten his start in the late 1930s writing poetry, fusing modern psychology with Sufism and existentialism, and searching for "the secret of the emotional power of the Qur'an" or its "affective logic" [*al-manṭiq al-wijdānī*]. His studies convinced him that emotions blossomed from Qur'anic recitation because of the rhythms, the selection of words with "specific sonic properties," and the visual scenery which "fills the eye and the ear, senses and imagination, emotions and thought." Convinced the romance of language could help reenchant hearts hardened by mechanical industrialism, Qutb saw language and feelings as the wellspring of action. As he described, only ideas married to feelings could generate the "emotional heat" capable of driving change.[28]

Figure 6.1 Moral Metaphors in Egypt: The Wolf in Pasha's Clothing.

A cover illustration from *al-Fajr al-Jadid*, printed at the time of the 1946 demonstrations, uses a moral metaphor to warn against Prime Minister Isma'il Sidqi Pasha. Depicted as a wolf, the prime minister stands atop a copy of the unpopular Anglo-Egyptian Treaty, holding a stick to "maintain security... and extreme nationalism" (a jab at the Muslim Brotherhood's partnership with the Sidqi Administration).

Source: *Al-Fajr al-Jadīd* 24, March 6, 1946, in IISH ARCH02315/Folder 97. Tali'a al-'Ummal Collection, International Institute of Social History, Amsterdam.

Moral Maps: The Dance Club, the Shaykh, and the Sinner Repentant

Moral emotions were one way that activists tried to jolt audiences from slumber; redrawing moral maps was another potent technology of protest. Moral maps—also called moral cartographies, moral geographies, or normative geographies—linked spaces to specific roles, scripts, divisions of time, and value judgments.[29] A 1950 article by *al-Risala* editor Ahmad Hasan al-Zayyat, for instance, mapped nakedness onto spaces like the bathroom and the bedroom, and onto social roles like husband and wife, doctor and patient.[30] Such shared maps made for an orderly society (and kept chests, breasts, and balls out of spaces like schools, playgrounds, and malls).

When contesting the social order, activists told stories that transgressed these moral maps. In 1940s Egypt, for example, dance club patrons imagined cabarets as erotic entertainment spaces made for uncovering (at least so long as the nakedness was professionalized in the person of the dancer and confined to the stage). But "Shaykh in a Dance Club" challenged this space by sending in a shaykh, who astutely argues in his sermon that men have the power to remake space by changing their behavior. When one lusts in the mosque, the mosque becomes like a club, and when nightclub patrons pray, the club becomes a religious space. The story then relocates the men to the mosque and remaps the appropriate space for women (and their nakedness): by the end of story, the dancer returns to the home to become a wife and mother.[31]

In Egypt, activist clubs contested different spaces depending on their political outlook. More conservative publications (like *al-Risala*, *Misr al-Fatah*, *Shabab Sayyidna Muhammad*, *al-Da'wa*, and *Majallat al-Azhar*) shared a common concern with media, leisure, and entertainment spaces. One passionate attack on the media, for instance, appeared in a 1945 article written by Sayyid Qutb (who had not yet joined the Muslim Brotherhood). After relating various tales of iniquity (describing a woman leaving the house to cheat on her husband and a girl in a restaurant with a male suitor), Qutb ended by asking "What pushed this generation into the abyss?" His answer: magazines, popular music, and films. (Qutb later added that the radio also needed to be cleansed of perverted, wretched creatures like ʿAbd al-Wahhab and Farid al-Atrash for singing that the world was a "cigarette and a drink.")[32] Misr al-Fatah, the Muslim Brotherhood, and Shabab Sayyidna Muhammad similarly criticized media and entertainment spaces.[33]

Besides magazines, theaters, and nightclubs, there was another "paradise of Satan" that worried Egyptian moralists. This den of iniquity, where pleasure-seekers frolicked in filth was … the beach! "The beach is Satan's Paradise, which gathers together a thousand Adams and a thousand Eves," wrote Kamil Mahmud Habib in 1949. Bringing together individuals unfettered by *ḥayāʾ* and *khajal* (conscience-shame and blushing-shame), "The beach in summer is a playground of immorality and theater of moral depravity … the saltwater washes away nothing but decency and pride."[34] Muslim Brotherhood leader Salih ʿAshmawi included the beach (alongside co-ed parties and magazines) in a list of things decaying the Egyptian nation.[35] Sayyid Qutb found the beach so odious he included it in a five-part series on Egyptian moral collapse, which ran in *al-Risala* in 1946. In the series, he described the beach as representing all the symptoms of moral decline: there was a private beach for corrupt aristocrats who did not speak Arabic; Egyptian celebrities visiting the beach (representing the decrepitude of popular music); and a magazine photographer taking pictures of half-dressed women.[36]

What made beaches the source of so much moral anxiety in the 1940s and 1950s? This question was echoed in one 1949 anti-beach morality tale, "Goddess of the Beach," in which the narrator posed a similar question: "What possible harm could it do to throw off one's shackles for an hour to enjoy the breeze of life … there on the seashore, where the world ripples with beauty and fun, and the earth undulates with youth and movement?" As the story continued, feeling bound by "chains of manhood and family," a husband went to the lay on the ocean sands. There, he saw a beautiful girl, and he was instantly enchanted with this "Goddess of the Beach." Like a fever she occupied his thoughts, until one night the man gave in to temptation and visited the casino. But when the dancer came onstage to perform, the young man was dismayed. It was "my girl," the narrator exclaimed, "She—the Goddess of the Beach! … a dancer from among the 'fancy girls,'[37] who breathes poison into the hearts of men, to steal from man his masculinity and money and strip the husband from his wife and children. She—the servant of Satan, who wants to destroy the home and break up the family."[38]

The beach was thus part of a pattern in Egyptian moralizing, which linked entertainment and leisure practices with harms to the household. As the foundational space for social (re)production, the household was where marital dyads produced new members of society, where children were socialized, and where gender norms and divisions of labor were defined. Egyptian moralists thus spilled buckets of ink worrying how new leisure practices would affect the family. The usually sober and dry *Majallat al-Azhar*, for instance, published an article in which Shaykh Mustafa al-Sawi lamented that restaurants and cafes were dangerous spaces. Restaurants had caused women to abandon the kitchen, Sawi complained, and now "the 'Queen of Cooking' has died in the brains of women and girls." From this, he concluded that "I think that the house is on the road to destruction, family building on the path to wreckage, and morals descending to the depths of depravity."[39]

On the far end of this spectrum, Muhammad's Youth argued the only way to safeguard social reproduction was to keep women at home. To reinforce this moral map, the club printed two unique kinds of morality tales: "cautionary rape tales" and "tales of mixing and murder." In the first category came one 1949 news story about a shaykh and his daughter. The shaykh allowed his daughter to serve tea to guests who visited their home. However, there was a wolf among the flock: Mustafa ʿAbd Allah, who went to the shaykh's home not to worship, but to enjoy the beauty of the shaykh's daughter. Then one fateful day, ʿAbd Allah dragged the shaykh's daughter away. Thus, the writer moralized, "the shaykh paid the price of his daughter's honor, his own honor, and his dignity for neglecting God's moral precepts."[40] Another cautionary tale described how a mother abandoned her children so she could enjoy nights out at entertainment halls. As a result, a servant molested the woman's six-year-old daughter. Similar "news-stories-as-morality-tales" in the association's journal described a pregnant woman raped by her obstetrician; a daughter raped after she left the house without a veil; a wife raped after deciding to leave the house; and many other such stories.[41]

Shabab Sayyidna Muhammad's newspaper also published many stories about "mixing and murder," which described how gender mixing in beaches and clubs would lead to adultery, murder, rape, disease, chaos, and crime.[42] For instance, in a series entitled "scandals [*faḍā'iḥ*] of [gender] mixing and unveiling"—the journal related sordid news stories full of bloodshed and betrayal caused by co-ed mingling.[43] In one story, a woman's jealous husband murdered her and her (also married) lover at a bar; as *Shabab Sayyidna Muhammad* moralized, the newspapers had not mentioned the real reason for the murders, which was "mixing and unveiling."[44] Another story (about the killing of a Saudi and the dancer accompanying him in a club) explained that "this is the natural result of what happens in dance clubs and cabarets," which "threaten morality, honor, and peoples' souls."[45] These stories—which often appeared preceding or following open letters to government ministers—imparted a twofold moral lesson. First, members of the opposite sex should not mix (not even with relatives), and second, the government was failing in its duty to protect both Egyptian homes and the "house of Egypt" (the nation).[46]

Since Muhammad's Youth activists positioned themselves as being more saintly than the shaykhs (criticizing the Muslim Brotherhood and al-Azhar for their laxity), the group argued not only against clubs and bars, but against universities. Universities, the association claimed, were dangerous spaces. As evidence, the paper printed stories about a girl impregnated by her professor, and another girl seduced by her tutor.[47] Writing to the Ministry of Education in 1949, the society complained that male and female students were sitting next to one another in class and mixing in the courtyards at Fu'ad University. In the letter, the group demanded university doors be closed to women and strict dress codes be imposed (including banning lipstick "and other manifestations of malice and pornography"). As the paper explained, "Equality between boys and girls in the type of education [they receive] … has led to the decline of education and morality, as well as distanced girls from their natural place, which is the home."[48] Small news items—like a story about female graduates crying in response to news that government ministries were not hiring women—reinforced this master narrative about the place of women in society.[49]

The Moral Geography of Communist Morality Tales

While conservative activists fretted about the home, Egyptian communists told stories about different spaces: farms, factories, and shops.[50] As communist articles explained, it was the countryside where peasants lived in ignorance, poverty, and disease while "feudal exploiters" took advantage of their labor. And it was the countryside where tenant farmers worked the ground but ceded the profits to landlords.[51]

While the characters in conservative morality tales were usually family members (husbands, wives, and daughters), and while the villains of conservative stories were usually entertainers and wayward women, communist stories featured a different cast of characters. Communist protagonists were typically workers and farmers, and many stories involved children (to inspire sympathy in readers). Communist villains, meanwhile, were wealthy employers, landowners, and men of religion.[52]

Communist morality tales also differed emotionally from the stories of social conservatives. If Muhammad's Youth insisted the world was a disgusting, dangerous, and frightening place, the Workers' Vanguard told tragic sagas of suffering and woe. One story followed a poor father and son in a slum. In the tale, the father slaved away in a shoe workshop, only to die of tuberculosis. After the father's death, his young son took his father's place in the factory. He continued breaking his back on the wheels of injustice—then died of tuberculosis, just like his father. Other stories followed a man returning to his natal village to find it in abject poverty, and a poor girl working in a cotton field.[53] Most tales contrasted the lives of rich and poor: the Workers' Vanguard magazine *al-Fajr al-Jadid*, for instance, printed a story comparing the lives of two girls (one rich, one poor) born on the same day. The poor girl's mother is taken to nurse the rich girl, leaving the poor girl malnourished. This pattern of injustice continues, ending with a final juxtaposition: the rich girl rides the train, the poor girl is found dead by the tracks.[54]

Another communist parable, printed in *al-Fajr al-Jadid*, illustrated how communist activists used emotions to criticize the social order. According to the parable, one winter's night a suffering peasant healing from a broken leg was released from the hospital. With no means of transportation, he was forced to hobble back to his hut through the bitter cold. As he limped home in misery, the happy sounds of a great feast echoed in the air.

The next morning, the peasant's dead body was found on the roadside. Grieved, other peasants of the village organized a funeral. However, as the funeral procession passed down the road, it encountered a rich man in his luxury car.

The rich man's driver respectfully stopped—but the rich man became angry and shouted at the inconvenience. While the rich man cursed and raged, the driver of the car was overcome with emotion and shed tears for the dead man.[55]

As a morality tale based on emotional displays, the communist parable juxtaposed the feelings of rich and poor. The poor were shown upright by their appropriate affective displays: the peasants honor the dead, and the driver models proper grieving behavior. In contrast, the abhorrent emotions of the wealthy illustrated their depravity: the partygoers celebrate while the poor suffer, and the rich man rages at the funeral—deplorable violations of Egyptian display rules (which prescribed solemnity and respect for the dead).[56]

What was unusual about these tales (especially considering the communist emphasis on revolutionary activism) was the weak action scripts. The peasants and workers in *al-Fajr al-Jadid*'s morality tales did not revolt, rebel, or resist—they slaved and died. Articles declared the workers had an elect role to play, but morality tales typically ended with the protagonist's death. A political sketch from April 1946 vividly illustrated this concept: it showed two men (Egypt and the Sudan) in the position of Samson, jointly toppling the columns of colonization. However, like the tale of Samson, the sketch implied the destruction would end in self-sacrifice: the building collapses on the mens' heads.[57]

No call to arms followed the tales. Instead, communist stories worked to inspire pity for the poor. This likely reflected *al-Fajr al-Jadid*'s intellectual readership, and the tradeoff that the journal made for its publishing license. The paper's editor Yusuf Darwish was a lawyer, and understood that to avoid prosecution according to §§171 and 174 of the Egyptian Penal Code, the journal could not print any incitement to crime or anything promoting the "overthrow of the ruling order."[58]

Despite *al-Fajr al-Jadid*'s quietism, the activists who produced the paper were heavily engaged in trade union activism, and signs of resistance appeared in smaller underground papers. In these illegal circulars, short news stories appeared about factories exploiting workers—and workers fighting back through strikes or union organizing. Still, the stories were more often tragedies than triumphal epics: resistance overwhelmingly ended with firings and arrests.

One exception to this corpus of passive and tragic scripts was the communist tale "Wings of Wax," an adaptation of the Icarus legend. The story concerned three friends (two men and a beautiful young lady) who visit an artist's studio. At the studio, they view a painting of a woman, bound and beaten atop a high hill. Surveying the painting, none of the men see any hope in the piece: as the artist explains, the bound woman is like the bourgeoisie—self-imprisoned.

The demoralized painter laments that "People who live on high occupy every surface … they want freedom, but as soon as they reach the door, they return to their prison—confused and disconcerted about whether it was wise [to go back to captivity] or leap into the abyss." But the young woman sees the enchained woman as a symbol of the poor, and with tears in her eyes asks, "How did I not notice the suffering of the miserable woman?" She also sees hope in the paint, arguing the woman is fighting her chains. One of her male friends, a young intellectual, has a different response: shaken by the painting, he becomes inexplicably angry and storms off.

Thus, two friends are left to view the final painting *Wings of Wax*. The painter leads them to a dark corner and a curtain rises, revealing a massive canvas. There in dark impassioned strokes, the painter has retold the Greek tale of Icarus, who made wings of wax to flee from his prison. In the artist's version of the story, Icarus "desired the sun, he went to her … but his wings melted, and Icarus, lover of the sun, enemy of slavery, plunged down and died, shrouded in the remnants of his wings of wax."[59] Unwilling to accept the painter's bleak outlook, the young lady asks if the glimmer on the horizon of the canvas is hope; but the painter replies in the negative. As he asks rhetorically, from where would such a light come?

By now, the sun is setting, so the two friends leave the painter in his gloom and head home. On their way back they come to a crossroads. One side is a calm and quiet road meandering toward the horizon; the other side is a busy road, where a group of provincial workers are returning from a hard day's labor, happily singing songs. One of the workers bumps into the young lady, but she is unperturbed. "Are you going on this road?" her friend asks, pointing to the calmer route. But with a laugh of beautiful youthfulness, the girl says no. "I will take this street"—the road with the workers.[60]

Of all the tales, "Wings of Wax" was notable as one of the few stories involving a female protagonist in an agentic role. The story was also rare among Egyptian communist tales, in that it involved both affective action scripts (grief for the suffering, hope for the future) and a concrete action script ("take the path of the workers"). There were also implied scripts like "break your chains" and "take a leap" (although these actions were still ambivalently described as dangerous, difficult, and deadly).

Overall, "Wings of Wax" was also an interesting study in how activists reprised older morality tales in a new key. In its oldest extant form, the story of Icarus (as told by the Roman poet Ovid) was a "listen to your parents" tale involving a boy and his father. The father instructs Icarus to stay the middle course between the earth and the sun—but Icarus ignores parental advice and flies too high. His downfall is thus caused by filial disobedience and failing to stay within the limits. The Greek tale is about obedience, not about escaping imprisonment.[61] But *al-Fajr al-Jadid*'s story of the ill-fated flyer discarded this moral, transforming Icarus into a symbol of the communist activist (a "lover of the sun, enemy of slavery").

There was admittedly an elite bias to "Wings of Wax" or "The Communist Icarus," reflecting *al-Fajr al-Jadid*'s authors and readership. The workers were a background feature, while the depressed painter, hopeful lady, her male friend, and the intellectual (clinging to his books) were all central. The male characters were negative examples of depressed or squabbling intellectuals (likely a veiled condemnation of the Workers' Vanguard's rivals in Iskra and the EMNL).

Because Egyptian communist articles were usually authored anonymously and newspapers read surreptitiously, there is little information on how these communist morality tales were received. One glimpse at reception, however, suggests the affective appeals met with mixed reviews. As Nawal al-Saʿdawi remembered, in 1946 when she was fifteen she became friends with a girl named Samiyya at their boarding school. Samiyya was in Iskra. As Nawal recalled, the communist activist always worked to elicit a certain emotional posture from Nawal: Samiyya "always made me feel guilty, as though we were responsible for the British occupation of Egypt … or for the widespread poverty, ignorance and disease." Samiyya's emotional appeals even earned her an unflattering nickname: "All the girls in the dormitory insisted on calling her Boo Boo Effendi."[62]

Later during her third year of medical school at Fuʾad University, Nawal had another encounter with communist activists. It was autumn 1951, and all the clubs on campus were making speeches. Nawal remembered little about the speeches—except for a speech by an excellent Muslim Brotherhood speaker, who told the story of how God sent a spider to weave a web over the mouth of a cave to hide the Prophet Muhammad while he was fleeing Mecca. Nawal also remembered that her friends believed communism was "atheism, heresy, corruption and immorality," and therefore kept a safe distance from the communist in their class, Yusuf Idris. One day, however, Nawal met another Marxist—medical student Ahmad Hilmi. Ahmad edited a small communist paper named *Shuʿlat al-Tahrir* and had written a short story for the paper called "The Boy and the Dog," so he gave Nawal a copy.

Like many other communist morality tales, "The Boy and the Dog" highlighted the suffering of the poor and had a child protagonist to inspire pity. But while "Boo Boo Effendi's" newspaper had not inspired Nawal to the guilt the paper intended, Hilmi's story had the desired effect. "Fifty years have gone by since then," Nawal later wrote, "but I still carry a vivid picture in my memory, that of a small crippled boy and a small crippled dog sitting side-by-side as they eat out of a dustbin."

Later sitting with Ahmad in a seminar, she remembered Yusuf Idris approaching them. Yusuf told Ahmad: "You know I read your short story 'The Boy and the Dog.' When I go to sleep at night I see the crippled dog and the crippled boy ... I felt it was more effective than a hundred political articles dealing with poverty."[63]

Conclusion: The Dog's Birthday Party (and Other Moral Totems)

Overall, large Egyptian journals and magazines of the 1940s and 1950s (including *al-Risala*, *al-Fajr al-Jadid*, and *al-Da'wa*) printed well-developed morality tales and parables in their pages. Faced with smaller operating budgets and constraints on page space, newsletters like *Kifah al-Sha'b*, *al-Muqawama al-Sha'biyya*, and *Kifah al-Umma* focused on publishing short news items and true stories that could be imbued with moral lessons. These "small stories" illustrated how political associations used everyday happenings and "talking about others" to craft group identities and notions of "us" and "them"—a process that typically involved flattening female characters, business owners, and religious leaders into one-dimensional foils.[64]

Narratives like "Shaykh in a Dance Club" were also notable for how they maneuvered emotions, social maps, metaphors, and vocabularies of virtue and vice[65] to move men to action. "Shaykh in a Dance Club" used shame and pride displays to challenge the ruling order and communicate messages about "dangerous" and "safe" spaces. The tale employed metaphors to "represents things as in a state of activity,"[66] describing club patrons as "flies swarming around" (a metaphor that asked readers to wrinkle their nose, clean house, and shoo away or exterminate the flies). The most important action script was saved for last: as the final line of the morality tale exclaimed, "If only a shaykh would enter every dance club! If only a shaykh would enter the Ministry of Education!"[67] Here then was the moral of the story: an action script encouraging religious functionaries to leave their usual spaces and enter the halls of government.[68]

Egypt's different political trends shared these strategies in common; but there were quantitative and qualitative differences in how groups deployed moral lexicons. Cluster I terms of contamination, for instance, proved popular among most activists, no matter their ideological bent. But social conservatives packed their journals with vocabulary from Clusters I–V, while Egyptian communists tended to limit themselves to Clusters I and IV (contamination appeals and high/low contrasts), shunning Clusters II and III (terms of deviation and terms of exposure).

Communists also tended to speak in a factual-informative or "rational" mode—a reflection of the scientific epistemologies from which they drew their authority and truth-claims. While this made communist papers look less moralistic on the surface, a close reading of communist papers revealed two other valuative lexicons at work, which a standard review of Arabic moral vocabulary (Figure 2.4) missed. Egyptian communists, it turned out, preferred to communicate value judgments using terms of flaw (e.g., ignorant, deaf, blind, ill) and naturalistic dualisms (e.g., darkness/dawn, grow/wither, live/die). The name of the Workers' Vanguard organ (*The New Dawn*, or *al-Fajr al-Jadid*) was a case in point. This naturalistic moral code also appeared in poetry: as communist poet Wasfi al-Bunni wrote in *al-Fajr al-Jadid*, "The *dawn* approaches / We are the *light* that drives out the *darkness*."[69] Thus, one could add to the Arabic moral lexicon a "Cluster VI: Terms of Flaw" and a "Cluster VII: Naturalistic Idioms."

Similar vocabularies of virtue and vice (and similar emotions-concepts) are found across different languages, historical contexts, and cultures.[70] This isomorphy likely stems from the fact that humans in different societies share similar experiences with their environments (like the rising and setting of the sun, encounters with invasive insects, and the hot feeling that accompanies the release of adrenaline and changes in cardiac activity and blood flow). As a result, learning to recognize moral and emotional discourses highlights how individuals can share similar imaginaries, while creatively adapting moral and emotional metaphors to individual and local experiences.

Ultimately, reading Egyptian morality tales thus helps outline a theoretical approach for understanding emotions and other types of "moral talk" in political narratives. For instance, when reading morality tales in campaigns, it is important to ask questions regarding narrative structure, moral maps, and emotions (see Figure 6.2). Approaching activist campaigns in this way yields many insights. Conservative groups usually told stories about protecting the home, and featured weak husbands and shameless women—an inversion of the affective order imagined by Egyptian conservatives. Communist stories, on the other hand, were set in the workplace or street, where the wealthy reveled and workers slaved and died. Action scripts tended to be reflexive (asking readers to change their mind) or affective (working to inspire guilt or compassion in middle- and upper-class readers).

Despite the different settings of their stories, activists occasionally shared morality tales in common. *Al-Fajr al-Jadid*, for instance, wrote about a servant girl raped by her master (although the communist action script aimed to stoke anger against the ruling classes, not engender fears about female chastity like Muhammad Youth's rape tales). The journal further protested the capitalist

Narrative Structure

- Which stories (and whose stories) are shared?
- How is the story emplotted (e.g., is it a tragedy, comedy, romance, adventure)?
- What characters and objects appear in the story?
- How does the narrative structure time? (What is the story's start point and end point? Is the story a progress narrative, a restoration narrative, or something else?)

Moral Maps

- Which spaces or geographies does the speaker describe? (What is the setting of the story?)
- Where does the speaker place characters and objects on this map?
- What roles, hierarchies, and categories are mentioned?
- What value judgments are made about different objects, characters, spaces, or behaviors?
- Does the speaker support or challenge any roles, spaces, or emotions?
- What moral vocabularies (and metaphors) are used? What does this tell us about the speaker's worldview and valuing of different people, places, and things?

Emotions

- Which emotions are described in the narrative?
- How are emotions attached or attributed to characters?
- How are emotions attached or associated with different spaces?
- Which emotions does the speaker perform?
- Which emotions does the speaker try to cue from the audience? What are the speaker's strategies for trying to produce emotion?
- How does the audience receive, reject, or negotiate these emotional cues?
- How does the speaker adhere to (or violate) affective norms?

Scripts

- Which prescriptive (do this) and proscriptive (don't do that) scripts does the speaker communicate? (What is the speaker asking the audience to think, feel, or do?)
- What scripts (emotional, temporal, behavioral, or otherwise) are embedded in the narrative?
- What metaphors appear, and how do these metaphors entreat action (and filter information)?

Figure 6.2 Considerations for Analyzing Morality Tales.

commodification of the body and denounced the popular paper *Akhbar al-Yawm* for trading sex like a commodity.[71]

The Muslim Brotherhood also shared stories with communists. A parable in *al-Da'wa* related the tragic tale of a tenant farmer exploited by a landowner, and ended with the farmer leaving his land in tears then dying.[72] News items in *al-Da'wa* and *al-Ikhwan al-Muslimun* similarly recounted stories about bosses mistreating employees. Finally, the groups shared a common contempt for Egyptian elites and British administrators. A Muslim Brotherhood story, for instance, described Egyptian politicians building ivory palaces, buying up large tracts of agricultural land, partying in clubs, and relaxing in European resorts while workers starved in a factory.[73]

As a last site of overlap, most activist associations chose certain behaviors, spaces, and characters as "moral totems." Each totem—be it the dancer, the ivory tower intellectual, the Muslim shaykh, or the rich boss—represented a certain deviant type, a "whole spectrum of problems and aberrations."[74] Muhammad's Youth selected the famous historian 'Afaf Lutfi al-Sayyid [Marsot] (a history student at the American University of Cairo at the time) as one of its moral totems. Announcing it would provide readers with a "real idea of the kind of education" being offered by American University, an institution that "works to destroy every virtue," the paper wrote in scandalous tones that "this university throws a birthday party—not for any great man—but for the dog of Lutfi al-Sayyid Pasha's daughter ['Afaf]!!" Describing professors and students enjoying the dog's birthday cake while "the vast majority of the nation writhes in starvation," the paper asked rhetorically "is there any greater scorn and wanton negligence than this?"[75]

Turning the dog's birthday into a straw man representing the wealthy Pasha, the birthday thus became a symbol of elite depravity. In the same way, the dancer represented the collapse of the family, the businessman represented economic exploitation, the university signified the "liberal agenda," and shorts represented foreign occupation and Westernization. Whatever the case, producing the desired outrage involved flattening human and institutional complexity, so the problem could be viewed as symbolic and homogeneous (rather than human and heterogeneous).

Ultimately, shared totems, myths, and emotions were thus an integral part of political claims-staking. By weaving moral totems into disturbing narratives, activists worked to stoke anger and mobilize change. And by laying claim to the problematic nature of certain activities, activists positioned themselves as guardians over certain spaces and activities.[76] The Brotherhood and Muhammad's

Youth positioned themselves as guardians of the family by telling stories about the home and entertainment spaces, and communists positioned themselves as the guardians of the workplace by telling stories about bosses and employees.

Nevertheless, there was "significant ideological fluidity" and exchange in 1940s Egypt, as Giedre Šabasevičiute points out. In those years political associations across the political spectrum "employed a shared language to denounce established elites" and borrowed arguments about social problems from one another. Sayyid Qutb, as an anti-establishment intellectual that freely sampled many protest discourses, was emblematic of this overlap. As a result, it is perhaps unsurprising that Qutb increasingly emerged as a dominant figure in protest politics and debates about decolonization—with rising star Naguib Mahfouz hailing him in 1945 as "the voice of the new generation" in Egypt.[77]

But most contested behaviors, roles, and spaces that appeared in communist and Islamist papers continued to be tolerated in Egyptian society. These moral stalemates formed either because no consensus could be reached about whether the behavior was truly harmful, or because practices were tied up in political and economic interests. Entering the month of October 1951, this was where Egyptian activist associations stood: unified in their belief that the ruling order must change, but locked in stalemate over how a new Egypt society should look. Thus, activists dutifully carried on performing emotions, hoping to win enough hearts to redraw the moral map. Few suspected that a thousand miles away, a political crisis at an Iranian oilfield was about to capsize the Egyptian status quo: a war for British evacuation was about to begin, and all emotions brought to arms.

7

Paul Revere's Ride through the Suez Canal

The 1951 Revolution

On October 3, 1951, a political earthquake rocked Egypt: the British evacuated the oil complex at Abadan, Iran. Within days, the Egyptian press buzzed with calls for British evacuation of the Suez Canal Zone. Watching events unfold, a British telegram warned that Egyptian newspapers were drawing conclusions from the British evacuation of Abadan, and reporting that "Egypt must draw a lesson from Iran's firm stand … the British [can] not stand up to force." On October 8, Wafd prime minister Mustafa al-Nahhas moved to transform the Abadan evacuation into political momentum: he announced in a speech to the nation that Egypt would unilaterally abrogate the 1936 Anglo-Egyptian Treaty.[1]

The treaty abrogation had a colossal effect on nationalist activism. On the morning of October 16, Cairo area university students took trains, busses, and cars, and poured into Isma'iliyya on the west bank of the Suez Canal. The battle for the Canal Zone—known to Egyptians as the "1951 Revolution" and "Liberation Struggle," and to the British as the "Suez Emergency"—had begun.

This anti-colonial struggle for British evacuation would pull in broad participation. Activists from the Muslim Brotherhood, Misr al-Fatah, the DMNL, the woman's organization Bint al-Nil, and the Women's Committee for Popular Resistance (launched by that "Communist Aristocrat" with the forty dresses, Inji Aflatun) all joined the struggle. This broad movement of *fidā'īyīn* [commandos, lit: self-sacrificers] launched anti-British paramilitary attacks, with the aim of achieving Egyptian national liberation.

Western journalists wove the Suez Emergency that autumn into an Orientalist myth about emotional hysteria in the East. A *New York Times* article painted the Egyptian prime minister's decision to abrogate the 1936 Treaty as a product of "his impetuosity, his sentimentalism, his irritable explosions," emotional flaws that were "100 percent Egyptian."[2] Rejecting this easy reading, this chapter returns to the 1951 Revolution to ask critical questions. What were the emotions of the moment, and how were feelings entangled in the Canal Struggle? How did Egyptians navigate the constraints of affective regimes and engage in affective diplomacy? And what stories circulated in this moment of uncertainty, when the revolution was still being written and different futures appeared within reach?

Building on studies in contentious politics and debates in fourth- and fifth-generation revolutionary theory, this chapter argues that rather than representing an uncontrolled explosion, journalists and activists expended an enormous amount of affective labor fanning the flames of the 1951 Revolution. This labor would be broadly shared, for moving beyond the craft newsletters and club journals of communist and Islamist associations, in autumn 1951 the revolutionary movement went mainstream. The "press of thighs and bosoms" (as Qutb had called it)[3]—popular magazines like *Akhir Sa ʿa, al-Musawwar*, and *al-Ithnayn*—turned their pens to war.

This mainstream endorsement of revolution would mark an important development. *Akhir Sa ʿa* (est. 1934) was part of the Akhbar al-Yawm publishing empire; the magazine was royalist but otherwise politically unaligned. *Al-Musawwar* (est. 1922) and *al-Ithnayn* (est. 1934), on the other hand, were owned by the Dar al-Hilal publishing house; the magazines were mildly Wafdist but "politically prudent," not endorsing any political party. Their reach was extensive: estimated circulation in 1944 for *al-Musawwar* and *al-Ithnayn* stood at around 60,000 and 90,000 copies.[4]

As a result, when the politically prudent press trumpeted the arrival of the 1951 Revolution that October, they made a significant contribution to making it a reality. Specifically, crafting the 1951 Revolution would involve an emotional boot camp, as emotions usually inhibited and impugned in Egyptian society as undesirable in peacetime—emotions like anger, hatred, and passion—had to be mobilized and legitimized for war. As a result, Egyptian editorialists worked to smelt and shape righteous indignation, build emotional connections with audiences, suppress fear of mortal risk, and rebuff British charges of fanaticism. The story of how Egyptians marshaled feelings that year thus proves informative, revealing how activists train emotions for war and engage adversaries on the emotional front.

Celebration at a Funeral: The Making of Egypt's First "Blessed Movement"

In the Canal Zone, trouble had been brewing since the student–worker protests of 1946. British Prime Minister Clement Attlee had responded to the 1946 demonstrations with a promise to evacuate Suez by September 1949. However, the Canal proved difficult to quit. At the time, the Suez Canal Zone was the largest military base in the world, hosting some 50,000–90,000 troops on any given year. With the developing Cold War increasing the strategic importance of Suez and officials worrying how an evacuation might damage British prestige, the British government thus postponed promises to evacuate.[5]

Despite British determination to hold on to Suez as the "jugular vein" of empire, world events fueled Egyptian hopes that Britain would take her final bow. Britain relinquished Transjordan in 1946, quit India and Pakistan in 1947, and lowered the Union Jack in the Mandate of Palestine in 1948. The event that rocked Egypt, however, came in March 1951: the Iranian parliament passed legislation nationalizing the Anglo-Iranian Oil Company. After an extended diplomatic crisis, on October 3, 1951, the British evacuated the oil complex at Abadan—a retreat the Associated Press lamented as the "1951 Dunkerque" the following day.[6]

Looking to repeat the British evacuation, five days later Prime Minister Nahhas asked a joint session of Egyptian Parliament to unilaterally abrogate the 1936 Anglo-Egyptian Treaty. His speech told the sordid tale of Britain's unsuccessful colonizations in America, India, and Iran, and highlighted the fact that America herself had canceled the Anglo-American Treaty in 1884.[7] Afterward, the US ambassador in Cairo cabled Washington. Unconvinced by the prime minister's stories, he dourly reported:

> [The speech] at first surprised and then almost hysterically delighted personal and radio audiences of [Egyptian] Senators, Deputies, newspapermen, and, incidentally, the people of Egypt. … The emotions of the moment were as irrational as the actions which the Prime Minister recommended, but there was no doubt then, and there has not been since, that regardless of the consequences and with no heed to the future … Egypt was behind the Prime Minister to a man.[8]

He added that in parlors and political clubs across the city, lamps were burning all night as Egyptians met to discuss the implications of the abrogation and decide what to do next.

The following morning, an elated crowd—among whom were Wafd heavyweights like Minister of Public Works ʿUthman Muharram Pasha and Minister of Social Affairs ʿAbd al-Fattah Hasan Pasha—gathered to celebrate in front of the old British barracks building at Qasr al-Nil. In their suits and ties, they symbolically smashed the building with pickaxes. Egyptian parliament ratified the abrogation that week, and *al-Ithnayn* captured the nation's joy with images of Egyptians smiling, dancing, playing instruments, and exchanging congratulatory kisses (a practice that echoes Anny Gaul's characterization of high-fives as a "physical acknowledgement and extension of a shared emotional experience") (see Figure 7.1).[9]

Along with the abrogation, major political parties and associations began mobilizing every revolutionary script in the Egyptian cultural canon. This involved a process of drawing attention to tales of war and resistance, and actively ignoring or bypassing peacetime scripts. For instance, the fact it was Muharram (a holy month in which fighting was forbidden according to Islamic law) was ignored. Instead, politicians analogically intercalated other chronoscapes, appealing to Laylat al-Qadr [the Night of Power or Destiny]—a night on the Islamic calendar when the heavens open, prayers are answered, and blessings rain down. (Notably, this was not the first time that leaders had rewritten chronoscapes—in antiquity, Muslims had simply exchanged the months of Muharram and Safar to avoid the prohibition against fighting during Muharram.)[10] The day of abrogation (October 8, 1951) was also collapsed with the Holiday of the National Struggle (13 November), which commemorated the 1919 Revolution. Egyptians were already working to construct a new revolution by chronologically linking it to the previous one.[11]

Along with these temporal negotiations, Egyptian politicians, journalists, and activist associations began invoking jihad scripts authorizing armed struggle. Some Egyptians called for a nationalist jihad: in this mode, on October 8 Egyptian politicians on the floor of Parliament described the treaty abrogation as Egypt's declaration of a national jihad, and the progressive women's rights organization Daughters of the Nile issued its own call to jihad few days later. Even progressive magazines like *al-Ithnayn* and *al-Musawwar* (infamous in conservative circles for their photos of bikini-clad women, beauty pageants, and fashion tips) announced that Egypt had declared jihad, and called on the people to prepare for sacrifice and struggle.[12] The Muslim Brotherhood issued its own general declaration calling for jihad on October 11, and al-Azhar shaykhs circulated a similar statement.[13]

Appeals to revolutionary scripts—particularly the 1919 Revolution—were also already on the lips of Egyptians. Comparisons with 1919 dotted the October 10 issue of *Akhir Lahza.* One editorialist reassured readers that "in 1919, Egypt was a thousand times weaker than she is today, and Britain a thousand times stronger," but still Egypt triumphed then (as she would triumph now).[14] A few days later, prominent politician and *al-Musawwar* editor Fikri Abaza proudly declared a new "revolutionary movement," framing it as a struggle between shame and dignity.[15] Most importantly, on October 15, *al-Ithnayn* printed an

Figure 7.1 Egyptians Celebrate the Treaty Abrogation.

At the top, Prime Minister Nahhas carries the coffin of the 1936 Treaty, while "Egypt" (the woman in the short black skirt) and the people celebrate with music and ululations. At the bottom, primary and secondary school students cheer the treaty abrogation and exchange congratulatory kisses.

Source: (Top to Bottom) "'Al-Jināzah' Allatī Shuʿīat b-al-Zaghārīd" and "Furḥat al-Shabāb," *al-Ithnayn* 905, October 15, 1951, 2, 8. Courtesy of Cornell University Library.

interview with 1919 veteran and YMMA president General Muhammad Salih Harb, who called on *fidāʾīyīn* to take the next steps; the general announced that one million Egyptians and Sudanese must sacrifice their lives, so the other 29 million citizens could live free.[16] One's of Egypt's most respected military men had given the green light for war.

A movement coalesced in the Canal Zone the following day. That Tuesday morning (October 16), Cairo area university students took trains, busses, and cars and poured into the city of Isma'iliyya. Converging in the square near the train station at 8 o'clock in the morning, the students began their march. As the demonstration moved through town, the students' confidence grew, and shouts expanded to throwing rocks and setting British cars and busses ablaze. The students then surrounded the British base commissary (NAAFI) and set it on fire. By afternoon, the British military went on the offensive and forced protesters out of the downtown, at the cost of one Egyptian policeman and three Egyptian civilians killed, many more wounded. The same day, thousands of students in Cairo gathered at the statue of nationalist icon Mustafa Kamil to chant anti-colonial slogans, and protestors in Alexandria convened at Sa'd Zaghlul Square (named for the hero of the 1919 Revolution) to chant "Down with colonialism!" Police dispersed the demonstration with clubs and live fire.[17]

A fifth fatality was added that evening, when following the end of a demonstration in Port Sa'id, eleven-year-old Nabil Mansur snuck out of his home in his pajamas, crawled under the Golf Course Camp barbed wire, and tried to set British tents on fire. He woke the guards and was shot. Bystander testimonies from townspeople who recovered his bullet-riddled body by the barbed wire were graphic and devastating.[18]

The "five coffins" of those killed that day would become a poignant rallying cry for anti-colonial sentiment. (Inji Aflatun's painting *We Cannot Forget* (1951) reimagined the suffering and resolve to resist that engulfed the funeral.) Facing diplomatic pressure, Prime Minister Nahhas and other government officials implored Egyptians to stand down, "remain calm," "be patient," and let the government pursue diplomatic solutions. *Akhir Lahza* printed the affective appeal, but undercut it by printing an editorial cartoon by Alexander Sarukhan that satirized the government's change of tune. The sketch featured Prime Minister Nahhas summoning the genie of "public opinion" from the lamp to throttle a tattered-looking John Bull—and the genie refusing to return to his bottle.[19] *Akhir Sa'a* journalists did their part that Wednesday by lampooning the prime minister's corruption, pointing out weak points in British supply lines, and printing a suggestive article about how the British feared guerrilla warfare.[20]

On Thursday October 18, the American ambassador in Cairo telegrammed Washington to report that the press and Egyptian activist societies were thus not cooperating with the prime minister's directive to remain calm. The bodies of those killed in the protests had been prominently displayed in the Egyptian press to stir sentiment, and Muslim Brotherhood irregulars would be arriving in Suez the following morning "to avenge Egyptians killed by the British."[21] A day later, the Friday cover of *al-Musawwar* declared "Egypt Announces Jihad!"[22]

The crisis could not have come at a worse time for British prime minister Clement Attlee's Labour government—the election was scheduled for October 25. Moreover, for over a month Conservative campaigns had ridiculed the weakness and timidity of the Attlee government.[23] The reprisal was therefore swift and extreme. Attlee ordered an immediate airlift of the British 16th Parachute Brigade to Egypt. On October 17, he further set in motion the seizure of all vital infrastructure points along the Canal: electricity stations, waterworks, communications lines, bridges, and railroads. The most famous strike was the Battle of al-Firdan Bridge; British soldiers launched a pre-dawn attack on the bridge watchhouse, killing one Egyptian guard and an Egyptian soldier.[24] The coup de force, however, was an embargo on all Suez–Cairo oil shipments—that lifeline supplying two thirds of Egyptian gasoline and cooking oil. The embargo sparked mass panic, a run on shops, and immediate shortages. As Egyptian police scrambled to protect gas stations, on October 24 *Akhir Lahza* published a cartoon that showed Attlee commanding British soldiers to pour gasoline on Egypt. The caption read "kindle the fire more, so they see it in London and know we are colonists just like the Conservatives!"[25]

The embargo poured fuel on the fire just as the paper predicted—and a day later Attlee lost the election; Churchill stepped into office. Moreover, a revolutionary mood filled the air. That week Egyptians ripped down signs with English lettering and whistled whenever British forces passed. Even Egypt's main lifestyle magazines printed lessons on urban warfare.[26] Newspapers described how all Egypt was preparing for battle. The Saʿdist Party discussed mobilizing volunteers in a "popular jihad against colonialism," and a few thousand Socialist Party (Young Egypt) activists registered in Liberation Battalions (despite leader Ahmad Husayn still being in jail). The YMMA demanded weapons from the government, and the Muslim Brotherhood met to draft a plan for paramilitary mobilization.[27]

Finally on October 26, a group of workers and students marched to the office of MP Hamid al-ʿAfifi to demand the government commence armed resistance against the British. Flustered, ʿAfifi said they would need to train in combat before any such confrontation. When the protesters demanded action, the MP suggested they leave their names. Paper was produced, and in the resulting signup rush, some 5,000 volunteers (including many veterans of the Palestine War and a group of female students) registered for one of the first official "Liberation Battalions."

At a loss, the government tapped Egyptian Army General ʿAziz al-Misri to supervise the training: in an interview, al-Misri called the guerrilla campaign this "blessed movement," and compared it to revolutionary movements in the United States, Ireland, and Spain.[28]

Mobilizing Morality Tales: From Paul Revere's Ride to "Juha's Nail"

Hand-in-hand with this physical mobilization came an explosion of storytelling, as Egyptians worked to provide positive signaling for armed resistance and appeal to international audiences. These appeals started with Nahhas's abrogation speech: *al-Musawwar* printed the speech on October 12, and a few pages after the speech printed a double-page spread (with photos) about Paul Revere's Ride and the American Revolution. In the article, Egyptian historian and Suez native Dr. Husayn Muʾnis recounted the history of the Boston Massacre (1770), the Boston Tea Party (1773), and the Liberty Tree. He also translated into Arabic one of the final stanzas of Henry Wadsworth Longfellow's iconic poem "Paul Revere's Ride":

> You know the rest. In the books you have read,
> How the British Regulars fired and fled,—
> How the farmers gave them ball for ball,
> From behind each fence and farm-yard wall,
> Chasing the redcoats down the lane,
> Then crossing the fields to emerge again,
> Under the trees at the turn of the road,
> And only pausing to fire and load.[29]

At the end of the poem, Muʾnis moralized that he wished the setting for the poem had been Egypt and its protagonists Egyptian farmers—but "those Redcoats" were still in the Nile Valley.[30] He was invoking a clear action script: the Suez Canal was calling her Minutemen to action; the British were coming. And come they did: five days after the election, Churchill ordered the 3rd Infantry Battalion to relocate from Cyprus to Suez, under the joint command of General Brian Robertson and Lieutenant-General George Erskine, made responsible for peacekeeping operations in Canal Zone.[31]

American history appeared again in *al-Ithnayn*'s special "Holiday of the National Struggle" [Eid al-Jihad] edition. The issue gave a short history of "The

Star-Spangled Banner" as an anthem of freedom and displayed a quote from Patrick Henry's famous 1775 speech: "Is life so dear, or peace so sweet, as to be purchased at the price of chains and slavery?! I know not what course others may take; but as for me, give me liberty or give me death!"[32]

A multi-page spread in the same issue delved into greater detail, recounting stories about five heroes of freedom that fought the British: George Washington, Éamon de Valera (an Irish Republican famous for his participation in the Easter Rising), Mohammad Mossadegh (the Iranian leader responsible for the Abadan evacuation), Gandhi, and Joan of Arc. The story of George Washington was boiled down to elements pertinent to the Egyptian situation: as the article described, the American founding father first fought French expansion in the Ohio Valley (just as Egyptians had fought French expansion in the Nile Valley). Washington had then "energetically worked to call these [American] states to unite in jihad and declare war against British trade" before leading the "American mujahidin" and American "Liberation Army" against the British. Ultimately, Washington had defeated the colonists and victoriously forced their evacuation. The author added that he hoped this history lesson would remind present-day Americans of the suffering inflicted by British imperialism.[33]

As the appeals demonstrate, Egyptians hoped to evoke sympathy from the Americans, remind them of their own suffering, and connect the pride of the American independence struggle to the pride Egyptians felt for their country. In part, these appeals reflected hope that the United States might remember her history and prove an ally in the anti-colonial struggle. Invoking the American Revolution may have additionally represented an attempt to reassure the United States that the Egyptian movement was neither anti-Western nor anti-democratic, but rather a genuine popular movement seeking liberation from a tyrannical occupier. Egyptian diplomats understood that a negative American response to the crisis might derail the nascent Egyptian movement; Egypt needed US allies. Whatever the motives, these efforts at emotional diplomacy would be in vain: American diplomats stood by the British and shunned the "Egyptian Minutemen," disappointing Egyptian hopes.

Local audiences, meanwhile, were treated to both cosmopolitan stories from around the globe and affective narratives from folk tradition. For instance, on October 18, the Modern Egyptian Theater Troupe opened its fall season with a patriotic performance in the Royal Opera House. Seeking to fuel the revolutionary momentum, they staged an adaptation of an Arab trickster tale: "Juha's Nail" [*Mismār Juḥā*].[34] This revolutionary version of "Juha's Nail" was set during the Turkish occupation of Iraq; and like the original trickster tale, the plot revolved around a clever ruse. Juha concocts a plan with his nephew to rouse the people to revolt against the Turkish occupier. The plan is to sell a house—but the sale comes with one condition. Whoever buys the property must allow Hammad to retain ownership of a single nail in the house's wall.[35]

In the play, Juha and Hammad put the plan in action: Hammad sells the home. Then, he drives the homeowners crazy. Day and night he arrives on their doorstep and demands to visit his nail. The new owners are so incensed by Hammad that the case goes to court. There, the homeowners confront Hammad and demand he remove his nail.

As the case reaches a climax, Hammad appears on the stand and reveals the reason for his subterfuge. In a stirring speech, he declares that the townspeople see his "little nail" as a great injustice, but they miss the "big nail": Turkish rule over the country! Their eyes opened to the injustice of the foreign "nail" in Iraq, the people revolt, and the occupier is forced to withdraw his troops from the country.[36]

"Juha's Nail" included a clear script for revolt; but the tale also communicated a series of emotional prompts. During the trial, Juha describes the nail as an affront to the homeowner's dignity; and Juha and Hammad work to arouse the anger of the people. The popular magazine *Akhir Sa ʿa* described other emotional cues from the play, in an article published a day after Cairo's million-man march of November 13. Juha felt *ḍīq* [distress] seeing the occupier feeding off the bounty of his country, "and felt the people in his country needed a living example, to symbolize the usurper and stir up a spirit of rebellion and revolution. So he crafted this story—the story of the house." This was how Egyptians should feel in response to British occupation. The article also made explicit the moral lesson embedded in the play: "The story of the nail—the real nail and the imagined nail—is the story of the unending occupation … the Suez Canal and the joint defense [treaty] … they are all nails the usurper slyly inserted into the house to harass [*muḍāyiqa*] the owners."[37]

Despite the creative refitting of "Juha's Nail" to analogize the revolutionary context, the old trickster tale was atypical among the morality tales that circulated that October and November. Historical events that could be hammered and shaped into morality tales were far more popular source material. The Indian national struggle, having achieved victory only a few years prior in 1948, was one prominent point of comparison. Gandhi had already been a popular figure in Egypt for a long time: in the interwar period he had visited Cairo, and was frequent front-page news in Egypt for his anti-British resistance activities.[38] Now in 1951, stories about Gandhi and calls to follow his model of passive resistance were splashed across the Egyptian magazine pages. *Al-Ithnayn* focused on the lack of rifles and tanks available to the Indian national movement. Nonetheless, Gandhi had a "strong spirit," which enabled him to lead a jihad of civil disobedience, boycott, and noncooperation, the magazine explained.[39] A leaflet in Port Saʿid, meanwhile, called on citizens to join the fight for freedom as Gandhi had done to free India.[40]

Different moral lessons were read into the Joan of Arc legend. One writer moralized that even a peasant—and a girl, nonetheless!—could score a victory against the British. The legend was further distilled into a lesson about the dual struggle against external invasion and internal corruption. As the article explained, armed with "firm faith in God and an unshakeable confidence in France's right to freedom," this teenage girl had "triumphed over the schemes of the king's retinue, the doubts of politicians, and the conceit of the men of the army," and led her people against the British invaders, striking blow after blow to the pride of the English army.[41]

Other articles lionized the Swiss heroes Arnold von Winkelried and William Tell, described Montenegro's liberation struggle against the Turks, and celebrated Venezuela's struggle against the Spanish Empire.[42] An article in *al-Ithnayn*, for example, described how William Tell refused to bow to the hat of Habsburg-appointed ruler Albrecht Gessler, and how Tell was thus sentenced to shoot an apple off his son's head as punishment. Tell accomplished the legendary feat, but was treacherously enchained. As the article recounted, however, Tell cleverly escaped to "call his people to revolution against Austrian tyranny."[43] For its "Holiday of the National Struggle" edition, *al-Ithnayn* further printed short histories of various anthems of freedom, including "La Marseillaise," Tchaikovsky's "1812 Overture," and the anti-Russian nationalist hymn "Finlandia" by Sibelius.[44]

Egypt's own historical record was also selectively arranged to create a mythic history of liberation struggles. This revolutionary timeline started with Egypt's "first occupation" by the Hyksos and their expulsion by Ahmose I in the sixteenth century BCE. Next, the Frankish attempt to conquer Egypt during the Seventh Crusade was featured, followed by the attempted Tartar invasion (and its defeat by Egyptian forces at ʿAyn Jalut). The ʿUrabi Revolution of 1879 and nationalist struggles of Mustafa Kamil Pasha also received broad play.[45] Like the Muslim Brotherhood's selective reading of Islamic history from Chapter 4, this selective history of Egyptian revolts crafted a mobilizing myth for the popular movement.

Of course, no revolutionary event received as much attention as the 1919 Revolution. Almost every Egyptian news source linked the 1919 Revolution with the dawn of the "1951 Revolution," and pages were stuffed with articles, speeches, and stories from veterans of 1919. *Al-Risala* ran an eleven-part series on the 1919 Revolution, which ran from October 1951 to January 1952 and freely blended historical information with references to current events in the Canal Zone. An article in *al-Musawwar* even put the 1919 Revolution in conversation with the 1951 Revolution in a literal sense, publishing imaginary letters from 1919 to 1951 (including a letter from the late Saʿd Zaghlul to Mustafa al-Nahhas, and a letter from the Revolution of 1919 to the Revolution of 1951).[46]

The historical trauma of the 1906 Dinshaway massacre also made a return, most notably in the play "Red Dinshaway," which capped the theater season that December (see Figure 7.2). Directed by Zaki Tulaymat and written by Khalil al-Rahmi, the play framed the Canal Struggle as a family drama, involving a son who decides to join the Liberation Battalions. As the mother dreads the risks her son will face as a *fidāʾī*, the father undertakes to steel her patriotic resolve by reminding her of what happened in Dinshaway. The play then plunges into analepsis, traveling back to the events of Dinshaway—"the bloody wound on Egypt's dignity since 1906."[47]

The play was significant for collapsing the historical events of the Dinshaway massacre into the combat underway in the Canal Zone. More than an artistic device, this anachrony made past British atrocities present, so Egyptian guerrillas could answer them in Ismaʿiliyya (dubbed "modern Dinshaway"). The temporal collapse complete and British depravity established, a reviewer explained that "the play [then] takes us back to 'New Dinshaway,' where we see the young man with a new consciousness avenging his ancestors from 'Old Dinshaway.'"[48]

Egyptian revolutionary retellings of historical events thus followed distinct patterns. The emphasis on the 1919 Revolution transferred the political capital of the old revolutionary myth onto the new movement. The Crusades were occasionally invoked—but the analogy was not nearly as popular as it had been a few years earlier during the 1948 War (when stories of Salah al-Din and his reconquest of the Holy Land had been a prominent leitmotif). Retellings of the American Revolution were more popular and reflected hopes that the United States as the rising Cold War hegemon might remember her history and prove an ally in the anti-colonial struggle. The sparse use of the French Revolution, meanwhile, suggested lingering wounds from the Napoleonic invasion of Egypt and misgivings about the continued French colonization of North Africa. Finally, Egyptians shunned the Russian Revolution as revolutionary fodder—a signal to the United States that a sovereign Egypt could be trusted not to drift into the Communist Bloc.

Instead, Egyptians labored to use Western nationalist myths to stir up revolutionary sentiment, while reassuring potential allies—especially the United States—that the movement was anti-colonial, but neither anti-Western nor anti-democratic. In this way, Egyptian revolutionary self-fashioning sought to prove that the guerrilla struggle was part of a genuine popular movement seeking liberation, and that Egypt deserved a place at the table of nations. This mobilization of history by the Egyptians represented a quick-witted deployment of British history against the British Empire, and a skillful display of Cold War politicking.

In the long run, it would be "Red Dinshaway" and "Juha's Nail"—not Paul Revere's Ride—that proved the most enduring morality tales of the period. American diplomats denied Egyptians their sympathies and refused to acknowledge the burgeoning revolution; as a result, Egyptians quickly dropped Paul Revere's Ride from the revolutionary canon. In contrast, Dinshaway continued to be a site of memory, commemorated in Inji Aflatun's painting *The Dinshaway Massacre* (*c*. 1950s) and multiple films and books. "Juha's Nail" also went on to enjoy a long career in the anti-colonial imagination. A month before the Free Officers' Revolution of July 1952, a film version of the trickster tale hit Egyptian movie theaters. The trickster tale returned to the Egyptian stage in 1956 and 1957—during President Gamal ʿAbd al-Nasser's nationalization of the Suez Canal. The story also enjoyed transnational purchase: it became popular in Algeria and made its way to France, where it was used by Pierre Bourdieu to describe the linguistic legacies of colonization.[49]

Despite these lasting legacies, as of December 1951 it was unclear which (if any) of these myths would have sticking power. In the press, disagreement raged about whether morality tales, poetry, and literature were even useful to the armed struggle. Egyptian poet Muhammad ʿAbd al-Ghani Hasan argued that Egypt needed action not poetry, weapons not words in the war against the English.[50] Another reviewer thought "Juha's Nail" could have guided the public's emotions to revolutionary action—if it had been released a year earlier and received support from the government.[51]

"Juha's Nail" and "Red Dinshaway" were also not without critique. In December, ʿAli Mutawalli Salah argued both plays were terrible analogies for the Canal Struggle. The Juha tale was confusing, and implied that the British had a real legal claim over their "nail" (which they did not, since they had never "owned" Egypt in the first place). The Dinshaway analogy was equally ill-fitting: the massacre represented a shameful page in the nation's history, while in the present the nation was proudly fighting a revolution in the Canal Zone.[52]

Figure 7.2 "Red Dinshaway" Takes the Stage.

Actors dressed as British soldiers prepare to hang Egyptian peasants in a scene from the fall 1951 production of "Red Dinshaway."

Source: "Al-Mashāniq Dinshawāy ʿalá al-Masraḥ," *Ākhir Sāʿa* 894, December 12, 1951, 8. Hatcher Graduate Library, University of Michigan.

That said, Salah admitted that whatever the shortcomings of "Juha's Nail" and "Red Dinshaway," stories and words were important to the national struggle, and intricately intertwined with action and emotion. "Writers write to call readers to an act among acts; to stir in their souls an emotion of emotions." Citing a passage from Jean-Paul Sartre's 1948 essay "Qu'est-ce que la littérature?" he added that words "are loaded guns; and man—if he speaks, he shoots."[53]

As a final note, morality tales turned against others besides the British that year. Lèse-majesté cases against activists speaking against the king rose from a steady trickle that spring to a ferocious torrent by fall. Angered at the king's continued moral violations and dissatisfying passivity on issue of British evacuation, activists put the monarchy in the line of fire. Ahmad Husayn and Young Egypt were early to the range, starting with an article in *al-Ishtirakiyya* on January 25, 1951, publishing rumors (passed along by the father-in-law of a nightclub owner) that King Faruq sat with dancers and gambled. The article prompted the government to cancel the newspaper, but the cancellation lasted only as long as it took Husayn to launch another newspaper, *al-Sha'b al-Jadid*, in April 1951. Moreover, the cancellation itself was overturned by a sympathetic judge in June. Defiantly proclaiming "We do not recognize the crime of lèse-majesté," the society then released a barrage of anti-government articles, including "Who is Responsible for Defaming Egypt's Reputation," "Advice from a Big Gambler to Gamblers," "New Scandal," and two articles on "Expenditures of His Majesty's Court." These stories criticized the king's yacht expenditures, described millions of pounds spent on cars, and detailed the king's gambling and womanizing. More provocative was an article in July suggestively entitled "How the English Hung Charles I, King of England," and a September article "Revolution—Revolution—Revolution!" (which ran with the byline "Ministers or thieves, government or gang?").[54]

Nor was Misr al-Fatah the only outlet condemning the king's behavior. Censored *Akhir Sa'a* articles included stories detailing the king's squandering of funds, with one prominent contribution in September 1950 entitled "The King who Gambles." *New Brigade* [*al-Liwa' al-Jadid*] printed many outspoken articles by Fathi Radwan and others, criticizing the king's corruption; a fiery article in August 1951 carried the title "Satan Speaks," and a September article dubbed Egypt's government "The Era of Dogs."[55] Marxist tracts similarly complained about the king's depravity, with Khalid Muhammad Khalid landing in court for articles that season entitled "From the Palace to the Prison" and "The King on the Way to the Guillotine" (an article ostensibly about the French Revolution).[56] These morality tales—and their action scripts—did not bode well for the monarchy.

Disciplining Egyptian Emotions

At the same time Egyptians mobilized their storytelling energies against the British, they worked to cultivate certain emotions, suppress others, and emotionally discipline the popular movement. For instance, in a call to action at the end of October, Coptic politician and 1919 Revolution veteran Makram ʿUbayd called on Egyptians to conquer their fears; he further asked citizens to cast off the wrong type of hate and put on the right kind—a "holy hatred" that could help purify the nation. As he acknowledged, the British were killing Egyptians in the Canal Zone,

> But if the British think … they can terrorize us, they are wrong! We do not hate [*nukrahu*] shedding our blood for the sake of the homeland, because this blood will kindle the fire of holy malice [*nār al-ḥiqd al-muqaddas*] in the hearts of Egyptians, which will ultimately cleanse the land of the valley from every one of them.

The British could kill Egyptians, he declared, "but we will not be alarmed or afraid [*nafzaʿu aw nakhāfu*], and all of this will not move a hair on our heads."[57]

Humor helped reinforce the message of fearlessness. That fall, an entire corpus of Egyptian anecdotes ridiculing the British sprung up. These anecdotes—which can be filed under the collective heading "Tales of the Asinine English"—mocked British soldiers as buck-toothed, scrawny simpletons scared of their own shadows and easily duped. *Al-Ithnayn* reported that these jokes were popular among Egyptians in the Canal Zone, and a survey of the tales reveals that they typically featured the British being outwitted by Egyptian children (see Figure 7.3). The lesson was clear: if children could defeat the colonists, the British and their guns were nothing to fear. In fact, fear should be replaced by ridicule!

Egyptians also implored one another to restrain hatred and angry outbursts toward foreign civilians. On October 22, *al-Ithnayn* praised "this wonderful feeling" of national pride displayed in demonstrations, but added "the time has come for self-control." It then urged Egyptians to protect foreign lives and property, and not direct hostility toward foreigners in general.[58] As the American ambassador to Cairo reported, there were "a surprising rash of exhortations to keep calm" from Egyptians participating in the Ismaʿiliyya protest, as demonstrators encouraged one another to protest peacefully.[59] *Akhir Saʿa* also reported that the Wafd government had censored photographs of the dead, seized newspapers trying to promote guerrilla warfare, and canceled an Umm Kulthum concert on October 18 because of the zeal it might ignite. The editor of the magazine disagreed with these measures, and argued the government should be stoking the fires of resistance, not trying to quench them.[60]

As the British increased troop strength, reports poured in about provocations and British "terrorist incidents" in the Canal Zone. Villagers complained about soldiers ransacking homes in search of insurgents. Magazines reported British

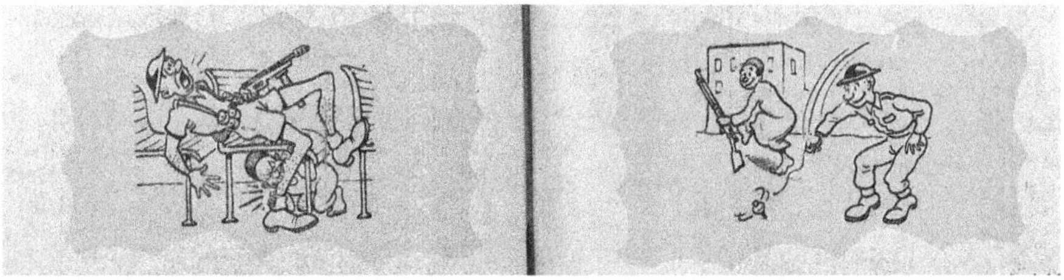

Figure 7.3 The Asinine English.

Cartoons and anecdotes in *al-Ithnayn* mocked British soldiers for being easily frightened fools. In these two drawings, Egyptian children best British soldiers with a painful bite on a bus (left) and the theft of a service weapon (right).

Source: "Hāʾulāʾ Hum… al-Junūd al-Majhūlūn!" *al-Ithnayn* 914, December 17, 1951, 3, 42–3. Courtesy of Cornell University Library.

piracy on the road to Suez—searches and seizures at roadside checkpoints, with British soldiers looting food, money, camera equipment, and other goods from Egyptian drivers and pedestrians. The press also carried shocking photos and stories. There was Umm Sabir, a grandmother shot and killed by a British soldier during a bus search (according to the Egyptian press, the elderly woman was shot either because she was walking too slowly or because she refused to let the soldier pat her down).[61] There were stories of young boys aged twelve and thirteen killed, a young woman who took a bullet in the leg, a nine-year-old boy shot, Egyptian police and military servicemen shot while in uniform (one while waiting for the bus), and an eleven-year-old boy whose head was severed from his body by machine-gun fire.[62] British emotional violations featured in these news stories: as one article explained, the British showed a cold "indifference to the people's feelings." During a stop-and-search, British soldiers had shot an unarmed civilian in the head and laughed.[63]

As military operations expanded, Egyptian leaders thus began arguing they were providing valuable affective services by controlling the anger of the populace. These emotional labors, they reasoned, were shielding the British from the consequences of their atrocities. In an interview with *al-Musawwar*, a local governor in Suez claimed that despite the British provocations, "I have been able to preserve security and maintain calm, and have stopped the wave of anger that is raging in the hearts of [Egyptian] citizens." A week later, an open letter acknowledged the emotional work that government leaders were expending: party leaders had "reined in the furious, enraged people" and were preventing the "hand of anger and wrath [*ghaḍab wa ghayẓ*]" from striking foreigners. An official in Port Sa'id similarly complained in an interview that it was exhausting trying to restrain local youth from confronting the British.[64]

Despite the attempts to wage a measured struggle, when the Churchill government announced another oil embargo on October 29 and the landing of an additional British infantry battalion the Canal Zone on October 30, there was broad consensus that it was time for Egypt to express her anger. *Al-Ithnayn*'s cover photo for October 29, entitled "Egypt's Anger!," both responded to British behavior and provided prescriptive signaling for how Egyptians should feel in response to the news.[65] At the same time, Egyptians insisted that their anger was not the cruel, barbaric anger of the British—but a righteous expression of masculinity and national dignity. *Al-Ithnayn* explained this distinction in its December 3 issue, entitled "The Anger of the Patient—or the Revolution that Rent the Stillness!" The issue naturalized Egyptian anger as an organic and natural response, explaining that after weeks of reports about British moral violations—looting, piracy, and attacks on women, children, and the elderly—Egypt's patient endurance of seventy years of British occupation was being replaced by a storm of righteous wrath. "Patience, however long it lasts, comes to an end. For every patient person has a moment of anger, where his patience and bearing explode into a destructive revolution and blow away [*ta'ṣifu*] those who stand in its way!"[66]

Still, Egyptians strove to maintain discipline. The Holiday of the National Struggle marches in Cairo and Alexandria on November 13 projected an image of orderliness, with participants organized in companies. The Cairo demonstration drew almost a million participants, and featured a procession of women, ranks of judges and lawyers, a brigade of university professors and deans, mixed ranks of al-Azhar students and Coptic Christians (to show religious unity) (see Figure 7.4), and units of army officers. Ahmad Husayn and the Socialist Party played a large role in organizing the Cairo demonstration (contacting different parties and professional organizations in the days prior), and some participants carried signs calling for the release of Muslim Brotherhood prisoners to fight the English.[67] Most astonishingly (considering the massive size of the protest), demonstrators marched in silent rows, per the instructions of newspaper articles and organizing meetings the night prior. The protest was also linked to other Cold War struggles: as one sign read: "Colonialism is being destroyed in Egypt, Iran, Marrakesh, Korea, and Vietnam!"[68]

Mass workers strikes also punctuated the first weeks of November. As Egyptian laborers quit their jobs in the Canal Zone en masse, departing workers explained in interviews that it was a combination of patriotism, pressure and

Figure 7.4 Muslims and Christians Send a Message about Religious Unity.

Coptic Christian and Muslim leaders march together in the demonstration of November 13, 1951. As printed in *al-Ithnayn*, the caption read "The Cross and the Crescent are everlasting in Love… We are all Egyptians, all fighters [*mujāhidūn*], there are no Copts, no Muslims—religion is for God and the nation for all." This last phrase was a popular slogan of the 1919 Revolution. On November 9, *al-Muṣawwar* similarly carried a photo of a Coptic priest and the vice president of the Young Men's Muslim Association (YMMA) reviewing the ranks of students volunteering for the Liberation Battalions. The religious leaders were part of a joint Muslim–Christian committee, formed to coordinate resistance and rebuff British charges that the movement was an Islamic movement being directed by Muslim fanatics.

Source: *Al-Ithnayn* 910, November 19, 1951, 22. Courtesy of Cornell University Library.

threats from anti-colonial activists, and the fact that life in the Canal Zone had become unbearable that drove them away. They were tired of British military checkpoints, bosses taking advantage of the crisis to withhold salaries, being searched for weapons, having their magazines and newspapers and lunches seized as suspicious contraband, and receiving death threats from British residents. The Egyptian government scrambled to find some 40,000–60,000 workers new jobs and housing, while British troops arrested Egyptian military officers and foremen at Fayed Station, Geneifa Station, and Abu Sultan Station for inciting the walkouts.[69]

Association newsletters contributed to the struggle by calling on Egyptian youth to arm themselves "by any means" and using affective signals to encourage students to join the movement. Articles shamed those who purchased British products or went to work in the Canal Zone; there were also appeals to masculine pride. In a special editorial for *al-Da ʿwa*, for instance, Sayyid Qutb declared that "Every young man who joins a battalion … he is a young man who has earned his manhood." He further declared that through their sacrifices, Egyptian youth would cleanse themselves of luxury and selfishness—and after the battle, volunteers would be men "of whom the nation is proud."[70] Dissatisfied with such rhetoric and determined that the movement should not only be men, women from the association Bint al-Nil formed an all-female battalion as well. Reporting on the sixty-member all-female battalion, the Egyptian press commented on the fact the women had refused to serve as nurses and taken up arms.[71]

In that first month of the conflict, a few Muslim Brotherhood and Young Egypt cells, as well as at least one DMNL group, thus headed off to the Canal Zone to participate in resistance activities. Some activists distributed boycott literature to Egyptian merchants, some intimidated shopkeepers and other "collaborators" not participating in strikes, and some distributed threatening leaflets to British residents to sow fear and hasten evacuation. Determined to fight the British, the boldest participated in sniping and sabotage operations, cutting telephone lines and damaging railroad tracks. Notably, students also created a secret cell to monitor paramilitary units, so infiltrators would not join and perpetrate attacks that the English might use to discredit the movement.[72]

At the start of November, the Socialist Party, the National Party, and the Ikhwan opened recruiting and training centers for volunteers. Notably, the Wafd newspaper *al-Misri* and journal *Ruz al-Yusuf* opened their offices as recruitment centers as well. However, even as training commenced, the Wafd government pressured student groups to exercise self-restraint and wait for the signal. The Wafdist Youth agreed to honor the directive, and in the name of unity the Saʿdist Party youth committee followed suit. Extra-parliamentary clubs were unhappy about the delay, but open carrying was illegal and guns were in short supply—so at least some measure of government support would be needed for armed struggle.[73] Consequently, in mid-November most paramilitary momentum still seemed to come not from Cairo, but from towns along the Canal, where villagers tired of British sweeps and patrols formed local self-defense groups. Despite the publicity dedicated to the liberation battalions, the bulk of volunteers stayed behind in the capital—training and waiting and demanding that the government distribute weapons to fight the British.[74]

Conclusion: The Affective Politics of the Egyptian Revolution

As the early days of the Canal Struggle show, feelings were an important part of the fight for decolonization. British administrators justified occupation by painting anti-colonial activists as fanatics seized by primitive and violent passions, and Egyptian policymakers had to strategically respond to these narratives. Revolutionary mobilization thus involved complex emotional negotiations. Politicians, political associations, individuals, international actors, and newspapers (looking to sell papers) all had their own affective agendas, which sometimes complemented and sometimes conflicted with government prerogatives. Thus, "heterogeneous actors with different backgrounds, perceptual abilities, and motives about what is going on, what should be done to respond to the crisis, and who should do it" grappled to shape an emergent revolution.[75]

The Suez struggle thus shines a beacon on how feelings both limit and ignite revolutions. Fourth-generation revolutionary theory, for instance, shows how structures limit social movements. Emotional regimes similarly constrain revolutionary takeoff. For Egypt in the 1950s, both local and international norms governed anger—so justifying revolution meant explaining why the time for patience had passed. A sense of futility and fear also limited the desire to rebel. However, at a certain juncture revolutionaries gauged the emotional state of their peers, and considered: which emotions are preventing change? And which emotions are needed to impel action?

What is impressive here is the flexibility of the *emotional regulation repertoire*. Egyptians demonstrated a broad ability to modulate emotional responses and advance different interpretations of emotional states. They disciplined sentiments and were highly attuned to what the international press was saying about the movement (with Egyptian magazines regularly reviewing what British, French, Italian, and American newspapers were printing about Egypt). There was thus rich evidence of affective context sensitivity, or "the ability to perceive impinging demands and opportunities from the situational context … and determine the most appropriate [emotional] regulatory strategy."[76]

Applying fifth-generation revolutionary theory further draws attention to the emotional payouts and emotional cultures of 1951. Activists did advertise that volunteers would reap pride and joy from commitment to the national struggle. But was an emergent Cold War emotional culture in play? Reviewing the evidence, Egyptians felt themselves to be in a moment of solidarity with other anti-colonial struggles in Iran, India, Ireland, and Korea—and yet the door remained open for the United States, Switzerland, and even France to share common sentiment.

One thing is clear: the 1951 Revolution rebelled against oversimplistic imperial imaginaries of "Middle Eastern emotions." The anti-colonial movement gained traction not because a wave of hysteria suddenly seized Egypt, but because enterprising Egyptians leveraged a particular historic moment and expended a tremendous amount of emotional labor in pursuit of policy goals.[77] Activists nurtured hope, suppressed fear, and shared stories of former shame and recovered pride. They used affective diplomacy to appeal to international sympathies and gave emotive performances to draw attention to outrage-inducing violations.[78] So what went wrong? Why would the revolution end in a world of rubble and ash?

8

"Those Who Jest in a Time of Gravity"

Emotional Appeals and the Cairo Fire

On January 26, 1952, the Cairo city center went up in flames, bringing the popular movement to a crashing halt. But the relationship between events in the Canal Zone and the infamous fire-setting in the capital—as well as the identities and motives of the perpetrators—has long remained a historical mystery. Martial law and press censorship limited documentary traces about the fire, and the Egyptian government's official inquest was rushed to a conclusion and compromised by political interests. What is known about the events of January 26 thus comes from the British Residency's investigation and interviews after the fact. Scholarly studies have since helped fill in some blanks: in 2012, for instance, Nancy Reynolds examined the fire as an act of protest against foreign goods and elite consumer culture.[1]

There are still many aspects of the fire-setting which remain unexplored, however. For instance, some accounts of the fire-setting parroted old colonial lines about the crowd's emotions: a cable to London after the fire described "destruction by howling incendiary mobs."[2] But contradictory evidence circulates. Ralph Stevenson, the British ambassador in Cairo, witnessed the flames that fated day and voiced his firm belief that the crowd's emotions had been far from frenzied. As he argued a few days after the fire, "It would be idle to pretend that these riots were the spontaneous manifestation of popular emotion. The organization of the many different gangs, their discipline and their very carefully concerted action could only have been the result of plans laid long beforehand."[3]

So what emotions engulfed Cairo that fateful day? Did the fire-setting represent uncontrolled emotions, a more measured attempt at world-building, or something else? Answering these questions is important because the British government, the Egyptian government, and the Free Officers would all use the emotional excesses of the Cairo Fire as cause to terminate the anti-colonial movement and clamp down on the political associations. Returning to the scene helps reconstruct events that day—and raises questions about culpability in the wake of emotional engineering.

The Suez Massacre and Operation Flatten

Despite the press already celebrating the 1951 Revolution as the end of the British Empire in Egypt, Churchill and the Conservatives were not ready to relinquish the Canal. As a result, behind the scenes the British conspired with the king to depose the Wafd government. For perhaps the first time, however, British negotiators could not find a willing Egyptian partner. Rejecting the offer to take over the prime minister's seat, ʿAli Mahir bluntly told the English that no Egyptian politician could politically survive such a partnership. A cartoon in *al-Ithnayn* echoed his sentiment, showing Churchill shocked that all the hands of the Egyptian "octopus" were holding weapons, leaving no hand to shake.[4]

The Wafd, meanwhile, attempted to negotiate a storm of conflicting demands. Facing intense British and American pressure to maintain the status quo ante, the Wafd dispatched 1,000–1,500 auxiliary police to the Canal to restore calm. The gambit was a failure; the police were reported to be participating in nighttime paramilitary raids alongside Canal Zone residents unhappy about their homes being ransacked by British soldiers searching for guerrilla fighters.[5]

The Wafd thus found itself in an awkward position. In asserting the right to armed struggle against a foreign occupier, the liberation movement was challenging the government's monopoly on force and jeopardizing British–Egyptian relations (a concern *al-Ithnayn* mocked by asking "What relations?").[6] But the press's heroizing of the Liberation Battalions and the October martyrs made it difficult for the Wafd to repudiate the movement without ceding its nationalist credentials. As a result, the Wafd experimented with different strategies. In late October and early November, Minister of Interior Fuʾad Siraj al-Din Pasha organized a government council to discuss bringing the paramilitary groups under the aegis of the state. At the same time, the Wafd announced it would have auxiliary police shoot unauthorized commandos in the Canal Zone.[7]

Police declined to enforce the directive. Moreover, a few days after the Holiday of the National Struggle demonstrations on November 13, battles in Port Saʿid and Ismaʿiliyya rendered the government's position untenable. The Port Saʿid skirmish erupted the evening of November 17. According to Egyptian witnesses, six drunk British soldiers robbed a cigarette kiosk and the next door sandwich shop at gunpoint. Their night on the town, however, turned sour when one of the soldiers shot in the air, waking up people sleeping. One of the angry sleepers came down and grabbed the gun. In the ensuing scuffle, the soldiers sprayed the street with bullets—and a passerby heading home from work fell to the ground, fatally wounded. As the neighborhood turned out to fight, Egyptian auxiliary police entreated the British commander to withdraw troops from the neighborhood to prevent a blowup, but instead soldiers from the nearby camp turned out to raid the quarter. The night finally ended when Egyptian police convinced the British commander to withdraw his men and allow Egyptian officers to run weapons sweeps themselves. However, tensions remained high the next day, as *fidāʾīyīn* met with residents, erected barricades, and lined up garbage trucks across the avenue to repel an expected British attack.[8]

Further up the canal, the "Second Battle of Ismaʿiliyya" or the "Battle of the Auxiliary Police" [*Bulūk al-Niẓām*] was far more serious. Contradictory accounts swirled about the spark, but it seems on November 17, British troops tried to detain a guard. When the guard resisted arrest, the British either fired first or were fired upon. Whatever happened, it escalated into a battle in downtown Ismaʿiliyya. The following day, British command sent troops to storm the auxiliary police post by the park. Egyptian police resisted, and in the firefight that ensued five Egyptian officers, five Egyptian civilians, and seven British soldiers died; some two dozen bystanders were wounded.[9]

The public outcry and wave of threats that followed were so intense that General Erskine immediately undertook a mass evacuation of British families and civilians from Ismaʿiliyya. As a result, in the following weeks British soldiers took "civvie jobs" like manning sewage stations.[10] Meanwhile back in Cairo, the Wafd government was buffeted by rising public demand for armed struggle and finally opened a six-week military training course for students under the aegis of the Battalion Command Council.[11] In the last week of November, Young Egypt volunteers thus appeared in *Akhir Saʿa* at a government-aligned camp for commandos. Under the oversight of 1948 veteran General ʿAziz al-Misri, they learned to climb walls, shoot rifles, and wriggle under barbed wire.[12]

While students trained, tensions ran high in the Canal Zone. Commandos avenged the Ismaʿiliyya deaths with almost daily attacks on British troops. A terse telegraph to Washington from American secretary of state Dean Acheson warned that the British were thus engaged in their own battle to emotionally discipline their men. "Bodies Brit[ish] soldiers being dragged from Sweet Water Canal, and temper of troops rising."[13]

Tensions boiled over on December 3. For weeks British commanders had accused the Egyptian police of inciting worker walkouts and arming *fidāʾīyīn*. So when an Egyptian police vehicle broke down in front of a railway workshop (a sensitive military asset), a British unit opened fire on the vehicle. Townspeople rushed to aid the officers and trapped workers, resulting in a pitched battle that left twenty Egyptians dead. The violence continued the following day, when a funeral attempted to cross a bridge in violation of a military cordon. The British opened fire on the procession, killing fifteen. *Al-Ithnayn* described the event as the "Suez Massacre"; *Akhir Lahza* angrily blamed the deaths on the Wafd government's eternal calls for calm, placing the article next to a photo of a panicked man on the bridge carrying his bleeding child.[14]

The same day as the funeral fatalities, commandos ambushed and killed two British guards traveling through the village of Kafr ʿAbduh on their way to the water filtration plant. On December 5, General Erskine thus signed an order for "Operation Flatten." As dawn broke the morning of December 7 thousands of British troops—backed by tanks, artillery pieces, bulldozers, and armored vehicles—surrounded the village of Kafr ʿAbduh. Then, they systematically razed the town to the ground.

In a telegram, Churchill personally congratulated Erskine for the successful operation.[15] The British press, meanwhile, explained the operation was "Not Punitive but a Necessary Military Measure" to build a bypass road and reported the operation had been successfully "completed without incident."[16] The aerial photographs taken before and after the destruction of the village spoke of road design for a water filtration plant and showed no people in frame (see Figure 8.1); this narrative strategy divorced the operation from its human cost and precluded any emotional response to the event. In contrast, the Egyptian press showed pictures of the idyllic, palm-tree encircled village before its destruction. Then, scenes showed images of children crying, villagers searching the rubble of their homes for salvage, and homeless families (see Figure 8.2). The operation left approximately 1,500 civilians homeless.[17]

Overall, the Suez Massacre and the razing of Kafr ʿAbduh poured fuel on both anti-British and anti-government sentiment. By now, the British Embassy was reporting that their Canal Zone garrison had swelled to some 64,000 men. Estimated death tolls at the start of December stood at 70 Egyptians killed, 253 wounded since October. The Egyptian estimates were higher, listing 117 killed and 438 wounded.[18] In Cairo crowds turned against the king, shouting anti-monarchy slogans. Egyptians also turned on the Wafd with fury for not defending Kafr ʿAbduh. Worried, the Wafd suspended the right to public

Figure 8.1 "Operation Flatten" or the Construction of Pegasus Avenue.

As depicted in the British press, the destruction of the village of Kafr ʿAbduh was a distant, unsentimental affair involving highway engineering.

Source: *The Illustrated London News*, December 29, 1951, 1057. © Illustrated London News Ltd/Mary Evans.

assembly, recalled the Egyptian ambassador from London, and donated 100,000 Egyptian pounds to the Liberation Battalions.[19]

Through December, guerrilla strikes increased sharply, with events like the December 14 train bombing and commando attacks on railroads and bridges along the Canal. General Robertson requested permission to hold summary trials and executions—but Churchill refused the request. He worried that summary executions would infuriate the international community.[20]

Faced with growing pressure to act, around Christmas the Wafd cabinet announced the right to bear arms (legalizing the open carrying of pistols and

Figure 8.2 The Razing of Kafr ʿAbduh.

As depicted in the Egyptian press, the destruction of the village of Kafr ʿAbduh was a human tragedy. Magazine photographs showed the picturesque hamlet encircled by palm groves, followed by images of the town occupied by British troops and bulldozers reducing homes to rubble. Articles also humanized the tragedy by showing images of displaced families and printing human interest stories about individuals affected. Egyptian media reported that 1,500 villagers were left homeless.

Source: *Al-Muṣawwar* 1419, December 21, 1951, 9. (For additional images, see also *al-Muṣawwar* 1418, December 14, 1951, 20, 22.) University of Washington Libraries.

small rifles),[21] and university campuses in Cairo became visible sites for youth army drills and guerrilla training. The courtyards of Fuʾad University, Ibrahim Pasha University, and al-Azhar University filled with students jostling to join the Liberation Battalions. In *al-Musawwar*, students at Fuʾad University (with majors ranging from law and literature to medicine and engineering) learned to throw Molotov cocktails in the courtyard, pharmacy and science students reported their success building bombs, and images showed students happily putting one another in headlocks (see Figure 8.3).[22]

Figure 8.3 Commando Training on Campus.

Students at Fu'ad University jump barbed wire and learn to climb buildings on campus as part of a three-week accelerated training course to prepare them to fight for their country in the Canal Zone.

Source: (Left) *Ākhir Sā'a* 896, December 26, 1951, 8; (Right) *Al-Muṣawwar* 1420, December 28, 1951, 16. Hatcher Graduate Library, University of Michigan and University of Washington Libraries.

The Muslim Brotherhood played a prominent role in the training movement although their position as usual was ambiguous. The group's new leader, moderate Hasan al-Hudaybi, had been welcomed with a royal audience in early November and kept students mostly in line by vaguely emphasizing the importance of struggle and need for proper training. Like most mainstream magazines, the Brotherhood's newspaper *al-Da'wa* implored readers to stand side-by-side with their Christian brothers, warning that the British hoped to accuse Egyptians of religious fanaticism.[23] However, the club remained coiled with tension. At the same time it called for unity, *al-Da'wa* stoked hostility toward "spies and traitors." In this broad category, it listed the Egyptian government (withholding arms from the popular movement), Egyptian elites (maintaining economic ties with the British), British and Jewish civilians (controlling Egypt's economy, stockpiling weapons, and humiliating Egyptians by teaching white superiority over "colored" men), and Greek and Italian civilians (running Egyptian banks and industry according to colonial interests).[24]

But, this outlook of besieged hostility masked a deep vulnerability. Still recovering from internal civil war and the death of al-Banna, the society remained divided. Hudaybi upon taking office had sidelined *al-Daʿwa* editor and ex-Special Section leader Salih ʿAshmawi and his more militant faction of Muslim Brothers (which included the Jeep Case defendants). The Brotherhood considered them members and ʿAshmawi retained his grip on *al-Daʿwa*. However, Muslim Brotherhood General Secretary ʿAbd al-Hakim ʿAbidin broadcast an announcement that *al-Daʿwa* did not reflect the Ikhwan's official position, and warned other members to be wary of the Special Section old guard. Ahmad ʿAdil Kamal was given a desk job in Cairo preparing a curriculum for recruits wanting to fight in the Canal Zone. Unable to join the fighting, he bitterly described the new Brotherhood Battalions as upstarts. Worse yet, he felt the new leadership was using the Liberation Battalions to prove the Special Section could be phased out.[25]

Despite the Special Section's complaints, the Brotherhood claimed it contributed more men and arms to the struggle than other organizations in those months—and their claims were likely not misplaced. The Brotherhood had been founded in Ismaʿiliyya and had a major presence in the city; as a result, members quickly converted the society's headquarters there into volunteer centers. Moreover, the Brotherhood counted amongst its members many veterans of the 1948 War (like Hasan Dawh and Yusuf Talʿat), who were prominent on rosters of volunteers who signed up to fight and helped train new recruits.[26]

Nevertheless, the Brothers encountered suspicion from other volunteers that fall. At Fuʾad University, Muslim Brotherhood student leader Hasan Dawh was charged with running the military drills on campus. A 1948 war veteran, Dawh appeared prominently in *al-Musawwar* helping train volunteers.[27] However, the leader remembered encountering students concerned that the Brotherhood might try to impose their ideologies on the anti-colonial struggle. As a result, Dawh said he felt pressured to foreswear partisanship, and in his first speech on campus declared "I do not represent the Ikhwan movement inside the university or during the battle." He attributed the suspicion to the "violent setbacks" the association had experienced in 1948.[28]

The Liberation Battalions were also pressured not to display partisan club banners or insignia, so as not to give the British government ammunition to discredit the movement as anything other than an expression of the popular will. These concerns about the aesthetics of Muslim Brotherhood involvement were valid: *Akhir Lahza* grumbled that the British were back to their usual tricks, trying to discredit the Canal Struggle by claiming the movement had religious goals. The newspaper also noted the British were justifying their increase of troop strength in the Canal Zone by claiming the soldiers were needed to safeguard Suez against Soviet and Muslim Brotherhood infiltration.[29]

But as the year came to a close, students headed off for Suez. In the first week of January, guerrilla attacks and battles between *fidāʾīyīn* and British troops were reported in Ismaʿiliyya, Port Saʿid, Abu Suwayr, and at various British camps and infrastructure points along the Canal.[30] Estimates varied to how many student volunteers traveled to the Canal Zone in those weeks. Misr al-Fatah announced it had 10,000 volunteers—the British estimated the club's recruitment strength at one-tenth that figure. A Muslim Brotherhood commander reported that they recruited and trained 500 young men in the first two months, and more after that. But each young man and woman that went took their lives in their hand—and many did not return. As Egyptian communist Nawal El Saʿdawi described, her first love (a fellow medical student in her biochemistry lab at Fuʾad University) was one of the young men who went to fight in the Canal Zone that autumn. Before he departed, he slipped her a note promising that while he was away, "Your image will always be before my eyes." A few weeks later, he was killed.[31]

Operation Eagle and Black Saturday

The Battle of Tell al-Kabir on January 12 and 13 marked yet another bloody episode in Egypt's struggle. Claiming the town was harboring terrorists, the British prepared to occupy the symbolic site, where General Ahmad ʿUrabi had made his last stand before British occupation in 1882. The battalion from Fuʾad University cut the rail line (for the tenth time that season) but were ultimately surrounded, with students Ahmad al-Manisi (Muslim Brotherhood), ʿUmar Shahin (Muslim Brotherhood), and ʿAbd al-Hamid ʿAbd Allah killed in the battle. ʿUmar Shahin's funeral in Cairo the next day was a national event attended by the university deans, professors, and students as well as various politicians; it was followed by anti-palace demonstrations by high school and college students in Cairo.[32]

Such was the climate in the weeks leading up to the Cairo Fire. Fury—expressed against the British occupation, the Wafd government, and increasingly the Palace—was a prominent sentiment. However, one anomaly stands out when looking at the moral and emotional appeals that preceded fire: the surprising scarcity of appeals to contamination and purification. Considering purity appeals often accompany fire-setting, book-burning, and other acts of ritual immolation this is unusual. Purity discourses may have circulated by word of mouth and in back rooms; but at least in the press, calls to cleanse Cairo were not central to the narrative of the city's sins.

Instead of purification appeals, a different kind of moral narrative was prominent in the weeks leading up to the fire: the idea that Cairo's elites were scorning the sacrifice of young men and women fighting in the Canal Zone, by celebrating in entertainment halls and failing to take the appropriate affective posture. As Ahmad Husayn declared in a December article:

> Will you continue, O you ministers, will you continue, O you Mustafa al-Nahhas, to live in scandal, wealth, joy, and illuminations? Will our cinemas and theaters and our cabarets stay open? … The anger that now stirs up the people … looks for an exit to express itself…. If the government continues [in its actions] … the explosion will be directed against the government itself and will overthrow it.[33]

In a December 15 proclamation, Muslim Brotherhood leader Hasan al-Hudaybi further argued: "It is *unfair* that supporters of the Muslim Brotherhood should fight and sacrifice their lives for the sake of their country, while others spend their time in places of amusement."[34]

Condemnations of Cairo were repeated in the two weeks leading up to the fire, with activists denouncing those who engaged in selfish behaviors while their brothers fought. Twelve days before the fire, Bahija al-Minshawi, secretary of the Muslim Women's Society in Cairo, wrote:

> Spoiled, drunk Cairo has not yet woken up. Deafened by the entertainment and hubbub, she has not heard the sound of bullets in the Suez Canal; in her frivolities and her pleasures, her foolishness and her clamor, [Cairo] continues, as if nothing had happened …. Hasn't this dangerous and stormy period been enough to make Cairo limit her evils—for entertainment halls, theaters, bars, and nightclubs to curb their extravagances … in honor of this blood spilt for Egypt?[35]

The idea of "happy Cairo" violating affective display rules, celebrating while others suffered, was particularly well-articulated in an article entitled "Those Who Jest in a Time of Gravity," by Anwar al-Maʿaddawi. In the editorial for *al-Risala*, Maʿaddawi wrote:

> On Saturday night, January 5, 1952 … wretched Suez cried out in pain, listening to the sound of bullets, [while] happy Cairo overflowed with pleasure, listening to the sound of Umm Kulthum! There was a funeral, and there was a wedding—there was blood, and there was singing. …. [And] what do people say about this happy, cheerful capital that knows no shame [*ḥayāʾ*]?

As Ma'addawi explained, he had expected that Egyptian cities would rally to the aid of Suez, that Egyptian souls would be united in the cry of the homeland. "I was waiting for all this and more—but insolent Cairo moved me from the world of beautiful fantasy to the world of ugly reality … My blood boils in my veins, and I search for the man that owns an executioner's whip, but I do not find him."[36]

Five days before the fire, Sayyid Qutb lent his voice to the chorus of condemnations, publishing an article provocatively entitled "Fire … Blood." Denouncing the behavior of the idle rich in the face of the bloodshed in the Canal Zone, Qutb wrote:

> The people do not demand that those affluent, bloated, impudent men, in their pleasures, render a blood tax to this valley … [the people] do not demand they sacrifice their precious blood! Not to die as the martyrs die! … [The people] demand only a *fair* portion of that which is spent at wine tables and evening shows![37]

In the days leading up to January 26, the British were being thoroughly excoriated in the press and in the streets. There was a student walkout and demonstrations for martyred classmates on January 20; students chanted against the monarchy, set a tramcar on fire, and pelted the police with stones. A British sweep of a cemetery in Isma'iliyya on January 21 had Egyptians crying desecration, and resulted in a handful of deaths and hundreds of arrests.[38] In an article for *al-Risala* that same day, Qutb described the colonizers as extreme deviants and role-violators, calling them criminal, barbaric, heinous, savages, betrayers, and enemies of humanity.[39] On January 22, an illustrated brochure entitled "British Atrocities in the Canal Zone" circulated to stoke outrage.

In a pivotal moment, the Wafd Minister of Interior gave a speech on January 23, in which he called the behavior of British troops in the Canal Zone "barbarous." "Things have gone beyond the point where mere protests are of avail," Siraj al-Din declared. "Women were turned into the streets half-clothed and taken to camps where their fate is still unknown. Mosques were desecrated, cemeteries profaned, great numbers of Egyptians killed or wounded and crucified on trees."[40] These stories—a shaykh killed while praying, women violated, mosques and cemeteries profaned, bodies desecrated—sent a clear message: the British had violated all boundaries. They had crossed the lines of gender, sacred space, religion, justice, and humanity itself.

The ill-fated moment came at dawn on January 25. British command put into action "Operation Eagle," an attempt to seize and disarm (at gunpoint) the Egyptian auxiliary police in Ismaʿilyya. The British knew the move might backfire and cause "major disturbances"—so they repositioned naval ships in the Mediterranean and moved up the readiness timeline for a possible evacuation of British citizens and the military occupation of Cairo. However, they pushed the plan forward despite the risks.[41]

In the British estimate, "Operation Eagle" that Friday was a "very tidy operation." At around six in the morning, Brigadier Robert Exham surrounded the police station with Centurion tanks, armored vehicles, and infantry, and via loudspeaker ordered the Egyptian auxiliary police to surrender. At 6:20 am, the police chief called the Minister of Interior to ask for instructions. Siraj al-Din, remembering the fallout from Kafr ʿAbduh, told them to stand their ground. According to the Egyptian story, Captain Mustafa Rifʿat thus sent his response back to Exham: "The British won't receive anything from us except dead bodies."[42]

At approximately 7:00 am British tanks opened fire. They bombarded the building for four hours, until the police ran out of ammunition. When the shooting stopped, four British soldiers and fifty Egyptian policemen lay dead. The scenes of their uniformed bodies lined up in rows on the street appalled Egyptians: that evening, the Wafd cabinet discussed expelling the entire British community from Egypt and appropriating all British assets. The British press, meanwhile, called the action "bold but wise," the beginning of a new Crusade marking "a mighty reaffirmation of Imperial destiny."[43]

The next morning—January 26—the Egyptian auxiliary police amassed for a demonstration in front of ʿAbdin Palace around 10 am. They were joined by local university students from Fuʾad University and al-Azhar University, who marched to the Palace to demand the government distribute weapons to fight the British. The spark came around noon. As the morning protesters began to disperse, part of the crowd passed through Opera Square, where some Egyptian officers were sitting on the balcony of Casino Badiʿah. Members of the crowd began shouting at the officers for "not being in the front ranks in Ismaʿiliyya."[44] As the fight continued, demonstrators stormed through the front doors of the casino. Inside, they overturned chairs and tables, threw furniture off the terrace, and set the furniture ablaze (see Figure 8.4).

The spark was only the beginning. From noon until six o'clock that evening, groups of young men systematically moved from business to business in the city center, lighting shops, cinemas, tourism offices, bars, and clubs on fire. Witnesses reported that this was not a mass movement or popular uprising. Instead, it was a campaign undertaken by gangs of well-organized, middle-class young men in suits. The fire-raisers were familiar with the security measures of the shops they attacked, and came prepared with an oxyacetylene torch, paraffin, and trucks carrying hay and petrol. The gangs carried pre-compiled lists of stores to target, and witnesses recalled that the men told them they had "orders" to attack various locations. Moving methodically from site to site, the young vigilantes broke doors and windows, entered shops, spread petrol across the premises, and set the stores ablaze. Then, they moved on to the next location. As the British Embassy reported, the riots were thus far from a "spontaneous manifestation of popular emotion. The organization of the many different gangs, their discipline and their very carefully concerted action could only have been the result of plans laid long beforehand."[45]

The arsonists targeted bars and clubs offering alcoholic beverages, shops selling luxury goods, and places where Western entertainment was available.

Figure 8.4 The Cairo Fire of 26 January 1952.

An anonymous photographer captures the start of the fire that consumed downtown Cairo on "Black Saturday." Men can be seen up on the balcony, while protesters on the ground burn furniture thrown from the terrace.

Source: "Min Hunā Ibtada'at al-Kārithah," *al-Musawwar* 1427, February 15, 1952, 13. University of Washington Libraries.

Although most of the targeted businesses were not British-owned, most traded in British goods.[46] One report speculated that "the cinemas, the Pasha's clubs, the bars and cabarets, frequented by the idle rich were attacked more as part of the morality drive begun by the Muslim Brotherhood, and the big stores from a general feeling that their prices make them establishments only for [the rich]."[47]

The targeting of theaters, bars, and nightclubs, the argument with the soldiers on the terrace of the Casino Badiʿah, and the articles that preceded the fire all suggested that the gangs were punishing "spoiled, drunk Cairo." The targeting of the celebrating soldiers could also be read as an attempt to enforce Egyptian affective regimes, which dictated gravity in the face of suffering. And while the Egyptian military was applauded for stopping the conflagration, it was also undutiful soldiers—out of role, out of place, and taking the wrong affective posture—who had been the original target of aggression on the casino terrace.

In the end, 750 buildings were damaged and twenty-six people killed as the gangs moved through the European downtown, torching visible reminders of colonial presence. But who was responsible for the fire? For a moment, Western officials blamed the Poles, circulating a Red Scare rumor that the Polish Embassy had given "truckloads of dynamite to the arsonists."[48] Once Cold War paranoia wore off, most pointed fingers at the Egyptian government—specifically, the Wafd and its Minister of Interior, Siraj al-Din Pasha. The British Residency, for instance, maintained that the emotions of the Cairo Fire had been "the direct consequence of their [the Wafd and Siraj al-Din's] policy of inciting the population."[49] In other words, the fire had been the product of the Wafd's emotional labors.

Egyptian popular gossip and apocryphal tales indicted Egyptian leaders for their behavior the day of the fire, weaving Black Saturday into a morality tale of government corruption. As the city center went up in flames, Nahhas had purportedly been receiving a pedicure, Siraj al-Din engrossed in a private land deal (or soaking in the bath, or smoking cigars by other accounts). King Faruq had feasted at a banquet, dining while Cairo burned.[50] Egyptian activists also blamed the British—claiming the colonists were responsible either directly (by having orchestrated the fire as pretense for enforcing martial law) or indirectly (by inflaming Egyptian emotions with the police massacre of January 25).[51] The Free Officers, for instance, circulated a tract calling the fire an imperialist coup and conspiracy aimed at quenching the nationalist movement.[52]

The association Muhammad's Youth circulated an article a few months later intimating a different opinion. The society indirectly suggested Cairo had been punished for her violation of display rules. Echoing the idea of Cairo singing while fighters in the Canal died, the journal wrote: "The blood of the martyrs was running in rivers, villages utterly annihilated—and at the same time, singing spread over the horizons, and bars and dance clubs were packed with thousands."[53]

Direct responsibility, of course, belonged to the smartly dressed gangs of middle-class vigilantes. British investigators concluded that the fireraisers had been members of Misr al-Fatah and the Muslim Brotherhood; some of Young Egypt's green armbands were reportedly spotted. Communist activists supported this reading in *al-Muqawama al-Sha'biyya*, charging Ahmad Husayn with being "at the head of the reactionary forces that burned the city of Cairo."[54] The destruction of foreign establishments, bars, entertainment venues, and luxury shops was particularly in keeping with Misr al-Fatah's rhetoric, guardianship claims over entertainment space, and modus operandi (bar-sacking as a sentence against foreigners and Egyptian elites who imitated British dress and manners).

In other words, in many ways the Cairo Fire was the physical actualization of moral claims and narratives that had been circulating for months. It is possible the fire represented a loss of emotional control or a failure of emotional discipline. However, considering the targeting of specific institutions and the consistency with well-established political claims and discourses, it seems more likely the fire represented an intentional rejection of calm and an attempt to remake the moral map of downtown Cairo. The months of emotional tilling and sowing that preceded the fire—countless conversations, articles, images, fliers, gestures, stories, and speeches dedicated to turning sentiment against cabarets, theaters, foreign clothing, and other visible marks of British cultural and economic occupation—further undermine the idea that the emotions of the day were fully spontaneous.

The Muslim Brotherhood's ongoing power struggles between 'Ashmawi and Hudaybi may have contributed to the fire-setting decision as well. Following the fire, Hasan al-Hudaybi immediately released a statement condemning the perpetrators and affirming that the Muslim Brotherhood was committed to "jihad through legal means."[55] But one of Hudaybi's advisors reported to the British Residency that Brotherhood factions had been involved:

> Farkhani confirms that some of the gangs operating in Cairo on 26th January were formed by the Moslem Brotherhood. They had attacked the bars and cafes but not the cinemas. *Hodeibi [Hudaybi] was losing his grip and had been unable to control many of the members,* although in present circumstances he hoped to regain control.[56]

As Farkhani's report hinted, the fire may have been ʿAshmawi and the Special Section's attempt at challenging their marginalization, Hudaybi's leadership, and the society's increasingly moderate stance. But the Brotherhood liaison maintained that most of the men had been Misr al-Fatah members, equipped and given police protection by the Wafd Minister of Interior, Siraj al-Din Pasha. As Farkhani explained, the Minister had been expecting Ahmad Husayn's men to execute a "normal riot"—not set the city on fire.[57]

In later interviews, Salih ʿAshmawi, Ahmad Husayn, and their confederates all denied involvement (although witnesses claimed they had seen Ikhwan member Ibrahim Karrum start the Opera Square fire). Instead, the associations pointed fingers at the British, the king, and the king's Iron Guard.[58] Based on the venues attacked and the articles circulating before the fire, however, it is reasonable to think Young Egypt and the Muslim Brotherhood's *al-Daʿwa* group were attempting to use the Canal Struggle to reinvigorate their guardianship claims over Cairo's entertainment spaces. The action scripts that appeared in their newspapers certainly pointed toward violence: Husayn's article in December claimed an explosion would overthrow the government if the cabarets remained open, and five days before the inferno Qutb had called for a "burning fire between us and them [the British]."[59]

The Wafd also played a role, whether directly or indirectly. As the revolution developed, the party alternated between attempts to suppress the movement (by selling calm) and attempts to head it (by selling outrage). Moreover, Minister of Interior Siraj al-Din's provocative speech three days before the fire urged Egyptians to respond to British provocations by taking steps beyond "mere protest." Internal party dynamics could have played a role: Siraj al-Din was a powerful Wafd minister who competed with party leader Mustafa al-Nahhas Pasha for influence, and the minister may have been preparing an internal challenge to Prime Minister Nahhas. Finally, the party had a history of allying with Young Egypt when it wanted paramilitary muscle on the street. The evidence remains circumstantial, but the minister's support of Young Egypt (if it is true) may have constituted part of this cycle.

The emotions of that week, however, illustrate how outrage operated both as a constraint and an opportunity for Egyptian politicians and activists. As Todd Hall points out, the "enraged speech of a policymaker—be it stemming from personal outrage, calculated performative outrage, or a combination of the two" can have unexpected consequences, as other actors in the system respond to the display, choose to amplify the emotion, and change their risk assessments for certain behaviors.[60] In other words, like other political maneuvers, affective strategies have spillover effects.

Complicating the picture is the fact that politicians often intentionally introduce narrative gaps to maintain plausible deniability. Like a puzzle piece waiting to be placed, ambiguities in political directives

> introduce interpretive dynamism by enabling multiple possible readings … there is no single, univocal meaning to be recovered … it also means that any specific interpretation can be denied while also enabling messages to be communicated which might be considered unacceptable if stated explicitly. This combination of deniability and multivocality highlights the central importance of gaps in "dog whistle" politics.[61]

The metaphors and emotions that the Minister of Interior, Young Egypt activists, and Muslim Brotherhood pundits invoked could certainly be read as enthymemes, providing a road map for action. Alternately, such media might have merely given arsonists the impression that popular or governmental support existed for vigilantism. Either way, some level of culpability exists. But in the end, we may never know who started the fire and whether someone gave a direct order to purge the downtown of colonial influence. Because there was strong social opprobrium directed toward the perpetrators of the fire—and because the fire terminated both the popular movement and the 1951 Revolution—nobody admitted responsibility. The British Embassy maintained there was "no reasonable doubt" that Ahmad Husayn and Misr al-Fatah were "the principle designers and executors of the main destruction." But they added "there is no actual proof."[62]

The Military's Blessed Movement

Whoever the perpetrator, the fire-raising had lasting effects. The Wafd government was dismissed on January 27 for its failures in preventing and responding to the January 26 conflagration. The new, palace-aligned government used the fire as pretense to round up some 181 suspected rioters, looters, and auxiliary policemen, as well as hundreds of Egyptian activists representing a variety of political views (communists, the Muslim Brotherhood, the Nationalist Party, Misr al-Fatah, and others). Finally, the government clamped down on the Liberation Battalions, confiscating arms and ending the popular movement. The 1951 Revolution was over.

In the following months, a series of minority-party "salvation ministries" took office: the governments of ʿAli Mahir (January 27–March 1, 1952),

Ahmad al-Hilali (March 2–June 29, 1952), Husayn Sirri (July 2–20, 1952), and Ahmad al-Hilali (July 22–23, 1952). However, with a lack of public confidence in the regime, the Wafd in the opposition, and the Palace working to increase its power over the premiership, no government could enact substantial reforms or make headway on the British question. As a result, in the last six months before the Free Officers' coup of July 23, the prime minister's office changed hands four times (making for a grand total of over one dozen government turnovers in ten years).

Meanwhile, the deployment of the army to quell the fire emboldened young activists in the officer corps. Officers had already organized underground cells to amass weapons and help train paramilitary volunteers in the Canal Zone. Now, "The army seemed to step up as a defender of the nation … the one force capable of imposing order," Marxist officer Khalid Muhyi al-Din wrote. The officers "had saved the country, and if the army had moved the night of the Cairo Fire on 26 January for the king's benefit—why not move for their own benefit?"[63]

The Free Officers shared many myths with the young activists that undertook anti-colonial campaigns in the late 1940s. The officers pointed to the founding shame of February 4, 1942, and the duty of cleansing the country from colonialism and its collaborators.[64] By only mentioning vague goals (such as liberating Egypt and eliminating traitors), the Free Officers attracted a broad membership: Gamal Abdel Nasser had been affiliated with Young Egypt, the Muslim Brotherhood, and the DMNL; ʿAbd al-Munʿim ʿAbd al-Raʾuf and Husayn Hammuda hailed from the Muslim Brotherhood; and Khalid Muhyi al-Din had joined the Muslim Brotherhood and Iskra before committing to the communist DMNL. Muhammad Anwar al-Sadat, meanwhile, said during those years he had "joined every single political party in Egypt."[65]

The Free Officers thus built on established networks and discourses. They cooperated with the Brotherhood in paramilitary training and borrowed Roneo machines from the DMNL, printing anti-government tracts to circulate in the mess hall. Their ideological program represented a mélange of influences and tried to strike a balance between the socialist agenda of its Marxist members and the social conservativism of the Brotherhood and Young Egypt.[66]

Interestingly, where contamination and purification appeals were lacking in the Cairo Fire, they were in abundance in tracts released by the Free Officers. In autumn 1951, a joint DMNL–Free Officers tract listed as its first objective "The extermination of foreign colonialism and its servants—the traitors—from the Nile Valley." As the tract argued, "These traitors must be rooted out in order to cleanse the country."[67] A pamphlet of March 22, 1952, similarly called for cleansing, warning "We will never advance, and the army will not walk on the right path, until it purifies itself of colonial henchmen."[68]

Already in late January 1952, the British Foreign Office was nervous. A few days before Mahir's resignation, a dispatch to the British Embassy in Cairo asked: "Will there be a revolution in Egypt?"[69] A week later, the British Embassy replied back that the British government should expect a coup, rather than a revolution: "[S]ince the fall of the Wafd Government [on 27 January], *it has become likely that the immediate effect of a failure [in negotiations securing British evacuation] … will be a military dictatorship* rather than an immediate outbreak of revolution."[70] Still, the British refused to evacuate.

Behind the scenes, the United States was more actively encouraging a coup. The day after the Cairo Fire, CIA deputy director Allan Dulles met agent Kermit Roosevelt (whose later claim to fame would be spearheading the Operation Ajax coup against Mohammed Mossadegh). The two discussed pressuring the king to implement reforms or backing a military overthrow of King Faruq by a "strong man." Dubbed "Project FF" (short for "Fat Fucker," the Americans' nickname for the portly king), in March Roosevelt visited Cairo and purportedly met with the Free Officers to express American support for a coup.[71]

The precipitating event for the coup came on July 16: King Faruq dissolved the board of the Officers' Club. In the army, there was fear the king's next move would be to arrest officers suspected of disloyalty.[72] After debating for three days, the conspirators decided to launch a coup d'état and set a date in early August. Events were moving quickly, however. The next day (July 20), Prime Minister Sirri resigned, and the Free Officers learned that Hilali would return to power in a few days. Concerned Hilali's new minister of war would purge the ranks of the army, the officers moved up their timeline.

Even as the officers conspired, however, the British Embassy was optimistic. A telegram to London reported that the Palace was

> now far more confident of the future than he had been at any time in the last six months …. [The King's advisor] Hafez Afifi had heard rumors of impending trouble in the country and of agitation by the partisans of Ahmad Husayn, but did not set much store by them …. [I]f the new Government … is successful in dealing with the trouble in the army, there is a reasonable chance that the next few months will be uneventful. Hafez Afifi himself is planning to go away for a holiday in Europe in mid-August.[73]

That same evening, the Free Officers launched their coup. They arrested their commanding officers, rallied the units at their command, and marched through Cairo. They seized control of bridges and roads, took over military barracks and headquarters, and commandeered the radio station. As a result, on the morning of July 23, 1952, Egyptians found themselves "waking up to khaki"—tan military uniforms, tanks parked in front of government ministries, and military planes flying overhead.[74]

Within thirty-six hours, calls and messages of support poured in from other army units, university staff and students, nationalist clubs, and trade unions. Trapped in Ras al-Tin Palace in Alexandria, King Faruq had little choice but to acknowledge the new regime. Three days later, he was presented with an abdication proclamation. He was allowed to board his yacht and sailed off into exile.[75]

In his wake, he left a military government charged with purifying the nation of factionalism and corruption. As the order investing the new head-of-state declared:

> Today, our dearest homeland urgently needs to establish its structure on a firm and sound foundation .... The Blessed Movement, whose standard you carry, is but an expression of the hopes held in the hearts of a noble people. ... Therefore, we have seen fit to invest you [General Muhammad Naguib] with the charge of governance, and entrust the premiership to you ... so the country can soon enjoy parliamentary life, *free from stain and flaw*.[76]

It is said that when institutions fail the test of justice, "morality acquires new flag-bearers."[77] The Muslim Brotherhood, Misr al-Fatah, the DMNL, the Wafd, and many other groups attempted to seize the standard of social order and moral reform in late monarchial Egypt. However, after July 23, 1952, the right to bear the flag of public morality was not seized by any of these clubs, but by a vigilante cadre from the ranks of the state: the "Blessed Army Movement."

9

Conclusion

Emotions and Protest in the Cold War Middle East

Oh Suez Canal,
Oh Zamzam …
Symbol of tolerant brotherhood
We dug you as a tool
Conveying hope …
A connection of love
From the brotherhood of mankind
Expanding wide
In purity and kindness
Not enmity or animosity

We've connected through tears
Water with water
We've connected the two seas
Closing the distance.

ʿAbd al-Laṭīf al-Nashār,
"Al-Fidāʾī," *Majallat al-Risāla* 962,
December 10, 1951, 1402.

The eminent historian John Darwin once quipped that British imperial histories used soft watercolors to paint decolonization as "effected over tea in an atmosphere of sweetness and light."[1] Meanwhile, third-world nationalists trumpeted decolonization as won with a flag and a gun. But juxtaposing Islamist and communist clubs in early Cold War Egypt overturns both the tea-table fairy tale and the flag-and-gun epic. The 1951 Revolution ambiguously interlaced victory and tragedy with attempts at friendship and revolt. The failed revolution also demonstrated how the disentanglements of decolonization were often not peaceful, not triumphal, and not fully resolved with a stroke of the pen and a handshake. Decolonization involved a fraught process of weeding colonialism out of political institutions, commerce, culture, and emotions, as well as pitched battles over the shape of the postcolonial order. And complete decolonization would prove an impossibility: after years of contact, colonialization had left its marks on bodies, cultures, and institutions.[2]

If we pull at the loose threads attached to myths about the "Rise of Nationalism," "Rise of Communism," and "Islamic Awakening," these scholarly narratives also unravel. Admittedly, historians inherited the terminology of social movements "rising" and "awakening" from the sources: militants trumpeted the "rise of communism" and the "rise of Islam" to assert the natural, inevitable, and irresistible nature of their mythic movements. Moreover, many activists *experienced* their movements as awakenings, because they were undergoing a worldview shift that woke them to new perspectives. Their establishmentarian adversaries also spoke of rising tides and irrepressible awakenings—albeit to warn against lurking threats and dormant powers.

Even so, using this language to describe Cold War movements is misleading. By describing a thing (be it Islam, communism, nationalism, etc.) as rising, it becomes an impersonal and all-powerful force that is everywhere and nowhere. Such language cloaks human agency and bids us pay no attention to the man behind the curtain. But no wave of emotion suddenly sparked anti-colonial movements. No faceless proletariat or Islamic consciousness suddenly "awakened." For as Michael Walzer writes, "the annoying word 'rise,' which seems to denote some collective and impersonal ascent, actually conceals a vast amount of painful human endeavor requiring willfulness, calculation, nerve, and perhaps above all an anxious, introspective discipline and self-control."[3]

Islamism and communism gained traction because enterprising individuals expended a tremendous amount of blood, sweat, and tears constructing movements brick by brick from available resources. Ideological "-isms" were painstakingly crafted and marketed to meet the needs of specific demographics. Associations toiled to build networks, signal moral sincerity, connect with others, and model new worlds. Al-Banna himself reflected on this labor-intensive process of ideological production in December 1948, in one of his final interviews before his assassination. "We have spent twenty years *making people understand* that Islam is a religion and a state: not a religion of worship and reclusion, but a religion of jihad and *niḍāl* [struggle]."[4]

For Egyptian political organizations of the 1940s, these world-building efforts produced ambiguous results. Egyptian communists told a tale in which Jews, Copts, women, and black Egyptians had a role to play in the national story. However, factionalism and anti-communist campaigns rendered their morality tale inert. The onset of the Cold War and the British decision to carve out a Jewish state in the Mandate of Palestine further damaged the movement and pushed many Egyptian communists (and Egyptian Jews) outside the tightening circle of Egyptian identity.

Meanwhile, the Muslim Brotherhood hoped their Islamic revival would purify the political sphere of corruption. Their story (and the performances of love and brotherhood that accompanied it) succeeded in making a theocratic state "thinkable" for many Egyptians. However, the moral compromises the Brotherhood made to remain competitive, as well as the society's decision to push muscular masculinity and elevate Egypt's ethnic and religious majority (Arab Muslims) often marginalized Egyptian Christians, Greeks, Jews, and women.

In the end, neither myth succeeded in overturning Egypt's ruling order. However, Islamist and communist associations did contribute to toppling the monarchy: when the Free Officers began constructing a myth to justify their military coup, they built up from the stories already circulating. Myths like the "Shame of 4 February" and King Faruq's banqueting while Cairo burned helped undermine the legitimacy of the *ancien régime*—and the Free Officers took their mandate from these myths.

Charting a middle path between extra-parliamentary societies, after 1952 the Free Officers constructed their platform on pan-Arabism and "Islamic socialism." This positioned the regime as a moderate middle between "communist atheism" and Islamic traditionalism.[5] But despite carving out a third way for Egypt, the Free Officers' story persisted in making Arab ethnicity the cornerstone of Egyptian identity, inadvertently marginalizing Egyptian Copts and Jews. Ironically then, one of the largest constrictions of Egyptian identity occurred not at the hands of the Muslim Brotherhood or Young Egypt, but under the Free Officers. However, as the new regime rationalized, the military was bringing Egypt out of the darkness and into the light, out of slavery and into the free world.[6]

Yet in the years after the July 23 coup/1952 Revolution, many Egyptians rejected the military's romance of a revolution achieved. The British remained in the Canal Zone, and as the United States and Britain pressured the new regime to join the Middle East Defense Organization (MEDO), Egyptian pundits denounced the Cold War defense pact as another attempt at "empire by treaty." Sayyid Qutb was one of the critics. In an article published three months after the coup, he argued that despite the military's self-congratulations, the war against colonization was far from won. The British were still commanding the Canal, foreign practices still spreading in Egyptian schools, and Egyptian newspapers still idolizing foreign culture. Egypt might have a new government, Qutb declared, but those who revered the West were still slaves of "spiritual colonialism, which shackles our feelings even as we revolt against political colonialism!" Such men—the "colonized of the heart"—dipped their pens "in the ink of shame and disgrace, to glorify the white man who tramples our neck with his boots."[7]

Echoing Frantz Fanon's *Black Skin, White Masks* (published earlier that year), Qutb argued that Egypt would never be free until Egyptians fought decolonization on the emotional front.

> In America, they talk about "the white man" as though they were talking about a half-God, and they talk about "colored folk" like us Egyptians (and Arabs in general) as though they were talking about a half-human! … Yet here [in Egypt], we … look at the white man with a reverent gaze …

The solution, Qutb explained, was to break the affective shackles of the West.

> Our schoolchildren must *turabbī* [teach and elevate] their feelings, and open up their minds to the white man's injustices and the white man's contemptibleness [*ḥaqāra*]. In our community, the goal of education must be liberation from the white man's influence, the white man's greed, and the white man's disdain. Here, the goal of education must be liberation from the white man's sway—not only political and economic, *but also social, emotional, and intellectual.*
>
> … The white man disgracefully exploits us and exploits our homeland, and it is our duty to steel our nerves and *mobilize our feelings* against him. … *We cannot overcome colonialism unless we smash it in our feelings*—and smash along with it the mechanisms that crush our faith in ourselves. …
>
> And the day we tear down colonialism in this way, razing it from our souls and our minds; the day our blood boils with holy hatred for everything European or American; the day we crush under our feet everything that shackles us to the wheel of colonialism—then and only then will we win our full freedom—because we will have obtained freedom within.[8]

Qutb's appeal fell on deaf ears in the government. The Free Officers had a diplomatic imperative to cultivate Western allies and avoid being pigeonholed as part of the Soviet camp—and for the moment, that took precedence over satisfying demands for cultural and emotional liberation.

Meanwhile, American diplomats noted with relief that following the Free Officers coup, British strategists had "decided in December 1952 that the Canal Zone base, though still valuable, was no longer indispensable" thanks to advances in nuclear weapons technologies. Churchill was still calling any agreements with Egypt "appeasement" and describing the situation as "Munich on the Nile"—but the British prime minister had, according to the official in charge of Middle Eastern affairs at the Foreign Office, "dropped his previous idea that we could not possibly [evacuate] until a lot of people had been killed."[9] Instead the Foreign Office expressed in February 1953 that "It is useless ... to maintain troops [in the Canal Zone] simply to be shot at." That same month, Deputy Prime Minister Anthony Eden described the problem as one of manpower: "Military occupation [can] be maintained by force, but in the case of Egypt the base upon which it depends is of little use if there is no local labor to man it." Paramilitary attacks and workers strikes, Peter Hahn concludes, had "rendered the base practically unmanageable."[10]

As a result, discussions began for the British to relinquish Suez. Negotiations proceeded in a climate of political uncertainty: the new regime began dissolving Egyptian political parties and associations, and on January 23, 1953, the military created a one-party state by establishing the Liberation Rally. The Free Officers offered Muslim Brotherhood ideologue Bahi al-Khuli (famous for articulating Islam as a "third-way" doctrine) a liaison position, and offered Sayyid Qutb the position of general secretary. Understanding the jobs were a way to dissolve the Brotherhood into the Liberation Rally, both men refused. Within a month, Qutb formalized his membership with the Muslim Brotherhood and took over editorship of the society's newspaper, effectively renouncing any hopes of government appointment.[11]

The regime's consolidation campaign continued. In spring and summer 1953, the Revolutionary Command Council arrested Wafdist and communist activists, and staged show trials in autumn. In March 1954, General Nasser arrested General Naguib after an internal power struggle, and in April new censorship laws muzzled the media. By September 1954, the Nasser regime purged universities and the judiciary. Fittingly, the government also invested in narratives and mythmaking, establishing the Storytelling Club [*Nādī al-Qiṣṣa*] and Supreme Council for the Protection of Arts, Literature and Social Science.[12]

Amidst these changes, in October 1954 President Gamal ʿAbdel Nasser signed a new Anglo-Egyptian Treaty with Britain. The treaty agreed to a twenty-month staged evacuation of the Canal Zone—but controversially allowed for British re-occupation in case of foreign interference with Canal traffic.[13] Just over a week after the signing, an assassination attempt targeted Nasser for his "act of treason."

The regime response was swift. Suspecting the Muslim Brotherhood—which by now was the only remaining power bloc besides the Liberation Rally—the Free Officers launched a war against the Brothers, arresting thousands of members including guide Hasan al-Hudaybi. A rushed show trial found the high-profile leaders guilty and sentenced them to death by hanging. Hudaybi received a last-minute pardon, allowing him to spend the last nineteen years of his life in prison (until his death in 1973). Retired judge and lawyer ʿAbd al-Qadir ʿAwda was not so fortunate. He and five others ascended the gallows on December 7, 1954. With his last words, the judge beseeched God: "make my blood a curse upon the men of the revolution." In Egypt, the execution was met with "stunned and horrified silence."[14]

Hysterics and Fanatics: The Emotions of Revolution

The men were outlived by the lasting effects of the revolution that failed, and the debates about emotions that had circulated in the 1940s and early 1950s. Once upon a time, the Egyptian doctor Muhammad Wilaya and reader Mustafa Jabir had debated the motives driving individuals who sacrificed themselves for a cause. In their 1942 disagreement, Dr. Wilaya characterized self-sacrificers as "hysterics" who masochistically enjoyed suffering for their creed.[15]

To interrogate profiles like Dr. Wilaya's, this study set out to map the affective environment of political associations and untangle the emotions of anti-colonial protest. Egyptian and British pundits saw activists as fanatics; but it turned out that those same Egyptian activists also used charges of emotionality to devalue their own competitors. The Muslim Brotherhood argued that Westernized elites were letting their passions run wild, while the Workers' Vanguard described the Brothers as fanatics stoking the passions of the ignorant masses. Emotionalism thus constituted part of the moral vocabulary. But in fact, Egyptian activists shared the same rationalist discourses as the culture at large. They disciplined emotions, discussed which sentiments befit sound moral citizens, and worked to advertise and influence demand for socio-affective goods like belonging, pride, and security.[16]

Their process of "producing emotions" deserves special attention. A study by Susanne Stadlbauer found that to elicit sentiment, Arabic-speakers *code-switch*, using *ʿāmmīyya* (dialectical Arabic) and poetic *fuṣḥá* (literary Arabic).[17] Based on this study, I would add that convincing others to share an emotional state involved other strategies: tonal changes, emotions-words, rhythm and rhyme,

metaphors, adjectives and sensory descriptions, stories, and first- and second-person pronouns. Speakers increased gaze-holding and competed to convince audiences that affective displays were sincere. Campaigners encouraged chanting and repetitious synchrony (the collective repetition of movements and vocalizations).[18] And when asking audiences to feel, Arabic speakers modeled what it looked like to "feel moved," coordinating facial expressions and gestures. James Jasper groups some of these strategies under the heading of *prosody*, or "all the variations in intonation or melody, the pauses and stresses, the intensity or timbre of our speech—all of which is … crucial in displaying emotions intelligibly."[19]

However, most of these affective "production rules" were implicit. Activists intuitively landed on protest slogans with rhythm and rhyme; advice columns offered fragmentary tips on how to write a tragic tearjerker of a tale. Sayyid Qutb's recipe for emotions-making in literature, for instance, told writers to (1) fill their palettes with painted phrases and vibrant words to compose a colorful portrait for the reader, (2) choose words that plunge the reader into deep, fathomless connotations, and (3) create cadence and rapped tapped rhythm with word structure.[20] But even when emotional production rules were made explicit, evoking feelings remained part social learning, part trial-and-error, and part intuition regarding the sensibilities of one's audience—and stimulating the desired emotional response from someone else was never guaranteed.

Politics and protest thus involved vast amounts of emotional labor. The Egyptian communist paper *al-Tatawwur*, for instance, recognized that building a new society required re-teaching emotions. As the paper exclaimed, "we must establish a school to teach people *how to be angry* and *what to be angry about*."[21] Political campaigns thus involved many emotional performances and "outbursts," which helped pierce busy environments and attract attention. Groups further specialized in affective postures: Egyptian communists publicized pity for the poor and outrage about exploitation, while Young Egypt and Muslim Brotherhood members stoked anger and disgust toward depraved entertainment and leisure activities. But in general, moral emotions constituted a shared language and social technology for negotiating norms—even if the conclusions were worlds apart.[22]

What of Wilaya's argument that those who sacrificed masochistically enjoyed suffering and craved attention? In fact, attention and status may have yielded some emotional payouts; but Egyptian activists more frequently described enjoying the social environment, certainty, and sense of meaning they gained from their work—not the pain and suffering. Muslim Brotherhood member

Jamal Fawzi, for instance, described the society's ideology as something that brought him joy. In a poem entitled "My Idea," he wrote "I was content with her ... /I lived for her/Her protection sheltered me/*I found happiness with her*."[23]

Organizations like the Muslim Brotherhood and Workers' Vanguard worked hard to co-produce these socio-affective payouts for members. To facilitate group cohesion and strong attachments, they scheduled social events and encouraged members to use similar gestures, vocabularies, and emotional styles.[24] Some organizations leveraged more costly and coercive bonding strategies, requiring members to share personal information, pressuring members to wear similar clothes, limiting contact with kin, or recruiting individuals separated from kin.

Emotionally, love talk was a glue that fortified bonds. For instance, al-Banna taught members of the Muslim Brotherhood to love God and "Love one another, and jealously guard your bond, as it is the key to your strength and the pillar of your success."[25] And members said they experienced such teachings of love and light as profoundly elevating. As seventeen-year-old Jabir Qumayhah eulogized in a 1951 poem on al-Banna's legacy, "And when I heard him say/Oh friends, God is the be-all, end-all/I saw light dawn on the horizon/ ... /And all eyes swim in light/And the Earth—oh Earth!—becomes a sky."[26]

These experiences of love must not be dismissed; but they should come with a word of caution. Love-driven commitments are sometimes just as problematic as hate and guilt-driven commitments. Love sets hearts aflame and moves men assuredly toward the "utopian horizon"[27]—but G. Arunima, Patricia Hayes, and Premesh Lalu point out that the promises of the "revolutionary romance" are rarely fulfilled. "For the most part, the present speaks of revolutions that did not make one free, struggles that provided only incomplete citizenship, and domains of life, and selfhood ... still marked by inequality and injustice."[28]

Sara Ahmed is even more skeptical; she argues that the "loveable object" or idealized community—be it the nation, the race, the religion, or the company—is often loved only because it is recognized as similar to oneself. We long for a community that will recognize us and welcome us and reciprocate love back to us. However, Ahmed warns that affection based on similarity often deteriorates into an exercise in exclusion, manipulation, and hate. Once the lines of love are drawn around the likeminded, there is no exit, and people of difference become a threat. The very existence of difference is interpreted as a form of hatred toward the beloved object—and the supposed "hatred" of others then used to justify extreme actions to defend the community "in the name of love."[29]

Revolutionary emotions thus illustrate that negative and positive emotions are not incompatible: in protest movements anger exists alongside hope, and

the two work in tandem to energize the decision to revolt.[30] Moreover, the 1951 Revolution reflects how that many emotional payouts were highly individualized and historically specific. Muslim Brotherhood members in Cairo reported that membership made them feel valued during an era of urbanization, when rural emigrants arriving in the city struggled with their lack of means and felt demeaned by city-dwellers who shamed them for their provincial habits. Communist activists in Egypt described different affective payouts. Sharif Hatata—educated, ethnically mixed, and elite—said communism helped him feel connected to other Egyptians. "Belonging to an upper-class family with an English mother … I had a need not to feel alienated."[31] Avraham Farhi similarly described how as an Egyptian Jew, communism gave him both a sense of community and a sense of reach beyond that small community.

> We were a group of young *lycée* students … we were very similar: we spoke French and shared common ideals and perspectives …. Marxism gave us the identity that we were lacking. Belonging to Marxism meant to belong to the international proletariat … we felt as an integral part of the big world, not as members of a small community.[32]

Notably, while activists spoke at length about the benefits of membership (and while organizations freely advertised these benefits)—members vigorously rejected the accusation they had embraced the cause for selfish gain. The Ikhwan, for instance, solemnly pledged:

> [T]he mission of the Muslim Brotherhood is a pure and unblemished one. It has aspired to such heights of purity that it has transcended the limits of merely personal ambition: it has held material gain in contempt, abandoned all selfish impulses and goals.[33]

Members likely felt that acknowledging payouts would vindicate critics. Acknowledging payouts might have also devalued the organization's altruistic claims (and losing that sense of altruism would have in turn devalued the sense of meaning that political associations provided). The moral and affective economy of activism hinged on societies maintaining member belief that the group was pursuing pro-social goals. When organizations showed themselves to be self-serving, it devalued the sense of pride and accomplishment the group offered—and this led to membership flight (as Young Egypt and the Muslim Brotherhood discovered at various junctures).

The fact that activists benefited from activism should not be taken as evidence that altruism claims were disingenuous, however. Study after study has found that selfishness is *negatively* correlated to high-cost behaviors like rebellion and armed insurgency; individuals who dedicate themselves to a cause do so out of a sincere belief that their actions will benefit their kin group, party, or community.[34] In line with these findings, Egyptians indicated time and time again that their sacrifices were for Egypt, the Islamic umma, or some other shared community.

In the end, campaigning thus emerged as a high risk, high reward activity. The emotional payouts of striving together were high—but many Egyptian protestors spent years of their life in prison: such was the fate of Muslim Brotherhood activists like Ahmad ʿAdil Kamal, Hasan al-Jamal, and Mustafa Mashhur, and Egyptian communist activists Henri Curiel, Inji Aflatun, and Diane Fawzy-Rossano. Communist activist Mubarak ʿAbduh Fadl was expelled from al-Azhar, kicked out of his home, and by age twenty-six had spent more than four years of his life in Egyptian prisons and concentration camps.[35] Other activists paid the ultimate price. Muslim Brotherhood activists ʿAdil Ghanim (a medical student at ʿAyn Shams University, son of Professor Muhammad Ghanim) and ʿUmar Shahin (a humanities student at Fuʾad University) joined a liberation battalion and traveled to the Canal Zone to fight the British. In January 1952 they returned home in caskets. Leaving out their affiliation, *al-Musawwar* reported that they died for Egypt, and that was all.[36]

Stories and Social Movements

Building on the theme of revolutionary emotions, the study also asked how activists muster stories to stir sentiments. Wilaya argued (citing German psychologist Emil Kraepelin) that self-sacrificers build elaborate fantasies in which they play the role of hero or victim. Then the activist "distorts facts to make them fit his personal desires."[37]

In fact, Dr. Wilaya's comments about building fantasies (and conforming reality to fit them) sounded strikingly similar to the organizational narratives that activists recited. Islamist and communist activists did structure, filter, and interpret information through the lens of myth. Wilaya also correctly noted that organizational myths allowed members to take on meaningful roles: an activist could become a soldier of God, a bringer of light, or a member of the revolutionary vanguard. The doctor's analysis thus contained some truth, even if it was embedded in a heavy helping of normativity.

Rather than constituting pure fantasy, however, stories were socially important for mobilizing and coordinating action. In a study of Coptic activism in Egypt,

Sana Hasan once wrote that "the function of myths is not just to interpret the past in a way that strengthens group solidarity, but to alter behavior. In other words, myths lead to action."[38] Michel de Certeau similarly hypothesized that stories open a theater for (and legitimize) dangerous behaviors.[39] This study pinpointed *how* activists used myths to move men to action through a process of "intense, chaotic, and ambiguous storytelling practices."[40] Action scripts laid out cognitive-behavioral paths. Temporal scripts attempted to interrupt habits, create grand ruptures, and encourage individuals to act out change, thus transforming myths into *mythomoteurs*. Personal stories gave individuals a place in the world, imparted a sense of purpose, and inspired people to reach this "ideal self." And shared stories expressed common values, unified individuals, and provided a schema for making sense of events. Stories were thus inwoven in the fabric of society and self. So intimate was this bond that literary theorist Jacqueline Rose concludes that "fantasy is not therefore antagonistic to social reality; it is its precondition or psychic glue."[41]

In short, myths and their emotions were not so much pathology as they were a socio-cognitive technology: tools for dialogically constructing groups around shared values and identities. And like most technologies, myths were inherently ambiguous. As potent acts of creation they were keys to a new world—but whether those keys unlocked the gates of heaven or the gates of hell was rarely clear.[42]

While it can thus be tempting to pathologize the myths and emotions of groups we dislike, it is important to take stories seriously. Myths and emotions emerge from specific political, economic, social, and historical contexts. Dehumanizing activists as fools of passion only serves to mystify the structures in which they are embedded, the stories they use to construct their worlds, and the emotions they embrace. Rather than dismiss the myths of others, we should consider instead how those narratives map paths for action, structure and filter information, and reward and bind those who embrace the story.

It is also important to recognize that myths are not unique to religious and political movements: organizations of many types used narratives to produce meaning and direct behavior. Consider the elaborate myths and corporate personality cults surrounding "self-made" men like Henry Ford, Steve Jobs, Jeff Bezos, and Elon Musk. The story that legitimizes their wealth (and the American corporate system as a whole) is a familiar fable:

> The young men (it is always men) have an idea: "killer" hard or software that will change everything. Rejecting traditional educational and career paths, defying business orthodoxies, they devote themselves to its development. Holed up in

> their garage/basement/industrial loft, they max out their relatives' credit cards and dispense with most trappings of normal adult life … Their obsession bears fruit … The twenty-something visionaries from the garage/basement/industrial loft are now richer than they ever imagined.[43]

Professions like nursing and teaching are similarly fueled by their own myths of meaning, which offer workers the satisfaction of being a superhuman helper or masterful mind.[44]

Such myths may be built around a seed of truth—but the story becomes problematic when it is used to mystify power relations, camouflage costs, or preclude fair compensation. Paying attention to the intersection of myths and emotions thus helps us recognize how powerbrokers use emotional narratives to manufacture consent, and what affective benefits and costs we incur from such commitments. For as Paula Ioanide observes our emotional investments can often override our financial interests.[45] Learning to navigate the emotional and moral thicket of hard-to-understand political groups, religious movements, or business structures helps explain how something "unthinkable" becomes thinkable and even attractive.

Learning emotional and moral navigational skills also holds up a lantern to how we use emotions to persuade others. By considering emotions a type of argument, we learn to recognize when others are trying to solicit our moral and emotional immune systems. How (and on whose bodies) are we asked to act out boundary-patrolling emotions like anger and disgust? How are love and pride used to create hierarchies and defy established regimes? Why do certain moral or emotional metaphors crawl beneath the skin and sting the nerves?

Finally, the Egyptian experience illuminates the fact that terms like "emotional," "radical," and "extreme" often constitute moral discourses rather than stable categories. When a politician, journalist, or scholar talks about "radicalism," they contribute to the creation of social norms and moral geographies. By describing things as "extreme," we differentiate unreasonable emotions, unacceptable protest, illegitimate aggression, and repulsive religious practices from practices deemed reasonable, safe, and beneficial. But like all boundary-policing efforts, such discourses can become entangled in guardianship claims. Naming and claiming something as "radical" invests the speaker with the right to judge (and implies that the speaker-as-judge is rational, reasonable, and unimpeded by their own guiding narratives and emotional commitments). However, caution is needed, because history is littered with failed radicalism claims that never caught on (like Shabab Sayyidna Muhammad's attempt to declare universities as radical spaces of gender-mixing).

The fact that conversations about "fanaticism" and "emotionalism" represent a form of moral debates is significant for scholars. It means that no study can close the book on "radicalism" or "extremism"—because debates over behavior "beyond the acceptable limits" serve an important social function. Such debates establish boundaries and are an important field where political claimants attempt to stake out protectorates. Moreover, it means "radical," "fanatical" behaviors may never be fully banished from society—because testing and debating boundaries is a normal part of social ecosystems (even if the process is often contested, and in some cases, violent).

From the 1951 Suez Crisis to the 1956 Suez Crisis

In many ways, the legacy of Egypt's tumultuous 1940s was calamitous. During the late monarchy, British occupation destabilized multiple Egyptian governments, fueled the growth of extra-parliamentary associations like the Muslim Brotherhood, and legitimized and normalized paramilitary violence by non-state actors. In those years, various Egyptian governments sought to strengthen the military by buying surplus weapons from the United States or Czechoslovakia—but British intrusion shuttered the sales, leaving the state both weak and obsessed with asserting military strength. British military intervention in the Canal Zone pushed Egypt toward socialist commitment (see Figure 9.1). The failure of the anti-colonial movement and burning of Cairo fertilized the soil for military rule. And decades into the Cold War, memories of British occupation would inform Egypt's staunch refusal to participate in joint-defense initiatives like the MEDO and the Baghdad Pact.

When British troops finally withdrew from the Suez Canal on June 13, 1956, Egyptians breathed a sigh of relief, thinking the book could be closed. But shortly thereafter, the United States retracted funding for the Aswan Dam. The decision led Nasser to nationalize the Suez Canal on July 26, 1956. Timed to coincide with the fourth anniversary since the fall of the monarchy, Nasser's speech to the nation framed the decision as helping fund the High Dam, safeguarding Egypt's economic independence, and eliminating the Suez Canal Company as a "state within a state."[46] A British Embassy official described the jubilant ten-minute ovation that followed the announcement, and the burlesque parade of a float in the shape of a "Sphinx swallowing a British soldier with the British flag sewn on his derrière."[47]

Nasser's nationalization plan horrified advisors, who immediately warned him about the fate of Mossadegh (overthrown in a CIA and MI-6-backed coup

Figure 9.1 Egyptian Perspectives of the Cold War.

British Prime Minister Winston Churchill points a bayonet at Miṣrī Effendi (the Egyptian "everyman") during the Canal Struggle of 1951 while US President Harry Truman looks on. Stalin smokes pipe in the background, while Egypt exclaims "I don't want to turn to the left… but you're the one pushing me there!"

Source: Alexander Ṣarūkhān, "English Politics in the Canal [Zone]," *Ākhir Sāʿa* 890, November 14, 1951, 4. Hatcher Graduate Library, University of Michigan.

in August 1953). As insurance, in the weeks following the nationalization Nasser therefore took pages from the 1951 Canal Struggle. On August 9, 1956, the revolutionary regime opened recruitment centers for student volunteers to join the National Liberation Army. But the expected British retaliation did not come, so Egyptians settled back to life as usual.[48]

Then suddenly on October 29, Israel invaded the Sinai Peninsula. In Nasser's war room there was confusion, then the dawn of understanding on October 31, when Britain and France commenced their seven-day bombing campaign of Cairo and Port Saʿid. The Tripartite Aggression—or triple invasion of Egypt by Britain, France, and Israel—had begun.[49]

Naming their gallant assault "Operation Musketeer" after Alexander Dumas' three musketeers, British and French fighter planes unleashed nearly 2,000 bombs on Egypt in a few days' time. Then starting November 5, the allies staged a naval and paratrooper landing to occupy Port Saʿid. As the Egyptian army retreated from the Canal Zone to defend the capital, the Nasser government dumped crates of rifles in Port Sa'id streets. Residents took up arms, thinking the Third World War had begun. French paratroopers described executing a dozen "nuisance" fisherman out looking for a morning haul; a young Egyptian man in *al-Ahram* described watching his brother who had never held a rifle before "reduced to a heap of flesh underneath [a] tank." Ultimately, almost a thousand Egyptian civilians were killed before the arrival of UN peacekeeping forces on November 15. But Egyptians held the line.[50]

British historians debate whether the Suez withdrawal that followed represented the sun setting on the British Empire or continuity with previous policies (as Britain resumed her exploits in Jordan in 1958 and Kuwait in 1961).[51] Official Egyptian perspectives of 1956, meanwhile, cast Nasser in a hagiographical light. He had nationalized Suez, and sunk fifty-one boats, cranes, bridges, and dredgers in the Canal to block traffic as the imperialists advanced, sent the British economy into a tailspin, and won the day. Historians later concluded that Nasser's victory made him a symbol of anti-colonial resistance, propelled him to leadership in the Non-Aligned Movement, ushered in a "decade of Nasserite domination," and allowed him to further consolidate his regime against domestic opponents.[52]

But parallel threads connected the 1956 Suez Crisis with the 1951 Suez Crisis that came before. Once more *fidāʾīyīn*—including students from Fuʾad University (now renamed Cairo University)—traveled to the Canal Zone to fight. Once more Port Sa'id civilians took up arms against the British. And once more these struggles were masked by the regime. As Alia Mossallam explains, paradoxically the popular struggle in Port Sa'id became "one of the most 'remembered' events" of the 1956 Suez Crisis and one of the most silenced. The Nasser government celebrated the town's collective resistance—but silenced any narratives that might challenge the official story of military heroism playing the star role. Press coverage of the Anglo-French invasion reflected the government narrative: whereas in 1951 magazines poured out pictures of *fidāʾīyīn* and workers and villagers (and Wafd politicians), in 1956 pages were stuffed with images of Nasser, Egyptian army lieutenants, naval officers, air force captains, and military hardware.[53] Inji Aflatun, who resisted this narrative with *The Protest* (1958) and *Port Said* (1957) (depicting a child sitting by the body of her dead mother), was arrested in 1959.[54]

Throughout the Suez struggle of 1956, there was also a deep silence about the Suez struggle that came before. There were no celebratory comparisons, no calls to complete what had been started that fateful fall of 1951. If anything, the 1956 invasion cast a harsh light on the extent to which the 1951 Canal Struggle had become an event amputated from history. Stopping the British advance in 1956 was certainly steeped in emotional significance as a moment of recovered pride, as Elie Podeh points out.[55] But there was neither talk of the "shame of 1951" nor the "glories of 1951." There was only silence.

As the curtain fell on the 1950s, the military regime continued its rule—and Sayyid Qutb remained the thorn in their side. His prison poem compared Nasser to the false god Hubal and denounced Nasserism as a form of idolatry.[56] Qutb would thus remain in prison for nine years, until health problems finally spurred his release in 1964. That year, he revised the Muslim Brotherhood's Islamist myth one last time in light of regime violence. In *Ma'alim fi al-Tariq*, the Brotherhood spokesman divided the world into two camps: on one side, the people of darkness and *jāhiliyya* (the mass of unbelievers and so-called Muslims like Nasser), and on the other side, "we who have understood Islam and live in its atmosphere." Calling Islam "a revolution against earthy authority," he called men to crawl out of the darkness—stand up and revel in the light, "oceanic vastness" of faith and inhale freedom.[57] As Qutb implored, "we invite people to Islam because we love them and we wish them well, although they may torture us."[58] He was quickly rearrested.

By now the victories of 1956 were a decade gone, and military failures in Yemen meant the Nasser regime was weak and rotten with plots. Their patience with Sayyid Qutb at an end, the regime last detained the sixty-year-old social critic on August 9, 1966. After twenty days in prison, on August 29 the writer was taken to police headquarters. And there at approximately 3:00 am, Qutb and two other Brothers were quietly hung and buried in an unmarked grave.[59]

Myths and emotions, however, are not as easily buried as the men and women who embrace them. Consequently, Qutb would be remembered as "the most significant thinker of Islamic resurgence in the modern Arab world"—and in less kind readings as the father of modern jihadism.[60] Meanwhile, the Muslim Brotherhood and many groups like them would continue to nourish hopes of moral revival throughout the Cold War, their claims legitimized by the violence of US- and Soviet-backed authoritarian regimes. So in the end, the hopes of the dead would be born up from the ashes on the words and wings of stories and live on—carrying the banded ambiguities of myth up with them.

Notes

Chapter 1

1 Stefanie Wichhart, *Britain, Egypt, and Iraq during World War II: The Decline of Imperial Power in the Middle East* (London: I.B. Tauris, 2022), 82–7; Israel Gershoni, *Arab Responses to Fascism and Nazis: Attraction and Repulsion* (Austin: University of Texas Press, 2014), 185, 203.

2 Emphasis added. Muḥammad Ḥusnī Wilāyah, "al-Shakhṣiyyat al-histīriyya," *Majallat al-Risāla* 468, June 22, 1942, 639.

3 Muṣṭafā ʿAbd al-Majīd Jābir, "al-Fidāʾiyya," *Majallat al-Risāla* 470, July 6, 1942, 691.

4 Muḥammad Ḥusnī Wilāya, "al-Fidāʾiyya," *Majallat al-Risāla* 472, July 20, 1942, 731.

5 Muṣṭafā ʿAbd al-Majīd Jābir, "al-Fidāʾiyya Ayḍan," *Majallat al-Risāla* 474, August 3, 1942, 771–2.

6 Only a few forays into the field exist among scholars of the modern Middle East: Ellinor Morack has recovered accounts of fear and loathing in Greek-occupied republican Turkey, and Joseph Ben Prestel has studied emotions and urban space in nineteenth-century Cairo, for instance. See: Joseph Ben Prestel, *Emotional Cities: Debates on Urban Change in Berlin and Cairo, 1860–1910* (Oxford: Oxford University Press, 2017); Ellinor Morack, "Fear and Loathing in 'Gavur' Izmir: Emotions in Early Republican Memories of the Greek Occupation (1919–1922)," *International Journal of Middle East Studies* 49, no. 1 (February 2017): 71–89.

7 Sara Ahmed, *The Cultural Politics of Emotion*, 2nd ed. (Edinburgh: Edinburgh University Press, 2014), 72–8, 98; Edward W. Said, *Orientalism* (New York: Vintage Books, 1979); Edward W. Said, *Covering Islam* (New York: Vintage Books, 1997).

8 Florence Nightingale, *Letters from Egypt: A Journey on the Nile, 1849–1850* (New York: Grove Press, 1987 [First. ed. 1854]), 17, 24–5, 71, 81, 196–7.

9 The Athenaeum, *The Progress of Nations; Or, The Principles of National Development in Their Relation to Statesmanship, a Study in Analytical History* (London: Longman, Green, Longman, and Roberts, 1861), 147, 269–77, 610–11. Also see Margrit Pernau, "Great Britain: The Creation of an Imperial Global Order," in *Civilizing Emotions*, ed. Margrit Pernau and Helge Jordheim et al. (Oxford: Oxford University Press, 2015), 45–58.

10 "Egypt," *The Saturday Review* 1397, vol. 54, August 5, 1882, 164; Ben Prestel, *Emotional Cities*, 108–9.

11 Hamilton Fyfe notably described how the "typically Nationalist brain" was "easily inflamed." Hamilton Fyfe, *The New Spirit in Egypt* (London: William Blackwood and Sons, 1911), 116–19, 168.

12 Israel Gershoni and James P. Jankowski, *Egypt, Islam, and the Arabs: The Search for Egyptian Nationhood, 1900–1930* (Oxford: Oxford University Press, 1987), 41–4.

13 My thanks to Elizabeth Thompson for drawing my attention to Russell's account. See: Elizabeth F. Thompson, "The Paris Peace Conference as Counterrevolution in the Middle," Working Paper presented at the Roundtable *War and Revolution in the Middle East*, School of International Service at American University (Washington, DC: March 2023) and Sir Thomas Russell Pasha, *Egyptian Service 1902–1946* (London: John Murray, 1923), 191, 198.

14 Sir Thomas Russell Pasha, *Egyptian Service 1902–1946*, 201–3, 207.

15 Sir Thomas Russell Pasha, *Egyptian Service 1902–1946*, 197–8.

16 Ibid.

17 Stefanie Wichhart, *Britain, Egypt, and Iraq during World War II: The Decline of Imperial Power in the Middle East* (New York: I.B. Tauris, 2022), 4; Michael J. Cohen, "The Strategic Role of the Middle East after the War," in *Demise of the British Empire in the Middle East: Britain's Response to Nationalist Movements, 1943–55*, ed. Michael J. Cohen and Martin Kolinsky (London: Frank Cass, 1998), 23.

18 See, for instance, the military plans Pincher and Makefast (1946) and Broiler (1947). Peter L. Hahn, *The United States, Great Britain, and Egypt, 1945–1956: Strategy and Diplomacy in the Early Cold War* (Chapel Hill: University of North Carolina Press, 1991), 27–8, 53; Kyle J. Anderson, *The Egyptian Labor Corps: Race, Space, and Place in the First World War* (Austin: University of Texas Press, 2021), 33; Robert Tignor, *Capitalism and Nationalism at the End of Empire* (Princeton: Princeton University Press, 2015), 47, 56–7; Louise Kettle, *Learning from the History of British Interventions in the Middle East* (Edinburgh: Edinburgh University Press, 2018), 25, 57; Joel Beinin and Zachary Lockman, *Workers on the Nile: Nationalism, Communism, Islam, and the Egyptian Working Class, 1882–1954* (London: I.B. Tauris, 1988), 408.

19 Ibid.

20 Ibid.

21 "Anglo-Egyptian Negotiations," May 7, 1946, Parliamentary Debate, House of Commons, Vol. 422, https://hansard.parliament.uk/commons/ 1946-05-07/debates/5de5312a-e5a0-42da-8098-77839cb6a034/Anglo-EgyptianNegotiations (BritishForcesWithdrawal).

22 "Anger in Egypt," *The Times* 50848, August 25, 1947, 3; H.A.R. Gibb, *Modern Trends in Islam* [1947] (New York: Octagon Books, 1972), 113, 120, 136. The 1947 edition was a print of Gibb's Haskell Lecture, delivered at the University of Chicago in 1945. For other Arabists commenting on the Brotherhood as an example of

emotionalism, and more on the intellectual history of these debates, see: Israel Gershoni, "The Theory of Crisis and the Crisis in a Theory: Intellectual History in Twentieth-Century Middle Eastern Studies," in *Middle East Historiographies: Narrating the Twentieth Century*, ed. Israel Gershoni, Amy Singer, and Y. Hakan Erdem (Seattle: University of Washington Press, 2006), 138–50.

23 "Egypt and the Canal Zone," *The Economist* 161, no. 5642 (October 13, 1951): 867.

24 Jack A. Goldstone, "Toward a Fourth Generation of Revolutionary Theory," *Annual Review of Political Science* 4 (2001): 145.

25 The main treatments of the Canal Struggle are found in Michael Thornhill, *Road to Suez: The Battle of the Canal Zone* (Gloucestershire: Sutton Publishing, 2006) and Anne-Claire de Gayffier-Bonneville, "La guerre du canal 1951–1952," *Cahiers de la Méditerranée* 70 (June 2005): 111–36. Both contributions tell events from the perspective of British diplomatic documents. A few books tangentially cover activism surrounding the Canal Struggle. These include Selma Botman, *The Rise of Egyptian Communism, 1939–1970* (New York: Syracuse University Press, 1988); Tareq Ismael and Rifaʿat El-Saʿid, *The Communist Movement in Egypt, 1920–1988* (New York: Syracuse University Press, 1990); Rami Ginat, *A History of Egyptian Communism* (Boulder: Lynne Rienner, 2011); Ahmed Abdalla, *The Student Movement and National Politics in Egypt, 1923–1973* (Cairo: The American University in Cairo Press, 2008); and Nancy Y. Reynolds, *A City Consumed: Urban Commerce, the Cairo Fire, and the Politics of Decolonization in Egypt* (Stanford: Stanford University Press, 2012).

26 Joel Gordon, *Nasser's Blessed Movement: Egypt's Free Officers and the July Revolution* (New York: Oxford University Press, 1992), 9–12, 26–31, 47–51, 175–97. For examples of revisionist accounts, see Anouar Abdel-Malek, *Egypt: Military Society: The Army Regime, the Left, and Social Change under Nasser* (New York: Vintage Books, 1968); Mahmoud Hussein, *Class Conflict in Egypt, 1945–1970* (New York: Monthly Review Press, 1973).

27 Ibid.

28 See Thornhill, *Road to Suez* and de Gayffier-Bonneville, "La guerre du canal 1951–1952," 111–36.

29 The term is proposed by Jan C. Jansen and Jürgen Osterhammel in *Decolonization: A Short History*, trans. Jeremiah Riemer (Princeton: Princeton University Press, 2017), 25.

30 See, for instance, Harald Fischer-Tiné, ed., *Anxieties, Fear, and Panic in Colonial Settings: Empires on the Verge of a Nervous Breakdown* (Cham: Springer, 2016); Jane Lyndon, *Imperial Emotions: The Politics of Empathy across the British Empire* (Cambridge: Cambridge University Press, 2020).

31 Jan C. Jansen and Jürgen Osterhammel, *Decolonization: A Short History*, trans. Jeremiah Riemer (Princeton: Princeton University Press, 2017), 2–13; Ruth Craggs and Claire Wintle, eds., *Cultures of Decolonisation: Transnational Productions and*

Practices, 1945–70 (Manchester: Manchester University Press, 2016), 3; Neetu Khanna, *The Visceral Logics of Decolonization* (Durham: Duke University Press, 2020).

32 J.H. Denison, *Emotion as the Basis of Civilization* (New York: Charles Scribner's Sons, 1928), 274–7.

33 Ahmed, *The Cultural Politics of Emotion,* 72–8, 98.

34 Emphasis added. Ahmed, *The Cultural Politics of Emotion*, 72–8, 98.

35 James Jasper, *The Emotions of Protest* (Chicago: University of Chicago Press, 2018), 29.

36 Rob Boddice, ed., *Pain and Emotion in Modern History* (New York: Palgrave Macmillan, 2014), 3.

37 James P. Jankowski, *Egypt's Young Rebels: Young Egypt, 1933–1952* (Stanford: Hoover Institution Press, 1975); Richard P. Mitchell, *The Society of the Muslim Brothers* (Oxford: Oxford University Press, 1969); Brynjar Lia, *The Society of the Muslim Brothers in Egypt: The Rise of an Islamic Mass Movement, 1928–1942* (Reading: Ithaca Press, 1998).

38 Botman, *The Rise of Egyptian Communism, 1939–1970*; Joel Beinin, *Was the Red Flag Flying There?* (Berkeley: University of California Press, 1990); Irmgard Schrand, *Jews in Egypt: Communists and Citizens* (Münster: Lit Verlag, 2004); Ginat, *A History of Egyptian Communism*; Ismael and el-Saʿid, *The Communist Movement in Egypt, 1920–1988*; and Roel Meijer, *The Quest for Modernity: Secular Liberal and Left-Wing Political Thought in Egypt, 1945–1958* (New York: Routledge, 2002).

39 See, for instance: Mohammed M. Hafez, *Why Muslims Rebel: Repression and Resistance in the Islamic World* (Boulder: Lynne Rienner Publishers, 2003); Roger Hardy, *The Muslim Revolt: A Journey through Political Islam* (London: Hurst, 2010); Quintan Wiktorowicz, *Islamic Activism: A Social Movement Theory Approach* (Bloomington: Indiana University Press, 2004); Ferran Izquierdo Brichs, John Etherington, and Laura Feliu, eds., *Political Islam in a Time of Revolt* (Cham: Springer International, 2017).

40 Jasper, *The Emotions of Protest*, 18; Ahmed, *The Cultural Politics of Emotion*, 10–12.

41 Pioneers of this approach include scholars like Susan J. Matt, Peter Stearns, and William Reddy, as well as organizations like the Australian Research Council's Center for Excellence for the History of Emotions (focused on emotions in European history) and the Max Planck Institute for Human Development (which spearheads a History of Emotions Research Center). See: Susan J. Matt, "Current Emotion Research in History: Or, Doing History from the Inside Out," *Emotion Review* 3, no. 1 (January 2011): 117–24; Susan J. Matt and Peter N. Stearns, eds., *Doing Emotions History* (Urbana: University of Illinois Press, 2014); Carol Zisowitz Stearns and Peter N. Stearns, *Emotion and Social Change: Toward a New*

Psychohistory (New York: Holmes & Meier, 1988); Geoffrey Cocks and Travis L. Crosby, *Psycho/History: Readings in the Method of Psychology, Psychoanalysis, and History* (New Haven: Yale University Press, 1987).

42 Kathleen Vongsathorn, "Africa," in *The Routledge History of Emotions in the Modern World*, ed. Katie Barclay and Peter N. Stearns (New York: Routledge, 2023), 124.

43 Kishwar Rizvi, ed., *Affect, Emotion, and Subjectivity in Early Modern Muslim Empires* (Leiden: Brill, 2017); Nil Tekgül, *Emotions in the Ottoman Empire: Politics, Society and Family in the Early Modern Era* (London: Bloomsbury, 2023).

44 Barbara H. Rosenwein, *Emotional Communities in the Early Middle Ages* (Ithaca: Cornell University Press, 2006), 2.

45 William M. Reddy, *The Navigation of Feeling: A Framework for the History of Emotions* (Cambridge: Cambridge University Press, 2001), 129.

46 Jayne Morgan and Kathleen Krone, "Bending the Rules of 'Professional' Display: Emotional Improvisation in Caregiver Performances," *Journal of Applied Communication Research* 29, no. 4 (2001): 317–40; Keelah E.G. Williams and Art Hinshaw, "Outbursts: An Evolutionary Approach to Emotions in the Mediation Context," *Negotiation Journal* 34, no. 2 (April 2018): 165–86.

47 James M. Jasper, "Emotions and Social Movements: Twenty Years of Theory and Research," *Annual Review of Sociology* 37 (2011): 285–303. Frédéric Volpi and James M. Jasper's edited volume *Microfoundations of the Arab Uprisings* (Amsterdam: Amsterdam University Press, 2018), for instance, contains a few essays that focus on the collective identity dimensions of emotions in protest movements.

48 John W. Du Bois and Elise Kärkkäinen, "Taking a Stance on Emotion: Affect, Sequence, and Intersubjectivity in Dialogic Interaction," *Text & Talk* 32, no. 4 (2012): 439–46; Ahmed, *The Cultural Politics of Emotion*, 5; Jasper, *The Emotions of Protest*, 4.

49 June Price Tangney, Jeff Stuewig, and Debra J. Mashek, "Moral Emotions and Moral Behavior," *Annual Review of Psychology* 58 (2007): 347. Also see Reddy, *The Navigation of Feeling*, 16–17; Ross A. Thompson, "Emotional Regulation and Emotional Development," *Educational Psychology Review* 3, no. 4 (December 1991): 269–307; Jonathan Haidt, "The Moral Emotions," in *Handbook of Affective Sciences*, ed. R.J. Davidson et al. (Oxford: Oxford University Press, 2003), 852–70; Amanda Barrett Cox, "Correcting Behaviors and Policing Emotions: How Behavioral Infractions Become Feeling-Rule Violations," *Symbolic Interaction* 39, no. 3 (August 2016): 484–503.

50 Damian R. Murray and Mark Schaller, "The Behavioral Immune System: Implications for Social Cognition, Social Interaction, and Social Influence," in *Advances in Experimental Social Psychology*, Vol. 53, ed. James M. Olson and Mark P. Zanna (Cambridge: Academic Press, 2016), 75–129; Yoel Inbar and David

Pizarro, "Pollution and Purity in Moral and Political Judgment," in *Advances in Experimental Moral Psychology*, ed. Hagop Sarkissian and Jennifer Cole Wright (London: Bloomsbury, 2014), 111–25.

51 I use here Charles Tilly's concept of a social movement as "a sustained, organized public effort making collective claims on target authorities." Charles Tilly, *Regimes and Repertoires* (Chicago: University of Chicago Press, 2006), 53; Charles Tilly, *Social Movements, 1768–2004* (Boulder: Paradigm Publishers, 2004), 3.

52 Stephanie Downes et al., eds., *Feeling Things: Objects and Emotions through History* (Oxford: Oxford University Press, 2018).

53 Aḥmad Riḍā, *Muʿjam Matn al-Lugha* (Beirut: Dār Maktabat al-Ḥayāt, 1958–61), Vol. 2, 86–7, Vol. 3, 329–32, Vol. 4, 136–8, 429; Marek M. Dziekan, "The Categorisation of Emotions in the Classical Arabic Language. A Preliminary Lexicographical Study," in *Codes and Rituals of Emotions in Asian and African Cultures*, ed. Nina Pawlak (Warsaw: ELIPSA, 2009), 63–81; Hans Wehr, *A Dictionary of Modern Written Arabic*, 3rd ed., ed. J. Milton Cown (Ithaca: Spoken Language Services, 1976), 174–5, 473–4, 620–1, 721.

54 Ben Prestel, *Emotional Cities*, 114.

55 David Sander, "Models of Emotion: The Affective Neuroscience Approach," in *The Cambridge Handbook of Human Affective Neuroscience*, ed. Jorge Armony and Patrik Vuilleumier (New York: Cambridge University Press, 2013), 16–17; Scott E. Jacobs and James J. Gross, "Emotion Regulation in Education," in *International Handbook of Emotions in Education*, ed. Reinhard Pekrun and Lisa Linnenbrink-Garcia (New York: Routledge, 2014), 184–5; James J. Gross et al., "The Tie That Binds? Coherence among Emotion Experience, Behavior, and Physiology," *Emotion* 5, no. 2 (2005): 175–6, 187.

56 The link between emotions and motivational systems is reflected in the discussion about emotions as "motivated states." See: Carla Bagnoli, *Morality and the Emotions* (Oxford: Oxford University Press, 2011).

57 Susanne Stadlbauer, "Language Ideologies in the Arabic Diglossia of Egypt," *Colorado Research in Linguistics* 22 (June 2010): 1–19.

58 Narratives are a cognitive strategy for organizing information and making sense of experience: selecting events and placing them in sequence helps order information and endow it with meaning. In other words, stories structure information into chains of cause and effect (called "cognitive causal chains"). See: Christophe Heintz, "Cognitive History and Cultural Epidemiology," in *Past Minds: Studies in Cognitive Historiography*, ed. Luther H. Martin and Jesper Sørensen (London: Equinox, 2011), 13; Hayden White, *The Content of the Form: Narrative Discourse and Historical Representation* (Baltimore: Johns Hopkins University Press, 1987), 14; Louis O. Mink, "Narrative Form as a Cognitive Instrument," in *The Writing of History: Literary Form and Historical Understanding*, ed. Robert H. Canary and Henry Kozicki (Madison: University of Wisconsin Press, 1978), 131; Gérard

Genette, *Narrative Discourse: An Essay in Method [Discours du récit]* trans. Jane E. Lewin (Ithaca: Cornell University Press, 1980), 25–7.

59 Stefán Snævarr, *Metaphors, Narratives, Emotions: Their Interplay and Impact* (Amsterdam: Editions Rodopi, 2010), 321–4; Mariano Longo, *Emotions through Literature: Fictional Narratives, Society and the Emotional Self* (New York: Routledge, 2020), 81–4; Keith Oatley, *The Passionate Muse: Exploring Emotion in Stories* (Oxford: Oxford University Press, 2012), 74–5.

60 For instance, stories can promote neural coupling, or the synchronization of speaker-listener hemodynamic responses. See: Greg J. Stephens, Lauren J. Silbert, and Uri Hasson, "Speaker–Listener Neural Coupling Underlies Successful Communication," *PNAS* 107, no. 32 (August 2010): 14425–30; Lauren J. Silbert et al., "Coupled Neural Systems Underlie the Production and Comprehension of Naturalistic Narrative Speech," *PNAS* 111, no. 43 (October 2014): 4687–96; Raymond A. Mar, "The Neural Bases of Social Cognition and Story Comprehension," *Annual Review of Psychology* 62 (2011): 103–34; Raymond A. Mar, "The Neuropsychology of Narrative: Story Comprehension, Story Production and Their Interrelation," *Neuropsychologia* 42 (2004): 1414–34; Christopher J. Honey et al., "Not Lost in Translation: Neural Responses Shared across Languages," *Journal of Neuroscience* 32, no. 44 (October 2012): 15277–83.

61 Formally, a script is a behavioral heuristic or cognitive knowledge structure that guides action. Michel de Certeau describes scripts when he notes that myths "offer their audience a repertory of tactics for future use," or phrased differently, "repertories of schemas of action." Michel de Certeau, *The Practice of Everyday Life* (Berkeley: University of California Press, 1984), 23–4; Robert G. Lord and Mary C. Kernan, "Scripts as Determinants of Purposeful Behavior in Organizations," *The Academy of Management Review* 12, no. 2 (1987): 265–77.

62 See here David Herman's synthesis of cognitive science and narratology. David Herman, "Scripts, Sequences, and Stories: Elements of a Postclassical Narratology," *PMLA* 112, no. 5 (October 1997): 1046–59.

63 Elaine M. Bennett, "Storytelling and the Moral Tradition: An Examination of the Pedagogy of Storytelling for Moral Enculturation," in *The Many Facets of Storytelling: Global Reflections on Narrative Complexity*, ed. Melanie Rohse et al. (Leiden: Brill, 2013), 13–21; Robert Reich, "Four Morality Tales," in *Popular Culture: An Introductory Text*, ed. Jack Nachbar and Kevin Lause (Madison: University of Wisconsin Press, 1992), 111.

64 Specifically, I use here Émile Durkheim's definition of morality a "system of rules of conduct"—which belongs to a collectivity, is invested with authority and sacrality, is enforced by sanctions, is interpreted differently by "each individual moral conscience," helps determine conduct, and changes according to historical and social setting. Émile Durkheim, "The Determination of Moral Facts," in *Sociology and Philosophy*, trans. D.F. Pocock (New York: The Free Press, 1974), 35–62; Emilé

Durkheim, *Moral Education*, trans. E.K. Wilson and H. Schnurer (New York: Free Press, 1973), 24.

65 de Certeau, *The Practice of Everyday Life*, 89.

66 I use the terms "emotional economy" and "moral economy" as a metaphor for describing how emotions and values circulate. The concepts of "emotional economy" and "affective economy" are similarly used by Sara Ahmed, "Affective Economies," *Social Text* 22, no. 2 (2004): 117–39 and Paula Ioanide, *The Emotional Politics of Racism* (Stanford: Stanford University Press, 2015). Ioanide, for instance, uses the term to reflect how "emotions function much like economies; they have mechanisms of circulation, accumulation, expression, and exchange that give them social currency, cultural legibility, and political power." Other scholars have used the term "emotional economy" to mean something else: the role of emotions in economics, or the investment of commodities with emotional importance. See: Hazel Christie et al., "The Emotional Economy of Housing," *Environment and Planning A* 40 (2008): 2296–312. The term "moral economy" similarly has multiple meanings. As coined by E.P. Thompson and used by social historians, the term "moral economy" more frequently means *an economy that is moral*—that is, the normative beliefs that a society holds about virtuous buying and selling behavior. See: E.P. Thompson, *The Making of the English Working Class* (New York: Pantheon, 1964), 66–7.

67 Ewan Palmer, "Video of Kyle Rittenhouse Crying Viewed over 2 Million Times," *Newsweek*, November 11, 2021, https://www.newsweek.com/kyle-rittenhouse-crying-video-trial-1648249; Kjell Vowles and Martin Hultman, "Dead White Men vs. Greta Thunberg: Nationalism, Misogyny, and Climate Change Denial in Swedish far-right Digital Media," *Australian Feminist Studies* 36, no. 110 (2021): 414–31; Nino Antadze, "Moral Outrage as the Emotional Response to Climate Injustice," *Environmental Justice* 13, no. 1 (2020): 1–26.

Chapter 2

1 Robert Clewis, "What Is Kant's Theory of Humor?" in *Ethics in Comedy: Essays on Crossing the Line*, ed. Steven A. Benko (Jefferson: McFarland & Co., 2020), 48–50; Robert Clewis, *Kant's Humorous Writings: An Illustrated Guide* (London: Bloomsbury, 2020).

2 Meir Hatina, *ʿUlamaʾ, Politics, and the Public Sphere: An Egyptian Perspective* (Salt Lake City: University of Utah Press, 2010), 96; Vivian Ibrahim, *The Copts of Egypt: The Challenges of Modernisation and Identity* (London: I.B. Tauris, 2011), 86; S.S. Hasan, *Christians versus Muslims in Modern Egypt* (Oxford: Oxford University Press, 2003), 59–60, 72–6.

3 The term is Ziad Fahmy's.

4 Beth Baron, *Egypt as Woman: Nationalism, Gender, and Politics* (Berkeley: University of California Press, 2005), 109–12; Margot Badran, *Feminists, Islam, and the Nation: Gender and the Making of Modern Egypt* (Princeton: Princeton University Press, 1995), 47, 160, 172, 190–1.

5 See: Mounah Abdallah Khouri, *Poetry and the Making of Modern Egypt: 1882–1922* (Leiden: Brill, 1971), 77–90; Ziad Fahmy, *Ordinary Egyptians: Creating the Modern Nation through Popular Culture* (Stanford: Stanford University Press, 2011), 92–5, 134, 145–9, 161–4; Joel Beinin and Zachary Lockman, *Workers on the Nile: Nationalism, Communism, Islam, and the Egyptian Working Class, 1882–1954* (London: I.B. Tauris, 1988), 7–13, 26–7.

6 See §§ 102, 178, 188, of the Egyptian Penal Code of 1937. Al-Saʿīd Muṣṭafá al-Saʿīd, *Qānūn al-ʿUqūbāt al-Miṣrī: al-Ṣādir b-al-Qānūn Raqm 58 li-Sanat 1937* (Cairo: Maṭbaʿat Fatḥ Allāh al-Yās Nūrī wa-Awlādihi, 1937), 97, 104, 148, 160.

7 See §§ 178, 270–7 of the Egyptian Penal Code of 1937. Al-Saʿīd, *Qānūn al-ʿUqūbāt al-Miṣrī*, 219, 223–30. Most of the laws against corruption of youth were abolished by Law No. 68 of 1951.

8 These criminal categories existed in French law until the passage of the French Penal Code of 1994. See, for instance, the French Penal Code of 1810 and the Law of 19-July 22, 1791: *Code pénal de l'empire français* (Paris: l'Imprimerie impériale, 1810), 44, 50–2; Désiré Dalloz, *Jurisprudence du XIX*[e] *siècle, vol. 3* (Brussels: Chez H. Tarlier, 1828), 91–115.

9 The Egyptian Constitution of 1923 (officially, "Royal Decree No. 42 of 1923 on Establishing a Constitutional System for the Egyptian State"), was in force from 1923 to 1930, and 1935–52. See: *Amr Malakī Raqm 42 li-Sanat 1923 bi-Waḍʿ Niẓām dustūrī lil-Dawla al-Miṣriyya* (Cairo: al-Maṭbaʿat al-Amīriyya, 1950).

10 See §§ 160–1 of the Egyptian Penal Code of 1937. Al-Saʿīd, *Qānūn al-ʿUqūbāt al-Miṣrī*, 133–4.

11 Again, as the development of the Egyptian legal system was informed by European law, these statutes against blasphemy were not unusual, being found in most European legal codes of the eighteenth to twentieth century. And as was the case in Egypt, European blasphemy laws were generally linked to the idea of public goods, and prohibitions against incitement, libel, or disturbing the peace. For an example of blasphemy charges in conjunction with incitement charges, see, for instance, the 1950 blasphemy case against Khālid Muḥammad Khālid. Khālid Muḥammad Khālid, *Min Huna Nabdaʾ*, 12th ed. (Beirut: Jamīʿ al-Ḥuqūq Maḥfūẓa lil-Muʿalif, 1974), 11–12.

12 Peter E. Pormann, "The Arab 'Cultural Awakening (Nahda)', 1870–1950, and the Classical Tradition," *International Journal of the Classical Tradition* 13, no. 1 (Summer 2006): 3–4, 19–20; Michael Kreutz, "The Greek Classics in Modern Middle Eastern Thought," in *Judaism, Christianity, and Islam in the Course of History: Exchange and Conflicts*, ed. Lothar Gall and Dietmar Willoweit

(Munich: De Gruyter, 2016), 87–9; Israel Gershoni, "Imagining and Reimagining the Past: The Use of History by Egyptian Nationalist Writers, 1919–1952," *History and Memory* 4, no. 2 (Fall–Winter 1992): 12–29; Walter Armbrust, The Formation of National Culture in Egypt in the Interwar Period: Cultural Trajectories," *History Compass* 7, no. 1 (2009): 155–80.

13 Omnia El Shakry, *The Arabic Freud: Psychoanalysis and Islam in Modern Egypt* (Princeton: Princeton University Press, 2017), 1–4, 13–17.

14 Joseph Ben Prestel, *Emotional Cities: Debates on Urban Change in Berlin and Cairo, 1860–1910* (Oxford: Oxford University Press, 2017), 106–15.

15 See, for instance, Ṣiḍḍīq Shaybūb, "Sīgmūnd Frūyd," *Majallat al-Risāla* 380, October 14, 1940, 1573–4; Muḥammad Ḥusnī Wilāya, "al-Aḥlām," *Majallat al-Risāla* 447, January 26, 1942, 94–5.

16 Shawqi Ḍayf [alt: Ḍaif], "al-Shiʿr," *Majallat al-Risāla* 28, January 15, 1934, 9–11; Jamīl Ṣalībā, "Ṣifāt al-Nisāʾ al-Nafsīyya," *Majallat al-Risāla* 248, April 4, 1938, 566–8; Zakī Mubārak, "Ilá Duktūr Ṭaha Ḥusayn Bik," *Majallat al-Risāla* 346, February 19, 1940, 249–51; Aḥmad Abū Zayd, "al-Funūn al-Jamīla," *Majallat al-Risāla* 500, February 1, 1943, 93–4.

17 Ibid.; Shaybūb, "Sīgmūnd Frūyd," 1573–4.

18 Ibid.

19 Efraim Barak, "Egyptian Intellectuals in the Shadow of British Occupation," *British Journal of Middle Eastern Studies* 35, no. 2 (August 2008): 174–8; Gershoni, "Imagining and Reimagining the Past," 12–29; Israel Gershoni and James P. Jankowski, *Redefining the Egyptian Nation, 1930–1945* (Cambridge: Cambridge University Press, 1995), 2–7, 44–9, 57–8, 65.

20 Fahmy, *Ordinary Egyptians*, 33, 74–7; Gershoni and Jankowski, *Redefining the Egyptian Nation*, 63–4.

21 Anthony Gorman, *Historians, State and Politics in Twentieth Century Egypt: Contesting the Nation* (New York: Routledge, 2003), 36.

22 André Raymond, *Cairo*, trans. Willard Wood (Cambridge: Harvard University Press, 2000), 317–21.

23 Nancy Y. Reynolds, *A City Consumed: Urban Commerce, the Cairo Fire, and the Politics of Decolonization in Egypt* (Stanford: Stanford University Press, 2012).

24 Baron, *Egypt as Woman*, 109–12; Badran, *Feminists, Islam, and the Nation*, 47, 160, 172, 190–1.

25 Phil Hopkins, *Mass Moralizing: Marketing and Moral Storytelling* (Lanham: Lexington Books, 2015), 2, 11–16.

26 Marie Virolle, *Gestes d'Algérie* (Paris: Karthala, 2007); Geneviève Calbris, "Geste et parole," *Langue français* 68 (1985): 66–84; Robert A. Barakat, "Arabic Gestures," *Folklore* 6, no. 4 (Spring 1973): 749–93.

27 Iman Farag, "Private Lives, Public Affairs: The Uses of Adab," in *Muslim Traditions and Modern Techniques of Power*, ed. Armando Salvatore (New Brunswick: Transaction, 2001), 93–120.

28 See, for instance, Zakī Mubārak, "al-Ḥadīth dhū shujūn," *Majallat al-Risāla* 465, June 1, 1942, 578; ʿAbd al-Qādir al-Maghrabī, "al-Taṭawwur al-ijtimāʿī baʿda al-ḥarb," *Majallat al-Risāla* 617, April 30, 1945, 443–5; Sayyid Quṭb, "al-Lugha al-ʿArabiyya fī al-ʿālam al-islāmī," *Majallat al-Risāla* 965, December 31, 1951, 1469–70.

29 Fawwaz Al-Abed Al-Haq and Ahmad Khair Allah Al Sharif, "A Comparative Study of Some Metaphorical Conceptualizations of Happiness and Anger in English and Arabic" (Master's Thesis, Yarmouk University, 2007); Ahmad El-Sharif, "The Muslim Prophetic Tradition: Spatial Source Domains for Metaphorical Expressions," in *Religion Language and the Human Mind*, ed. Paul Chilton and Monika Kopytowska (Oxford: Oxford University Press, 2017), 263–93; Ahmed Abdul-Raheem, "Moral Metaphor and Gender in Arab Visual Culture: Debunking Western Myths," *Social Semiotics* (2019), DOI: 10.1080/10350330.2019.1604991. For examples of similar practices in English, French, and Persian, see: Shahrzad Pirzad Mashak et al., "A Comparative Study on Basic Emotion Conceptual Metaphors in English and Persian Literary Texts," *International Education Studies* 5, no. 1 (February 2012): 200–7; Fabienne Baider and Georgeta Cislaru, eds., *Cartographie des émotions* (Paris: Presses Sorbonne Nouvelle, 2013); Ad Foolen, "The Expressive Function of Language: Towards a Cognitive Semantic Approach," in *The Language of Emotions*, ed. Susanne Niemeier and René Dirven (Amsterdam: John Benjamins, 1997), 15–32.

30 George Lakoff and Mark Johnson, *Metaphors We Live By* (Chicago: University of Chicago Press, 1980), 105; Zoltán Kövecses, *Emotion Concepts* (New York: Springer-Verlag, 1990).

31 Here, Ricœur quotes Aristotle. Paul Ricœur, "The Metaphorical Process as Cognition, Imagination, and Feeling," *Critical Inquiry* 5, no. 1 (Autumn 1978): 144. Also see: Paul Ricœur, *The Rule of Metaphor: The Creation of Meaning in Language*, trans. Robert Czerny et al. (London: Routledge, 2004), 38.

32 Ahmad Elsharif, "The Muslim Prophetic Tradition: Spatial Source Domains for Metaphorical Expressions," in *Religion, Language, and the Human Mind*, ed. Paul Chilton and Monika Kopytowska (Oxford: Oxford University Press, 2018), 265.

33 For a brief explanation about the tradition of *adab* in Arab literature, see: Juan Eduardo Campo, "Adab," in *Encyclopedia of Islam* (New York: Facts on File, 2009), 11–12. Also see: Hoda Yousef, *Composing Egypt: Reading, Writing, and the Emergence of a Modern Nation, 1870–1930* (Stanford: Stanford University Press, 2016), 60; Richard Jacquemond, *Conscience of the Nation: Writers, State, and Society in Modern Egypt*, trans. David Tresilian (Cairo: The American University of Cairo Press, 2008) [covering the period from the 1952 coup forward].

34 Sayyid Muḥammad, *al-Taḥliyya wa-al-targhīb fī al-tarbiyya wa-al-tahdhīb*, 2nd ed. (Cairo: al-Maṭbaʿa al-Kubrá al-Amīriyya, 1896); Muḥammad Masʿūd, *al-Adab al-lāʿiq: sābiqan ādāb al-līyāqa* (Cairo: Maṭbaʿat al-Rābiṭa bi-Bāb al-Khalq bi-Miṣr, 1931), 18–19; Farag, "Private Lives, Public Affairs," 93–120.

35 For non-Arabophone examples of this, see T.O. Beidelman, *Moral Imagination in Kaguru Modes of Thought* (Bloomington: Indiana University Press, 1986). For a sociological explanation, see: William E. Thompson and Jennifer C. Gibbs, eds., *Deviance and Deviants: A Sociological Approach* (Oxford: Wiley Blackwell, 2017); Clifton D. Bryant ed., *Deviant Behavior: Readings in the Sociology of Norm Violation* (New York: Taylor and Francis, 1990).

36 Mona L. Russell, *Creating the New Egyptian Woman: Consumerism, Education, and National Identity, 1863–1922* (New York: Palgrave Macmillan, 2004); Reynolds, *A City Consumed.*

37 Liat Kozma, "White Drugs in Interwar Egypt: Decadent Pleasures, Emaciated Fellahin, and the Campaign against Drugs," *Comparative Studies of South Asia, Africa and the Middle East* 33, no. 1 (2013): 89–101; Khaled Fahmy, "Prostitution in Egypt in the Nineteenth Century," in *Outside In: On the Margins of the Modern Middle East*, ed. Eugene Rogan (London: I.B. Tauris, 2002), 77–103. ʿImād Hilāl, *Al-Baghāyā fī Miṣr: Dirāsa Tārīkhiyya Ijtimāʿiyya, 1834–1949* (Cairo: Al-ʿArabī li-l-Nashr wa-l-Tawzīʿ, 2001); Shaun T. Lopez, "The Dangers of Dancing: The Media and Morality in 1930s Egypt," *Comparative Studies of South Asia, Africa, and the Middle East* 24, no. 1 (2004): 97–105; Viola Shafik, "Prostitute for a Good Reason: Stars and Morality in Egypt," *Women's Studies International Forum* 24, no. 6 (2001): 711–25.

38 Lisa Pollard, "From Husbands and Housewives to Suckers and Whores: Marital-Political Anxieties in the 'House of Egypt', 1919–48," *Gender and History* 21, no. 3 (November 2009): 647–69; Hanan Kholoussy, *For Better, for Worse: The Marriage Crisis That Made Modern Egypt* (Stanford: Stanford University Press, 2010).

39 Indira Falk Gesink, *Islamic Reform and Conservatism: Al-Azhar and the Evolution of Modern Sunni Islam* (New York: I.B. Tauris, 2014); B.L. Carter, *The Copts in Egyptian Politics, 1918–1952* (Cairo: American University of Cairo Press, 1988); Eve M. Troutt-Powell, *A Different Shade of Colonialism: Egypt, Great Britain, and the Mastery of the Sudan* (Berkeley: University of California Press, 2003); Farag, "Private Lives, Public Affairs: The Uses of Adab," 93–120.

40 Beth Baron, *Egypt as Woman: Nationalism, Gender, and Politics* (Berkeley: University of California Press, 2007); Lisa Pollard, *Nurturing the Nation: The Family Politics of Modernizing, Colonizing, and Liberating Egypt, 1805–1923* (Berkeley: University of California Press, 2005).

41 See, for instance, Beth Baron, "Mothers, Morality, and Nationalism in Pre-1919 Egypt," in *The Origins of Arab Nationalism*, ed. Rashid Khalidi, Lisa Anderson, Muhammad Muslih, and Reeva S. Simon (New York: Columbia University Press, 1991), 271–88; Viola Shafik, "Prostitute for a Good Reason: Stars and Morality in Egypt," *Women's Studies International Forum* 24, no. 6 (2002): 711–25; Lopez, "The Dangers of Dancing," 97–105.

42 Aḥmad Amīn, "Kīmiyāʾ al-Afkār wa-l-ʿĀwaṭif," *Majallat al-Risāla* 103, June 24, 1935, 1007–8; Muḥammad Fahmī ʿAbd al-Laṭīf, "al-ʿĀṭifa," *Majallat al-Risāla* 275,

October 10, 1938, 1658–61; Shaybūb, "Sīgmūnd Frūyd," 1573–5; Muḥammad Ḥusnī Wilāya, "al-Shakhṣīyyat al-Histīriyya," *Majallat al-Risāla* 468, June 22, 1942, 639; Ḥamdī al-Ḥusaynī, "al-Ghazālī wa ʿIlm al-Nafs," *Majallat al-Risāla* 895, August 28, 1950, 970–1.

Chapter 3

1 See James Jacobs, "The War in North Africa, 1940–43: An Overview of the Role of the Union of South Africa," and Alan Jeffreys, "Training the Troops: The Indian Army in Egypt, Eritrea, and Libya, 1940–42," in *El Alamein and the Struggle for North Africa: International Perspectives from the Twenty-first Century*, ed. Jill Edwards (Cairo: American University in Cairo Press, 2012), 20–7, 38–50.
2 Didar Fawzy-Rossano, *Mémoires d'une militante communiste (1942–1990): du Caire à Alger, Paris et Genève, lettres aux miens* (Paris: Éditions l'Harmattan, 1997), 31, 39–53, 135; Gilles Perrault, *A Man Apart: The Life of Henri Curiel*, trans. Bob Cumming (London: Zed Books, 1987), 84, 133–5.
3 Ibid.
4 Aḥmad ʿĀdil Kamāl, *Al-Nuqaṭ Fawqa al-Ḥurūf: al-Ikhwān al-Muslimūn wa-l-Niẓām al-Khāṣṣ* (Cairo: Al-Zahrāʾ li-l-Iʿlām al-ʿArabī, Qism al-Nashr, 1989), 42–55.
5 ʿĀdil Kamāl, *Al-Nuqaṭ Fawqa al-Ḥurūf*, 42–55.
6 Ibid.
7 The *iftiqād* [inspection, check], was a popular technology of organization in the 1930s and 1940s. The Muslim Brotherhood used it in their recruiting; Coptic youth organizers also used it as a strategy. See: S.S. Hasan, *Christians versus Muslims in Modern Egypt* (Oxford: Oxford University Press, 2003), 79.
8 ʿĀdil Kamāl, *Al-Nuqaṭ Fawqa al-Ḥurūf*, 42–55.
9 Ahmed Helal, "Egypt's Overlooked Contribution to World War II," in *The World in World Wars: Experiences, Perceptions and Perspectives from Africa and Asia*, ed. Heike Liebau et al. (Ledien: Brill, 2010), 217–47; Artemis Cooper, *Cairo in the War, 1939–1945* (London: Hamish Hamilton, 1989), 112–19; Arthur Goldschmidt Jr., *Historical Dictionary of Egypt*, 4th ed. (Lanham: Rowman and Littlefield, 2013), 442.
10 Ibid.
11 My thanks to Dr. Mona Russell for sharing her family's memories of this game, while serving as a discussant at a panel at American University.
12 Farīda, Queen of Egypt.
13 Egypt's ruling political party.
14 Muṣṭafá Naḥḥās Pasha, the Egyptian prime minister and head of the Wafd.

15 English slang: Egyptian.

16 A recording of Henderson singing the song himself in March 1951 exists in the public trust, as part of an interview with Alan Lomax. See: Hamish Henderson, "The Ballad of King Faruk and Queen Farida," in *Ballads of World War II* (Glasgow: Caledonian Press, n.d.), 19–22; Hamish Henderson, Interview with Alan Lomax, London, March 6, 1951, T3266.0, Track 8, Association for Cultural Equity; http://research.culturalequity.org/get-audio-detailed-recording.do?recordingId=7171#. For other [equally bawdy] versions of the song and an anthropological interpretation of its meanings, see Les Cleveland, "Soldiers' Songs: The Folklore of the Powerless," *New York Folklore* 11, nos. 1–4 (1985): 79–97.

17 Ibid.

18 ʿImād Aḥmad Hilāl, *Al-Baghāyā fī Miṣr: Dirāsa Tārīkhiyya Ijtimāʿiyya, 1834–1949* (Cairo: Al-ʿArabī li-l-Nashr wa-l-Tawzīʿ, 2001); Hanan Hammad, "Between Egyptian 'National Purity' and 'Local Flexibility': Prostitution in al-Mahalla al-Kubra in the First Half of the 20th Century," *Journal of Social History* 44, no. 3 (Spring 2011): 768–4.

19 Mohammed Neguib, *Egypt's Destiny* (London: Victor Gollancz, 1955), 84–5. [English version predates the Arabic.]

20 Fawzy-Rossano, *Mémoires d'une militante communiste*, 52, 101.

21 Mubārak ʿAbdu Faḍl, "Mudhakkirāt," in Rifʿat Saʿīd, *Hākadhā Takallama al-Shuyūʿīyūn: Maḥāḍir Niqāsh, Taqārīr, Mudhakkirāt, Rasāʾil, Taḥqīqāt Qaḍāʿīyyah, Bayānāt Intikhābiyya* (Cairo: Sharikat al-Amal li-l-Ṭibāʿa wa-l-Nashr wa-l-Tawzīʿ, 1989), 125–6; ʿĀdil Kamāl, *Al-Nuqaṭ Fawqa al-Ḥurūf*, 123–79.

22 Judith A. Byfield, "Producing for the War," in *Africa and World War II*, ed. Judith A. Byfield et al. (Cambridge: Cambridge Universty Press, 2015), 37; Helal, "Egypt's Overlooked Contribution to World War II," 217–47.

23 Ibid.; Peter L. Hahn, *The United States, Great Britain, and Egypt, 1945–1956: Strategy and Diplomacy in the Early Cold War* (Chapel Hill: University of North Carolina Press, 1991), 56–7.

24 James Jankowski, "The View from the Embassy: British Assessments of Egyptian Attitudes during World War II," in *Arab Responses to Fascism and Nazism*, ed. Israel Gershoni (Austin: University of Texas Press, 2014), 171–94; Helal, "Egypt's Overlooked Contribution to World War II," 217–47.

25 Charles D. Smith, "4 February 1942: Its Causes and Its Influence on Egyptian Politics and on the Future of Anglo-Egyptian Relations, 1937–1945," *International Journal of Middle East Studies* 10 (1979): 453–79.

26 Sayyid Quṭb, "Ayna Inta Yā Muṣṭafā Kāmil?!" *Majallat al-Risāla* 648, December 3, 1945, 1309–10.

27 Khālid Muḥyī al-Dīn, *Wa-l-Ān Atakallam* (Cairo: Markaz al-Ahrām lil-Tarjama wa-al-Nashr, Mu'assasat al-Ahrām, 1992), 35.

28 Muḥammad Najīb, *Kuntu Ra'īs li-Miṣr: Mudhakkirāt Muḥammad Najīb* (Cairo: Al-Maktab al-Miṣrī al-Ḥadīth, 1984), 66.
29 Joel Gordon, *Nasser's Blessed Movement: Egypt's Free Officers and the July Revolution* (New York: Oxford University Press, 1992), 18–20.
30 "Report to the Empire Communist Parties Conference in London," 26 February to 3 March 1947, in *Communism*, FO 141/1158 [1947].
31 Makram ʿUbayd, *Al-Kitāb al-Aswad fī al-ʿAhd al-Aswad* (Cairo: Al-Markaz al-ʿArabī lil-Baḥth wa-al-Nashr, 1984 [First ed. 1943]).
32 Anwar Sadat, *In Search of Identity* (New York: Harper and Row, 1978), 58.
33 Rifʿat Saʿīd, *Tārīkh al-Munaẓẓamāt al-Yasāriyya al-Miṣriyya, 1940–1950* (Cairo: Dār al-Thaqāfa al-Jadīda, 1976), 89.
34 Interview with Mustafa Haykal, in Rifʿat Saʿīd, *Hākadhā Takallama al-Shuyūʿīyūn*, 212.
35 Laṭīfa al-Zayyāt interview with Selma Botman, 9 February 1980, Cairo. As quoted in Selma Botman, *The Rise of Egyptian Communism, 1939–1970*, 51–2.
36 Interview with Mustafa Haykal, in Rifʿat Saʿīd, *Hākadhā Takallama al-Shuyūʿīyūn*, 212; John Calvert, *Sayyid Qutb and the Origins of Radical Islamism* (Oxford: Oxford University Press, 2013), 186.
37 Anonymous, "al-Siyāsa fī Ḥadīqat al-Ḥayawān," *Ākhir Sāʿa* 719, August 4, 1948, 22.
38 See: Draft telegram from Lampson to Eden, March 20, 1936, FO 371/20108 and Kelly to Eden, June 4, 1936, FO 141/772, both quoted in Matthew H. Ellis, *King Me: The Political Culture of Monarchy in Interwar Egypt and Iraq* (MA thesis, Oxford University, 2005), 86–91. Also see Elie Podeh, *The Politics of National Celebrations in the Arab Middle East* (Cambridge: Cambridge University Press, 2011), 63–4.
39 Lampson to F.O., June 6, 1937, FO 371/20884, as quoted in Ellis, *King Me*, 91.
40 Lampson to F.O., July 5, 1937, FO 371/20884 and Lampson to F.O., July 29, 1937, FO 371/20884, as quoted in Ellis, *King Me*, 91–2.
41 See *al-Muṣawwar* 953, January 15, 1943. The British ambassador also noticed the new beard, and gave him "a good deal of chaff" about it. Sir Miles Lampson, *The Killearn Diaries, 1934–1946: The Diplomatic and Personal Record of Lord Killearn (Sir Miles Lampson), High Commissioner and Ambassador, Egypt*, ed. Trefor E. Evans (London: Sidgwick and Jackson, 1972), 246.
42 "Illī yaʿīsh yāmā yashūf!" See Muṣṭafá Naḥḥās, *Mudhakkirāt Muṣṭafá al-Naḥḥās: Rubʿ Qarn min al-Siyāsa fī Miṣr, 1927–1952, Vol. 2*, ed. Aḥmad ʿIzz al-Dīn (Cairo: al-ʿUṣūr al-Jadīdah, 2000).
43 Sayyid ʿAshmāwī, *Al-ʿAyb fī al-Dhāt al-Maṣūnah: Inhiyār Haybat hḤukm al-Fard al-Muṭlaq, al-Khidīwī, al-Sulṭān, al-Malik, Miṣr, 1882–1952* (Cairo: Markaz al-Maḥrūsa lil-Buḥūth wa-al-Tadrīb wa-l-Nashr, 1999), 205–18. For text of the Egyptian lèse-majesté clause, see § 179 of the Egyptian Penal Code of 1937, in al-Saʿīd, *Qānūn al-ʿuqūbāt al-Miṣrī*, 149–150. For a side-by-side comparison of the texts of Egyptian and French lèse-majesté laws, see § 162 of the Egyptian Penal

Code of 1883 and § 156 of Law No. 32 of 1922. Appendix 1 in ʿAshmāwī, *al-ʿAyb fī al-Dhāt al-Maṣūna*, 241.

44 ʿAshmāwī, *al-ʿAyb fī al-Dhāt al-Maṣūnah*, 207–18.

45 On the social and moral functions of gossip, see: Gary Alan Fine, "The Social Organization of Adolescent Gossip: The Rhetoric of Moral Evaluation," in *Children's Worlds and Children's Language*, ed. Jenny Cook-Gumperz et al. (Berlin: Mouton de Gruyter, 1986), 405–24; Niko Besnier, *Gossip and the Everyday Production of Politics* (Honolulu: University of Hawai'i Press, 2009); Tuulikki Pietilä, *Gossip, Markets, and Gender: How Dialogue Constructs Moral Value in Post-Socialist Kilimanjaro* (Madison: University of Wisconsin Press, 2007).

46 Murtaḍá al-Marāghī, *Gharāʾib min ʿAhd Fārūq wa Bidāyat al-Thawra al-Miṣriyya* (Beirut: Dār al-Nahār, 1976).

47 Jalāl ʿAllūba, *al-Malik wa-Amīr al-Baḥr: Mudhakkirāt Amīr al-Baḥr Ḥaḍrat Ṣāḥib al-ʿIzza Jalāl Bik ʿAllūba, Qāʾid al-Yūkhūt al-Malakiyya wa-Yāwir Jalālat al-Malik* (Cairo: Māks Jurūp, 1998), 64–9; Lampson, *The Killearn Diaries, 1934–1946*, 359–60; Hugh McLeave, *The Last Pharaoh: Farouk of Egypt* (New York: McCall Publishing Company, 1970).

48 The comment was most likely a slight to Fāʾiqa and Fatḥīya (in America) and Fawzīya (divorced). Fārūq's fourth sister, Fāʾiza, may not have been intended in the comment, as she was married at the time. See: FO 141/1303 (no. 14) and Ḥanafī al-Maḥallāwī, *Al-Malika Nāzlī* (Cairo: Al-Dār al-Miṣriyya al-Lubnāniyya, 1995), 209–15.

49 Aḥmad Ḥusayn, *Mudhakkirāt Aḥmad Ḥusayn Raʾīs Miṣr al-Fatāh* (Cairo: Al-Hayʾa al-Miṣriyya al-ʿĀmma li-l-Kitāb, 2007); ʿAshmāwī, *Al-ʿAyb fī al-Dhāt al-Maṣūna*, 223–4; James P. Jankowski, *Egypt's Young Rebels: Young Egypt, 1933–1952* (Stanford: Hoover Institution Press, 1975), 93–4.

50 Khaled Mohi El Din, *Memories of a Revolution: Egypt 1942* (Cairo: The American University in Cairo Press, 1995), 42–4.

51 "Min bayt al-ʿahara ʿala bayt al-ṭahara, yā Farīdah!" An alternate but similar chant was "Kharajat min bayt al-daʿāra ilá bayt al-ṭahāra," or "She [Farīda] went from the whorehouse to the house of purity." ʿAshmāwī, *al-ʿAyb fī al-dhāt al-maṣūna*, 214–15.

52 Aḥmad Ḥasan al-Zayyāt, "Mithl al-Miṣriyya al-ḥadītha," *Majallat al-Risāla* 468, June 22, 1942, 633–4. Lisa Pollard and Beth Baron have authored a few excellent studies that expand on this theme, examining how ideas about family, home, and motherhood played in to Egyptian nationalism in the nineteenth and twentieth centuries. See: Lisa Pollard, "From Husbands and Housewives to Suckers and Whores: Marital-Political Anxieties in the 'House of Egypt', 1919–48," *Gender and History* 21, no. 3 (November 2009): 647–69; Lisa Pollard, *Nurturing the Nation: The Family Politics of Modernizing, Colonizing, and Liberating Egypt, 1805–1923* (Berkeley: University of California Press, 2005); Beth Baron, "Mothers,

Morality, and Nationalism in Pre-1919 Egypt," in *The Origins of Arab Nationalism*, ed. Rashid Khalidi, Lisa Anderson, Muhammad Muslih and Reeva S. Simon (New York: Columbia University Press, 1991), 271–88; Beth Baron, *Egypt as Woman: Nationalism, Gender, and Politics* (Berkeley: University of California Press, 2007).

53 Zakī Mubārak, "al-Ṣawm ʿan al-Qāhira fī yawm al-ʿīd," *Majallat al-Risāla* 445, January 12, 1942, 32–3.

54 Pollard, *Nurturing the Nation*, 91–9, 171–94.

55 Pollard, "From Husbands and Housewives to Suckers and Whores," 661–5.

56 Makram ʿUbayd, *al-Kitāb al-Aswad fī al-ʿAhd al-Aswad*, 162, 264–73.

57 Abū Sayf Yūsuf, "Muqadima," in *Wathāʾiq wa Mawāqif min Tārīkh al-Yasār al-Miṣrī, 1941–1957* (Cairo: Sharikat al-Amal li-l-Ṭibāʿa wa-l-Nashr, 2000). [Henceforth, *Wathāʾiq*]; J. Heyworth-Dunne, *Religious and Political Trends in Modern Egypt* (Washington, DC, 1950), 30. (He provides a partial list of these organizations on pages 90–1 of the book).

58 Perrault, *A Man Apart*, 119–30.

Chapter 4

1 Abū al-Futūḥ ʿAfīfī, *Riḥlatī maʿa al-Ikhwān al-Muslimīn* (Cairo: Abū al-Futūḥ ʿAfīfī, 2003).

2 For more on narratives of "collective significance," see Arie Kruglanski et al., "Cognitive Mechanisms in Violent Extremism," *Cognition* 188 (July 2019): 119.

3 Cristine H. Legare and Mark Nielsen, "Imitation and Innovation: The Dual Engines of Cultural Learning," *Trends in Cognitive Sciences* 19, no. 11 (November 2015): 688–99.

4 Shaul Shalvi et al., "Self-Serving Justifications: Doing Wrong and Feeling Moral," *Current Directions in Psychological Science* 24, no. 2 (2015): 125–30.

5 James P. Jankowski, *Egypt's Young Rebels: Young Egypt, 1933–1952* (Stanford: Hoover Institution Press, 1975), 9–41; Israel Gershoni and James Jankowski, *Confronting Fascism in Egypt: Dictatorship versus Democracy in the 1930s* (Stanford: Stanford University Press, 2010), 234–65.

6 Israel Gershoni and James P. Jankowski, *Egypt, Islam, and the Arabs: The Search for Egyptian Nationhood, 1900–1930* (New York: Oxford University Press, 1983), 164–90; Jankowski, *Egypt's Young Rebels*, 9–41; Gershoni and Jankowski, *Confronting Fascism in Egypt*, 234–65.

7 Aḥmad Ḥusayn, *Imānī* (Cairo: n.p., 1936), 19–33.

8 Emphasis added, Ibid.

9 Emphasis added, Aḥmad Ḥusayn, *Niṣf Qarn maʿa al-ʿUrūba wa-Qadīyyat Filasṭīn* [1972], as translated by and quoted in Gershoni and Jankowski, *Egypt, Islam, and the Arabs*, 175.

10 Ines W. Jindra, *A New Model of Religious Conversion: Beyond Network Theory and Social Constructivism* (Leiden: Brill, 2014), 87–122. Also see: Henri Gooren, *Religious Conversion and Disaffiliation: Tracing Patterns of Change in Faith Practices* (New York: Palgrave Macmillan, 2010).

11 David A. Snow and Richard Machalek, "The Convert as a Social Type," *Sociological Theory* 1 (1983): 259–89; David A. Snow, "The Sociology of Conversion," *Annual Review of Psychology* 10 (1984): 167–90; Christy M. Ponticelli, "Crafting Stories of Sexual Identity Reconstruction," *Social Psychology Quarterly* 62, no. 2 (1999): 157–72; Sarah Hards, "Tales of Transformation: The Potential of a Narrative Approach to Pro-Environmental Practices," *Geoforurm* 43, no. 4 (June 2012): 760–71.

12 *Miṣr al-Fatāh* 33, September 12, 1945; *Miṣr al-Fatāh* 135, November 24, 1947; *Miṣr al-Fatāh* 222, January 2, 1950; Jankowski, *Egypt's Young Rebels*, 9–41.

13 Haggai Erlich, *Students and University in Twentieth Century Egyptian Politics* (London: Frank Cass, 1989), 108–25.

14 ʿAlī Shalabī, *Miṣr al-Fatāh wa Dawruhā fī al-Siyāsa al-Miṣriyya, 1933–1941* (Cairo: Dār al-Kitāb al-Jāmiʿī, 1982), 93–103.

15 Compare this with the abstract Islamic theological discussions in *al-Ikhwān al-Muslimīn* (which resumed printing in August 1942).

16 "The Young Egypt Party," Memorandum from Colonel G.J. Jenkins of May 18, 1944, Ref. 231/15/144, in *Young Egypt Party*, FO 141/951 [1944].

17 Ibid.; "Minutes," June 20, 1944, in *Young Egypt Party* FO/141/951 [1944].

18 "Memorandum" from Sir Walter Smart, June 9, 1944, Ref. 231/16/44 and Correspondence from Sir Walter Smart to Lieutenant General R.G.W.H. Stone, August 9, 1944, in *Young Egypt Party*, FO 141/951 [1944].

19 In Arabic: "al-Ḍarūrāt tubīḥu al-maḥẓūrāt" (necessity allows the forbidden). Dispatch from Colonel Jenkins, June 9, 1944, in *Young Egypt Party*, FO 141/951 [1944].

20 "Intelligence Report No. 449," November 4, 1944, Ref. 231/28/44, in *Young Egypt Party*, FO 141/951 [1944].

21 Jankowski, *Egypt's Young Rebels*, 93–4, 109–19.

22 *Miṣr al-Fatāh* no. 222, January 2, 1950.

23 Lit: "Bearer of the Turban of the Devout and Pious." The phrase was most famously applied to Wafdist Copt politician Makram ʿUbayd, who infamously fluctuated between liberal declarations and attempts to court the Muslim Brotherhood. ʿArafa ʿAbduh ʿAlī, "ʿIndamā Yaʿlū Sulṭān al-Kalima Fawq Kalima al-Sulṭān: Muḥammad al-Tābiʿī, Birins al-Ṣiḥāfa al-ʿArabiyya," *al-Ahrām al-ʿArabī*, March 21, 2017, http://arabi.ahram.org.eg/News/ 107310.aspx.

24 Ḥasan al-Banna, *Mudhakkirāt al-Daʿwa wa-l-Dāʿīyya* (Kuwait: Maktabat Āfāq, 2012 [First ed. 1950]), 8–26; Gudrun Krämer, *Hasan al-Banna* (London: Oneworld, 2013).

25 al-Banna, *Mudhakkirāt al-Da ʿwa wa-l-Dā ʿ īyya*, 43–85; Jamāl al-Banna, *Khiṭābāt Ḥasan al-Banna al-Shābb ilá Abīhi* (Cairo: Dār al-Fikr al-Islāmī, 1990), 43–4; Brynjar Lia, "Autobiography or Fiction? Ḥasan al-Banna's Memoirs Revisited," *Journal of Arabic and Islamic Studies* 15 (2015): 199–226.

26 Ibid.; Mehdi Sajid, "A Reappraisal of the Role of Muḥibb al-Dīn al-Khaṭīb and the YMMA in the Rise of the Muslim Brotherhood," *Islam and Christian–Muslim Relations* 29, no. 2 (2018): 195–200.

27 Johannes J.G. Jansen, "Ḥasan al-Banna's Earliest Pamphlet," *Die Welt des Islams* 32, no. 2 (1992): 254–8; Heather J. Sharkey, *American Evangelicals in Egypt: Missionary Encounters in an Age of Empire* (Princeton: Princeton University Press, 2008), 107; Beth Baron, *The Orphan Scandal: Christian Missionaries and the Rise of the Muslim Brotherhood* (Stanford: Stanford University Press, 2014), 85–150; Israel Gershoni, "The Muslim Brothers and the Arab Revolt in Palestine, 1936–39," *Middle Eastern Studies* 22, no. 3 (July 1986): 381–2.

28 Notably, *al-Ikhwān al-Muslimīn*'s first issue listed al-Khaṭīb as the journal's director, Shaykh Ṭanṭāwī Jawharī as the editor, and al-Banna as the "editor of the religious section." Sajid, "A Reappraisal of the Role of Muḥibb al-Dīn al-Khaṭīb," 203. Also see: Baron, *The Orphan Scandal*, 85–150; Sharkey, *American Evangelicals in Egypt*, 106–30; Maḥmūd ʿAssāf, *Ma ʿa al-Imām al-Shahīd Ḥasan al-Bannā* (Cairo: Maktabat ʿAyn Shams, 1993), 32–4; Richard P. Mitchell, *The Society of the Muslim Brothers* (Oxford: Oxford University Press, 1969), 185–8.

29 ʿAbd al-Fattah Muhammad el-Awaisi, *The Muslim Brothers and the Palestine Question 1928–1947* (London: Tauris, 1998); Gershoni, "The Muslim Brothers and the Arab Revolt in Palestine, 1936–9," 367–97.

30 Yūsuf al-Qaraḍāwī, *Ibn al-Qarya wa-l-Kuttāb: Malāmiḥ Sīra wa-Masīra* (Cairo: Dār al-Shurūq, 2002), 20.

31 See Krämer, *Hasan al-Banna*, [n.p.]; Mitchell, *The Society of the Muslim Brothers*, 328–9; Gershoni and Jankowski, *Redefining the Egyptian Nation*, 16; Zakarīyā Bayyūmī, *al-Ikhwān al-Muslimūn wa-l-Jamā ʿāt al-Islāmiyya fī al-Ḥayāt al-Siyāsiyya al-Miṣriyya, 1928–1948* (Cairo: Maktabat Wahbah, 1979), 85–7.

32 Giedre Šabasevičiute, *Sayyid Qutb: An Intellectual Biography* (Syracuse: Syracuse University Press, 2021), 139–40.

33 Brynjar Lia, *Society of the Muslim Brothers in Egypt: The Rise of an Islamic Mass Movement, 1928–1942* (Reading: Ithaca Press, 1998), 170.

34 Jābir Qumayḥah, *Dhikrayātī ma ʿa Da ʿwa al-Ikhwān fī al-Manzila Daqahliyya* (Giza: Markaz al-I ʿlām al- ʿArabī, 2009).

35 ʿAssāf, *Ma ʿa al-Imām al-Shahīd Ḥasan al-Bannā*, 226–7.

36 Lia, *Society of the Muslim Brothers*, 103–8; Mitchell, *The Society of the Muslim Brothers*, 31.

37 Aḥmad ʿĀdil Kamāl, *al-Nuqaṭ Fawqa al-Ḥurūf: al-Ikhwān al-Muslimūn wa-l-Niẓām al-Khāṣṣ* (Cairo: Al-Zahrāʾ li-l-I ʿlām al- ʿArabī, Qism al-Nashr, 1989), 78–90.

38 Khālid Muḥyī al-Dīn similarly wrote "Honestly, Ḥasan al-Banna possessed the unique ability to persuade and infiltrate the souls of his listeners." Khālid Muḥyī al-Dīn, *Wa-l-Ān Atakallam* [And Now I Speak] (Cairo: Markaz al-Ahrām li-l-Tarjama wa-al-Nashr, Mu'assasat al-Ahrām, 1992), 44.

39 Jābir Qumayḥah, *Dhikrayātī ma'a Da'wa al-Ikhwān fī al-Manzila Daqahliyya* (Giza: Markaz al-I'lām al-'Arabī, 2009).

40 Anwar al-Jundī, "Ḥasan al-Bannā, al-Rajul al-Qur'ānī," *Majallat al-Risāla* 982, April 28, 1952, 462–3.

41 Ḥasan al-Bannā, "Bayna al-Ams wa-l-Yawm," *Majmū'at Rasā'il al-Imām al-Shahīd Ḥasan al-Bannā* (Dār al-Ḥaḍāra al-Islāmiyya, 1980), 93–108. Unless otherwise noted, page numbers henceforth refer to the *rasā'il* as printed in this edition.

42 Ibid.

43 R. Stephen Humphreys, "Qur'anic Myth and Narrative Structure in Early Islamic Historiography," 217–90; Mansoor Moaddel, *Islamic Modernism, Nationalism, and Fundamentalism: Episode and Discourse* (Chicago: University of Chicago Press, 2005), 215–20.

44 Ḥasan al-Bannā, "Hal naḥnu qawm 'amaliyūn?" *Majmū'at Rasā'il al-Imām al-Shahīd Ḥasan al-Bannā* (Dār al-ḥaḍārah al-Islāmīyyah, 1980), 81.

45 Jamāl al-Dīn 'Abd al-Fattāh and 'Abd al-Karīm Manṣūr eds., *Qaḍīyat Sayyārat al-Jīb, al-Ḥaythīyāt wa Naṣṣ al-Ḥukm* (Cairo: Dār al-Fikr al-Islāmī, 1951), 61.

46 Ḥasan al-Bannā, "Ilá Ay Shay' Nad'ū al-Nās?" 42; Ḥasan al-Bannā, "Risāla al-Ta'ālīm," 369.

47 The verse in its entirety: "For each one is successive before and behind him who protect him by the decree of God. Indeed, God will not change the condition of a people until they change what is in themselves. And when God intends for a people ill, there is no repelling it. And there is not for them besides him any patron." (Surāt al-Ra'd 13:11) See: Ḥasan al-Bannā, "Ilá Ay Shay' Nad'ū al-Nās?" 45; Ḥasan al-Bannā, "Naḥwa al-Nūr," 282; Ḥasan al-Bannā, "Risāla al-Mu'tamar al-Khāmis," 116.

48 Emphasis added. Ḥasan al-Bannā, "Bayna al-Ams wa-l-Yawm," 103–4; Ḥasan al-Bannā, "Naḥwa al-Nūr," 275–6.

49 Ḥasan al-Bannā, "Niẓarāt Thalāth," in *Majmū'at Rasā'il al-Imām al-Shahīd Ḥasan al-Bannā* (Beirut: Dār al-Andalus, 1965). For a similar argument, see Muḥammad al-Ghazālī, *Min Hunā Na'lam ...!* (Cairo: Nahḍat Miṣr, 2005), 8.

50 Muḥammad Abū Bakir Ibrāhīm, "Al-Akhlāq al-Dīnīya fī al-Madāris," *al-Ikhwān al-Muslimūn* no. 8, 26 Dhū al-Qa'da 1361/December 5, 1942, 11 in IISH COLL00329/Folder 3.5; Ṣāliḥ 'Ashmāwī, "Hal ān al-Awān li-Ḥimāyat al-Ādāb wa-l-Taqālīd," *Majallat al-Mabāḥith* no. 29, 27 Sha'bān 1936 [sic, 1369]/June 13, 1950, 1 in IISH COLL00329/Folder 7.1.

51 Ḥasan al-Bannā, "Bayna al-Ams wa-l-Yawm," 110; Ḥasan al-Bannā, "Fī mu'tamar ṭalaba al-Ikhwān al-Muslimīn," 158–68; Ḥasan al-Bannā, "Naḥwa al-Nūr," 276–81; Ḥasan al-Bannā, "Risāla al-Mu'tamar al-Khāmis," 119.

52 "Al-minhāj al-ṣaḥīḥ: wa qad *wajadahu* al-Ikhwān fī kitāb Allāh …" Emphasis added. Ḥasan al-Bannā, "Daʿwatunā," *Majmūʿat Rasāʾil al-Imām al-Shahīd Ḥasan al-Bannā* (Beirut: Dār al-Ḥaḍāra al-Islāmīyya, 1980), 30.

53 The entirety of the verse reads "Fight them until there is no *fitna* and the religion is all for God. But if they cease, then indeed God is Seeing." The antecedent of the pronoun "them" is "those who have disbelieved" [*ladhīna kafarū*], from āyah 38. This scripture is often compared to Qur'an 2:193 (Sūrat al-Baqarah) "Fight them until there is no *fitna* and the religion is for God. But if they cease, then there is to be no aggression except against the oppressors." The antecedent of the pronoun "them" in this verse is "those who fight you" [*alladhīna yuqatilūnakum*], from āyah 190 of the same sūrah.

54 Again, the verse as a whole reads "O mankind, indeed We have created you from male and female and made you peoples and tribes that you may know one another. Indeed, the most noble of you in the sight of God is the most righteous of you. Indeed, God is Knowing and Acquainted." Ḥasan al-Bannā, "Naḥwa al-Nūr," 278–9.

55 Ḥasan al-Bannā, "Bayna al-Ams wa-l-Yawm," 108–9.

56 "Naḥwa al-Nūr" contains the most comprehensive statement of the Ikhwān's political program. The tract was compiled from earlier Brotherhood tracts, and sent to King Fārūq, Prime Minister Naḥḥās Pasha, and other Egyptian leaders in summer 1936. It was also reprinted as an open letter around the same time. The letter was at once self-promotion, a condemnation of the Egyptian political system, and an open bid for power. It began: "We submit [this message], and place ourselves, our talents, and all we have at the disposal of any organization or government that wants to make strides toward progress and advancement with an Islamic nation." Ḥasan al-Bannā, "Naḥwa al-Nūr," 294.

57 Ibid., 291–4. For similar statements concerning revision of Egyptian laws, see Ḥasan al-Bannā, "Ilá Ay Shayʾ Nadʿū al-nās?" 48.

58 Ḥasan al-Bannā, "Naḥwa al-Nūr," 291–3.

59 Ḥasan al-Bannā, "Risāla al-Taʿālīm," 368–9.

60 Ibid.

61 Aḥmad ʿĀdil Kamāl, *al-Nuqaṭ fawqa al-ḥurūf*, 73–4.

62 Jābir Qumayḥah, *Dhikrayātī maʿa Daʿwa al-Ikhwān fī al-Manzila Daqahliyya* (Giza: Markaz al-Iʿlām al-ʿArabī, 2009).

63 Ṭaha Saʿd ʿUthmān interview with Irmgard Schrand, Shubrā al-Khaymah, November 1999, in Irmgard Schrand, *Jews in Egypt: Communists and Citizens* (Münster: Lit Verlag, 2004), 238.

64 Ḥasan Dawḥ, *25 ʿĀman fī Jamāʿah*, 21–3.

65 Muḥammad Labīb al-Būhī, "Khiṭāb," *al-Ikhwān al-Muslimūn* 8, 26 Dhū al-Qaʿdah 1361/December 4, 1942, 17 in IISH COLL00329/Folder 3.5.

66 Quotations are from the English version, which adheres closely enough to the Arabic to make a retranslation redundant. Nonetheless, the Arabic will be cited for

reference. Anwar Sadat, *In Search of Identity* (New York: Harper and Row, 1978), 8–9; Anwar Sādāt, *al-Baḥth ʿan al-Dhāt: Qiṣṣat Ḥayātī* (Cairo: al-Maktab al-Miṣrī al-Ḥadīth, 1978), 16–17.

67 Ḥasan al-Bannā, "Ilá Ay Shayʾ Nadʿū al-Nās?," 46.

68 Here I have quoted the translation by William Shepard; however, to avoid superimposing a particular understanding of "capital" over Quṭb's original phrasing, I have provided terms from the original Arabic as well. William Shepard, *Sayyid Qutb and Islamic Activism: A Translation and Critical Analysis of Social Justice in Islam* (Leiden: Brill, 1996), 1, and Sayyid Quṭb, *Al- ʿAdāla al-Ijtimāʿiyya fī al-Islām* (Beirut: Dār al-Shurūq, 1995), 7.

69 Sam Huston, "'Monks by Night and Knights by Day': Ḥasan al-Banna, *Tarbīya*, and the Embodied Ethics of the Early Muslim Brotherhood," *Religion Compass* 12, no. 7 (2018): 5.

70 Julia A. Clancy-Smith, *Rebel and Saint: Muslim Notables, Populist Protest, Colonial Encounters (Algeria and Tunisia, 1800–1904)* (Berkeley: University of California Press, 1994), 216.

71 ʿĀdil Kamāl, *Al-Nuqaṭ Fawqa al-Ḥurūf*, 51–2, 59–61, 85–94.

72 See Ḥasan al-Bannā, "Hal Naḥnu Qawm ʿAmaliyūn?" and "Risāla al-Muʾtamar al-Khāmis."

73 Ḥasan al-Bannā, "Daʿwatunā," 29; Ḥasan al-Bannā, "Daʿwatunā fī Ṭawr Jadīd," 232–3.

74 Ḥasan al-Bannā, "Daʿwatunā fī Ṭawr Jadīd," 232–3.

75 ʿĀdil Kamāl, *Al-Nuqaṭ Fawqa al-Ḥurūf*, 51–2, 59–61, 85–94.

76 Ḥasan al-Bannā, "Risāla al-Taʿālīm," 360.

77 Ḥasan al-Bannā, "Hal Naḥnu Qawm ʿAmaliyūn?" 75.

78 Muḥammad Ḥasan Aḥmad (pseud. for ʿAbd al-Raḥman ʿAbd al-Nāṣir), *Al-Ikhwān al-Muslimūn fī al-Mīzān* (Cairo: n.p., 1946), 13–21, 43.

79 Ḥasan al-Bannā, "Daʿwatunā," 13–14, 25.

80 Aḥmad ʿAbd al-Majīd, *Al-Ikhwan wa- ʿAbd al-Nāṣir: al-Qiṣṣa al-Kāmila li-Tanẓīm 1965* (Cairo: Al-Zahrāʾ, 1991), 26.

81 Al-Banna's tracts "To What Do We Summon the People?" (1936), "Towards the Light" (1936), and "Our Call" (1937), for instance, all worked to define the Brotherhood's position vis-à-vis the national question, rejecting Pharaonism and other nationalisms based on geography and race. Wilson Chacko Jacob, *Working Out Egypt: Effendi Masculinity and Subject Formation in Colonial Modernity, 1870–1940* (Durham: Duke University Press, 2011), 109–10, 312.

82 Mitchell, *The Society of the Muslim Brothers*, 13–14, 275–91.

83 For an extended discussion of this, see: Gershoni and Jankowski, *Confronting Fascism in Egypt*, 210–33.

84 Maḥmūd Muḥammad ʿAbd al-Ḥalīm, *Al-Ikhwān al-Muslimūn, Aḥdath Sanaʿat al-Tārīkh: Ruʾya min al-Dākhil, Juzʾ 1* (Alexandria: Dār al-Daʿwa, 1994), 124–8.

85 Mitchell, *The Society of the Muslim Brothers*, 17–19; Muhammad el-Awaisi, *The Muslim Brothers and the Palestine Question 1928–1947*; Gershoni, "The Muslim Brothers and the Arab Revolt in Palestine, 1936–9," 367–97.
86 For a discussion of this, see Laurence R. Iannaccone, "Why Strict Churches Are Strong," *American Journal of Sociology* 99, no. 5 (March 1994): 1180–211.
87 Al-Azhar graduate Ḥāfiẓ Salāmah, a shaykh with a following in the Canal Zone, would also become a member of the society. Mitchell, *The Society of the Muslim Brothers*, 17–19.
88 Lia, *The Society of the Muslim Brothers in Egypt*, 255–6.
89 "Report: Abdul Kader Mukhtar," Dispatch from the Cairo City Police to the British Embassy, April 28, 1944, in *Young Egypt Party*, FO 141/951 [1944]; J. Heyworth-Dunne, *Religious and Political Trends in Modern Egypt* (Washington, DC: n.p., 1950), 40–1; Muḥammad Ṣābir ʿArab, *Ḥādith 4 Fibrāyir 1942 wa-l-Ḥayāh al-Siyāsiyya al-Miṣriyya* (Cairo: Dār al-Maʿārif, 1985), 284–5.
90 Lia, *The Society of the Muslim Brothers in Egypt*, 249.
91 Al-Bahī al-Khūlī, *Islām, lā Shuyūʿiyya wa lā Raʾsmāliyya* (Cairo: Dār al-Kitāb al-ʿArabī, 1951 [First ed. 1947]); "Al-Tafsīr wa-l- ʿUlūm al-Qurʾān," *al-Shihāb*, February 1948, 15–16.
92 Šabasevičiute, *Sayyid Qutb*, 97–8, 109–12.
93 Sayyid Quṭb, "al-Kutla al-Islāmiyya fī al-Mīzān al-Dawlī," *Majallat al-Risāla* 949, September 10, 1951, 1021–3; Sayyid Quṭb, "al-ʿĀlam al-Islāmī Ḥaqīqa Wāqiʿa," *Majallat al-Risāla* 966, January 7, 1952, 10–12; Sayyid Quṭb, "al-Ṭarīq ilá al-Kutla al-Thālitha," *Majallat al-Risāla* 976, March 17, 1952, 293–5; Sayyid Quṭb, "Ghubār ḥawla al-Kutla al-Islāmiyya!" *Majallat al-Risāla* 981, April 12, 1952, 433–4. Also see: Sayyid Quṭb, *Maʿrakat al-Islām wa-l-Raʾsmāliiyya* (Cairo: Maktabat Wahbah, 1951).
94 Šabasevičiute, *Sayyid Qutb*, 122–3.
95 Sir Ronald Campbell to Michael R. Wright, Dispatch 88/4/49G, in Communism in Egypt, FO 371/73476 [1949].
96 Ḥasan al-Bannā, *Majmūʿat Rasāʾil al-Imām al-Shahīd Ḥasan al-Bannā* (Beirut: Dār al-Ḥaḍāra al-Islāmīyya, 1980), 338–50; Ḥasan al-Bannā, "Ilá Ay Shayʾ Nadʿū al-Nās?" 48; Ḥasan al-Bannā, "Naḥwa al-Nūr," 291–4.
97 Mitchell, *The Society of the Muslim Brothers*, 13–14, 275–91.
98 Botman, *The Rise of Egyptian Communism, 1939–1970*, 59–60.
99 Ibid.; See the folder *Egypt*, FO 950/24 [1946]; "Anti-British Rioting in Cairo," *Illustrated London News*, March 2, 1946, 232; "Anti-British Riots in Cairo: Scenes of the Disorders Which Have Threatened Anglo-Egyptian Relations," *Illustrated London News*, March 9, 1946, 260–1.
100 ʿĀdil Kamāl, *Al-Nuqaṭ Fawqa al-Ḥurūf*, 133–5, 175.
101 Ahmed Abdalla, *The Student Movement and National Politics in Egypt, 1923–1973* (Cairo: The American University in Cairo Press, 2008), 68–77; Joel Beinin and Zachary Lockman, *Workers on the Nile: Nationalism, Communism, Islam, and the*

Egyptian Working Class, 1882–1954 (London: I.B. Tauris, 1988), 369–72. For more details on the vicissitudes of the Brotherhood–Ṣidqī alliance, see Malak Badrawi, *Isma'il Sidqi (1875–1950): Pragmatism and Vision in Twentieth Century Egypt* (Surrey: Curzon Press, 1996), 148–60.

102 Muḥyī al-Dīn, *Wa-l-Ān Atakallam* [And Now I Speak], 47.

103 Schrand, *Jews in Egypt*, 237–9.

104 Letter No. 903 from the British Embassy, Cairo to the Foreign Office, London, July 29, 1946, in *Egypt*, FO 950/24 [1946]; 'Ādil Kamāl, *Al-Nuqaṭ Fawqa al-Ḥurūf*, 184–91.

105 Muḥammad Ḥasan Aḥmad (pseud. for 'Abd al-Raḥman 'Abd al-Nāṣir), *Al-Ikhwān al-Muslimūn fī al-Mīzān* (Cairo: n.p., 1946); "Al-Taḍlīl bi-Ism al-Waḥdah," [1946] in IISH ARCH02315/Folder 56; Muḥsin Muḥammad, *Man Qatala Ḥasan al-Bannā?* (Cairo: Dār al-Shurūq, 1987), 193–5.

106 "Lā Fāshiyya wa-lā Ikhwān, wa-lā Tijāra bi-l-Adyān!" See: Fārūq al-Qāḍī, *Fursān al-Āmal: Ta'ammul fī al-Ḥarakat al-Ṭullābiyya al-Miṣriyya* (Cairo: Markaz al-Buḥūth al-'Arabiyya, 2000), 248.

107 Lia, "Autobiography or Fiction? Ḥasan al-Banna's Memoirs Revisited," 202–3.

108 Letter No. 903 from the British Embassy, Cairo to the Foreign Office, London, 29 July 1946, in *Egypt*, FO 950/24 [1946]; 'Ādil Kamāl, *al-Nuqaṭ Fawqa al-Ḥurūf*, 184–91.

109 Lia, "Autobiography or Fiction? Ḥasan al-Banna's Memoirs Revisited," 202–3; Barbara Zollner, *The Muslim Brotherhood: Hasan al-Hudaybi and Ideology* (New York: Routledge, 2009), 12.

110 Vivian Ibrahim, *The Copts of Egypt: The Challenges of Modernisation and Identity* (London: I.B. Tauris, 2011), 92–3, 212–13; Muḥammad, *Man Qatala Ḥasan al-Bannā?*, 193–5.

111 Ibid.; "Turāthunā" in *Wathā'iq*, 146; "Taḥāluf lā Yanqaṭi' bayna al-Raj'īya wa-l-Isti'mār," [1948] in *Wathā'iq*, 211–13.

112 Ṣāliḥ 'Ashmāwī, "Ḥawla al-Murshid al-'Āmm," *al-Da'wa* 28, 11 Dhū al-Qa'da 1370/August 13, 1951, 11 and 'Abd al-'Azīz Kāmil, "al-Jabhat al-Dākhiliyya," *al-Da'wa* 26, 27 Shawwāl 1370/July 13, 1951, 6 in IISH COLL00329/Folder 7.1.

113 "I'tiqāl al-Ustādh Aḥmad Ḥusayn," *al-Da'wa* 26, 27 Shawwāl 1370/July 31, 1951, 6 in IISH COLL00329/Folder 7.1; "Bayna al-Ṣuḥuf wa-l-Kutub wa-l-Ḥayāh," *al-Fajr al-Jadīd* 1, May 16, 1945, 20 in IISH ARCH02315/Folder 97; "Safāla … Ākhir Sā'a," *Shabāb Sayyidinā Muḥammad* 211, 20 Shawwāl 1368/August 15, 1949, 7 in IISH COLL00329/Folder 2.5; "al-Ṣuḥuf al-Khalī'a," *Shabāb Sayyidinā Muḥammad* 229, 21 Ramaḍān 1369/July 7, 1950, 11 in IISH COLL00329/Folder 2.5.

114 'Ādil Kamāl, *al-Nuqaṭ Fawqa al-Ḥurūf*, 238–9.

115 "Summary of a Report Submitted by Abdel Rahman Ammar Bey, Under Secretary of State, Ministry of the Interior, to the Prime Minister, which Led to the Publication of Military Proclamation No. 63 Dissolving the Ikhwan al Muslimin," in *Arab Societies: Ikhwan el Muslimin*, FO 141/1271 [1948].

116 ʿĀdil Kamāl, *Al-Nuqaṭ Fawqa al-Ḥurūf*, 277–80; Luṭfī ʿUthmān, *Qaḍīyat Maqtal al-Nuqrāshī Bāshā* (Cairo: Maṭbaʿat al-Tawakkul, 1950), 15–16; Mitchell, *The Society of the Muslim Brothers*, 63–7.

117 ʿĀdil Kamāl, *Al-Nuqaṭ Fawqa al-Ḥurūf*, 325.

118 "Al-Īmān Qaydu al-Fatki," *al-Asās bi Tārīkh*, January 2, 1949, as reprinted in *Jamharat Maqālāt al-ʿAllāma al-Shaykh Aḥmad Muḥammad Shākir* (Riyadh: Dār al-Riyāḍ, 2005), 472–5; Aḥmad Muḥammad Shākir, *Taqrīr ʿan Shuʾūn al-Taʿlīm wa-al-Qaḍāʾ*, 47–50.

119 ʿUthmān, *Qaḍīyat Maqtal al-Nuqrāshī Bāshā*, 78–89, 87–91, 117–19.

120 Ibid., 26–37.

121 Having one's papers "sent to the Mufti" is a euphemism in Egypt for prescribing the death penalty. It was a customary part of Ottoman *kanun* law, which involved declaring the perpetrator a *sai bil' fesad* [fomenter of evil/corruption]. The Mufti would sign off on the execution with a fatwa [fetva]; a clause in the fatwa stipulated that the authority for the order was in the hands of the sovereign. This was an acknowledgment that sovereignty continued to reside with sultan, not the Mufti himself. See: Haim Gerber, *State, Society, and Law in Islam: Ottoman Law in Comparative Perspective* (New York: State University of New York Press, 1994), 97–100. For other instances of this practice in Egypt, see Malak Badrawi, *Political Violence in Egypt 1910–1925* (New York: Routledge, 2013).

122 ʿUthmān, *Qaḍīyat Maqtal al-Nuqrāshī Bāshā*, 78–89, 87–91, 117–19, 208–27.

123 The main charge was the violation of §87 of the Egyptian Penal Code, "conspir[ing] to overturn by force the state's constitution, form of government, or system of monarchial succession." Maḥmūd Ṣabbāgh, *Ḥaqīqat al-Tanẓīm al-Khāṣṣ wa-Dawruhu fī Daʿwat al-Ikhwān al-Muslimīn* (Cairo: Dār al-Iʿtiṣām, 1988); ʿAbd al-Fattāh and Manṣūr eds., *Qaḍīyat Sayyārat al-Jīb*, 13–23, 46–77.

124 "Qaḍīyat Sayyārat al-Jīb," *al-Daʿwa* 2, 29 Rabīʿa al-Thānī 1370/February 6, 1951, 12–13 in IISH COLL00329/Folder 7.1; ʿAbd al-Fattāh and Manṣūr eds., *Qaḍīyat Sayyārat al-Jīb*, 13–23, 46–77; Zollner, *The Muslim Brotherhood*, 18–19; Al-Saʿīd Muṣṭafā al-Saʿīd, *Qānūn al-ʿUqūbāt al-Miṣrī: al-Ṣādir b-al-Qānūn Raqm 58 li-Sanat 1937* (Cairo: Maṭbaʿat Fatḥ Allāh al-Yās Nūrī wa-Awlādihi, 1937), 98; ʿĀdil Kamāl, *Al-Nuqaṭ Fawqa al-Ḥurūf*, 245–9.

125 ʿAbd al-Fattāh and Manṣūr eds., *Qaḍīyat Sayyārat al-Jīb*, 91–3.

126 Ibid.

127 "Al-Hujūm ʿalá al-Salām," *al-Muqāwamat al-Shaʿbiyya* no. 7, August 27, 1951, in IISH ARCH02315/Folder 111.

128 Sayyid Quṭb, "al-Kutla al-Islāmiyya fī al-Mīzān al-Dawlī," *Majallat al-Risāla* 949, September 10, 1951, 1021–3; Sayyid Quṭb, "al-ʿĀlam al-Islāmī Ḥaqīqa Wāqiʿa," *Majallat al-Risāla* 966, January 7, 1952, 10–12; Sayyid Quṭb, "al-Ṭarīq ilá al-Kutla al-Thālitha," *Majallat al-Risāla* 976, March 17, 1952, 293–5; Sayyid Quṭb, "Ghubār

Ḥawla al-Kutla al-Islāmiyya!" *Majallat al-Risāla* 981, April 12, 1952, 433–4. Also see: Quṭb, *Maʿrakat al-Islām wa-l-Raʾsmāliyya.*

129 For a literature review of studies on "filter bubbles," see Axel Bruns, "Filter Bubble," *Internet Policy Review* 8, no. 4 (2019): 1–14.

130 Emphasis added. Leon Festinger et al., *When Prophecy Fails* (Minneapolis: University of Minnesota Press, 1956), 3.

Chapter 5

1 Henri Curiel, *Pages autobiographiques: une contribution à l'histoire de la naissance du Parti Communiste Égyptien de 1940 à 1950* (Typescript, 1977), vi–viii, 12–14, 27 in IISH ARCH01722/Folder 402; Didar Fawzy-Rossano [Diane Rossano], *Mémoires d'une militante communiste (1942–1990): du Caire à Alger, Paris et Genève, lettres aux miens* (Paris: Éditions l'Harmattan, 1997), 31, 42–3.

2 Raymond Aron, "Aventures et mésaventures de la dialectique," *Preuves* 59 (January 1956): 5, as quoted by Tony Judt, *Past Imperfect: French Intellectuals, 1944–1956* (Berkeley: University of California Press, 1992), 159. Also see the accounts in Rifʿat Saʿīd, *Hākadhā Takallama al-Shuyūʿīyūn: Maḥāḍir Niqāsh, Taqārīr, Mudhakkirāt, Rasāʾil, Taḥqīqāt Qaḍāʿiyya, Bayānāt Intikhābiyya* (Cairo: Sharikat al-Amal li-l-Ṭibāʿa wa-l-Nashr wa-l-Tawzīʿ, 1989).

3 Gilles Perrault, *A Man Apart: The Life of Henri Curiel*, trans. Bob Cumming (London: Zed Books, 1987), 36–7, 49–51; Fawzy-Rossano, *Mémoires d'une militante communiste*, 42–3.

4 Fawzy-Rossano, *Mémoires d'une militante communiste*, 48–9, 62, 65.

5 Curiel, *Pages autobiographiques*, 34–7; Perrault, *A Man Apart*, 95.

6 Report from Colonel G.J. Jenkins, Head of Security Intelligence Middle East (SIME) in Cairo, to F.H. Tomlyn, Cairo Embassy, Ref. No. DS(E) 200/128, in *Arab Societies: Democratic Movement for National Liberation*, FO 141/1272 [1948].

7 Mubārak ʿAbduh Faḍl, "Mudhakkirāt," in Rifʿat Saʿīd, *Hākadhā Takallama al-Shuyūʿīyūn*, 125–6.

8 Laṭīfa al-Zayyāt in interview with Selma Botman, 1980. As quoted in Selma Botman, "The Experience of Women in the Egyptian Communist Movement, 1939–1954," *Women's Studies International Forum* 11, no. 2 (1988): 120.

9 Irmgard Schrand, *Jews in Egypt: Communists and Citizens* (Münster: Lit Verlag, 2004), 210.

10 Mubārak ʿAbduh Faḍl, "Mudhakkirāt," in Rifʿat Saʿīd, *Hākadhā Takallama al-Shuyūʿīyūn*, 125–6.

11 Fawzy-Rossano, *Mémoires d'une militante communiste*, 37–8.

12 Sharīf Ḥatāta in interview with Selma Botman, February 28, 1980, Cairo. As quoted in Selma Botman, *The Rise of Egyptian Communism, 1939–1970* (New York: Syracuse University Press, 1988), 50–1.

13 Schrand, *Jews in Egypt*, 212–13; Botman, *The Rise of Egyptian Communism*, 51.

14 Interview with Sulaymān al-Rifāʿī, January 12, 1976, Cairo, in Rifʿat Saʿīd, *Hākadhā Takallama al-Shuyūʿīyūn*, 109–22.

15 Nawal El Saadawi, *A Daughter of Isis: The Autobiography of Nawal El Saadawi*, trans. Sherif Hetata (London: Zed Books, 1999), 209–24.

16 Ibid.; "44 inculpés de communisme devant la cour martiale," *Affaire des "44"* (1954), p. 5 in IISH ARCH01722/Folder 149; Mubārak ʿAbduh Faḍl, "Mudhakkirāt," in Rifʿat Saʿīd, *Hākadhā Takallama al-Shuyūʿīyūn*, 123–79.

17 Al-Qalʿa counted around 150 members (*c.* 1945–1946). Smaller breakaway groups such as the Marxist League (al-ʿUsbat al-Mārksiyya; est. 1946, founder Fawzī Jurjis) counted only around sixty members.

18 Rifʿat Saʿīd, *Tārīkh al-Ḥarakat al-Shuyūʿiyya al-Miṣriyya*, al-Mujallad 3 (Cairo: 2007), 503–4; Tareq Y. Ismael and Rifaʿat el-Saʿid, *The Communist Movement in Egypt, 1920–1988* (Syracuse: Syracuse University Press, 1990), 53–64; Rami Ginat, *A History of Egyptian Communism* (Boulder: Lynne Rienner, 2011), 231–4; Perrault, *A Man Apart*, 143.

19 Fawzy-Rossano, *Mémoires d'une militante communiste*, 111. See, for instance, *Scripting Revolution*, on interpretations and innovations on the revolutionary script that emerged from the French Revolution. The text is also interesting as a *Begriffsgeschichte* (conceptual history), a field that strongly intersects with cognitive history. Keith Michael Baker and Dan Edelstein, eds., *Scripting Revolution: A Historical Approach to the Comparative Study of Revolutions* (Stanford: Stanford University Press, 2015), 3–4.

20 For poems invoking some of these dualities, see: Waṣfī al-Bunnī, "Ṣidq al-Shiʿr," *al-Fajr al-Jadīd* 3, June 16, 1945, 14; Muḥammad Kamāl, "al-Fajr al-Jadīd," *al-Fajr al-Jadīd* 22, February 20, 1946, 2; and Muḥammad Kamāl, "Hadhihi al-Thawra," *al-Fajr al-Jadīd* 23, February 28, 1946, 7, all in IISH ARCH02315/Folder 97.

21 See, for instance: *al-Khubz wa-l-Ḥurriyya* 1, February 1949, in "Communism in Egypt" FO 371/374/76 [1949]; *Maḥkamat Jināya Miṣr: Raqm al-Qaḍiyya 2021 al-Juzʾ al-Thānī* (Miṣr al-Qadīma, 1951), in IISH ARCH02693/Folder 2.

22 "Hadhihi Aṣwāt al-Jāmiʿa wa-l-Maʿāhid," *al-Fajr al-Jadīd* 23, February 28, 1946, 8 and Dīmitrī Jurjus, "Talaqqāhu al-Ṭarīq," *al-Fajr al-Jadīd* 10, October 1, 1945, 22–3 in IISH ARCH02315/Folder 97; "Akhbār ʿummālīyah," *Kifāḥ al-Shaʿb* 42, July 15, 1949, 2–3 in IISH ARCH02315/Folder 104; "Muʾāmarat Khabītha li-Ḍarb al-ʿUmmāl wa-l-Fallāḥīn," *al-Muqāwamat al-Shaʿbiyya* 11, October 24, 1951, 2 in IISH ARCH02315/Folder 111; "La lutte ideologique" and "al-Kifāḥ al-Aydiyūlūjī," (1953), pp. 11–12 in IISH ARCH01722/Folder 333.

23 See, for instance, Anwār Kāmil's anti-Stalinist pamphlet "Opium of the People" (1948).

24 This may have been a borrowing from Maurice Thorez's influential 1936 speech and 1938 pamphlet *Communistes et catholiques, la main tendue* (Paris: Éditions du Comité populaire de propagande, 1938), which made the same argument.

However, Egyptian communists often refrained from openly citing European sources. Emphasis added. ʿAbd al-Mughnī Saʿīd, *Asrār al-Siyāsat al-Miṣriyyat fī Rubʿ Qarn* (Cairo: Dār al-Ḥurrīyyah, 1985), 58–9; Piotr H. Kosicki, *Catholics on the Barricades: Poland, France, and "Revolution," 1891–1956* (Stanford: Stanford University Press, 2018), 52–3.

25 Mārsīl Shīrīzī [Mārsīl Isrāʾīl] *Awrāq Munāḍil Īṭālī fī Miṣr* (Cairo: Dār al-ʿĀlam al-Thālith, 2002), 145–6.

26 See, for instance, the DMNL tract quoted in Letter from Ronald Campbell to Ernest Bevin, April 25, 1948, Dispatch No. 215 (501/50/48), in *Development of Communism in Egypt*, FO 371/69250 [1948].

27 Muḥammad ʿAbd al-Maʿbūd Jubaylī and Shuhudī ʿAṭīyya al-Shāfiʿī, *Ahdāfunā al-Waṭaniyya* (Cairo: Dār Miṣr al-Maḥrūsa, 2004 [First ed. 1945]), 40–5.

28 "Akhbār ʿUmmāliyya," *Kifāḥ al-Shaʿb* 42, July 15, 1949, 2–3 in IISH ARCH02315/Folder 104.

29 "Limādhā Yaslaḥūna al-Ikhwān?" *Kifāḥ al-Shaʿb* 26, March 8, 1948, 2 in IISH ARCH02315/Folder 102.

30 K.Sh. [pseud.], "al-Ittiḥād al-Masīḥī al-Markazī baʿd al-Ikhwān al-Muslimīn," *Kifāḥ al-Umma* 24, February 16, 1948, in *Wathāʾiq*, 211–12.

31 Abū Sayf Yūsuf, "Ṣadd al-Hujūm al-Rajʿī al-Istiʿmārī Yataṭallaba Taghyīr Usus Munāhaḍa al-Istiʿmār," *al-Fajr al-Jadīd* 27, March 27, 1946, in *Wathāʾiq*, 81.

32 See *Kifāḥ al-Umma* articles from 1948 in "Taḥāluf lā Yanqaṭiʿ bayna al-Rajʿiyya wa-l-Istiʿmār," [1948] in *Wathāʾiq*, 205–13; "Turāthunā," Handwritten lecture on notebook paper, 1948 in *Wathāʾiq*, 146, 183.

33 *Al-Muqāwama al-Shaʿbīyah*, for instance, reported in 1951 that the government was encouraging the Brotherhood to form armed brigades to fight workers and farmers. "Muʾāmara Khabītha li-Ḍarb al-ʿUmmāl wa-l-Fallāḥīn," *al-Muqāwama al-Shaʿbiyya* no. 11, October 24, 1951, 2 in IISH ARCH02315/Folder 111.

34 As quoted in Beinin and Lockman, *Workers on the Nile*, 369–70.

35 Muḥammad Ḥasan Aḥmad (pseud. for ʿAbd al-Raḥman ʿAbd al-Nāṣir), *Al-Ikhwān al-Muslimūn fī al-Mīzān* (Cairo: n.p., 1946), 13–21, 43.

36 Botman, *The Rise of Egyptian Communism*, 40–71; Ismael and el-Saʿid, *The Communist Movement in Egypt*, 54.

37 Shīrīzī [Mārsīl Isrāʾīl] *Awrāq Munāḍil Īṭālī fī Miṣr*, 145–6.

38 Meeting notes of May 22, 1950, in *Maḥkamat Jināya Miṣr*, 154–5, in IISH ARCH02693/Folder 2.

39 Curiel, *Pages autobiographiques*, 23–5, 29–30.

40 See, for instance: "Barnāmaj al-Lajna al-Waṭaniyya bi-Ḥayy al-Azhar," January 1952 in IISH ARCH02315/Folder 50; Mubārak ʿAbduh Faḍl, "Mudhakkirāt," in Rifʿat Saʿīd, *Hākadhā Takallama al-Shuyūʿīyūn*, 125–6.

41 Letter from Ronald Campbell to Ernest Bevin, April 25, 1948, Dispatch No. 215 (501/50/48), in *Development of Communism in Egypt*, FO 371/69250 [1948].

42 Zakī Salāma (pseud.), "Nushū' Fikrat Allāh wa Taṭawwuruhā," *al-Taṭawwur*, February 1940, 27–9.
43 Sa'īd, *Asrār al-Siyāsat al-Miṣriyyat fī Rub' qarn*, 58–9; Schrand, *Jews in Egypt*, 113.
44 Schrand, *Jews in Egypt*, 210, 237–8.
45 Muṣṭafā Haykal, in Rif'at Sa'īd, *Hākadhā Takallama al-Shuyū'īyūn*, 211; 'Alī 'Abd al-Rāziq, *al-Islām wa-Uṣūl al-Ḥukm: Baḥth fī al-Khilāfa wa-l-Ḥukūma fī al-Islām* (Cairo: Maṭba'at Miṣr Shirka Musāhama Miṣriyya, 1925), 64.
46 Botman, *The Rise of Egyptian Communism*, 10.
47 Interview with Muṣṭafā Haykal, in Rif'at Sa'īd, *Hākadhā Takallama al-Shuyū'īyūn*, 211–23; Schrand, *Jews in Egypt*, 241.
48 Sa'ādat Muḥammad al-'Ashmāwī Bik, "Hal Nataṭala' ilá Fajr Jadīd fī al-Iṣlāḥ," *al-Ikhwān al-Muslimūn*, January 31, 1945, 3–5.
49 Schrand, *Jews in Egypt*, 206–12.
50 Thurayā Shākir in an interview with Irmgard Schrand, in Schrand, *Jews in Egypt*, 212–13. Also see Ginat, *A History of Egyptian Communism*, 282.
51 As Khālid Ḥamza explained, Ṭalī'at al-'Ummāl later had to remix the sections, as it had the effect of isolating the group's female members.
52 Report from Colonel G.J. Jenkins, Head of Security Intelligence Middle East (SIME) in Cairo, to F.H. Tomlyn, Cairo Embassy, Ref. No. DS(E) 200/128, in *Arab Societies: Democratic Movement for National Liberation*, FO 141/1272 [1948].
53 Curiel, *Pages autobiographiques*, 23–5, 29–30.
54 Ismael and el-Sa'id, *The Communist Movement in Egypt*, 45; Joel Beinin, "Exile and Political Activism: The Egyptian-Jewish Communists in Paris, 1950–9," *Diaspora: A Journal of Transnational Studies* 2, no. 1 (Spring 1992): 73–94.
55 Laṭīfa al-Zayyāt in interview with Selma Botman, 1980. As quoted in Botman, "The Experience of Women in the Egyptian Communist Movement, 1939–1954," 124–5.
56 See, for instance: *Wathā'iq*, 88, 201, 218, 220, 616; Rif'at Sa'īd, *Hākadhā Takallama al-Shuyū'īyūn*, 246.
57 "Al-'Ummāl fī Kifāḥihum al-Jamāhīrī al-Siyāsī," in *Wathā'iq*, 638.
58 Emphasis added. "Marra Ukhrá, Naḥnu wa Yahūd Miṣr," *Miṣr al-Fatāh*, November 24, 1947, 7.
59 "Ḍabṭ Murāsalāt ma'a Mūskū … wa Taqārīr Khaṭīra!" *Ākhir Sā'a* 701, March 31, 1948, 8–9.
60 "Shuyū'iyya Arstuqrāṭiyya … Am Waṭaniyya?" *Ākhir Sā'a* 701, April 28, 1948, 7; Muḥammad al-Tābi'ī, "Anā Shuyū'ī?" *Ākhir Sā'a* 704, April 21, 1948, 6.
61 Fawzy-Rossano, *Mémoires d'une militante communiste*, 69–72; Perrault, *A Man Apart*, 127.
62 Ibid.; Perrault, *A Man Apart*, 149.
63 Pierre Bourdieu, "The Social Conditions of the International Circulation of Ideas," in *Bourdieu: A Critical Reader*, ed. Richard Shusterman (Oxford: Blackwell, 1999), 224.

64 Internal EMNL [Hameto-Shar] memo regarding the newspaper *al-Jamāḥīr*, "The Newspaper: Its Task … Its Possibilities … Its Duties," Ref. No. DS(E) 330/6 and 20/2/24, July 1947, p. 5, in *Communism*, FO 141/1158 [1947].

65 Schrand, *Jews in Egypt*, 210–12.

66 Ibid., 152–3.

67 Ibid., 105.

Chapter 6

1 Abridged version. ʿAlī al-Ṭanṭāwī, "Shaykh fī Marqaṣ!" [part 1], *Majallat al-Risāla* 673, May 27, 1946, 574–5; ʿAlī al-Ṭanṭāwī, "Shaykh fī Marqaṣ!" [part 2], *Majallat al-Risāla* 674, June 3, 1946, 599–601.

2 Joel Gordon, *Nasser's Blessed Movement: Egypt's Free Officers and the July Revolution* (New York: Oxford University Press, 1992), 28–30, 205.

3 In Arabic: أعدى أعدائك نفسك التي بين جنبيك

4 Zakī Mubārak, "Aʿdā al-Aʿdāʾ!" *Majallat al-Risāla* 448, February 2, 1942, 115–16.

5 Ibid.

6 "Zakī Mubārak," *Al Jazeera*, December 23, 2014, https://www.aljazeera.net/encyclopedia/icons/2014/12/23/مبارك-زكي

7 "Al-Barīd al-Adabī," *Majallat al-Risāla* 451, February 23, 1942, 251.

8 Damian R. Murray and Mark Schaller, "The Behavioral Immune System: Implications for Social Cognition, Social Interaction, and Social Influence," in *Advances in Experimental Social Psychology* Vol. 53, ed. James M. Olson and Mark P. Zanna (Cambridge: Academic Press, 2016), 75–129; Yoel Inbar and David Pizarro, "Pollution and Purity in Moral and Political Judgment," in *Advances in Experimental Moral Psychology*, ed. Hagop Sarkissian and Jennifer Cole Wright (London: Bloomsbury, 2014), 111–25.

9 June Price Tangney, Jeff Stuewig, and Debra J. Mashek, "Moral Emotions and Moral Behavior," *Annual Review of Psychology* 58 (2007): 347. Also see William M. Reddy, *The Navigation of Feeling: A Framework for the History of Emotions* (Cambridge: Cambridge University Press, 2001), 16–17; Ross A. Thompson, "Emotional Regulation and Emotional Development," *Educational Psychology Review* 3, no. 4 (December 1991): 269–307; Jonathan Haidt, "The Moral Emotions," in *Handbook of Affective Sciences*, ed. R.J. Davidson et al. (Oxford: Oxford University Press, 2003), 852–70; Amanda Barrett Cox, "Correcting Behaviors and Policing Emotions: How Behavioral Infractions Become Feeling-Rule Violations," *Symbolic Interaction* 39, no. 3 (August 2016): 484–503.

10 Formally, moral socialization is the process by which individuals "learn to adopt the norms, values, attitudes, and behaviors accepted and practiced" in one's social circles. See: Emilé Durkheim, *Moral Education*, trans. E.K. Wilson and H. Schnurer

(New York: Free Press, 1973); Peter Robert Sawyer, *Socialization to Civil Society* (Albany: State University of New York Press, 2005), 38–9. For an overview of definitions of socialization, as well as debates and different approaches to the topic, see the entries for: "Socialization," "Agents of Socialization," and "Primary Socialization" in *The Concise Encyclopedia of Sociology*, ed. George Ritzer and J. Michael Ryan (Oxford: Wiley-Blackwell, 2011), 588–92.

11 Susan J. Matt, "Current Emotion Research in History: Or, Doing History from the Inside Out," *Emotion Review* 3, no. 1 (January 2011): 117–24.

12 Reddy, *The Navigation of Feeling*, 129.

13 The concepts and definitions in this and the paragraphs that follow are based on a review of the journals and magazines *Majallat al-Risāla*, *al-Ithnayn*, *al-Muṣawwar*, *Ākhir Sā ʿa*, and *al-Da ʿwa* (followed by a cross-comparison of those terms and descriptions to Arabic dictionary definitions and *al-Lisān al- ʿArab*). Unfortunately, the list of articles used to arrive at these concepts is too extensive to list article by article, but many of the individual articles are listed throughout this book. Statements on the frequency of various terms, as well as statements about how emotions move the body, are similarly based on readings of Egyptian journals, followed by keyword searches to confirm or deny patterns noticed in the readings. Note that beneath these broad trends, there was much diversity in the emotional expressions of individual authors. See: Muḥammad ibn Mukarram Ibn Manẓūr, *al-Lisān al- ʿArab*, 15 vols. (Beirut: Dār Lisān al- ʿArab, 1955–6); *Al-Munjid fī al-Lugha wa-l- ʿAlām* (Beirut: Dār al-Mashriq, 2005); Al-Fīruzābādī, *Al-Qāmūs al-Muḥīṭ* (Beirut: Al-Risāla, 2015); Hans Wehr, *A Dictionary of Modern Written Arabic*, 3rd ed., ed. J. Milton Cown (Ithaca: Spoken Language Services, 1976); Marek M. Dziekan, "The Categorisation of Emotions in the Classical Arabic Language: A Preliminary Lexicographical Study," in *Codes and Rituals of Emotions in Asian and African Cultures*, ed. Nina Pawlak (Warsaw: ELIPSA, 2009), 63–81.

14 For an interesting description of *sadma* in conversation with Freud and Breuer, see Fāʾiza ʿAlī Kāmil, "Al-Nisyān fī Naẓar al-Taḥlīl al-Nafsī," *Majallat al-Risāla* 948, September 3, 1951, 997–9.

15 ʿAlī al-Ṭanṭāwī, "Shaykh fī Marqaṣ!" [part 1], *Majallat al-Risāla* 673, May 27, 1946, 574–5.

16 See for instance Fadwá ʿAbd al-Fattāḥ Ṭuqān, "Lan Yaqʿud al-Aḥrār ʿan Thaʾrhum," *Majallat al-Risāla* 844, May 9, 1949, 1321 and Sayyid Quṭb, "al-Ḍarībat al-Dhull," *Majallat al-Risāla* 989, June 16, 1952, 657–8.

17 For an outstanding and thorough description of Arabic shame concepts, see Nader al-Jallad, "The Concept of 'Shame' in Arabic: Bilingual Dictionaries and the Challenge of Defining Culture-Based Emotions," *Language Design* 12 (2010): 31–57. See, for instance: Sayyid Quṭb, "Ayna Inta Yā Muṣṭafā Kāmil?!" *Majallat al-Risāla* 648, December 3, 1945, 1309–10; Ḥusayn Yūsuf, "Naʿlinuhā Mudawwiyya ʿĀliyya: Hādhihi al-Ḥafalāt mā Hiya illā Fāḥisha Munaẓẓama wa Shuyūʿiyya

Ṣārikha," *Shabāb Sayyidinā Muḥammad* 226, 24 Rajab 1369/May 12, 1950, 2, 11 in IISH COLL00329/Folder 2.5.

18 al-Jallad, "The Concept of 'Shame' in Arabic," 47.

19 Ibid., 35–54.

20 For a good article contrasting *ʿizza* and *dhull*, see Aḥmad Amīn, "al-ʿIzza," *Majallat al-Risāla* 137, February 17, 1936, 241–4. For comments on the twisted nose, see Dziekan, "The Categorisation of Emotions in the Classical Arabic Language," 70.

21 Ḥamid Badr, "Hunā Mawḍiʿ al-Gharābah," *Majallat al-Risāla* 923, March 12, 1951, 312.

22 Sayyid Quṭb, "Min Laghw al-Ṣayf: Ṣarāṣīr … !" [part 2], *Majallat al-Risāla* 683, August 6, 1946, 856–8.

23 John Calvert, *Sayyid Qutb and the Origins of Radical Islamism* (Oxford: Oxford University Press, 2013), 108–9.

24 Paul Ricœur, *The Rule of Metaphor: The Creation of Meaning in Language*, trans. Robert Czerny et al. (London: Routledge: 2004), 101, 224.

25 See, for instance, Sayyid Quṭb, "Min Laghw al-Ṣayf: Hāʾulāʾ al-Aristuqrāṭ," [part 4], *Majallat al-Risāla* 687, September 2, 1946, 961–3.

26 Aḥmad Amīn, "Kīmiyāʾ al-Afkār wa-l-ʿAwāṭif," *Majallat al-Risāla* 103, June 24, 1935, 1007–8.

27 Ḥasan [pseud.], "ʿUlamāʾ!" *Majallat al-Risāla* 994, July 21, 1952, 797.

28 Giedre Šabasevičiute, *Sayyid Qutb: An Intellectual Biography* (Syracuse: Syracuse University Press, 2021), 61, 67–81, 197.

29 Timothy Cresswell, *In Place/Out of Place: Geography, Ideology, and Transgression* (Minneapolis: University of Minnesota Press, 1996), 48–9.

30 Aḥmad Ḥasan al-Zayyāt, "Adab al-Mujūn," [part 3], *Majallat al-Risāla* 885, June 19, 1950, 680.

31 ʿAlī al-Ṭanṭāwī, "Shaykh fī Marqaṣ!" [part 2], *Majallat al-Risāla* 674, June 3, 1946, 599–601.

32 Sayyid Quṭb, "Ṣuwar min al-Jīl al-Jadīd," *Majallat al-Risāla* 622, November 4, 1945, 579–80; Sayyid Quṭb, "Akhrisū Hadhihi al-Aṣwāt al-Danisa," *Majallat al-Risāla* 1003, September 22, 1952, 1049–50; Giedre Šabasevičiute, "Sayyid Qutb and the Crisis of Culture in Late 1940s Egypt," *International Journal of Middle East Studies* 50 (2018): 94. Also see: Sayyid Quṭb, "Min Laghw al-Ṣayf: Mufāraqāt … !" [part 5], *Majallat al-Risāla* 689, September 16, 1946, 1017–19.

33 For instance, after the magazine *Ākhir Sāʿa* published a photo of a woman sitting naked among the trees (with the caption "Waiting for Adam"), *Shabāb Sayyidnā Muḥammad* denounced the baseness [*safāla*] of the magazine, asking "how long will these filthy [*danisa*] newspapers continue to corrupt the nation's morals and spread debauchery and immorality [*daʿāra wa fujūr*] on their pages?" "Safāla … Ākhir Sāʿa," *Shabāb Sayyidinā Muḥammad* 211, 20 Shawwāl 1368/August 15, 1949, 7 in IISH COLL00329/Folder 2.5. Also see: "Mujūn wa Istihtār," *Miṣr al-*

Fatāh 135, November 24, 1947; Ṣāliḥ ʿAshmāwī, "Ilḥād fī al-ʿAqīda wa Ibāḥiyya fī al-Aʿmāl," *al-Ikhwān al-Muslimūn* 6, 28 Shawwāl 1361/November 7, 1942, 3–4 in IISH COLL00329/Folder 3.5. For similar complaints about cinemas, see: Raḍwān Maḥmūd Naṣr, "al-Sīnimā," *Shabāb Sayyidinā Muḥammad* 284, 19 Rajab 1371/ April 14, 1952, 11 in IISH COLL00329/Folder 2.6; Sayyid Quṭb, "Min Laghw al-Ṣayf: Sūq al-Raqīq," [part 3], *Majallat al-Risāla* 685, August 19, 1946, 911–12; Nafīsa al-Shaykh, "al-Barīd al-Adabī: Risālat al-Sīnimā fī Tarbiyyat al-Shuʿūb," *Majallat al-Risāla* 992, July 7, 1952, 765–6; Maḥmūd Sāmī Aḥmad, "al-Masraḥ al-Miṣrī," *Majallat al-Risāla* 867, February 13, 1950, 186–7.

34 Kāmil Maḥmūd Ḥabīb, "Ṣuwar min al-Ḥayāh: Jannat al-Shayṭān!" *Majallat al-Risāla* 846, September 19, 1949, 1362–3; Kāmil Maḥmūd Ḥabīb, "Ṣuwar min al-Ḥayāh: ʿAlá al-Shāṭiʾ," *Majallat al-Risāla* 892, August 7, 1950, 880–1.

35 Ṣāliḥ ʿAshmāwī, "Ilḥād fī al-ʿAqīda wa Ibāḥīya fī al-Aʿmāl," *al-Ikhwān al-Muslimūn* 6, 28 Shawwāl 1361/November 7, 1942, 4 in IISH COLL00329/Folder 3.5.

36 Sayyid Quṭb, "Min Laghw al-Ṣayf: ilá al-Iskandariyya" [part 1], *Majallat al-Risāla* 681, July 22, 1946, 796–8; Sayyid Quṭb, "Min Laghw al-Ṣayf: Ṣarāṣīr … !" [part 2], *Majallat al-Risāla* 683, August 6, 1946, 856–8; Sayyid Quṭb, "Min Laghw al-Ṣayf: Sūq al-Raqīq," [part 3], *Majallat al-Risāla* 685, August 19, 1946, 911–12; Sayyid Quṭb, "Min Laghw al-Ṣayf: Hāʾulāʾ al-Aristuqrāṭ," [part 4], *Majallat al-Risāla* 687, September 2, 1946, 961–3; Sayyid Quṭb, "Min Laghw al-Ṣayf: Mufāraqāt … !" [part 5], *Majallat al-Risāla* 689, September 16, 1946, 1017–19.

37 Archaic term for a high-end prostitute or escort.

38 Kāmil Maḥmūd Ḥabīb, "Ṣuwar min al-Ḥayāh: Rabbat al-Shāṭiʾ," *Majallat al-Risāla* 847, September 26, 1949, 1395–6.

39 Muṣṭafá al-Ṣāwī, "Fī Ikhtilāṭ al-Jinsayn," *Majallat al-Azhar* 12, no. 8 (1941/1360), 503–5. Also see: Abū al-Wafā al-Marāghī, "Nadhīr min al-Gharb," *Majallat al-Azhar* 21, no. 2 (1949/1359), 144–6.

40 "Al-Shayṭān Yaghrī," *Shabāb Sayyidinā Muḥammad* 211, 20 Shawwāl 1368/August 15, 1949, 4 in IISH COLL00329/Folder 2.5.

41 Muḥammad Fahmī ʿAbd al-Wahāb, "Fasād fī al-Niẓām wa-l-Tafrīṭ fī al-Ḥuqūq wa Tadahwur fī al-Akhlāq: Anṣār al-Marʾa fī Fujūrihā … Hum Adhnāb al-Mustaʿmirīn," *Shabāb Sayyidinā Muḥammad* 215, 2 Muḥarram 1369/October 25, 1949, 1, 5 in IISH COLL00329/Folder 2.5; Yūsuf, "Naʿlinuhā Mudawwiyya ʿĀliyya," 2, 11 in IISH COLL00329/Folder 2.5.

42 "Mādhā fī ʿĀṣimat al-Islām!" *Shabāb Sayyidinā Muḥammad* 287, 8 Shaʿbān 1371/ May 3, 1952, 7 in IISH COLL00329/Folder 2.6.

43 "Min Faḍāʾiḥ al-Sufūr wa-l-Ikhtilāṭ," *Shabāb Sayyidinā Muḥammad* 282, 2 Rajab 1371/March 28, 1952, in IISH COLL00329/Folder 2.6.

44 Yūsuf, "Naʿlinuhā Mudawwiyya ʿĀliyya," 2, 11 and "al-Sufūr wa-l-Ikhtilāṭ," *Shabāb Sayyidinā Muḥammad* 266, 23 Ṣafar 1371/November 23, 1951, 4, both in IISH COLL00329/Folder 2.6.

45 "ʿAlá Hāmish al-Akhbār," *Shabāb Sayyidinā Muḥammad* 289, 28 Shaʿbān 1371/ May 23, 1952, 5 in IISH COLL00329/Folder 2.6.

46 Lisa Pollard, "From Husbands and Housewives to Suckers and Whores," 648–9.

47 Ḥusayn Yūsuf, "Naʿlinuhā Mudawwiyya ʿĀlīyya: Hādhihi al-Ḥafalāt mā Hiya illā Fāḥisha Munaẓẓama wa Shuyūʿiyya Ṣārikha," *Shabāb Sayyidinā Muḥammad* 226, 24 Rajab 1369/May 12, 1950, 2, 11 in IISH COLL00329/Folder 2.5; Saʿūd Muṣṭafá al-Ḥafīf, "Iḥdharū al-Taraddī fī al-Hawiyya," *Shabāb Sayyidinā Muḥammad* 289, 28 Shaʿbān 1371/May 23, 1952, 11 in IISH COLL00329/Folder 2.6.

48 "Min Shabāb Sayyidinā Muḥammad ilá maʿālī wazīr al-maʿārif," *Shabāb Sayyidinā Muḥammad* 211, 20 Shawwāl 1368/August 15, 1949, 6 in IISH COLL00329/ Folder 2.5.

49 "Ilá Rajul al-Sāʿa: Maʿālī Aḥmad Mursī Badr Bik, Wazīr al-Maʿārif," *Shabāb Sayyidinā Muḥammad* 215, 2 Muḥarram 1369/August 25, 1949, 9 and "Khirījāt al-Zirāʿa Yabkīna!" *Shabāb Sayyidnā Muḥammad* 211, 20 Shawwāl 1368/August 15, 1949, 5, both in IISH COLL00329/Folder 2.5; Saʿūd Muṣṭafá al-Ḥafīf, "Iḥdharū al-Taraddī fī al-Hawiyya," *Shabāb Sayyidinā Muḥammad* 289, 28 Shaʿbān 1371/2,May 3, 1952, 11 in IISH COLL00329/Folder 2.6.

50 "Aṣḥāb al-ʿUmmāl Yuḥāwilūna Inqāṣ al-Ujūr bi-Shattá al-Ṭuruq," and "al-Kifāḥ al-Yawmī fī al-Maṣāniʿ," *Kifāḥ al-Umma*, September 20, 1948, 4–5 in IISH ARCH02315/Folder 106; "Akhbār ʿUmmāliyya," *Kifāḥ al-Shaʿb* 42, July 15, 1949, 2–3 in IISH ARCH02315/Folder 104.

51 Henri Curiel, "Lettre à mes compatriotes," (1951), 1–3 in IISH ARCH01722/ Folder 329; "Fī Dawāʾir āl Sirāj al-Dīn," *Kifāḥ al-Umma*, July 15, 1948, 5 in IISH ARCH02315/Folder 106.

52 See, for instance: "Akhbār ʿUmmāliyya," *Kifāḥ al-Shaʿb* 42, July 15, 1949, 2–3 in IISH ARCH02315/Folder 104; "Muʾāmara Khabītha li-Ḍarb al-ʿUmmāl wa-l-Fallāḥīn," *al-Muqāwama al-Shaʿbiyya* 11, October 24, 1951, 2 in IISH ARCH02315/ Folder 111.

53 Laṭīfa al-Zayyāt, "Qiṣṣa: Mawkib al-Ḥayāh," *al-Fajr al-Jadīd* 9, September 16, 1945, 22–3; "Ibn al-Fallāh," [pseud. "Son of the Peasant"], "Ḥaṣād," *al-Fajr al-Jadīd* 2, June 1, 1945, 17, 19; Laṭīfa al-Zayyāt, "Allāh Yurīdu," *al-Fajr al-Jadīd* 1, May 16, 1945, 16; all in IISH ARCH02315/Folder 97.

54 Anwar al-Mashrī, "Muʾminah," *al-Fajr al-Jadīd* 13, November 1945, 20–1, all in IISH ARCH02315/ Folder 97.

55 Dīmitrī Jurjus, "Talaqqāhu al-Ṭarīq," *al-Fajr al-Jadīd* 10, October 1, 1945, 22–3 in IISH ARCH02315/ Folder 97.

56 See, for instance: another funeral-themed morality tale by Najātī Ṣidqī, "Umthūla Qiṣaṣṣiyya …," *Majallat al-Risāla* 699, November 25, 1946, 1317–18.

57 *Al-Fajr al-Jadīd* 30, April 17, 1946, in IISH ARCH02315/Folder 97.

58 See, for instance: Yūsuf Darwīsh's court records following his 1950 arrest for communist activism. The case is both dull and legally astute: the lawyer spends

most of the file refusing to answer questions, denying any involvement in the production of communist propaganda, denying the chain of custody of documents found in his residence, and stating for the record that he has been mistreated in police custody. *Maḥkamat Jināya Miṣr: Raqm al-Qaḍiyya 2021 al-Juzʾ al-Thānī* (Miṣr al-Qadīmah, 1951), in IISH ARCH02693/Folder 2. Also see §§171, 174 of the Egyptian Penal Code of 1937. Al-Saʿīd Muṣṭafā al-Saʿīd, *Qānūn al-ʿUqūbāt al-Miṣrī: al-Ṣādir bi-l-Qānūn Raqm 58 li-Sanat 1937* (Cairo: Maṭbaʿat Fatḥ Allāh al-Yās Nūrī wa-Awlādihi, 1937), 140–1, 143–7.

59 The painter interprets these wings as "civilization": men tried to use civilization to gain freedom, but "civilization covered people's bodies and covered their souls."

60 A.R.Ṣ. [probably Aḥmad Rushdī Ṣāliḥ], "Ajniḥa min al-Shamaʿ," *al-Fajr al-Jadīd* 2, June 1, 1945, 18–19 in IISH ARCH02315/Folder 97.

61 In Ovid's version of the tale, Icarus' father "Instruit et natum 'Medio' que, 'ut limite curras, Icare …'" (Lines 203–4) and "hortaturque sequi …" (Line 215), but Icarus "deseruitque ducem" (Line 224). For the entire passage, see: Lines 183–235 of Ovid, *Metamorphoses Book VIII*, ed. A.S. Hollis (Oxford: Oxford University Press, 1983), 7–9, 59.

62 Nawal El Saadawi, *A Daughter of Isis: The Autobiography of Nawal El Saadawi*, trans. Sherif Hetata (London: Zed Books, 1999), 209–24.

63 Saadawi, *A Daughter of Isis*, 273–8; Nawal El Saadawi, *Walking through Fire: The Later Years of Nawal El Saadawi*, trans. Sherif Hetata (London: Zed Books, 2009), 250–1.

64 Alexandra Georgakopoulou, *Small Stories, Interaction, and Identities* (Amsterdam: John Benjamins, 2007), 119–20; Alex Georgakopoulou et al., eds., *Small Stories Research: Tales, Tellings, and Tellers across Contexts* (New York: Routledge, 2024); Hayden White, "The Value of Narrativity in the Representation of Reality," in *On Narrative*, ed. W.J.T. Mitchell (Chicago: University of Chicago Press, 1980), 19–23.

65 "Shaykh in a Dance Club" mostly invoked Cluster I terms of contamination and decay (e.g., dirt/*rijs*, filth/*danas*, and mud/*ḥamʾa*) and Cluster II terms of deviation and breaking (e.g., straying/*ḍalāl*, immorality/*fujūr*, sin/*ithm*, and error/*khaṭīʾah*.) See: ʿAlī al-Ṭanṭāwī, "Shaykh fī Marqaṣ!" [part 1], 574–5; ʿAlī al-Ṭanṭāwī, "Shaykh fī Marqaṣ!" [part 2], 599–601.

66 Ricœur, *The Rule of Metaphor*, 48.

67 ʿAlī al-Ṭanṭāwī, "Shaykh fī Marqaṣ!" [part 2], 599–601.

68 ʿAlī al-Ṭanṭāwī, "Shaykh fī Marqaṣ!" [part 1], 574–5; ʿAlī al-Ṭanṭāwī, "Shaykh fī Marqaṣ!" [part 2], 599–601.

69 Emphasis added. Waṣfī al-Bunnī, "Ṣidq al-Shiʿr," *al-Fajr al-Jadīd* 3, June 16, 1945, 14 in IISH ARCH02315/Folder 97.

70 See, for instance: an Algerian example at FLN-ALN, *Avenir* 34, n.d. [c. 1958], in SHD GR 1H 2590/D1.

71 Muḥammad ʿAlī al-Laythī, "al-Sayyid al-Ṣaghīr," *al-Fajr al-Jadīd* 27, March 27, 1946, 19–20, in IISH ARCH02315/Folder 97; Šabasevičiute, "Sayyid Qutb and the Crisis of Culture in Late 1940s Egypt," 94.

72 "Nihāyat ʿĀbid al-Arḍ," *al-Daʿwa* 2, 29 Rabīʿa al-Thānī 1370/February 6, 1951, 15 in IISH COLL00329/Folder 7.1.

73 M.F., "Faṣl 1200 ʿĀmil," *al-Daʿwa* 26, 27 Shawwāl 1370/July 31, 1951, 14; "Ismaʿū li-Haʾulā," *al-Daʿwa* 39, 13 Ṣafar 1371/November 13, 1951, both in IISH COLL00329/Folder 7.1.

74 Stanley Cohen, *Folk Devils and Moral Panics: The Creation of the Mods and Rockers* (London: Routledge, 2002), 51–5.

75 "ʿĪd Mīlād!!" *Shabāb Sayyidinā Muḥammad* 224, 15 Jumādá al-Ākhirah 1369/4 April 1950, 5 in IISH COLL00329/Folder 2.5.

76 Sean P. Hier, "Thinking beyond Moral Panic: Risk, Responsibility, and the Politics of Moralization," *Theoretical Criminology* 12, no. 2 (2008): 176, 180–1; Cohen, *Folk Devils and Moral Panics.*

77 Šabasevičiute, "Sayyid Qutb and the Crisis of Culture in Late 1940s Egypt," 87–95; Šabasevičiute, *Sayyid Qutb: An Intellectual Biography*, 112.

Chapter 7

1 Inward Telegram No. 202 from Lieutenant-General G. Erskine (Ismailia) to Sir R. Stevenson, No. 2/8, October 16, 1951, in *Disorder in Ismailia*, FO 141/1439 [1951], in *BDEEP* Series B, Volume 4, Part II, 234–5; *Ākhir Laḥẓa* 198, October 10, 1951, 1–5; *al-Muṣawwar* 1409, October 12, 1951, 6–9.

2 Albion Ross, "Mood of the Egyptians Compound of Many Forces," *New York Times*, October 12, 1951, 147; "Egypt and the Canal Zone," *The Economist* 161, no. 5642, October 13, 1951, 867.

3 Giedre Šabasevičiute, "Sayyid Qutb and the Crisis of Culture in Late 1940s Egypt," *International Journal of Middle East Studies* 50 (2018): 94.

4 Israel Gershoni and James P. Jankowski, *Confronting Fascism in Egypt: Dictatorship versus Democracy in the 1930s* (Stanford: Stanford University Press, 2011), 89–91.

5 In 1951, the Egyptian magazine *al-Muṣawwar* cited two reports, one that claimed the garrison was 40,000 strong, another that reported it was 70,000 men strong (see: "Al-Muʿāhada al-Mashʾūma," *al-Muṣawwar* 1411, October 26, 1951, 14). The British reported their garrison strength as follows:

Spring 1947–90,000
Fall 1948–47,000
Fall 1951–64,000
Spring 1952–80,000

Michael T. Thornhill, *Road to Suez: The Battle of the Canal Zone* (Stroud: Sutton Publishing, 2006), 5, 16–17, 46, 70.

6 "British Retreat from Abadan is 1951 Dunkerque," *Chicago Tribune*, October 4, 1951, 9.

7 *The Egyptian Case, As Presented in the October 8, 1951 Speech of Mustafa el-Nahas Pasha* (Washington, DC: Egyptian Information Bureau, 1951).

8 Jefferson Caffery, Cairo, October 9, 1951, "The Ambassador in Egypt (Caffrey) to the Department of State," Dispatch 651.74/10-951, No. 921, Ref No. 911 in *Foreign Relations of the United States, 1951*, The Near East and Africa, Vol. V, ed. William Z. Slany (Washington, DC: United States Government Printing Office, 1982), 392–5.

9 *Al-Muṣawwar* 1409, October 12, 1951, 10; Anny Gaul, "Egypt, Laughter, and the History of Emotions," the Queen Mary Centre for the History of the Emotions at the Queen Mary University of London, March 7, 2016, https://emotionsblog.history.qmul.ac.uk/2016/03/egypt-laughter-and-the-history-of-emotions/.

10 Ṣaḥīḥ al-Bukhārī, *The Early Years of Islam* [*Kitāb al-Jāmiʿ al-Ṣaḥīḥ*], trans. Muhammad Asad (Selangor: Islamic Book Trust, 2013), 147.

11 "Al-Yaʾsu Ḥurr! Wa-l-Rajāʾu ʿAbd!" *al-Muṣawwar* 1409, October 12, 1951, 6–9; "Miṣr Taʿlinu al-Jihād min Jadīd!" *al-Muṣawwar* 1409, October 12, 1951, 8–9.

12 "Nidāʾ Ittiḥād Bint al-Nīl," *Ākhir Laḥẓa* 198, October 10, 1951, 4; Fikrī Abāẓa, "Badaʾa al-Kifāḥ!" *al-Muṣawwar* 1409, October 12, 1951, 6.

13 Anne-Claire de Gayffier-Bonneville, "La guerre du canal 1951–1952," *Cahiers de la Méditerranée* 70 (June 2005): 111–36.

14 *Ākhir Laḥẓa* 198, October 10, 1951, 1, 5.

15 Abāẓa, "Badaʾa al-Kifāḥ!" 6.

16 *Ākhir Laḥẓa* 198, October 10, 1951, 1, 5; Abāẓa, "Badaʾa al-kifāḥ!," 6; Ṣāliḥ Ḥarb, "Fal-Yataʾakhkhar al-Siyāsīyūn Khuṭwa wa li-Yataqaddam al-Fidāʾīyūn Khaṭawāt!" *al-Ithnayn* 905, October 15, 1951, 8.

17 *Ākhir Laḥẓa* 200, October 17, 1951, 1–5.

18 For one testimony, see Nūrhān Muṣṭafá, "Qiṣṣat suquṭ āṣghar shahīd fī Būrsaʿīd ʿĀm 1951," *al-Maṣrī al-Yawm*, December 2, 2016, https://lite.almasryalyoum.com/extra/123036. *Al-Muṣawwar* 1412, November 2, 1951, 1–2; Inward Telegram No. 202 from Lieutenant-General G. Erskine (Ismailia) to Sir R Stevenson, No. 2/8, October 16, 1951, in *Disorder in Ismailia*, FO 141/1439 [1951], in *BDEEP* Series B, Volume 4, Part II, 234–5; Walter S. Gifford, London, October 16, 1951–6pm, "The Ambassador in the United Kingdom (Gifford) to the Department of State," Telegram No. 641.74/10-1651 in *Foreign Relations of the United States, 1951*, The Near East and Africa, Vol. V, 403–4.

19 *Ākhir Laḥẓa* 200, October 17, 1951, 1, 3–4.

20 *Ākhir Sāʿa* 886, October 17, 1951, 3–4.

21 Jefferson Caffrey, Cairo, October 18, 1951, "The Ambassador in Egypt (Caffrey) to the Department of State," Telegram No. 519 in *Foreign Relations of the United States, 1951*, The Near East and Africa, Vol. V, 404.

22 *Al-Muṣawwar* 1410, October 19, 1951, 1.

23 Peter L. Hahn, *The United States, Great Britain, and Egypt, 1945–1956: Strategy and Diplomacy in the Early Cold War* (Chapel Hill: University of North Carolina Press, 1991), 133.

24 Their names are listed as Ibrāhịm ʿAbd al-Nabī and Mr. Muḥammad Munāṣirī. "Al-Ṭarīq ka-Annahu Khaṭṭ Qanāl," *Ākhir Sāʿa* 889, November 7, 1951, 6; ʿAbd al-Raḥmān Rāfiʿī, *Muqaddimāt Thawrat 23 Yūlyū Sanat 1952* (Cairo: Dār al-Maʿārif, 1987), 54.

25 "Yawm al-Shuhadāʾ," *Ākhir Laḥẓa* 202, October 24, 1951, 4–5; Walter S. Gifford, London, October 16, 1951–6pm, "The Ambassador in the United Kingdom (Gifford) to the Department of State," Telegram No. 641.74/10-1651 in *Foreign Relations of the United States, 1951*, The Near East and Africa, Vol. V, 403–4; Hahn, *The United States, Great Britain, and Egypt*, 133.

26 See *al-Ithnayn* 90, October 22, 1951; *Ākhir Sāʿa* 887 and *Ākhir Laḥẓa* 202 of October 24, 1951; *al-Muṣawwar* 1411, October 26, 1951.

27 "Miṣr Kulluhā Tataʾahhabu li-Maʿrakat al-Taḥrīr," *al-Muṣawwar* 1411, October 26, 1951, 13.

28 "Mawlid Katāʾib al-Taḥrīr," *al-Muṣawwar* 1411, October 26, 1951, 29.

29 "Paul Revere's Ride," in *Henry Wadsworth Longfellow: Poems and Other Writings*, ed. J.D. McClatchy (New York: Penguin Putnam, 2000), 365; Dr. Ḥusayn Muʾnis, "Bawsṭin … Maḥd al-Ḥurriyya al-Amrīkiyya," *al-Muṣawwar* 1409, October 12, 1951, 20–1, 38.

30 Dr. Ḥusayn Muʾnis, "Bawsṭin … Maḥd al-Ḥurriyya al-Amrīkiyya," 20–1, 38.

31 "Churchill Sends Division to Troubled Mideast," *United Press International*, October 30, 1951, https://www.upi.com/Archives/1951/10/30/Churchill-sends-division-to-troubled-Mideast/2542004412147/; Thornhill, *Road to Suez*, 49.

32 *Al-Ithnayn* 909, November 12, 1951, 9, 18.

33 "Khamsa Kāfaḥū … Fahazamūhā!" *al-Ithnayn* 909, November 12, 1951, 20–1, 43.

34 ʿAlī Aḥmad Bākathīr provided the script, and Zakī Ṭulaymāt directed. For other examples of Juḥā tales, including tales of Juḥā as a judge, see Salma Khadra Jayyusi ed., *Classical Arabic Stories: An Anthology* (New York: Columbia University Press, 2010).

35 ʿAbbās Khaḍir, "Masraḥiyya 'Mismār Juḥā,'" *Majallat al-Risāla* 956, October 29, 1951, 1230–2; Anwār Fatḥ Allāh, "Mismār Juḥā," *Majallat al-Risāla* 957, November 5, 1951, 1267–9.

36 ʿAlī Aḥmad Bākathīr, *Mismār Juḥā: Masraḥiyya Fukāhiyya fī Sitta Munāẓir* (Cairo: Maktabat Miṣr, 1985), 75, 91–2, 102–4.

37 "Juḥā ... Baṭal min Abṭal al-Taḥrīr!" *Ākhir Sāʿa* 890, November 14, 1951, 12–13.

38 See, for instance: *al-Fajr al-Jadīd* 23, February 27, 1946 in IISH ARCH02315/ Folder 97.

39 "Khamsa Kāfaḥū ... Fahazamūhā!" *al-Ithnayn* 909, November 12, 1951, 20–1, 43.

40 "Nidāʾ Ayyuhā al-Muwāṭin al-Ḥurr," *al-Ithnayn* 908, November 5, 1951, 20.

41 "Khamsa Kāfaḥū ... Fahazamūhā!" *al-Ithnayn* 909, November 12, 1951, 20–1, 43.

42 "Ṣuwar min Buṭūla," *al-Ithnayn* 916, December 31, 1951, 24–5.

43 "Min Qiṣaṣ al-Kifāḥ al-Shaʿbī: Rafaḍa an Yuḥayyī Qubbaʿat al-Ḥākim!" *al-Ithnayn* 909, November 12, 44–5.

44 "Kayf Wulidat al-Ḥān al-Ḥurrīyah!" *al-Ithnayn* 909, November 12, 18–19.

45 See, for instance: M. al-Shihābī, "Miṣr al-Mujāhidah," *al-Ithnayn* 908, November 5, 1951, 22; ʿAbbās Maḥmūd al-ʿAqqād, "Bayna ʿUrābī wa Saʿd Zaghlūl wa Muṣṭafá Kāmil," *al-Ithnayn* 909, November 12, 1951, 4–5.

46 See *Majallat al-Risāla* 956, October 29, 1951 [Part 1] to Majallat al-Risāla 969, January 28, 1952 [Part. 11]; "Min 'al-ākhira' ilá al-dunyā," *al-Muṣawwar* 1418, December 14, 1951, 9; Fikrī Abāẓah, "Mawākib al-Dhikrayāt wa-l-Muqāranāt bayna 'Thawra' wa 'Thawra,'" *al-Ithnayn* 916, December 31, 1951, 8–9.

47 Zakī Ṭulaymāt, "al-Masraḥ al-Miṣrī fī Khidmat al-ʿAqīdat al-Waṭaniyya," *Majallat al-Risāla* 961, December 3, 1951, 1378–9.

48 ʿAbbās Khiḍr, "al-Adab wa-l-Fann fī Usbūʿ," *Majallat al-Risāla* 963, December 17, 1951, 1430–1; ʿAlī Mutawallī Ṣalāḥ, "al-Masraḥ al-Miṣrī fī Khidmat al-ʿAqīdat al-Waṭaniyya," *Majallat al-Risāla* 963, December 17, 1951, 1435–6.

49 Pierre Bourdieu, "Le Clou de Djeha. Des contradictions linguistiques léguées par le colonisateur, entretien avec Didier Eribon," *Hommes et Migrations* 991, May 15, 1980, 37–43.

50 Muḥammad ʿAbd al-Ghanī Ḥasan, "Min Ṣawt al-Shuʿarāʾ:ʿalá Ṭalaqāt al-Madāfiʿ," *Majallat al-Risāla* 960, November 26, 1951, 1343–4.

51 Ṣalāḥ, "Juḥā ... Baṭal min Abṭal al-Taḥrīr!" 12–13.

52 ʿAlī Mutawallī Ṣalāḥ, "al-Masraḥ al-Miṣrī fī Khidmat al-ʿAqīdat al-Waṭaniyya," 1435–6.

53 ʿAlī Mutawallī Ṣalāḥ, "al-Adab wa Ṭalaqāt al-Madāfiʿ," *Majallat al-Risāla* 961, December 3, 1951, 1369–70. Also see: Tawfīq al-Ḥakīm, "al-Fann ... wa-l-Jihād al-Qawmī," *al-Ithnayn* 913, December 10, 1951, 13.

54 For an extensive list of lèse-majesté cases against *Rūz al-Yūsuf*, *Akhbār al-Yawm*, and many other papers, see: Sayyid ʿAshmāwī, *al-ʿAyb fī al-Dhāt al-Maṣūna*, 218–24.

55 See: Aḥmad Ḥusayn, *Fī Ẓilāl al-Mashnaqa* (Cairo: Sharikat al-Tawzīʿ al-Miṣriyya, 1953); Fatḥi Raḍwān, "al-Shaytān Yatakallamu," *al-Liwāʾ al-Jadīd*, August 28, 1951; Fatḥi Raḍwān, "ʿAhd al-Kilāb," *al-Liwāʾ al-Jadīd*, September 25, 1951; Fatḥi Raḍwān, "Fakhr al-Baḥr," *al-Liwāʾ al-Jadīd*, June 26, 1951.

56 (Translation of *al-Khubz wa al-Ḥurriyya* 1, February 1949) in "Communism in Egypt" FO 371/374/76, 1949.
57 Makram ʿUbayd, "Risāla min al-Shaykh al-Thāʾir ilá al-Fatan al-Thāʾir," *al-Ithnayn* 907, October 29, 1951, 4–5.
58 "Kunnā fī al-Qanāl," "Hākadhā Quṭaʿnā al-Injilīz," *al-Ithnayn* 906, October 22, 1951, 4; "Hākadhā Quṭaʿnā al-Injilīz," *al-Ithnayn* 906, October 22, 1951, 9.
59 Jefferson Caffrey, Cairo, October 27, 1951–7pm, "The Ambassador in Egypt (Caffrey) to the Department of State," Telegram No. 641.74/10-27151 in *Foreign Relations of the United States, 1951*, The Near East and Africa, Vol. V, 412–13.
60 Muḥammad al-Tābiʿī, "Ayna Mawqifukum …" *Ākhir Sāʿa* 889, November 7, 1951, 3.
61 "Umm Ṣābir," *al-Ithnayn* 910, November 19, 1951, 1–2, 18.
62 "Al-Qarsana fī Tarīq al-Suways," *al-Ithnayn* 907, October 29, 1951, 6–7; "Baṭal fī al-Ḥādiyya ʿAsharah," *al-Ithnayn* 907, October 29, 1951, 8–9; "Ḍaḥāyā … Abriyāʾ," *al-Muṣawwar* 1411, October 26, 1951, 9; "Luṣūṣ," *al-Muṣawwar* 1412, November 2, 1951, 5.
63 "Barīṭānīyān Yuṣibān Miṣrīyan," *al-Muṣawwar* 1411, October 26, 1951, 10.
64 "Al-Qanāl Yataḥawwal ilá Burkān Thāʾir!" *al-Muṣawwar* 1411, October 26, 1951, 8; "Khiṭābāt Maftūḥah," *al-Muṣawwar* 1412, November 2, 1951, 5; *al-Ithnayn* 909, November 12, 1951, 11.
65 Al-Ithnayn 907, October 29, 1951; Hahn, *The United States, Great Britain, and Egypt, 1945–1956*, 134.
66 "Ṣūrat al-Ghilāf," *al-Ithnayn* 912, December 3, 1951, 5.
67 "Wuzarāʾ Miṣr Yaqdamūna 14 Nūfimbir," *al-Muṣawwar* 1413, November 9, 1951, 30.
68 *Ākhir Laḥẓa* 209, November 13, 1951, 1, 4; *al-Muṣawwar* 1418, December 14, 1951, 11.
69 "Al-ʿUmmāl," *al-Muṣawwar* 1412, November 2, 1951, 12, 36; "Al-ʿUmmāl," *al-Ithnayn* 910, November 19, 1951, 11; "Faltukmil al-Hukuma Birrahā Haʾulāʾ b-al-Abṭāl," *al-Muṣawwar* 1416, November 30, 1951, 18–19. Ismaʿiliyya–based military historian Aḥmad Muṣṭafá Fayṣal, has recently recovered documents on these days, which can be found at Amīra ʿAbd al-Ḥakīm, "66 ʿĀman ʿalá Jalāʾ Jundī Ākhir al-Injlīzī," *al-Bawābah*, June 18, 2022, https://www.albawabhnews.com/4599145.
70 Sayyid Quṭb, "Sibāq ilá al-Taḍḥiyya wa-l-Fidāʾ," *al-Daʿwa* 39, 13 Ṣafar 1371/ November 13, 1951, 3 in IISH COLL00329/Folder 7.1; "Tasallaḥu … bi-Kull Wasīlah," *Shabāb Sayyidinā Muḥammad* 266, 23 Ṣafar 1371/November 23, 1951, 1 in IISH COLL00329/Folder 2.6.
71 *Al-Muṣawwar* 1414, November 16, 1951, 10–11; *Al-Ithnayn* 915, December 24, 1951, 15.
72 "Hayʾāt Būrsaʿīd Tatʿudu," *al-Ithnayn* 908, November 5, 1951, 10.
73 Ibid., 10.

74 "Qarṣanāt al-Injilīz Mustamirra fi-l-Qanāl," *al-Muṣawwar 1414,* November 16, 1951, 8–9; "Al-Sharqiyya!" *al-Ithnayn* 910, November 19, 1951, 8–9; "Ḥarb al-Manshūrāt!" *al-Ithnayn* 908, November 5, 1951, 20–1; *al-Ithnayn* 915, December 24, 1951; James P. Jankowski, *Egypt's Young Rebels: Young Egypt, 1933–1952* (Stanford: Hoover Institution Press, 1975), 100; Ahmed Abdalla, *The Student Movement and National Politics in Egypt, 1923–1973* (Cairo: The American University in Cairo Press, 2008), 78; de Gayffier-Bonneville, "La guerre du canal 1951–1952," 111–36.

75 B.E. Aguirre, Dennis Wenger, and Gabriela Vigo, "A Test of the Emergent Norm Theory of Collective Behavior," *Sociological Forum* 13, no. 2 (1998): 302.

76 Philippa-Sophie Connolly et al., "A Regulatory Flexibility Perspective on Positive Emotion," in *The Oxford Handbook on Positive Emotion and Psychopathology*, ed. June Gruber (Oxford: Oxford University Press, 2019), 53. Also see G.A. Bonanno and C.L. Burton, "Regulatory Flexibility: An Individual Differences Perspective on Coping and Emotion Regulation," *Perspectives on Psychological Science* 8 no. 6 (2013): 591–612.

77 Todd Hall, *Emotional Diplomacy: Official Emotion on the International Stage* (Ithaca: Cornell University Press, 2015), 192–3.

78 Dario Páez et al., "Psychosocial Effects of Perceived Emotional Synchrony in Collective Gatherings," *Journal of Personality and Social Psychology* 108, no. 5 (2015): 711–29; Christian Von Scheve and Mikko Salmela, eds., *Collective Emotions* (Oxford: Oxford University Press, 2014); Arie Kruglanski, *The Motivated Mind: The Selected Works of Arie W. Kruglanski* (New York: Routledge, 2018); Paul Pierson, *Politics in Time: History, Institutions, and Social Analysis* (Princeton: Princeton University Press, 2004), 51–2.

Chapter 8

1 Nancy Y. Reynolds, *A City Consumed: Urban Commerce, The Cairo Fire, and the Politics of Decolonization in Egypt* (Stanford: Stanford University Press, 2012).

2 Telegram from John Rathbone Hayes Jones, Cairo to Winston Churchill, London, January 31, 1952, Ref. No. D 13966, Code JE 1481/4 in *Claims against Egypt for Compensation for Injury and Damage Suffered as a Result of the Cairo Riots*, FO 371/97024.

3 Telegram No. 318 from Ambassador Ralph Stevenson, Cairo, to the Foreign Office, London, February 5, 1952, Code JE 1018/52 in *Egyptian Political Events Leading to the Military Coup d'État of General Neguib*, FO 371/96872.

4 Michael T. Thornhill, *Road to Suez: The Battle of the Canal Zone* (Gloucestershire: Sutton Publishing, 2006), 42–6; "Naḥnu wa-l-Injilīz," *al-Ithnayn* 910, November 19, 1951, 25.

5 Letter No. 1012/9/52 from the British Embassy, Cairo to the Foreign Office, London, January 24, 1952, in *Egyptian Political Events Leading to the Military Coup d'État of General Neguib*, FO 371/96871 [1952].

6 *Al-Ithnayn* 914, December 17, 1951.

7 Aḥmad Ḥusayn, *Mudhakkirāt Aḥmad Ḥusayn, Ra'īs Miṣr al-Fatāh* (Cairo: al-Hay'a al-Miṣriyya al-'Āmma li-l-Kitāb, 2007), 184–7; "Hay'āt Būrsa'īd Tat'udu," *al-Ithnayn* 908, November 5, 1951, 10.

8 "Ḥaḍarnā al-Ma'ārik al-Ismā'īliyya wa-l-Qanāl," *al-Muṣawwar* 1415, November 23, 1951, 8–9.

9 "Ḥaḍarnā al-Ma'ārik al-Ismā'īliyya wa-l-Qanāl," 9–11; Jamāl al-Ḥarajjī, "1,000 'Ā'ila Brīṭāniyya Ghādarū al-Ismā'īliyya …" *al-Yawm al-Sabā'*, November 20, 2019. Also see articles from *al-Balāgh* and *al-Miṣrī* compiled by Wasīm 'Afīfī at "Buṭūlāt al-mi'at yawm al-mansiyya qabl ma'rakat al-Isma'iliyya," *al-Mīzān*, https://elmeezan.com/%d9%82%d8%b5%d8%a9-%d8%b9%d9%8a% d8%af-%d8%a7%d9%84%d8%b4%d8%b1%d8%b7%d8%a9/.

10 "Qiṣṣat al-Jalā' 'an Ismā'īliyya," *Ākhir Sā'a* 895, November 28, 1951, 3–5; Thornhill, *Road to Suez*, 46.

11 Members of the council included: General 'Azīz al-Miṣrī (1948 veteran), Ḥasan 'Izzat, Wajīh Abāẓa (Free Officer), '(Fr al-Ḥamīd Ṣādiq, 'Aṭiyya Ṣābir Muḥammad, Abd al-Raḥman Abāẓa, Tawfīq al-Malṭ. Jamāl 'Azzām, Midḥat 'Āṣim, Aḥmad Abū al-Fataḥ (Wafd journalist), and Iḥsān 'Abd al-Quddūs (journalist). General Jalāl Nadā (1948 veteran) was also involved. See: Sharīf 'Ārif, "Al-Ikhwān fī Millafāt al-Būlīs al-Sīyāsī," *al-Miṣrī al-Yawm*, January 8, 2013, https://www.almasryalyoum.com/news/details/1754197.

12 *Ākhir Laḥẓa* 211, November 21, 1951, 1; "'Azīz al-Miṣrī Yaqūlu li-Katā'ib al-Taḥrīr 'Silāḥukum Ẓalām al-Layl wa Barīq al-Khanājir,'" *Ākhir Sā'a* 895, November 28, 1951, 8–9.

13 Dean Acheson to the Department of State, Rome, November 26, 1951–10pm, "The Secretary of State to the Department of State," Telegram No. 740.5/11-2651 in *Foreign Relations of the United States, 1951*, The Near East and Africa, Vol. V, 427.

14 "15 Qatīlan fī Ma'rakat al-Suways al-Thāniyya," *Akhir Laḥẓa* 210, December 5, 1951, 1; *al-Muṣawwar* 1417, December 7, 1951; *al-Ithnayn* 914, December 17, 1951, 10–11, 26.

15 Thornhill, *Road to Suez*, 50–2.

16 "Not Punitive but a Necessary Military Measure: The Building of 'Pegasus Avenue,'" *Illustrated London News*, December 22, 1951, 1022–3; "Before and after the Building of 'Pegasus Avenue,'" *Illustrated London News*, December 29, 1951, 1057.

17 *Al-Muṣawwar* 1418, December 14, 1951; and "Hākadhā Ya'īshu al-Ḍaḥāyā al-Musta'mir" and "Al-Qiṣṣa al-Dāmiyya," *al-Ithnayn* 914, December 17, 1951, 17, 24–5.

18 Michael Mason, "'The Decisive Volley': The Battle of Ismailia and the Decline of British Influence in Egypt, January–July, 1952," *The Journal of Imperial and Commonwealth History* 19, no. 1 (1991): 49.

19 Thornhill, *Road to Suez*, 49–51.

20 Ibid.

21 "Qānūn Ḥaml al-Silāḥ al-Jadīd," *Ākhir Laḥẓa* 221, December 26, 1951, 18.

22 "ʿAzīz al-Miṣrī Yaqūlu li-Katāʾib al-Taḥrīr 'Silāḥukum Ẓalām al-Layl wa Barīq al-Khanājir,'" 8–9; "Shabāb al-Jāmiʿa fī-l-Ṣaff," *Ākhir Laḥẓa* 217, December 12, 1951, 12; "Katībat al-Jāmiʿa Tatawajjahu ilá al-Qanāl," *Ākhir Sāʿa* 896, December 26, 1951, 8–9; "Tastaṭīʿu an Takūna Fidāʾīyan baʿd 21 Yawman!" *al-Muṣawwar* 1420, December 28, 1951, 1, 16–17.

23 "Raʾīs al-Ikhwān al-Muslimīn fī-l-Ḥaḍrat al-Malakiyya," *Ākhir Laḥẓa* 211, November 21, 1951, 1; *al-Daʿwa* 39, 13 Ṣafar 1371/November 13, 1951 and *al-Daʿwa* 47, 10 Rabīʿ al-Thānī 1371/January 8, 1952 in IISH COLL00329/Folder 7.1.

24 Ibid.

25 Aḥmad ʿĀdil Kamāl, *al-Nuqaṭ Fawqa al-Ḥurūf: al-Ikhwān al-Muslimūn wa-l-Niẓām al-Khāṣṣ* (Cairo: Al-Zahrāʾ li-l-Iʿlām al-ʿArabī, Qism al-Nashr, 1989), 329, 335; "Al-Idhāʿa..!"*al-Daʿwa* 47, 10 Rabīʿ al-Thānī 1371/January 8, 1952, 1 in IISH COLL00329/Folder 7.1.

26 Ḥasan Dawḥ, *Ṣafaḥāt min Jihād al-Shabāb al-Muslim* (Cairo: Dār al-Iʿtiṣām, 1979).

27 "Tastaṭīʿu an takūna fidāʾīyan baʿda 21 yawman," 16–17.

28 Ibid.; Kāmil al-Sharīf, *Al-Muqāwama fī Qanat al-Suways* (Cairo: Dār al-Wafāʾ, 2000), 74.

29 *Ākhir Laḥẓa* 207, November 7, 1951, 2.

30 See articles from *al-Balāgh* and *al-Miṣrī* compiled by Wasīm ʿAfīfī at "Buṭūlāt al-miʾat yawm al-mansiyya qabl maʿrakat al-Ismāʿīliyya," *al-Mīzān*, https://elmeezan.com/%d9%82%d8%b5%d8%a9-%d8%b9%d9%8a% d8%af-%d8%a7%d9%84%d8%b4%d8%b1%d8%b7%d8%a9/.

31 al-Sharīf, *al-Muqāwama fī Qanat al-Suways*, 91; Nawal El Saadawi, *Walking through Fire* (London: Zed Books, 2009), 34.

32 ʿAbd al-Raḥmān Rāfiʿī, *Muqaddimāt Thawrat 23 Yūlyū Sanat 1952* (Cairo: Dār al-Maʿārif, 1987), 106–7; "al-Tel al-Kabīr" and "Miṣr Tushayyiʿu Shuhadāʾ al-Jāmiʿa al-Arbaʿa," *al-Muṣawwar* 1423, January 18, 1952, 1, 9–11.

33 Emphasis added. Anne-Claire Kerbœuf, "The Cairo Fire of 26 January 1952 and the Interpretations of History," in *Re-Envisioning Egypt 1919–1952*, ed. Arthur Goldschmidt et al. (Cairo: American University in Cairo Press, 2005), 194–216.

34 Ibid.

35 "Al-Barīd al-Adabī," *Majallat al-Risāla* 963, December 17, 1951, 1438–9.

36 [Lit: "The Jesters in a Time of Gravity!"]. Anwar al-Maʿaddāwī, "al-Hāzilūn fī Waqt al-Jidd!" *Majallat al-Risāla* 967, January 14, 1952, 41–2.

37 Emphasis added. The term *nār* can mean "fire" or "gunfire." Quṭb's other uses of the term in the article (i.e. "the fire of holy hatred," "they turn blood to water, and fire to cold"; "just try to extinguish the burning fire between us and them") suggest it should be translated "fire." Sayyid Quṭb, "Nār … Dam," *Majallat al-Risāla* 968, January 21, 1952, 69–70.

38 Rāfiʿī, *Muqaddimāt thawrat 23 Yūlyū Sanat 1952*, 93–6; Anne-Claire de Gayffier-Bonneville, “La guerre du canal 1951–1952,” *Cahiers de la Méditerranée* 70 (June 2005): 111–36.

39 Quṭb, “Nār … Dam,” 69–70.

40 The crucifixion narrative also appeared in other accounts. See, for instance: Rāfiʿī, *Muqaddimāt Thawrat 23 Yūlyū Sanat 1952*, 95–6. “Report of the British Committee of Inquiry into the Riots in Cairo on the 26 January 1952,” in *Egyptian Political Events Leading to the Military Coup d'État of General Neguib*, FO 371/96873 [1952].

41 “Memorandum of Conversation, by the Acting Assistant Secretary of State for Near Eastern, South Asian, and African Affairs (Berry),” Ref. No. 641.74/1-2552, No. 951 in *Foreign Relations of the United States, 1952-1954*, The Near and Middle East, Vol. IX, Part 2, ed. John P. Glennon (Washington, DC: United States Government Printing Office, 1986), 1753-4; Michael T. Thornhill, “Britain and the Collapse of Egypt's Constitutional Order, 1950–52,” *Diplomacy and Statecraft* 13, no. 1 (2002): 138.

42 Rāfiʿī, *Muqaddimāt Thawrat 23 Yūlyū Sanat 1952*, 95–9; Thornhill, *Road to Suez*, 57–9.

43 Ibid.; Mason, “‘The Decisive Volley,’” 49–50.

44 “The Rioting and Organized Fire Raising in Cairo on 26 January,” Chancery (Cairo) to African Department, January 31, 1952, in *Egyptian Political Events Leading to the Military Coup d'État of General Neguib*, FO 371/96871 [1952].

45 Telegram No. 318 from Cairo to Foreign Office, February 5, 1952, in *Egyptian Political Events Leading to the Military Coup d'État of General Neguib*, FO 371/96872 [1952]; “Minutes,” March 1, 1952, in *Egypt and Sudan*, FO 371/96873 [1952].

46 “Report of the British Committee of Inquiry into the Riots in Cairo on the 26 January 1952,” in *Egyptian Political Events Leading to the Military Coup d'État of General Neguib*, FO 371/96873 [1952]; “The Rioting and Organized Fire Raising in Cairo on 26 January,” Chancery (Cairo) to African Department, 31 January 1952, in *Egyptian Political Events Leading to the Military Coup d'État of General Neguib*, FO 371/96871 [1952].

47 Ibid.

48 Peter L. Hahn, *The United States, Great Britain, and Egypt, 1945–1956: Strategy and Diplomacy in the Early Cold War* (Chapel Hill: University of North Carolina Press, 1991), 139–42.

49 Sir Anthony Eden, Secretary of State for Foreign Affairs, Address to the House of Commons, 29 January 1952, in FO 371/96871 [1952]. For similar statements, also see the dispatches and reports in FO 371/96872 and FO 371/96873 [1952].

50 Ibid.; “Kul Hadha wa-l-Qāhira Taḥtariq!” *Ākhir Sāʿa* 907, March 12, 1952, 4–5.

51 Jamāl al-Sharqāwī, *Ḥarīq al-Qāhira: Qarār Ittihām Jadīd* (Cairo: Dār al-Thaqāfa al-Jadīda, 1976).

52 Khālid Muḥyī al-Dīn, *Wa-l-Ān Atakallam* (Cairo: Markaz al-Ahrām lil-Tarjama wa-al-Nashr, Mu'assasat al-Ahrām, 1992), 120.

53 "Waqaʿat al-Waqʿah … Falā Yāʾis, wa lā Qunūṭ, wa lā Khunūʿ, wa lā Istislām," *Shabāb Sayyidnā Muḥammad* no. 283, 9 Rajab 1371/April 4, 1952, 7 in IISH COLL00329/Folder 2.6.

54 "Aḥmad Ḥusayn wa ʿIṣābat Majallat al-Malāyīn," *al-Muqāwama al-Shaʿbiyya*, July 1952, 8 in IISH ARCH02315/Folder 111.

55 Ḥasan al-Huḍaybī, "Bayān al-Murshid al-ʿĀmm li-l-Ikhwān al-Muslimīn," January 26, 1952 (printed in *al-Daʿwa*), in Jamāl al-Sharqāwī, *Ḥarīq al-Qāhirah*, 921–2.

56 Dispatch 1012/15/52 from the British Embassy in Cairo to the Foreign Office, 18 February 1952, in *Egyptian Political Events Leading to the Military Coup d'État of General Neguib*, FO 371/96872 [1952].

57 Emphasis added. Dispatch No. 1012/15/52 from the British Embassy, Cairo, to the African Department, Foreign Office, London, February 18, 1952, Ref., Code JE 1018/78 in *Egyptian Political Events Leading to the Military Coup d'État of General Neguib*, FO 371/96872 [1952].

58 See the interviews with Ṣāliḥ ʿAshmāwī, Aḥmad Ḥusayn, Ḥasan Dawḥ, and others in al-Sharqāwī, *Ḥarīq al-Qāhirah*.

59 Quṭb, "Nār … Dam," 69–70.

60 Todd H. Hall, "On Provocation: Outrage, International Relations, and the Franco–Prussian War," *Security Studies* 26, no. 1 (2017): 1–29.

61 Neil Sadler, *Fragmented Narrative: Telling and Interpreting Stories in the Twitter Age* (New York: Routledge, 2022), 88–92.

62 Dispatch No. 1012/15/52 from the British Embassy, Cairo, to the African Department, Foreign Office, London, February 18, 1952. Ref., Code JE 1018/78 in *Egyptian Political Events Leading to the Military Coup d'État of General Neguib*, FO 371/96872 [1952].

63 Khālid Muḥyī al-Dīn, *Wa-l-ān Atakallam*, 118–19.

64 See, for instance, Nasser's interview with *al-Ahram* on the First Anniversary of the Revolution, July 22, 1952, http://nasser.bibalex.org/Speeches/browser.aspx?SID=47

65 Anwar El Sadat, *In Search of Identity* (New York: Harper and Row, 1978), 59; "Ahdāf al-Ḍubbāṭ al-Aḥrār," [Autumn 1951] in Muḥyī al-Dīn, *Wa-l-Ān Atakallam*, 94–5; Joel Gordon, *Nasser's Blessed Movement* (Oxford: Oxford University Press, 1992), 44–50.

66 Muṣṭafá ʿAbd al-Majīd Naṣīr et al., *Thawrat Yūliyū wa-l-Ḥaqīqa al-Ghāʾiba* (Cairo: al-Hayʾa al-Miṣriyya al-ʿĀmma li-l-Kitāb, 1997), 136–60; Chapter 6 of ʿAbd al-Munʿim ʿAbd al-Raʾūf, *Arghamtu "Fārūq" ʿalá al-tanāzul ʿan al-ʿArsh: Mudhakkirāt* (Cairo: al-Zahrāʾ li-l-Iʿlām al-ʿArabī, 1988); Ḥusayn Ḥammūda, *Asrār Ḥarakat al-Ḍubbāṭ al-Aḥrār wa-l-Ikhwān al-Muslimūn* (Cairo: al-Zahrāʾ li-l-Iʿlām al-ʿArabī, 1985), 73–5; Muḥyī al-Dīn, *Wa-l-ān atakallam*, 84–6.

67 "Ahdāf al-Ḍubbāṭ al-Aḥrār," in Muḥyī al-Dīn, *Wa-l-ān Atakallam*, 94–5. For similar tracts and discourses, see the Free Officer tracts from January 1952 and March 1952: "Qāwamū al-Ṭughyān … wa Dāfaʿū ʿan al-Shaʿb," [1952] in Appendix 8, ʿAbd al-Majīd Naṣīr et al., *Thawrat Yūliyū wa-l-Ḥaqīqa al-Ghāʾiba,* 171–3.

68 *Ṣawt al-Ḍubbāṭ al-Aḥrār* 7, March 22, 1952, in Appendix 8, ʿAbd al-Majīd Naṣīr et al., *Thawrat Yūliyū wa-l-Ḥaqīqa al-Ghāʾiba,* 176–8. Also see: "Yā Rijāl al-Jaysh, Yā Abnāʾ al-Shaʿb," in Appendix 8, ʿAbd al-Majīd Naṣīr et al., *Thawrat Yūliyū wa-l-Ḥaqīqa al-Ghāʾiba,* 223–5.

69 Letter from R. Allen to M. J. Creswell on the Prospects of an Agreement, No. 365, February 26, 1952, in *Agreement with the Egyptians*, FO 371/96931 [1952], in *BDEEP* Series B, Vol. 4, Part II, 348–9.

70 Emphasis added. Letter (reply) from M. J. Creswell to R. Allen on the Implications of a Failure to Reach an Agreement, No. 365, March 4, 1952, in *Future Developments in Egypt*, FO 371/96931 [1952], in *BDEEP* Series B, Vol. 4, Part II, 349–51.

71 Matthew F. Holland, *America and Egypt: From Roosevelt to Eisenhower* (Westport: Praeger, 1996), 21–7; Hugh Wilford, *America's Great Game* (New York: Basic Books, 2013), 135–139.

72 Gamal Abdel Nasser, Interview with *al-Ahram* on the First Anniversary of the Revolution, July 22, 1952, Bibliotecha Alexandrina, http://nasser.bibalex.org/Speeches/browser.aspx?SID=47; al-Dīn, *Wa-l-ān atakallam*, 124–5.

73 Inward Telegram No. 1059, from M.J. Creswell to the Foreign Office, on a Meeting with Hafez Afifi, No. 72, July 22, 1952, in *Outcome of the Latest Crisis in Egypt*, FO 141/1453 [1952], in *BDEEP* Series B, Vol. 4, Part II, 437–8.

74 Thornhill, *Road to Suez*, 87–9.

75 Muḥyī al-Dīn, *Wa-l-Ān Atakallam*, 131–62.

76 Emphasis added. "Amr Malakī Raqm 10, li-Sanat 1952," Wizārat al-Liwāʾ Muḥammad Najīb, 7 Sibtambir 1952–18 Yūniyū 1953, Bibliotheca Alexandrina. Available at: http://naguib.bibalex.org/DocumentForm.aspx

77 Nandini Sundar, "Vigilantism, Culpability, and Moral Dilemmas," *Critique of Anthropology* 30, no. 1 (April 2010): 116–17.

Chapter 9

1 John Darwin, "Decolonization and the End of Empire," in *The Oxford History of the British Empire Vol. 5: Historiography*, ed. Robin W. Winks (Oxford: Oxford University Press, 1998), 554.

2 Omnia El Shakry, "The Vexed Archives of Decolonization in the Middle East," *American Historical Review* 120 (2015): 925; Yoav Di-Capua, "The Intellectual Revolt of the 1950s and 'The Fall of the *Udabāʾ*,'" in *Commitment*

and Beyond: Reflections on/of the Political in Arabic Literature since the 1940s, ed. Friederike Pannewick and Georges Khalil (Wiesbaden: Ludwing Reichert, 2015), 89; Dietmar Rothermund, *The Routledge Companion to Decolonization* (New York: Routledge, 2006), 30–1.

3 Michael Walzer, *The Revolution of the Saints* (New York: Harvard University Press, 1968), 20.

4 Emphasis added. Interview with Ḥasan al-Banna, "Hal al-Shaykh Ḥasan al-Banna Zaʿīm Qawī wa Māhir?" *Rūz al-Yūsuf* 1070, December 15, 1948. He further describes both Muslim and non-Muslim opposition to the Ikhwānid combination of religion and politics in Ḥasan al-Bannā, "Fī Muʾtamar Ṭalaba al-Ikhwān al-Muslimīn," 158–68.

5 P.J. Vatikiotis, "Islam and the Foreign Policy of Egypt (1965)," in *Arab and Regional Politics in the Middle East* (New York: Routledge, 2015), 32–4, 38; Jesse Ferris, *Nasser's Gamble: How Intervention in Yemen Cause the Six-Day War and the Decline of Egyptian Power* (Princeton: Princeton University Press, 2013), 33–5, 185, 255–7; Yvonne Yazbeck Haddad, *Contemporary Islam and the Challenge of History* (Albany: State University of New York Press, 1982), 366–9.

6 See, for instance, Nāṣir's speeches "Kalimat al-Bikbāshī Jamāl ʿAbd al-Nāṣir fī Jāmiʿat Fūʾād al-Awwal bi-munāsabat yawm al-shuhadāʾ," Cairo, November 15, 1952, "Kalimat al-bikbāshī Jamāl ʿAbd al-Nāṣir fī hayʾat al-Taḥrīr fī Shibīn al-Kum Munūfiyya," February 23, 1953; "Taṣrīḥ al-Bikbāshī Jamāl ʿAbd al-Nāṣir ilá Mudīr Wakālat Anbāʾ Miṣr bi-l-Qāhirah," March 1, 1953 (all available through the Bibliotheca Alexandrina and the Gamal Abdel Nasser Foundation Archive). Also see: Joel Gordon, *Nasser's Blessed Movement* (Oxford: Oxford University Press, 1992), 77–81.

7 Sayyid Quṭb, "ʿAdūnā al-Awwal: Al-Rajul al-Abyaḍ," *Majallat al-Risāla* 1009, November 3, 1952, 1217–19.

8 Emphasis added, Ibid.

9 William Roger Louis, *Ends of British Imperialism: The Scramble for Empire, Suez, and Decolonization* (New York: I.B. Tauris, 2006), 612–15.

10 Steve Morewood, "Prelude to the Suez Crisis: The Rise and Fall of British Dominance," in *Reassessing Suez 1956: New Perspectives on the Crisis and Its Aftermath*, ed. Simon C. Smith (Burlington: Ashgate, 2008), 29; Peter J. Beck, "Britain and the Suez Crisis: The Abadan Dimension," in *Reassessing Suez 1956*, 61; Peter L. Hahn, *The United States, Great Britain, and Egypt, 1945–1956: Strategy and Diplomacy in the Early Cold War* (Chapel Hill: University of North Carolina Press, 1991), 157–8.

11 John Calvert, *Sayyid Qutb and the Origins of Radical Islamism* (Oxford: Oxford University Press, 2013), 178–88.

12 Giedre Šabasevičiute, *Sayyid Qutb: An Intellectual Biography* (Syracuse: Syracuse University Press, 2021), 158.

13 Gordon, *Nasser's Blessed Movement*, 92–108; Barnaby Crowcroft, "Egypt's Other Nationalists and the Suez Crisis of 1956," *The Historical Journal* 59, no. 1 (March 2016): 260; Hahn, *The United States, Great Britain, and Egypt, 1945–1956*, 176.

14 Richard P. Mitchell, *The Society of the Muslim Brothers* (Oxford: Oxford University Press, 1969), 144–61.

15 Muḥammad Ḥusnī Wilāya, "al-Shakhṣīyyat al-Histīriyya," *Majallat al-Risāla* 468, June 22, 1942, 639; Muḥammad Ḥusnī Wilāya, "al-Fidā'iyya," *Majallat al-Risāla* 472, July 20, 1942, 731.

16 Paul Pierson, *Politics in Time: History, Institutions, and Social Analysis* (Princeton: Princeton University Press, 2004), 51–2; Gilbert Gottlieb, *Synthesizing Nature-Nurture: Prenatal Roots of Instinctive Behavior* (New York: Taylor and Francis, 1997), 57–9.

17 Susanne Stadlbauer, "Language Ideologies in the Arabic Diglossia of Egypt," *Colorado Research in Linguistics* 22 (June 2010): 1–19.

18 Dario Páez et al., "Psychosocial Effects of Perceived Emotional Synchrony in Collective Gatherings," *Journal of Personality and Social Psychology* 108, no. 5 (2015): 711–29; Arie Kruglanski, *The Motivated Mind: The Selected Works of Arie W. Kruglanski* (New York: Routledge, 2018). Christian Von Scheve and Mikko Salmela, eds., *Collective Emotions* (Oxford: Oxford University Press, 2014).

19 James Jasper, *The Emotions of Protest* (Chicago: University of Chicago Press, 2018), 18.

20 Sayyid Quṭb, "ʿAlá Hāmish al-Naqd," *Majallat al-Risāla* 696, November 4, 1946, 1216–18.

21 "Madrasah al-sukhuṭ," *al-Taṭawwur* 2, February 1, 1940, 7.

22 John A. Terrizzi Jr. et al., "Disgust: A Predictor of Social Conservatism and Prejudicial Attitudes toward Homosexuals," *Personality and Individual Differences* 49, no. 6 (October 2010): 587–92; John A. Terrizzi Jr., et al., "The Behavioral Immune System and Social Conservatism: A Meta-Analysis," *Evolution and Human Behavior* 34, no. 2 (March 2013): 99–108; Joshua M. Tybur et al., "Is the Relationship between Pathogen Avoidance and Ideological Conservatism Explained by Sexual Strategies?" *Evolution and Human Behavior* 36, no. 6 (November 2015): 489–97.

23 Emphasis added. "Fikratī," in Jamāl Fawzī, *al-Ṣabr wa-l-Thabāt: Nafathāt Mujāhid fī Sabīl Allāh: Dīwān Shiʿr* (Cairo: Dār al-Anṣār, 1980), 142–3.

24 This is sometimes called phenotype matching (using visual and auditory cues to recognize fellow group members). Hector Qirko, "Altruistic Celibacy, Kin-Cue Manipulation, and the Development of Religious Institutions," *Zygon* 39, no. 3 (September 2004): 681–706.

25 Ḥasan al-Bannā, "Bayna al-ams wa-l-yawm," in *Majmūʿat Rasāʾil al-Imām al-Shahīd Ḥasan al-Bannā* (Dār al-ḥaḍāra al-Islāmiyya, 1980), 111.

26 Jābir Qumayḥah, *Dhikrayātī maʿa Daʿwa al-Ikhwān fī al-Manzila Daqahliyya* (Giza: Markaz al-Iʿlām al-ʿArabī, 2009).

27 David Scott, *Conscripts of Modernity: The Tragedy of Colonial Enlightenment* (Durham: Duke University Press, 2004), 8, 135, 165–9.

28 G. Arunima, "Love and Revolution: An Introduction," in *Love and Revolution in the Twentieth-Century Colonial and Postcolonial World: Perspectives from South Asia and Southern Africa*, ed. G. Arunima et al. (Cham: Palgrave Macmillan, 2021), 5.

29 Sara Ahmed, *The Cultural Politics of Emotion*, 2nd ed. (Edinburgh: Edinburgh University Press, 2014), 42–4, 122–31.

30 José Manuel Sabucedo and Xiana Vilas, "Anger and Positive Emotions in Political Protest," *Universitas Psychologica* 13, no. 3 (July–Sept 2014): 829–38.

31 Sharīf Ḥatāta in interview with Selma Botman, February 28, 1980, Cairo. As quoted in Selma Botman, *The Rise of Egyptian Communism, 1939–1970* (New York: Syracuse University Press, 1988), 50–1.

32 Avraham Farhi interview with Rami Ginat, January 4 and February 3, 2005, Israel. As quoted in Ginat, *A History of Egyptian Communism*, 247.

33 "Daʿwatunā," in Ḥasan al-Bannā, *Majmūʿat Rasāʾil al-Imām al-Shahīd Ḥasan al-Bannā* (Damascus: Dār al-Ḥaḍāra al-Islāmiyya, 1980), 13.

34 Nichole Argo, "Why Fight?: Examining Self-Interested versus Communally-Oriented Motivations in Palestinian Resistance and Rebellion," *Security Studies* 18, no. 4 (2009): 651–80; Rachel L. Einwohner, "Opportunity, Honor, and Action in the Warsaw Ghetto Uprising of 1943," *American Journal of Sociology* 109, no. 3 (2003): 650–75; Jeremy Ginges and Scott Atran, "War as a Moral Imperative (Not Just Practical Politics by Other Means)," *Proceedings of the Royal Society B* 278 (2011): 2930–8.

35 "44 inculpés de communisme devant la cour martiale," *Affaire des "44"* (1954), 5 in IISH ARCH01722/ Folder 149; Mubārak ʿAbduh Faḍl, "Mudhakkirāt," in Rifʿat Saʿīd, *Hākadhā Takallama al-Shuyūʿīyūn: Maḥāḍir Niqāsh, Taqārīr, Mudhakkirāt, Rasāʾil, Taḥqīqāt Qaḍāʾīyya, Bayānāt Intikhābiyya* (Cairo: Sharikat al-Amal li-l-Ṭibāʿa wa-l-Nashr wa-l-Tawzīʿ, 1989), 125–79.

36 *Al-Muṣawwar* 1423 January 18, 1952, 1, 3, 12–13.

37 Wilāya, "al-Shakhṣīyyat al-Histīriyya," 639.

38 S.S. Hasan, *Christians versus Muslims in Modern Egypt* (Oxford: Oxford University Press, 2003), 61.

39 Michel de Certeau, *The Practice of Everyday Life* (Berkeley: University of California Press, 1984), 125–7.

40 Ann Starbæk Bager and Marianne Wolff Lundholt, "Organizational Storymaking as Narrative-Small-Story Dynamics," in *The Routledge Handbook of Counter-Narratives*, ed. Klarissa Lueg and Marianne Wolff Lundholt (New York: Routledge, 2021), 166–7.

41 Jacqueline Rose's *States of Fantasy* (1989), as quoted in Paula Ioanide, *The Emotional Politics of Racism* (Stanford: Stanford University Press, 2015), 18–19.

42 Emphasis added. Richard Feynman, "The Uncertainty of Science," in *The Meaning of It All* (New York: Perseus, 2009).

43 Sandford Borins and Beth Herst, *Negotiating Business Narratives: Fables of the Information Technology, Automobile Manufacturing, and Financial Trading Industries* (Toronto: Palgrave Macmillan, 2018), 13–19, 23–31.

44 Deborah Britzman, "Cultural Myths in the Making of a Teacher: Biography and Social Structure in Teacher Education," *Harvard Educational Review* 56, no. 4 (November 1986): 442–56.

45 Ioanide, *The Emotional Politics of Racism*, 3.

46 Gamal Abdel Nasser, Speech on the Fourth Anniversary of the Revolution (Nationalizing the Suez Canal), Alexandria, July 26, 1956, Bibliotheca Alexandrina, http://nasser.bibalex.org/TextViewer.aspx?TextID=SPCH-495-en

47 Scott Lucas, *Britain and Suez: The Lion's Last Roar* (Manchester: Manchester University Press, 1996), 46.

48 Mohamed H. Heikal, *Cutting the Lion's Tail: Suez through Egyptian Eyes* (New York: Arbor House, 1987), 124.

49 Keith Kyle, *Suez: Britain's End of Empire in the Middle East* (New York: I.B. Tauris, 2011), 132, 445–55, 462–3, 502–3, 643.

50 Ibid.

51 A.J. Stockwell, "Suez 1956 and the Moral Disarmament of the British Empire," in *Reassessing Suez 1956: New Perspectives on the Crisis and Its Aftermath*, ed. Simon C. Smith (Burlington: Ashgate, 2008), 232–6.

52 Yoram Meital, "Egyptian Perspectives on the Suez War," in *The 1956 War*, ed. David Tal (New York: Routledge, 2013), 200–4; Kyle, *Suez: Britain's End of Empire in the Middle East*, 484.

53 See *Ākhir Sā ʿa* 1150, November 7, 1956; *Ākhir Sā ʿa* 1151, November 14, 1956; *Ākhir Sā ʿa* 1152, November 21, 1956; *Ākhir Sā ʿa* 1153, November 28, 1956; *Ākhir Sā ʿa* 1154, December 4, 1956, *Ākhir Sā ʿa* 1155, December 12, 1956; and *Ākhir Sā ʿa* 1156, December 19, 1956.

54 Alia Mossallam, "Hikāyāt Sha ʿb—Stories of Peoplehood: Nasserism, Popular Politics and Songs in Egypt, 1956–1973" (PhD Dissertation, London School of Economics, 2021), 118–27; Betty LaDuke, "Egyptian Painter Inji Efflatoun: The Merging of Art, Feminism, and Politics," *NWSA Journal* 1, no. 3 (Spring, 1989): 480.

55 Elie Podeh, "Regaining Lost Pride: The Impact of the Suez Affair on Egypt and the Arab World," in *The 1956 War*, ed. David Tal (New York: Routledge, 2013), 210.

56 Sayyid Quṭb, "Hubal … Hubal," in *Al-A'māl al-Shi'riyyat al-Kāmila: Dirāsa fī Ash'ār Sayyid Quṭb*, ed. Ḥasan Ḥanafī (Damascus: Markaz al-Nāqid al-Thaqāfī, 2008), 279–80.

57 Šabasevičiute, *Sayyid Qutb: An Intellectual Biography*, 167, 201.

58 Sayyid Qutb, *Milestones* (Birmingham: Maktabah Publishers, 2006), 153–6.

59 Calvert, *Sayyid Qutb and the Origins of Radical Islamism*, 262–3.

60 El Shakry, "The Vexed Archives of Decolonization in the Middle East," 926–8.

Bibliography

Archives

Arabic Press Archives (Tel Aviv)
Bibliotheca Alexandrina (Alexandria)
Dār al-Kutub wa-l-Wathāʾiq al-Qawmiyya (Cairo)
Internationaal Instituut voor Sociale Geschiedenis/IISG (Amsterdam)
Library of Congress (Washington, DC)
National Archives (London)

Periodicals

Al-Ahrām
Ākhir Sāʿa
Al-Daʿwa
Al-Fajr al-Jadīd
Al-Hadaf
Al-Ikhwān al-Muslimūn
Al-Ithnayn
Kifāḥ al-Shaʿb
Kifāḥ al-Umma
Majallat al-Azhar
Majallat al-Ḍamīr
Majallat al-Hadaf
Majallat al-Risāla
Miṣr al-Fatāh
Al-Muqāwama al-Shaʿbiyya
Al-Muṣawwar
Al-Nadhīr
Al-Rāya
Shabāb Sayyidnā Muḥammad
Al-Ṣirāʿ al-Shaʿb
Al-Taṭawwur

Published Document Collections, Memoirs, and Poetry

ʿAbd al-Fattāh, Jamāl al-Dīn and ʿAbd al-Karīm Manṣūr, eds. *Qaḍiyyat Sayyārat al-Jīb, al-Ḥaythīyāt wa Naṣṣ al-Ḥukm*. Cairo: Dār al-Fikr al-Islāmī, 1951.

ʿAbd al-Ḥalīm, Maḥmūd Muḥammad. *Al-Ikhwān al-Muslimūn, Aḥdath Sanaʿat al-Tārīkh: Ruʾya min al-Dākhil, Juzʾ 1*. Alexandria: Dār al-Daʿwa, 1994.

ʿAbd al-Raʾūf, ʿAbd al-Munʿim. *Arghamtu "Fārūq" ʿalá al-Tanāzul ʿan al-ʿArsh: Mudhakkirāt*. Cairo: al-Zahrāʾ li-l-Iʿlām al-ʿArabī, 1988.

ʿAbd al-Rāziq, ʿAlī. *Al-Islām wa-Uṣūl al-Ḥukm: Baḥth fī al-Khilāfa wa-l-Ḥukūma fī al-Islām*. Cairo: Maṭbaʿat Miṣr Shirka Musāhama Miṣriyya, 1925.

Abdel-Nasser, Gamal. *The Philosophy of the Revolution*. Cairo: Mondiale Press, 1953.

Abū Sayf, Yūsuf, ed. *Wathāʾiq wa Mawāqif min Tārīkh al-Yasār al-Miṣrī, 1941–1957*. Cairo: Sharikat al-Amal li-l-Ṭibāʿa wa-l-Nashr, 2000.

ʿAfīfī, Abū al-Futūḥ. *Riḥlatī maʿa al-Ikhwān al-Muslimīn*. Cairo: Abū al-Futūḥ ʿAfīfī, 2003.

Aḥmad, Muḥammad Ḥasan. [pseud. for ʿAbd al-Raḥman ʿAbd al-Nāṣir]. *Al-Ikhwān al-Muslimūn fī al-Mīzān*. Cairo: n.p., 1946.

Al-Baghdādī, ʿAbd al-Laṭīf. *Mudhakkirāt ʿAbd al-Laṭīf al-Baghdādī*. Cairo: Al-Maktab al-Miṣrī al-Ḥadīth, 1977.

Al-Banna, Ḥasan. *Majmūʿat Rasāʾil al-Imām al-Shahīd Ḥasan al-Banna*. Beirut: Dār al-Ḥaḍāra al-Islāmiyya, 1980.

Al-Banna, Ḥasan. *Mudhakkirāt al-Daʿwa wa-l-Dāʿīyah*. Kuwait: Maktabat Āfāq, 2011 [First ed. 1950].

Al-Banna, Jamāl. *Khiṭābāt Ḥasan al-Banna al-Shābb ilá Abīhi*. Cairo: Dār al-Fikr al-Islāmī, 1990.

ʿAssāf, Maḥmūd. *Maʿa al-Imām al-Shahīd Ḥasan al-Banna*. Cairo: Maktabat ʿAyn Shams, 1993.

Curiel, Henri. *Pages autobiographiques: une contribution à l'histoire de la naissance du Parti Communiste Égyptien de 1940 à 1950*. Unpublished Typescript, 1977.

Dawḥ, Ḥasan. *Ṣafaḥāt min Jihād al-Shabāb al-Muslim*. Cairo: Dār al-Iʿtiṣām, 1979.

Dawḥ, Ḥasan. *25 ʿĀman fī Jamāʿah: Murūran bi-l-Ghābah*. Cairo: Dār al-Iʿtiṣām, 1983.

Al Dib, Mohamed Fathi. *Abdel Nasser et la révolution algérienne*. Paris: Éditions l'Harmattan, 1985.

Fawzī, Jamāl. *Al-Ṣabr wa-l-Thabāt: Nafathāt Mujāhid fī Sabīl Allāh: Dīwān Shiʿr*. Cairo: Dār al-Anṣār, 1980.

Fawzy-Rossano, Didar. *Mémoires d'une militante communiste (1942–1990) du Caire à Alger, Paris et Genève*. Paris: Éditions L'Harmattan, 1997.

Foreign Relations of the United States, 1952–1954: The Near and Middle East, Vol. IX, Part 2. Edited by John P. Glennon. Washington, DC: United States Government Printing Office, 1986.

Foreign Relations of the United States, 1951, The Near East and Africa, Vol. V. Edited by William Z. Slany. Washington, DC: United States Government Printing Office, 1982.

Fyfe, Hamilton. *The New Spirit in Egypt*. London: William Blackwood and Sons, 1911.

Al-Ghazālī, Muḥammad. *Min Hunā Na'lam … !*. Cairo: Nahḍat Miṣr, 2005 [First ed. 1951].

Gibb, H.A.R. *Modern Trends in Islam*. New York: Octagon Books, 1972 [First ed. 1947].

Ḥammūda, Ḥusayn. *Asrār Ḥarakat al-Ḍubbāṭ al-Aḥrār wa-l-Ikhwān al-Muslimūn*. Cairo: al-Zahrā' li-l-I'lām al-'Arabī, 1985.

Ḥanafī, Ḥasan, ed. *Al-A'māl al-Shi'riyyat al-Kāmila: Dirāsa fī Ash'ār Sayyid Quṭb*. Damascus: Markaz al-Nāqid al-Thaqāfī, 2008.

Heikal, Mohamed H. *Cutting the Lion's Tail: Suez through Egyptian Eyes*. New York: Arbor House, 1987.

Ḥusayn, Aḥmad. *Īmānī*. Cairo: n.p., 1936.

Ḥusayn, Aḥmad. *Mudhakkirāt Aḥmad Ḥusayn, Ra'īs Miṣr al-Fatāh*. Cairo: al-Hay'a al-Miṣriyya al-'Āmma li-l-Kitāb, 2007.

Jubaylī, Muḥammad 'Abd al-Ma'būd and Shuhudī 'Aṭīyya al-Shāfi'ī. *Ahdāfunā al-Waṭaniyya*. Cairo: Dār Miṣr al-Maḥrūsah, 2004 [First ed. 1945].

Kamāl, Aḥmad 'Ādil. *Al-Nuqaṭ Fawqa al-Ḥurūf: al-Ikhwān al-Muslimūn wa-l-Niẓām al-Khāṣṣ*. Cairo: al-Zahrā' li-l-I'lām al-'Arabī, 1989.

Khālid, Khālid Muḥammad. *Min Huna Nabda'*. Beirut: Jamī' al-Ḥuqūq Maḥfūẓa li-l-Mu'alif, 1974 [First ed. Cairo, 1950].

Al-Khūlī, al-Bahī. *Islām, lā Shuyū'iyya wa lā Ra'smāliyya*. Cairo: Dār al-Kitāb al-'Arabī, 1951.

Maḥkamat Jināya Miṣr: Raqm al-Qaḍiyya 2021. Cairo: Miṣr al-Qadīmah, 1951.

Al-Marāghī, Murtaḍá. *Gharā'ib min 'Ahd Fārūq wa Bidāyat al-Thawra al-Miṣriyya*. Beirut: Dār al-Nahār, 1976.

Markaz Wathā'iq wa-Tārīkh Miṣr al-Mu'āṣir. *Ightiyāl Amīn 'Uthmān*, edited by Nabīl 'Abd al-Ḥamīd Sayyid Aḥmad and Yuwāqīm Rizq Murquṣ. Cairo: Al-Hay'a al-Miṣriyya al-'Āmma li-l-Kitāb, 1992.

Muḥyī al-Dīn, Khālid. *Wa-l-Ān Atakallam*. Cairo: Markaz al-Ahrām li-l-Tarjama wa-l-Nashr, Mu'assasat al-Ahrām, 1992.

Najīb, Muḥammad. *Kuntu Ra'īs li-Miṣr: Mudhakkirāt Muḥammad Najīb*. Cairo: Al-Maktab al-Miṣrī al-Ḥadīth, 1984.

Naṣīr, Muṣṭafá 'Abd al-Majīd et al. *Thawrat Yūliyū wa-l-Ḥaqīqa al-Ghā'iba*. Cairo: Al-Hay'a al-Miṣriyya al-'Āmma li-l-Kitāb, 1997.

Neguib, Mohammed. *Egypt's Destiny*. London: Victor Gollancz, 1955.

Nightingale, Florence. *Letters from Egypt: A Journey on the Nile, 1849–1850*. New York: Grove Press, 1987 [First. ed. 1854].

Nu'mān, 'Alī Muṣṭafá. *Shāhid 'alá, Jihād al-Ikhwān al-Muslimīn fī Ḥarb Filasṭīn, 1948*. Cairo: Dār al-Tawzī' wa-l-Nashr al-Islāmiyya, 2002.

Al-Qaraḍāwī, Yūsuf. *Ibn al-Qarya wa-l-Kuttāb: Malāmiḥ Sīra wa Masīra*. Cairo: Dār al-Shurūq, 2002.

Qumayḥah, Jābir. *Dhikrayātī ma'a Da'wa al-Ikhwān fī al-Manzila Daqahliyya*. Giza: Markaz al-I'lām al-'Arabī, 2009.

Quṭb, Sayyid. *Maʿrakatunā maʿa al-Yahūd*. Cairo: n.p., 1950.
Quṭb, Sayyid. *Maʿrakat al-Islām wa-l-Raʾsmāliyya*. Cairo: Maktabat Wahbah, 1951.
Quṭb, Sayyid. *Al-ʿAdāla al-Ijtimāʿiyya fī al-Islām*. Beirut: Dār al-Shurūq, 1995.
Quṭb, Sayyid. *Milestones*. Birmingham: Maktabah Publishers, 2006.
Ramaḍān, ʿAbd al-ʿAẓīm. *Al-Ikhwān al-Muslimūn wa-l-Tanẓīm al-Sirrī*. Cairo: Maktabat Rūz al-Yūsuf, 1982.
Russell, Sir Thomas. *Egyptian Service 1902–1946*. London: John Murray, 1923.
El Saadawi, Nawal. *A Daughter of Isis: The Autobiography of Nawal El Saadawi*, translated by Sherif Hetata. London: Zed Books, 1999.
El Saadawi, Nawal. *Walking through Fire: The Later Years of Nawal El Saadawi*, translated by Sherif Hetata. London: Zed Books, 2009.
Ṣabbāgh, Maḥmūd. *Ḥaqīqat al-Tanẓīm al-Khāṣṣ wa-Dawruhu fī Daʿwat al-Ikhwān al-Muslimīn*. Cairo: Dār al-Iʿtiṣām, 1988.
Sādāt, Anwar. *Al-Baḥth ʿan al-Dhāt: Qiṣṣat Ḥayātī*. Cairo: Al-Maktab al-Miṣrī al-Ḥadīth, 1978.
Sādāt, Anwar. *In Search of Identity*. New York: Harper and Row, 1978.
Al-Saʿīd, Al-Saʿīd Muṣṭafá. *Qānūn al-ʿUqūbāt al-Miṣrī: al-Ṣādir bi-l-Qānūn Raqm 58 li-Sanat 1937*. Cairo: Maṭbaʿat Fatḥ Allāh al-Yās Nūrī wa-Awlādihi, 1937.
Saʿīd, Rifʿat. *Hākadhā Takallama al-Shuyūʿīyūn: Maḥāḍir Niqāsh, Taqārīr, Mudhakkirāt, Rasāʾil, Taḥqīqāt Qaḍāʾīyyah, Bayānāt Intikhābiyya*. Cairo: Sharikat al-Amal li-l-Ṭibāʿa wa-l-Nashr wa-l-Tawzīʿ, 1989.
Al-Sharīf, Kāmil. *Al-Muqāwama fī Qanat al-Suways*. Cairo: Dār al-Wafāʾ, 2000.
Shīrīzī, Mārsīl [Mārsīl Isrāʾīl]. *Awrāq Munāḍil Īṭālī fī Miṣr*. Cairo: Dār al-ʿĀlam al-Thālith, 2002.
ʿUbayd, Makram. *Al-Kitāb al-Aswad fī al-ʿAhd al-Aswad*. Cairo: Al-Markaz al-ʿArabī li-l-Baḥth wa-l-Nashr, 1984 [First ed. 1943].
ʿUthmān, Luṭfī. *Qaḍiyyat Maqtal al-Nuqrāshī Bāshā*. Cairo: Maṭbaʿat al-Tawakkul, 1950.

Secondary Sources

Abdalla, Ahmed. *The Student Movement and National Politics in Egypt, 1923–1973*. Cairo: The American University in Cairo Press, 2008.
Abu-Lughod, Lila. *Writing Women's Worlds: Bedouin Stories*. Berkeley: University of California Press, 1993.
Abu-Lughod, Lila. "Seductions of the 'Honor Crime.'" *Differences* 22, no. 1 (May 2011): 17–63.
Ackerman, Joshua M. and John A. Bargh. "The Purpose-Driven Life: Commentary on Kenrick et al. (2010)." *Perspectives on Psychological Science* 5, no. 3 (2010): 323–6.
Addington, Jean and Mariapaola Barbato. "Social Cognition in Those at High Risk for Psychosis." In *Social Neuroscience: Brain, Mind, and Society*, edited by Russell K. Schutt et al., 187–207. Cambridge: Harvard University Press, 2015.

Aguirre, B. E., Dennis Wenger, and Gabriela Vigo. "A Test of the Emergent Norm Theory of Collective Behavior." *Sociological Forum* 13, no. 2 (1998): 301–20.

Ahmed, Sara. "Affective Economies." *Social Text* 79, Vol. 22, no. 2 (Summer 2004): 117–39.

Ahmed, Sara. "Collective Feelings: Or, The Impressions Left by Others." *Theory, Culture & Society* 21, no. 2 (2004): 25–42.

Ahmed, Sara. "Declarations of Whiteness: The Non-Performativity of Anti-Racism." *Borderlands* 3, no. 2 (2004).

Ahmed, Sara. "The Nonperformativity of Antiracism." *Meridians* 7, no. 1 (2006): 104–26.

Ahmed, Sara. *The Cultural Politics of Emotion*, 2nd ed. Edinburgh: Edinburgh University Press, 2014.

Anderson, Kyle J. *The Egyptian Labor Corps: Race, Space, and Place in the First World War*. Austin: University of Texas Press, 2021.

Antadze, Nino. "Moral Outrage as the Emotional Response to Climate Injustice." *Environmental Justice* 13, no. 1 (2020): 21–6.

ʿArab, Muḥammad Ṣābir. *Ḥādith 4 Fibrāyir 1942 wa-l-ḥayāh al-siyāsiyya al-Miṣrīyya*. Cairo: Dār al-Maʿārif, 1985.

Argo, Nichole. "Why Fight?: Examining Self-Interested versus Communally-Oriented Motivations in Palestinian Resistance and Rebellion." *Security Studies* 18, no. 4 (2009): 651–80.

Armbrust, Walter. "The Formation of National Culture in Egypt in the Interwar Period: Cultural Trajectories." *History Compass* 7, no. 1 (2009): 155–80.

Armony, Jorge, and Patrik Vuilleumier, eds. *The Cambridge Handbook of Human Affective Neuroscience*. New York: Cambridge University Press, 2013.

Arunima, G. et al., eds. *Love and Revolution in the Twentieth-Century Colonial and Postcolonial World: Perspectives from South Asia and Southern Africa*. Cham: Palgrave Macmillan, 2021.

El-Awaisi, ʿAbd al-Fattah Muhammad. *The Muslim Brothers and the Palestine Question 1928–1947*. London: Tauris, 1998.

Badran, Margot. *Feminists, Islam, and the Nation: Gender and the Making of Modern Egypt*. Princeton: Princeton University Press, 1995.

Badrawi, Malak. *Ismaʿil Sidqi (1875–1950): Pragmatism and Vision in Twentieth Century Egypt*. Surrey: Curzon Press, 1996.

Badrawi, Malak. *Political Violence in Egypt 1910–1925*. New York: Routledge, 2013.

Bagnoli, Carla. *Morality and the Emotions*. Oxford: Oxford University Press, 2011.

Baider, Fabienne, and Georgeta Cislaru, eds. *Cartographie des émotions*. Paris: Presses Sorbonne Nouvelle, 2013.

Baker, Keith Michael, and Dan Edelstein, eds. *Scripting Revolution: A Historical Approach to the Comparative Study of Revolutions*. Stanford: Stanford University Press, 2015.

Bal, Mieke. *Narratology: Introduction to the Theory of Narrative*. Toronto: University of Toronto Press, 1999.

Bandura, Albert. *Social Foundations of Thought and Action: A Social Cognitive Theory.* Englewood Cliffs: Prentice Hall, 1986.

Bandura, Albert, et al. "Mechanisms of Moral Disengagement in the Exercise of Moral Agency." *Journal of Personality and Social Psychology* 71, no. 2 (1996): 364–74.

Bandura, Albert. "Moral Disengagement in the Perpetration of Inhumanities." *Personality and Social Psychology Review* 3, no. 3 (1999): 193–209.

Barak, Efraim. "Egyptian Intellectuals in the Shadow of British Occupation." *British Journal of Middle Eastern Studies* 35, no. 2 (August 2008): 173–86.

Barakat, Robert A. "Arabic Gestures." *Folklore* 6, no. 4 (Spring 1973): 749–93.

Barclay, Katie and Peter N. Stearns, eds. *The Routledge History of Emotions in the Modern World.* New York: Routledge, 2023.

Baron, Beth. "Mothers, Morality, and Nationalism in Pre-1919 Egypt." In *The Origins of Arab Nationalism*, edited by Rashid Khalidi et al., 271–88. New York: Columbia University Press, 1991.

Baron, Beth. *Egypt as Woman: Nationalism, Gender, and Politics.* Berkeley: University of California Press, 2005.

Baron, Beth. *The Orphan Scandal: Christian Missionaries and the Rise of the Muslim Brotherhood.* Stanford: Stanford University Press, 2014.

Barrett Cox, Amanda. "Correcting Behaviors and Policing Emotions: How Behavioral Infractions Become Feeling-Rule Violations." *Symbolic Interaction* 39, no. 3 (August 2016): 484–503.

Barthes, Roland. "Introduction à l'analyse structurale des récits." *Communications* 8, (1966): 1–27.

Bayyūmī, Zakarīyā. *Al-Ikhwān al-Muslimūn wa-l-Jamāʿāt al-Islāmiyya fī al-Ḥayāt al-Siyāsiyya al-Miṣriyya, 1928–1948.* Cairo: Maktabat Wahbah, 1979.

Beidelman, T.O. *Moral Imagination in Kaguru Modes of Thought.* Bloomington: Indiana University Press, 1986.

Beinin, Joel. *Was the Red Flag Flying There?.* Berkeley: University of California Press, 1990.

Beinin, Joel. "Exile and Political Activism: The Egyptian-Jewish Communists in Paris, 1950–9." *Diaspora: A Journal of Transnational Studies* 2, no. 1 (Spring 1992): 79–94.

Beinin, Joel. *The Dispersion of Egyptian Jewry: Culture, Politics, and the Formation of a Modern Diaspora.* Cairo: The American University of Cairo Press, 2005.

Beinin, Joel and Zachary Lockman. *Workers on the Nile: Nationalism, Communism, Islam, and the Egyptian Working Class, 1882–1954.* Cairo: The American University in Cairo Press, 1998.

Beissinger, Mark R. "Structure and Example in Modular Political Phenomena: The Diffusion of Bulldozer/Rose/Orange/Tulip Revolutions." *Perspectives on Politics* 5, no. 2 (2007): 259–76.

Bennett, Elaine M. "Storytelling and the Moral Tradition: An Examination of the Pedagogy of Storytelling for Moral Enculturation." In *The Many Facets of Storytelling: Global Reflections on Narrative Complexity*, edited by Melanie Rohse et al., 13–21. Leiden: Brill, 2013.

Ben Prestel, Joseph. *Emotional Cities: Debates on Urban Change in Berlin and Cairo, 1860–1910*. Oxford: Oxford University Press, 2017.

Besnier, Niko. *Gossip and the Everyday Production of Politics*. Honolulu: University of Hawai'i Press, 2009.

Blau, Peter M. and Joseph E. Schwartz. *Crosscutting Social Circles: Testing a Macrostructural Theory of Intergroup Relations*. New Brunswick: Transaction, 1997.

Bonanno, G. A. and C.L. Burton. "Regulatory Flexibility: An Individual Differences Perspective on Coping and Emotion Regulation." *Perspectives on Psychological Science* 8, no. 6 (2013): 591–612.

Borins, Sandford and Beth Herst. *Negotiating Business Narratives: Fables of the Information Technology, Automobile Manufacturing, and Financial Trading Industries*. Toronto: Palgrave Macmillan, 2018.

Botman, Selma. *The Rise of Egyptian Communism, 1939–1970*. New York: Syracuse University Press, 1988.

Bourdieu, Pierre. *Bourdieu: A Critical Reader*, edited by Richard Shusterman. Oxford: Blackwell, 1999.

Brichs, Ferran Izquierdo et al., eds. *Political Islam in a Time of Revolt*. Cham: Springer International, 2017.

Britzman, Deborah. "Cultural Myths in the Making of a Teacher: Biography and Social Structure in Teacher Education." *Harvard Educational Review* 56, no. 4 (November 1986): 442–56.

Bruns, Axel. "Filter Bubble." *Internet Policy Review* 8, no. 4 (2019): 1–14.

Bryant, Clifton D., ed. *Deviant Behavior: Readings in the Sociology of Norm Violation*. New York: Taylor and Francis, 1990.

Al-Bukhārī, Ṣaḥīḥ. *The Early Years of Islam* [*Kitāb al-Jāmiʿ al-Ṣaḥīḥ*], translated by Muhammad Asad. Selangor: Islamic Book Trust, 2013.

Burkholder, Amanda R. et al. "Intergroup Relationships, Context, and Prejudice in Childhood." In *Handbook of Children and Prejudice*, edited by Hiram E. Fitzgerald et al. Cham: Springer, 2019.

Calbris, Geneviève. "Geste et parole." *Langue français* 68, (1985): 66–84.

Calvert, John. *Sayyid Qutb and the Origins of Radical Islamism*. Oxford: Oxford University Press, 2013.

Carter, B.L. *The Copts in Egyptian Politics, 1918–1952*. Cairo: American University of Cairo Press, 1988.

Centola, Damon. *How Behavior Spreads*. Princeton: Princeton University Press, 2000.

Centola, Damon. "The Social Origins of Networks and Diffusion." *American Journal of Sociology* 120, no. 5 (March 2015): 1295–338.

De Certeau, Michel. *The Practice of Everyday Life*. Berkeley: University of California Press, 1984.

De Certeau, Michel. *Heterologies: Discourse on the Other*, translated by Brian Massumi. Minneapolis: University of Minnesota Press, 1986.

Choudhury, Suparna, and Jan Slaby, eds. *Critical Neuroscience*. Oxford: John Wiley and Sons, 2016.

Christensen, J.F., and A. Gomila. "Moral Dilemmas in Cognitive Neuroscience of Moral Decision-Making: A Principled Review." *Neuroscience and Biobehavioral Reviews* 36, (2012): 1249–64.

Christie, Hazel et al. "The Emotional Economy of Housing." *Environment and Planning A* 40, (2008): 2296–312.

Cikara, Mina, and Jay J. Van Bavel. "The Neuroscience of Intergroup Relations: An Integrative Review." *Perspectives on Psychological Science* 9, no. 3 (2014): 245–74.

Cikara, Mina, and Jay J. Van Bavel. "Intergroup Schadenfreude: Motivating Participation in Collective Violence." *Current Opinion in Behavioral Sciences* 3, (June 2015): 12–17.

Clancy-Smith, Julia A. *Rebel and Saint: Muslim Notables, Populist Protest, Colonial Encounters (Algeria and Tunisia, 1800–1904)*. Berkeley: University of California Press, 1994.

Cleveland, Les. "Soldiers' Songs: The Folklore of the Powerless." *New York Folklore* 11, nos. 1–4 (1985): 79–97.

Clewis, Robert. "What Is Kant's Theory of Humor?" In *Ethics in Comedy: Essays on Crossing the Line*, edited by Steven A. Benko, 40–56. Jefferson: McFarland & Co., 2020.

Clewis, Robert. *Kant's Humorous Writings: An Illustrated Guide*. London: Bloomsbury, 2020.

Cocks, Geoffrey, and Travis L. Crosby. *Psycho/History: Readings in the Method of Psychology, Psychoanalysis, and History*. New Haven: Yale University Press, 1987.

Cohen, Michael J. and Martin Kolinsky, eds. *Demise of the British Empire in the Middle East: Britain's Response to Nationalist Movements, 1943–55*. London: Frank Cass, 1998.

Cohen, Stanley. *Folk Devils and Moral Panics: The Creation of the Mods and Rockers*. London: Routledge, 2002.

Collins, Alan, and Colin Jennings. "A Club Good Perspective on Gangsters and Revolutionaries." Discussion Paper no. 88, University of Portsmouth. December 1996.

Cooper, Artemis. *Cairo in the War, 1939–1945*. London: Hamish Hamilton, 1989.

Craggs, Ruth and Claire Wintle, eds. *Cultures of Decolonisation: Transnational Productions and Practices, 1945–70*. Manchester: Manchester University Press, 2016.

Cresswell, Timothy. *In Place/Out of Place: Geography, Ideology, and Transgression*. Minneapolis: University of Minnesota Press, 1996.

Crowcroft, Barnaby. "Egypt's Other Nationalists and the Suez Crisis of 1956." *The Historical Journal* 59, no. 1 (March 2016): 253–85.

Darwin, John. "Decolonization and the End of Empire." In *The Oxford History of the British Empire Vol. 5: Historiography*, edited by Robin W. Winks, 541–57.Oxford: Oxford University Press, 1998.

Della Porta, Donatella. *Where Did the Revolution Go? Contentious Politics and the Quality of Democracy*. New York: Cambridge University Press, 2016.

Di-Capua, Yoav. "The Intellectual Revolt of the 1950s and 'The Fall of the *Udabā*'." In *Commitment and beyond: Reflections on/of the Political in Arabic Literature since the 1940s*, edited by Friederike Pannewick and Georges Khalil, 89–104. Wiesbaden: Ludwing Reichert, 2015.

Downes, Stephanie et al., eds. *Feeling Things: Objects and Emotions through History*. Oxford: Oxford University Press, 2018.

Du Bois, John W. and Elise Kärkkäinen. "Taking a Stance on Emotion: Affect, Sequence, and Intersubjectivity in Dialogic Interaction." *Text & Talk* 32, no. 4 (2012): 433–51.

Dunér, David, and Christer Ahlberger, eds. *Cognitive History: Mind, Space, and Time*. Berlin: De Gruyter Oldenbourg, 2019.

Durkheim, Emilé. *Moral Education*, translated by E. K. Wilson and H. Schnurer. New York: Free Press, 1973.

Durkheim, Emilé. "The Determination of Moral Facts." In *Sociology and Philosophy*, translated by D.F. Pocock, 35–62. New York: The Free Press, 1974.

Dziekan, Marek M. "The Categorisation of Emotions in the Classical Arabic Language. A Preliminary Lexicographical Study." In *Codes and Rituals of Emotions in Asian and African Cultures*, edited by Nina Pawlak, 63–81. Warsaw: ELIPSA, 2009.

Edwards, Jill, ed. *El Alamein and the Struggle for North Africa: International Perspectives from the Twenty-first Century*. Cairo: American University in Cairo Press, 2012.

Egerton, George. "Politics and Autobiography: Political Memoir as Polygenre." *Biography* 15, no. 3 (Summer 1992): 221–42.

Einwohner, Rachel L. "Opportunity, Honor, and Action in the Warsaw Ghetto Uprising of 1943." *American Journal of Sociology* 109, no. 3 (2003): 650–75.

Ellickson, Robert C. "The Market for Social Norms." *American Law and Economics Review* 3, no. 1 (Spring 2001): 1–49.

Ellis, Matthew H. *King Me: The Political Culture of Monarchy in Interwar Egypt and Iraq*. MA Thesis, Oxford University, 2005.

Erlich, Haggai. *Students and University in Twentieth Century Egyptian Politics*. London: Frank Cass, 1989.

Fahmy, Khaled. "Prostitution in Egypt in the Nineteenth Century." In *Outside In: On the Margins of the Modern Middle East*, edited by Eugene Rogan, 77–103. London: I.B. Tauris, 2002.

Fahmy, Ziad. *Ordinary Egyptians: Creating the Modern Nation through Popular Culture*. Stanford: Stanford University Press, 2011.

Farag, Iman. "Private Lives, Public Affairs: The Uses of Adab." In *Muslim Traditions and Modern Techniques of Power*, edited by Armando Salvatore, 93–120. New Brunswick: Transaction, 2001.

Fass, Paula S. "The Memoir Problem." *Reviews in American History* 34, no. 1 (2006): 107–23.

Ferris, Jesse. *Nasser's Gamble: How Intervention in Yemen Cause the Six-Day War and the Decline of Egyptian Power*. Princeton: Princeton University Press, 2013.

Festinger, Leon, et al. *When Prophecy Fails*. Minneapolis: University of Minnesota Press, 1956.

Feynman, Richard. *The Meaning of It All*. New York: Perseus, 2009.

Fine, Gary Alan. "The Social Organization of Adolescent Gossip: The Rhetoric of Moral Evaluation." In *Children's Worlds and Children's Language*, edited by Jenny Cook-Gumperz et al., 405–24. Berlin: Mouton de Gruyter, 1986.

Al-Fīruzābādī. *Al-Qāmūs al-Muḥīṭ*. Beirut: Al-Risāla, 2015.

Foolen, Ad. "The Expressive Function of Language: Towards a Cognitive Semantic Approach." *The Language of Emotions*, edited by Susanne Niemeier and René Dirven, 15–32. Amsterdam: John Benjamins, 1997.

Freitag, Ulrike, et al., eds. *Urban Violence in the Middle East: Changing Cityscapes in the Transition from Empire to Nation State*. New York: Berghahn Books, 2015.

Frimer, Jeremy A., and Lisa Sinclair. "Moral Heroes Look Up and to the Right." *Personality and Social Psychology Bulletin* 42, no. 3 (2016): 400–10.

De Gayffier-Bonneville, Anne-Claire. "La guerre du canal 1951–1952." *Cahiers de la Méditerranée* 70, (June 2005): 111–36.

Gazzaniga, Michael S., ed. *Handbook of Cognitive Neuroscience*. New York: Springer Science, 1984.

Genette, Gérard. *Narrative Discourse: An Essay in Method [Discours du récit]*, translated by Jane E. Lewin. Ithaca: Cornell University Press, 1980.

Georgakopoulou, Alexandra. *Small Stories, Interaction, and Identities*. Amsterdam: John Benjamins, 2007.

Georgakopoulou, Alexandra. et al., eds. *Small Stories Research: Tales, Tellings, and Tellers across Contexts*. New York: Routledge, 2024.

Gerber, Haim. *State, Society, and Law in Islam: Ottoman Law in Comparative Perspective*. New York: State University of New York Press, 1994.

Gershoni, Israel. "The Muslim Brothers and the Arab Revolt in Palestine, 1936–39." *Middle Eastern Studies* 22, no. 3 (July 1986): 367–97.

Gershoni, Israel. "Egyptian Liberalism in an Age of 'Crisis of Orientation': *Al-Risāla*'s Reaction to Fascism and Nazism, 1933–39." *International Journal of Middle East Studies* 31, (1999): 551–76.

Gershoni, Israel, ed. *Arab Responses to Fascism and Nazism*. Austin: University of Texas Press, 2014.

Gershoni, Israel and James P. Jankowski. *Egypt, Islam, and the Arabs: The Search for Egyptian Nationhood, 1900–1930*. New York: Oxford University Press, 1983.

Gershoni, Israel and James P. Jankowski. "Imagining and Reimagining the Past: The Use of History by Egyptian Nationalist Writers, 1919–1952." *History and Memory* 4, no. 2. (Fall–Winter 1992): 12–29.

Gershoni, Israel and James P. Jankowski. *Redefining the Egyptian Nation 1930–1945*. Cambridge: Cambridge University Press, 1995.

Gershoni, Israel, Amy Singer, and Y. Hakan Erdem, eds. *Middle East Historiographies: Narrating the Twentieth Century*. Seattle: University of Washington Press, 2006.

Gershoni, Israel and James Jankowski. *Confronting Fascism in Egypt: Dictatorship versus Democracy in the 1930s*. Stanford: Stanford University Press, 2010.

Gesink, Indira Falk. *Islamic Reform and Conservatism: Al-Azhar and the Evolution of Modern Sunni Islam*. New York: I.B. Tauris, 2014.

Gibb, H.A.R. *Modern Trends in Islam*. New York: Octagon Books, 1972.

Gigerenzer, Gerd, and Reinhard Selten. *Bounded Rationality: The Adaptive Toolkit*. Cambridge: The MIT Press, 2001.

Ginat, Rami. *The Soviet Union and Egypt, 1945–1955*. New York: Routledge, 1993.

Ginat, Rami. *A History of Egyptian Communism*. Boulder: Lynne Rienner, 2011.

Ginges, Jeremy and Scott Atran. "War as a Moral Imperative (Not Just Practical Politics by Other Means)." *Proceedings of the Royal Society B* 278, (2011): 2930–8.

Gintis, Herbert, et al., eds. *Moral Sentiments and Material Interests: The Foundation of Cooperation in Economic Life*. Cambridge: Massachusetts Institute of Technology, 2005.

Glass, Jennifer, Vern L. Bengtson, and Charlotte Chorn Dunham. "Attitude Similarity in Three-Generation Families: Socialization, Status Inheritance, or Reciprocal Influence?" *American Sociological Review* 51, no. 5 (October 1986): 685–98.

Goldschmidt Jr., Arthur, ed. *Historical Dictionary of Egypt*. 4th ed. Lanham: Rowman and Littlefield, 2013.

Goldstone, Jack A. "Toward a Fourth Generation of Revolutionary Theory." *Annual Review of Political Science* 4, (2001): 139–87.

Gollwitzer, Peter M., and John A. Bargh, eds. *The Psychology of Action: Linking Cognition and Motivation to Behavior*. New York: The Guilford Press, 1996.

Gomila, Toni, and Paco Calvo. "Directions for an Embodied Cognitive Science: Toward an Integrated Approach." In *Handbook of Cognitive Science: An Embodied Approach*, edited by Paco Calvo and Toni Gomila, 1–25. Oxford: Elsevier, 2008.

Gooren, Henri. *Religious Conversion and Disaffiliation: Tracing Patterns of Change in Faith Practices*. New York: Palgrave Macmillan, 2010.

Gordon, Joel. *Nasser's Blessed Movement: Egypt's Free Officers and the July Revolution*. New York: Oxford University Press, 1992.

Gorman, Anthony. *Historians, State and Politics in Twentieth Century Egypt: Contesting the Nation*. New York: Routledge, 2003.

Gottlieb, Gilbert. *Synthesizing Nature-Nurture: Prenatal Roots of Instinctive Behavior*. New York: Taylor and Francis, 1997.

Gottlieb, Gilbert and Carolyn Tucker Halpern. "A Relational View of Causality in Normal and Abnormal Development." *Development and Psychopathology* 14, (2002): 421–35.

Graesser, Arthur C., and Victor Ottati. "Why Stories? Some Evidence, Questions, and Challenges." In *Knowledge and Memory, Advances in Social Cognition Vol. 8*, edited by Robert S. Wyer, Jr., 121–32. New York: Psychology Press, 1995.

Gross, James J. et al. "The Tie That Binds? Coherence among Emotion Experience, Behavior, and Physiology." *Emotion* 5, no. 2 (2005): 175–90.

Gruber, June, ed. *The Oxford Handbook on Positive Emotion and Psychopathology*. Oxford: Oxford University Press, 2019.

Haddad, Yvonne Yazbeck. *Contemporary Islam and the Challenge of History*. Albany: State University of New York Press, 1982.

Hafez, Mohammed M. *Why Muslims Rebel: Repression and Resistance in the Islamic World*. Boulder: Lynne Rienner Publishers, 2003.

Hahn, Peter L. *The United States, Great Britain, and Egypt, 1945–1956: Strategy and Diplomacy in the Early Cold War*. Chapel Hill: University of North Carolina Press, 1991.

Haidt, Jonathan. "The Moral Emotions." In *Handbook of Affective Sciences*, edited by R.J. Davidson et al., 852–70. Oxford: Oxford University Press, 2003.

Hall, Todd. *Emotional Diplomacy: Official Emotion on the International Stage*. Ithaca: Cornell University Press, 2015.

Hall, Todd. "On Provocation: Outrage, International Relations, and the Franco–Prussian War." *Security Studies* 26, no. 1 (2017): 1–29.

Hammad, Hanan. "Between Egyptian 'National Purity' and 'Local Flexibility': Prostitution in al-Mahalla al-Kubra in the First Half of the 20th Century." *Journal of Social History* 44, no. 3 (Spring 2011): 768–74.

Al-Haq, Fawwaz Al-Abed and Ahmad Khair Allah Al Sharif. "A Comparative Study of Some Metaphorical Conceptualizations of Happiness and Anger in English and Arabic." Master's Thesis. Yarmouk University, 2007.

Hards, Sarah. "Tales of Transformation: The Potential of a Narrative Approach to Pro-Environmental Practices." *Geoforurm* 43, no. 4 (June 2012): 760–71.

Hardy, Roger. *The Muslim Revolt: A Journey through Political Islam*. London: Hurst, 2010.

Hasan, S.S. *Christians versus Muslims in Modern Egypt*. Oxford: Oxford University Press, 2003.

Hatina, Meir. *ʿUlamaʾ, Politics, and the Public Sphere: An Egyptian Perspective*. Salt Lake City: University of Utah Press, 2010.

Heikal, Mohamed Hasanein. *Sphinx and Commissar: The Rise and Fall of Soviet Influence in the Arab World*. New York: Harper and Row, 1978.

Helal, Emad Ahmed. "Egypt's Overlooked Contribution to World War II." In *The World in World Wars: Experiences, Perceptions and Perspectives from Africa and Asia*, edited by Heike Liebau et al., 217–47. Ledien: Brill, 2010.

Herman, David. "Scripts, Sequences, and Stories: Elements of a Postclassical Narratology." *PMLA* 112, no. 5 (October 1997): 1046–59.

Hesse, Carla. "The New Empiricism." *Cultural and Social History* 1, no. 2 (2004): 201–7.

Hexter, J.H. "Fernand Braudel and the *Monde Braudellien* ..." In *The Annales School: Critical Assessments*, edited by Stuart Clark, 30–84. London: Routledge, 1999.

Heyworth-Dunne, J. *Religious and Political Trends in Modern Egypt*. Washington, DC: n.p., 1950.

Hier, Sean P. "Thinking beyond Moral Panic: Risk, Responsibility, and the Politics of Moralization." *Theoretical Criminology* 12, no. 2 (2008): 173–90.

Hilāl, ʿImād. *Al-Baghāyā fī Miṣr: Dirāsa Tārīkhiyya Ijtimāʿiyya, 1834–1949*. Cairo: Al-ʿArabī li-l-Nashr wa-l-Tawzīʿ, 2001.

Hitlin, Steven and Stephen Vaisey, eds. *Handbook of the Sociology of Morality*. New York: Springer, 2010.

Hoffer, Eric. *The True Believer*. New York: HarperCollins, 2002.

Holland, Matthew F. *America and Egypt: From Roosevelt to Eisenhower*. Westport: Praeger, 1996.

Honey, Christopher J. et al. "Not Lost in Translation: Neural Responses Shared across Languages." *Journal of Neuroscience* 32, no. 44 (October 2012): 15277–83.

Hopkins, Phil. *Mass Moralizing: Marketing and Moral Storytelling*. Lanham: Lexington Books, 2015.

Humphreys, R. Stephen. "Qurʾanic Myth and Narrative Structure in Early Islamic Historiography." In *Tradition and Innovation in Late Antiquity*, edited by F.M. Clover and R.S. Humphreys, 271–90. Madison: University of Wisconsin Press, 1989.

Huston, Sam. "'Monks by Night and Knights by Day': Ḥasan al-Banna, *Tarbīya*, and the Embodied Ethics of the Early Muslim Brotherhood." *Religion Compass* 12, no. 7 (2018): 1–11.

Iannaccone, Laurence R. "Why Strict Churches Are Strong." *American Journal of Sociology* 99, no. 5 (March 1994): 1180–211.

Ibrahim, Vivian. *The Copts of Egypt: The Challenges of Modernisation and Identity*. London: I.B. Tauris, 2011.

Inbar, Yoel and David Pizarro. "Pollution and Purity in Moral and Political Judgment." In *Advances in Experimental Moral Psychology*, edited by Hagop Sarkissian and Jennifer Cole Wright, 111–125. London: Bloomsbury, 2014.

Ioanide, Paula. *The Emotional Politics of Racism*. Stanford: Stanford University Press, 2015.

Ismael, Tareq Y. and Rifaʿat el-Saʿid. *The Communist Movement in Egypt, 1920–1988*. New York: Syracuse University Press, 1990.

Jacob, Wilson Chacko. *Working Out Egypt: Effendi Masculinity and Subject Formation in Colonial Modernity, 1870–1940*. Durham: Duke University Press, 2011.

Jacobs, Scott E. and James J. Gross. "Emotion Regulation in Education." In *International Handbook of Emotions in Education*, edited by Reinhard Pekrun and Lisa Linnenbrink-Garcia, 183–201. New York: Routledge, 2014.

Jacquemond, Richard. *Conscience of the Nation: Writers, State, and Society in Modern Egypt*, translated by David Tresilian. Cairo: The American University of Cairo Press, 2008.

Al-Jallad, Nader. "The Concept of 'Shame' in Arabic: Bilingual Dictionaries and the Challenge of Defining Culture-Based Emotions." *Language Design* 12, (2010): 31–57.

Jankowski, James P. *Egypt's Young Rebels: Young Egypt, 1933–1952*. Stanford: Hoover Institution Press, 1975.

Jansen, Jan C. and Jürgen Osterhammel. *Decolonization: A Short History*, translated by Jeremiah Riemer. Princeton: Princeton University Press, 2017.

Jansen, Johannes J.G. "Ḥasan al-Banna's Earliest Pamphlet." *Die Welt des Islams* 32, no. 2 (1992): 254–8.

Jasko, Katarzyna et al. "Rebel with a Cause: Personal Significance from Political Activism Predicts Willingness to Self-Sacrifice." *Journal of Social Issues* 75, no. 1 (2019): 314–49.

Jasper, James. *The Art of Moral Protest: Culture, Biography, and Creativity in Social Movements*. Chicago: University of Chicago Press, 1995.

Jasper, James. "Emotions and Social Movements: Twenty Years of Theory and Research." *Annual Review of Sociology* 37, (2011): 285–303.

Jasper, James. *The Emotions of Protest*. Chicago: University of Chicago Press, 2018.

Jasper, James and Frédéric Volpi, eds. *Microfoundations of the Arab Uprisings*. Amsterdam: Amsterdam University Press, 2018.

Jayyusi, Salma Khadra, ed. *Classical Arabic Stories: An Anthology*. New York: Columbia University Press, 2010.

Jetten, Jolanda and Matthew J. Hornsey, eds. *Rebels in Groups: Dissent, Deviance, Difference, and Defiance*. Oxford: Wiley-Blackwell, 2011.

Jindra, Ines W. *A New Model of Religious Conversion: Beyond Network Theory and Social Constructivism*. Leiden: Brill, 2014.

Judt, Tony. *Past Imperfect: French Intellectuals, 1944–1956*. Berkeley: University of California Press, 1992.

Kahneman, Daniel. "Maps of Bounded Rationality: Psychology for Behavioral Economics." *The American Economic Review* 93, no. 5 (December 2003): 1449–75.

Katz, Mark N. *Revolutions and Revolutionary Waves*. New York: St. Martin's Press, 1999.

Katz, Mark N. "Cycles, Waves, and Diffusion." In *The Encyclopedia of Political Revolutions*, edited by Jack A. Goldstone, 126–27. New York: Routledge, 2014.

Kent, John. "The Egyptian Base and the Defence of the Middle East, 1945–55." *Journal of Imperial and Commonwealth History* 21, (September 1993).

Kerbœuf, Anne-Claire. "The Cairo Fire of 26 January 1952 and the Interpretations of History." In *Re-Envisioning Egypt 1919–1952*, edited by Arthur Goldschmidt et al., 194–216. Cairo: American University in Cairo Press, 2005.

Kholoussy, Hanan. *For Better, for Worse: The Marriage Crisis That Made Modern Egypt*. Stanford: Stanford University Press, 2010.

Khouri, Mounah Abdallah. *Poetry and the Making of Modern Egypt: 1882–1922*. Leiden: Brill, 1971.

Kosicki, Piotr H. *Catholics on the Barricades: Poland, France, and "Revolution," 1891–1956*. Stanford: Stanford University Press, 2018.

Kövecses, Zoltán. *Emotion Concepts*. New York: Springer-Verlag, 1990.

Kozma, Liat. "White Drugs in Interwar Egypt: Decadent Pleasures, Emaciated Fellahin, and the Campaign against Drugs." *Comparative Studies of South Asia, Africa and the Middle East* 33, no. 1 (2013): 89–101.

Krämer, Gudrun. *The Jews in Modern Egypt, 1914–1952*. London: I.B. Tauris, 1989.

Krämer, Gudrun. *Hasan al-Banna*. London: Oneworld, 2013.

Kreutz, Michael. "The Greek Classics in Modern Middle Eastern Thought." In *Judaism, Christianity, and Islam in the Course of History: Exchange and Conflicts*, edited by Lothar Gall and Dietmar Willoweit, 77–92. Munich: De Gruyter, 2016.

Kruglanski, Arie. *The Motivated Mind: The Selected Works of Arie W. Kruglanski*. New York: Routledge, 2018.

Kurtines William, M. and Jacob L. Gewirtz, eds. *Handbook of Moral Behavior and Development*. Hillsdale: Lawrence Erlbaum, 1991.

Jindra, Ines W. *A New Model of Religious Conversion: Beyond Network Theory and Social Constructivism*. Leiden: Brill, 2014.

LaDuke, Betty. "Egyptian Painter Inji Efflatoun: The Merging of Art, Feminism, and Politics." *NWSA Journal* 1, no. 3 (Spring, 1989): 474–85.

Lakoff, George and Mark Johnson. *Metaphors We Live By*. Chicago: University of Chicago Press, 1980.

Legare, Cristine H. and Mark Nielsen. "Imitation and Innovation: The Dual Engines of Cultural Learning." *Trends in Cognitive Sciences* 19, no. 11 (November 2015): 688–99.

Lévi-Strauss, Claude. "The Structural Study of Myth." *The Journal of American Folklore* 68, no. 270 (October–December 1955): 428–44.

Lia, Brynjar. *The Society of the Muslim Brothers in Egypt: The Rise of an Islamic Mass Movement, 1928–1942*. Reading: Ithaca Press, 1998.

Lia, Brynjar. "Autobiography or Fiction? Ḥasan al-Banna's Memoirs Revisited." *Journal of Arabic and Islamic Studies* 15, (2015): 199–226.

Longo, Mariano. *Emotions through Literature: Fictional Narratives, Society and the Emotional Self*. New York: Routledge, 2020.

Lopez, Shaun T. "The Dangers of Dancing: The Media and Morality in 1930s Egypt." *Comparative Studies of South Asia, Africa, and the Middle East* 24, no. 1 (2004): 97–105.

Lord, Robert G. and Mary C. Kernan. "Scripts as Determinants of Purposeful Behavior in Organizations." *The Academy of Management Review* 12, no. 2 (1987): 265–77.

Louis, William Roger. *Ends of British Imperialism: The Scramble for Empire, Suez, and Decolonization*. New York: I.B. Tauris, 2006.

Lucas, Scott. *Britain and Suez: The Lion's Last Roar*. Manchester: Manchester University Press, 1996.

Lueg, Klarissa and Marianne Wolff Lundholt, eds. *The Routledge Handbook of Counter-Narratives*. New York: Routledge, 2021.

Al-Maḥallāwī, Ḥanafī. *Al-Malika Nāzlī*. Cairo: al-Dār al-Miṣriyya al-Lubnāniyya, 1995.

Mallard, Graham. *Bounded Rationality and Behavioral Economics*. New York: Routledge, 2016.

Malti-Douglas, Fedwa. "Classical Arabic Crime Narratives: Thieves and Thievery in *Adab* Literature." *Journal of Arabic Literature* 19, no. 2 (1988): 108–27.

Ibn Manẓūr, Muḥammad ibn Mukarram. *Al-Lisān al-ʿArab*, 15, vols. Beirut: Dār Lisān al-ʿArab, 1955–6.

Mar, Raymond A. "The Neuropsychology of Narrative: Story Comprehension, Story Production and Their Interrelation." *Neuropsychologia* 42, (2004): 1414–34.

Mar, Raymond A. "The Neural Bases of Social Cognition and Story Comprehension." *Annual Review of Psychology* 62, (2011): 103–34.

Martin, Luther H. and Jesper Sørensen, eds. *Past Minds: Studies in Cognitive Historiography*. London: Equinox, 2011.

Mashak, Shahrzad Pirzad et al. "A Comparative Study on Basic Emotion Conceptual Metaphors in English and Persian Literary Texts." *International Education Studies* 5, no. 1 (February 2012): 200–17.

Mason, Michael. "'The Decisive Volley': The Battle of Ismailia and the Decline of British Influence in Egypt, January–July 1952." *The Journal of Imperial and Commonwealth History* 19, no. 1 (1991): 45–64.

Matt, Susan J. "Current Emotion Research in History: Or, Doing History from the Inside Out." *Emotion Review* 3, no. 1 (January 2011): 117–24.

Matt, Susan J. and Peter N. Stearns, eds. *Doing Emotions History*. Urbana: University of Illinois Pres, 2014.

Mayer, Thomas. *Egypt and the Palestine Question, 1936–1945*. Berlin: K. Schwarz, 1983.

McLeave, Hugh. *The Last Pharaoh: Farouk of Egypt*. New York: McCall Publishing Company, 1970.

Meijer, Roel. *The Quest for Modernity: Secular Liberal and Left-Wing Political Thought in Egypt, 1945–1958*. New York: Routledge, 2002.

Mink, Louis O. "Narrative Form as a Cognitive Instrument." In *The Writing of History: Literary Form and Historical Understanding*, edited by Robert H. Canary and Henry Kozicki, 129–49. Madison: University of Wisconsin Press, 1978.

Mitchell, Richard P. *The Society of the Muslim Brothers*. Oxford: Oxford University Press, 1969.

Moaddel, Mansoor. *Islamic Modernism, Nationalism, and Fundamentalism: Episode and Discourse*. Chicago: The University of Chicago Press, 2005.

Morack, Ellinor. "Fear and Loathing in 'Gavur' Izmir: Emotions in Early Republican Memories of the Greek Occupation (1919–1922)." *International Journal of Middle East Studies* 49, no. 1 (February 2017): 71–89.

Morgan, Jayne and Kathleen Krone. "Bending the Rules of 'Professional' Display: Emotional Improvisation in Caregiver Performances." *Journal of Applied Communication Research* 29, no. 4 (2001): 317–40.

Morris, Brandi S. et al. "Stories vs. Facts: Triggering Emotion and Action-Taking on Climate Change." *Climate Change* 154, nos. 1–2 (May 2019): 19–36.

Morsella, Ezequiel, John A. Bargh, and Peter M. Gollwitzer, eds. *Oxford Handbook of Human Action*. Oxford: Oxford University press, 2009.

Mossallam, Alia. "Hikāyāt Shaʿb – Stories of Peoplehood: Nasserism, Popular Politics and Songs in Egypt, 1956–1973." PhD Dissertation, London School of Economics, 2021.

Muḥammad, Muḥsin. *Man Qatala Ḥasan al-Bannā?* Cairo: Dār al-Shurūq, 1987.

Murray, Damian R. and Mark Schaller. "The Behavioral Immune System: Implications for Social Cognition, Social Interaction, and Social Influence." In *Advances in Experimental Social Psychology* Vol. 53, eds. James M. Olson, Mark P. Zanna, 75–129. Cambridge: Academic Press, 2016.

Oatley, Keith. *Such Stuff as Dreams: The Psychology of Fiction*. Oxford: Wiley-Blackwell, 2011.

Oatley, Keith. *The Passionate Muse: Exploring Emotion in Stories*. Oxford: Oxford University Press, 2012.

Ochsner, Kevin N. et al. "Functional Imaging Studies of Emotion Regulation: A Synthetic Review and Evolving Model of the Cognitive Control of Emotion." *Annals of the New York Academy of Sciences* 1251, no. 1 (March 2012): E1–E24.

Ochsner, Kevin N. and James J. Gross. "The Cognitive Control of Emotions." *Trends in Cognitive Sciences* 9, no. 5 (May 2005): 242–9.

Ovid. *Metamorphoses Book VIII*, edited by A.S. Hollis. Oxford: Oxford University Press, 1983.

Páez, Dario et al. "Psychosocial Effects of Perceived Emotional Synchrony in Collective Gatherings." *Journal of Personality and Social Psychology* 108, no. 5 (2015): 711–29.

Parsons, Laila. "Soldiering for Arab Nationalism: Fawzi Al-Qawuqji in Palestine." *Journal of Palestine Studies* 36, no. 4 (2007): 33–48.

Pennington, Donald C. *Social Cognition*. London: Routledge, 2000.

Pernau, Margrit and Helge Jordheim et al., eds. *Civilizing Emotions*. Oxford: Oxford University Press, 2015.

Perrault, Gilles. *A Man Apart: The Life of Henri Curiel*, translated by Bob Cumming. London: Zed Books, 1987.

Philipp, Thomas. "The Autobiography in Modern Arab Literature and Culture." *Poetics Today* 14, no. 3 (Autumn 1993): 573–604.

Pierson, Paul. *Politics in Time: History, Institutions, and Social Analysis*. Princeton: Princeton University Press, 2004.

Pietilä, Tuulikki. *Gossip, Markets, and Gender: How Dialogue Constructs Moral Value in Post-Socialist Kilimanjaro*. Madison: University of Wisconsin Press, 2007.

Pivetti, Monica et al. "Shame, Guilt, and Anger: Their Cognitive, Physiological, and Behavioral Correlates." *Current Psychology* 35, no. 4 (December 2016): 690–9.

Podeh, Elie. *The Politics of National Celebrations in the Arab Middle East*. Cambridge: Cambridge University Press, 2011.

Pollard, Lisa. *Nurturing the Nation: The Family Politics of Modernizing, Colonizing, and Liberating Egypt, 1805–1923*. Berkeley: University of California Press, 2005.

Pollard, Lisa. "From Husbands and Housewives to Suckers and Whores: Marital-Political Anxieties in the 'House of Egypt', 1919–48." *Gender and History* 21, no. 3 (November 2009): 647–69.

Ponticelli, Christy M. "Crafting Stories of Sexual Identity Reconstruction." *Social Psychology Quarterly* 62, no. 2 (1999): 157–72.

Popp-Baier, Ulrike. "Narrating Embodied Aims: Self-Transformation in Conversion Narratives: A Psychological Analysis." *Forum Qualitative Sozialforschung* 2, no. 3 (September 2001): 1–18.

Pormann, Peter E. "The Arab 'Cultural Awakening (Nahda)', 1870–1950, and the Classical Tradition." *International Journal of the Classical Tradition* 13, no. 1 (Summer 2006): 3–20.

Al-Qāḍī, Fārūq. *Fursān al-Āmal: Taʾammul fī al-Ḥarakat al-Ṭullābiyya al-Miṣriyya.* Cairo: Markaz al-Buḥūth al-ʿArabiyya, 2000.

Qirko, Hector. "Altruistic Celibacy, Kin-Cue Manipulation, and the Development of Religious Institutions." *Zygon* 39, no. 3 (September 2004): 681–706.

Abdul-Raheem, Ahmed. "Moral Metaphor and Gender in Arab Visual Culture: Debunking Western Myths." *Social Semiotics* 2019. DOI: 10.1080/10350330.2019.1604991.

Raymond, André. *Cairo*, translated by Willard Wood. Cambridge: Harvard University Press, 2000.

Reddy, William M. *The Navigation of Feeling: A Framework for the History of Emotions.* Cambridge: Cambridge University Press, 2001.

Reich, Robert. "Four Morality Tales." In *Popular Culture: An Introductory Text*, edited by Jack Nachbar and Kevin Lause, 110–20. Madison: University of Wisconsin Press, 1992.

Reid, Donald Malcolm. *Cairo University and the Making of Modern Egypt.* Cambridge: Cambridge University Press, 1990.

Reynolds, Nancy Y. *A City Consumed: Urban Commerce, the Cairo Fire, and the Politics of Decolonization in Egypt.* Stanford: Stanford University Press, 2012.

Ricœur, Paul. "The Metaphorical Process as Cognition, Imagination, and Feeling." *Critical Inquiry* 5, no. 1 (Autumn 1978): 143–59.

Ricœur, Paul. "Preface to Bultmann's *Jesus, mythologie et demythologization.*" In *Essays on Biblical Interpretation*, edited by Lewis Seymour Mudge, 31–46. Philadelphia: Fortress Press, 1980.

Ricœur, Paul. *The Rule of Metaphor: The Creation of Meaning in Language*, translated by Robert Czerny et al. London: Routledge, 2004.

Riḍā, Aḥmad. *Muʿjam Matn al-Lugha.* Beirut: Dār Maktabat al-Ḥayāt, 1958–61.

Ritzer, George and J. Michael Ryan, eds. *The Concise Encyclopedia of Sociology.* Oxford: Wiley-Blackwell, 2011.

Rizvi, Kishwar, ed. *Affect, Emotion, and Subjectivity in Early Modern Muslim Empires.* Leiden: Brill, 2017.

Roberts, M.J.D. "The Society for the Suppression of Vice and Its Early Critics, 1802–1812." *The Historical Journal* 26, no. 1 (1983): 159–76.

Rosenwein, Barbara H. *Emotional Communities in the Early Middle Ages.* Ithaca: Cornell University Press, 2006.

Rothermund, Dietmar. *The Routledge Companion to Decolonization.* New York: Routledge, 2006.

Russell, Mona L. *Creating the New Egyptian Woman: Consumerism, Education, and National Identity, 1863–1922.* New York: Palgrave Macmillan, 2004.

Sabaseviciute, Giedre. "Sayyid Qutb and the Crisis of Culture in Late 1940s Egypt." *International Journal of Middle East Studies* 50 (2018): 15–101.

Sabaseviciute, Giedre. *Sayyid Qutb: An Intellectual Biography.* Syracuse: Syracuse University Press, 2021.

Ṣabbāgh, Maḥmūd. *Ḥaqīqat al-Tanẓīm al-Khāṣṣ wa-Dawruhu fī Daʿwat al-Ikhwān al-Muslimīn*. Cairo: Dār al-Iʿtiṣām, 1989.

Sabucedo, José Manuel and Xiana Vilas. "Anger and Positive Emotions in Political Protest." *Universitas Psychologica* 13, no. 3 (July–September 2014): 829–38.

Sadler, Neil. *Fragmented Narrative: Telling and Interpreting Stories in the Twitter Age*. New York: Routledge, 2022.

Saʿīd, ʿAbd al-Mughnī. *Asrār al-Siyāsa al-Miṣriyya fī Rubʿ Qarn*. Cairo: Dār al-Ḥurriyya, 1985.

Said, Edward W. *Orientalism*. New York: Vintage Books, 1979.

Said, Edward W. *Covering Islam*. New York: Vintage Books, 1997.

Saʿīd, Rifʿat. *Tārīkh al-Munaẓẓamāt al-Yasāriyya al-Miṣriyya, 1940–1950*. Cairo: Dār al-Thaqāfa al-Jadīda, 1976.

Saʿīd, Rifʿat. *Tārīkh al-Ḥaraka al-Shuyūʿiyya al-Miṣriyya*. Cairo: Sharikat al-Amal, 2007.

Sajid, Mehdi. "A Reappraisal of the Role of Muḥibb al-Dīn al-Khaṭīb and the YMMA in the Rise of the Muslim Brotherhood." *Islam and Christian-Muslim Relations* 29, no. 2 (2018): 193–213.

Sander, David. "Models of Emotion: The Affective Neuroscience Approach." In *The Cambridge Handbook of Human Affective Neuroscience*, edited by Jorge Armony and Patrik Vuilleumier, 5–53. New York: Cambridge University Press, 2013.

Sawyer, Peter Robert. *Socialization to Civil Society*. Albany: State University of New York Press, 2005.

Schrand, Irmgard. *Jews in Egypt: Communists and Citizens*. Münster: Lit Verlag, 2004.

Scott, David. *Conscripts of Modernity: The Tragedy of Colonial Enlightenment*. Durham: Duke University Press, 2004.

Shafik, Viola. "Prostitute for a Good Reason: Stars and Morality in Egypt." *Women's Studies International Forum* 24, no. 6 (2001): 711–25.

Shākir, Aḥmad Muḥammad and ʿAbd al-Raḥman bin ʿAbd al-ʿAzīz bin Ḥammād al-ʿAql, ed. *Jamharat Maqālāt al-ʿAllāma al-Shaykh Aḥmad Muḥammad Shākir*. Riyadh: Dār al-Riyāḍ, 2005.

Shākir, Aḥmad Muḥammad and Ashraf Ibn ʿAbd al-Raḥīm, ed. *Taqrīr ʿan Shuʾūn al-Taʿlīm wa-l-Qaḍāʾ: Taqrīr Muqaddam li-Jalālat al-MalikAbd al-ʿAzīz Āl Sai>ʿūd, Sanat 1949*. Cairo: Maktabat al-Imām al-Bukhārī, 2009.

El-Shakry, Omnia. "Youth as Peril and Promise: The Emergence of Adolescent Psychology in Postwar Egypt." *International Journal of Middle East Studies* 43, (2011): 591–610.

El-Shakry, Omnia. "The Vexed Archives of Decolonization in the Middle East." *American Historical Review* 120, (2015): 920–34.

El-Shakry, Omnia. *The Arabic Freud: Psychoanalysis and Islam in Modern Egypt*. Princeton: Princeton University Press, 2017.

Shalabī, ʿAlī. *Miṣr al-Fatāh wa Dawruhā fī al-Siyāsa al-Miṣriyya, 1933–1941*. Cairo: Dār al-Kitāb al-Jāmiʿī, 1982.

El-Sharif, Ahmad. "The Muslim Prophetic Tradition: Spatial Source Domains for Metaphorical Expressions." In *Religion, Language, and the Human Mind*, edited by Paul Chilton and Monika Kopytowska, 263–93. Oxford: Oxford University Press, 2018.

Sharkey, Heather J. *American Evangelicals in Egypt: Missionary Encounters in an Age of Empire*. Princeton: Princeton University Press, 2008.

Shepard, William. *Sayyid Qutb and Islamic Activism: A Translation and Critical Analysis of Social Justice in Islam*. Leiden: Brill, 1996.

Shuleqitz, Malka Hillel, ed. *The Forgotten Millions: The Modern Jewish Exodus from Arab Lands*. London: Continuum, 2000.

Silbert, Lauren J. et al. "Coupled Neural Systems Underlie the Production and Comprehension of Naturalistic Narrative Speech." *PNAS* 111, no. 43 (October 2014): 4687–96.

Simonsen, Jørgen Bæk, ed. *Youth and Youth Culture in the Contemporary Middle East*. Aarhus: Aarhus University Press, 2005.

Skovgaard-Peterson, Jakob. *Defining Islam for the Nation*. Leiden: Brill, 1997.

Smith, Charles D. "4 February 1942: Its Causes and Its Influence on Egyptian Politics and on the Future of Anglo-Egyptian Relations, 1937–1945." *International Journal of Middle East Studies* 10, (1979): 453–79.

Smith, Sharon S. "From Violent Words to Violent Deeds? Assessing Risk from Threatening Communications." PhD dissertation, Georgetown University, 2006.

Smith, Simon C., ed. *Reassessing Suez 1956: New Perspectives on the Crisis and Its Aftermath*. Burlington: Ashgate, 2008.

Snævarr, Stefán. *Metaphors, Narratives, Emotions: Their Interplay and Impact*. Amsterdam: Editions Rodopi, 2010.

Snow, David A. "The Sociology of Conversion." *Annual Review of Psychology* 10, (1984): 167–90.

Snow, David A. and Richard Machalek. "The Convert as a Social Type." *Sociological Theory* 1, (1983): 259–89.

Sophocles. *Antigone*, translated by Reginald Gibbons and Charles Segal. Oxford: Oxford University Press, 2003.

Stadlbauer, Susanne. "Language Ideologies in the Arabic Diglossia of Egypt." *Colorado Research in Linguistics* 22, (June 2010): 1–19.

Staw, Barry M., et al. "Threat Rigidity Effects in Organizational Behavior: A Multilevel Analysis." *Administrative Science Quarterly* 26, no. 4 (December 1981): 501–24.

Stearns, Peter N., ed. *American Behavioral History: An Introduction*. New York: New York University Press, 2005.

Stearns, Peter N. *Childhood in World History*. New York: Routledge, 2006.

Stearns, Peter N. and Carol Zisowitz. *Emotion and Social Change: Toward a New Psychohistory*. New York: Holmes & Meier, 1988.

Steen, Ivan D. "Cleansing the Puritan City: The Reverend Henry Morgan's Antivice Crusade in Boston." *The New England Quarterly* 54, no. 3 (September 1981): 385–411.

Steffgen, George and Mario Gollwitzer, eds. *Aggressive Behavior*. Göttingen: Hogrefe & Huber, 2007.

Stephens, Greg J., Lauren J. Silbert, and Uri Hasson. "Speaker–Listener Neural Coupling Underlies Successful Communication." *PNAS* 107, no. 32 (August 2010): 14425–30.

Stone, Charles and Lucas Bietti, eds. *Contextualizing Human Memory: An Interdisciplinary Approach to Understanding How Individuals and Groups Remember the Past*. New York: Routledge, 2016.

Sundar, Nandini. "Vigilantism, Culpability, and Moral Dilemmas." *Critique of Anthropology* 30, no. 1 (March 2010): 113–21.

Al-Ṭabarī, Muḥammad Ibn Jarīr. *The History of al-Ṭabarī Vol. X: The Conquest of Arabia*, translated by Fred. M. Donner. Albany: State University of New York Press.

Tal, David, ed. *The 1956 War*. New York: Routledge, 2013.

Tangney, June Price, Jeff Stuewig, and Debra J. Mashek. "Moral Emotions and Moral Behavior." *Annual Review of Psychology* 58, (2007): 345–72.

Tekgül, Nil. *Emotions in the Ottoman Empire: Politics, Society and Family in the Early Modern Era*. London: Bloomsbury, 2023.

Terrizzi Jr., John A., et al. "Disgust: A Predictor of Social Conservatism and Prejudicial Attitudes toward Homosexuals." *Personality and Individual Differences* 49, no. 6 (October 2010): 587–92.

Terrizzi Jr., John A., et al. "The Behavioral Immune System and Social Conservatism: A Meta-Analysis." *Evolution and Human Behavior* 34, no. 2 (March 2013): 99–108.

Tignor, Robert. *Capitalism and Nationalism at the End of Empire*. Princeton: Princeton University Press, 2015.

Thompson, E.P. *The Making of the English Working Class*. New York: Pantheon, 1964.

Thompson, Elizabeth F. "The Paris Peace Conference as Counterrevolution in the Middle." Working Paper presented at the Roundtable *War and Revolution in the Middle East*, School of International Service at American University. Washington, DC: March 2023.

Thompson, Ross A. "Emotional Regulation and Emotional Development." *Educational Psychology Review* 3, no. 4 (December 1991): 269–307.

Thompson, William E. and Jennifer C. Gibbs, eds. *Deviance and Deviants: A Sociological Approach*. Oxford: Wiley Blackwell, 2017.

Thornhill, Michael T. "Britain and the Collapse of Egypt's Constitutional Order, 1950–52." *Diplomacy and Statecraft* 13, no. 1 (2002): 121–52.

Thornhill, Michael T. *Road to Suez: The Battle of the Canal Zone*. Stroud: Sutton Publishing, 2006.

Tilly, Charles. *The Politics of Collective Violence*. New York: Cambridge University Press, 2003.

Tilly, Charles. *Social Movements, 1768–2004*. Boulder: Paradigm Publishers, 2004.

Tilly, Charles. *Regimes and Repertoires*. Chicago: University of Chicago Press, 2006.

Troutt-Powell, Eve M. *A Different Shade of Colonialism: Egypt, Great Britain, and the Mastery of the Sudan*. Berkeley: University of California Press, 2003.

Tsang, Jo-Ann. "Moral Rationalization and the Integration of Situational Factors and Psychological Processes in Immoral Behavior." *Review of General Psychology* 6, no. 1 (2002): 25–50.

Tybur, Joshua M. et al. "Is the Relationship between Pathogen Avoidance and Ideological Conservatism Explained by Sexual Strategies?" *Evolution and Human Behavior* 36, no. 6 (November 2015): 489–97.

Underhill, James W. *Humboldt, Worldview and Language*. Edinburgh: Edinburgh University Press, 2009.

Vatikiotis, P.J. *Arab and Regional Politics in the Middle East*. New York: Routledge, 2015.

Vishkin, Allon, Yochanan Bigman, and Maya Tamir. "Religion, Emotion Regulation, and Well-Being." In *Religion and Spirituality across Cultures*, edited by Chu Kim-Prieto, 247–70. New York: Springer, 2014.

Voiklis, John and Bertram F. Malle. "Moral Cognition and Its Basis in Social Cognition and Social Regulation." In *Atlas of Moral Psychology*, edited by Kurt Gray and Jesse Graham. New York: The Guilford Press, 2018.

von Scheve, Christian and Mikko Salmela, eds. *Collective Emotions*. Oxford: Oxford University Press, 2014.

Vowles, Kjell and Martin Hultman. "Dead White Men vs. Greta Thunberg: Nationalism, Misogyny, and Climate Change Denial in Swedish Far-Right Digital Media." *Australian Feminist Studies* 36, no. 110 (2021): 414–31.

Walzer, Michael. *The Revolution of the Saints*. New York: Harvard University Press, 1968.

Wehr, Hans. *A Dictionary of Modern Written Arabic*, 3rd ed., edited by J. Milton Cown. Ithaca: Spoken Language Services, 1976.

White, Hayden. "The Value of Narrativity in the Representation of Reality." In *On Narrative*, edited by W.J.T. Mitchell. Chicago: University of Chicago Press, 1980.

White, Hayden. *The Content of the Form: Narrative Discourse and Historical Representation*. Baltimore: Johns Hopkins University Press, 1987.

Wichhart, Stefanie. *Britain, Egypt, and Iraq during World War II: The Decline of Imperial Power in the Middle East*. London: I.B. Tauris, 2022.

Wiktorowicz, Quintan. *Islamic Activism: A Social Movement Theory Approach*. Bloomington: Indiana University Press, 2004.

Wilford, Hugh. *America's Great Game: The CIA's Secret Arabists and the Shaping of the Modern Middle East*. New York: Basic Books, 2013.

Williams, Keelah E.G. and Art Hinshaw. "Outbursts: An Evolutionary Approach to Emotions in the Mediation Context." *Negotiation Journal* 34, no. 2 (April 2018): 165–86.

Wuthnow, Robert. *Meaning and Moral Order: Explorations in Cultural Analysis*. Berkeley: University of California Press, 1987.

Yaman, Hikmet. "The Concept of *Ḥikmah* in Early Islamic Thought." PhD dissertation, Harvard University, 2008.

Yousef, Hoda. *Composing Egypt: Reading, Writing, and the Emergence of a Modern Nation. 1870–1930*. Stanford: Stanford University Press, 2016.

Zeghal, Malika. "Religion and Politics in Egypt: The Ulema of al-Azhar, Radical Islam, and the State." *International Journal of Middle East Studies* 31, no. 3 (August 1999): 371–99.

Zigon, Jarrett. *Morality: An Anthropological Perspective*. New York: Berg, 2008.

Zollner, Barbara. *The Muslim Brotherhood: Hasan al-Hudaybi and Ideology*. New York: Routledge, 2009.

Index

Abadan 6, 117, 119
Abaza, Fikri 120
ʿAbbas Bridge demonstration 63–4
Abdel-Nasser, Gamal 5–6, 15, 129, 156, 163, 171–4
ʿAbdu Fadl, Mubarak 35, 77–80, 168
ʿAbd al-Ghani Hasan, Muhammad 129
ʿAbd al-Halim, Mahmud 62
ʿAbd Allah, Mustafa 105
ʿAbd al-Majid, Ahmad 61
ʿAbd al-Raziq, Shaykh ʿAli 86–7
ʿAbd al-Samiʿ, Husayn 33, 64
ʿAbidin, ʿAbd al-Hakim 146
abrogation treaty 117, 119–21
actionable metaphors 102
adab/ādāb 26, 28
affective economy 167, 182 n.66
al-ʿAfifi, Hamid 123
ʿAfifi, Abu al-Futuh 45
Aflatun, Inji 79, 88, 90–1, 117, 122, 129, 168, 173
Ahmad, Muhammad Sid 90
Ahmed, Sara 7, 166, 182 n.66
al-Ahram 2, 173
Akhir Lahza 120, 122–3, 142, 146
Akhir Saʿa 17–18, 22, 88–9, 118, 122, 126, 131–2, 141, 206 n.33
al-Akkad 80
ʿAli Mahir Pasha 36–7, 49, 61, 140, 155–6
ʿAli Pasha, Muhammad 39
Allfrey, Charles 41
American Revolution 124–5, 128
Amin, Ahmad 101–2
ʿāmmīyya (dialectical Arabic) 13
Anglo-Egyptian Treaty 103, 117, 119, 163
Arab emotions 8, 11
Arab Revolt 53, 61
ʿAshmawi, Salih 66, 68, 104, 146, 153–4
Asinine English 132–3
ʿAskariyya, Hamid 52
ʿAssaf, Mahmud 53
Aswan Dam 171
āṭifa (feeling, passion) 12, 59
Attlee, Clement 118–19, 123
Auxiliary Police *(Bulūk al-Niẓām)* 140–1, 150, 155
ʿAyb 99–100
al-Azhar 3, 21, 39, 51, 68, 80, 84–7, 97, 102, 106, 120, 134, 144, 150

al-Bagouri, Muhammad ʿUmar 28
The Ballad of King Faruk (Faruq) 34
al-Banna, Hasan 36, 43, 46, 51–7, 59–62, 64, 66–70, 72, 146, 160, 166
Baron, Beth 42, 190 n.52
basic emotions 30
Battle of El Alamein 31–2
The Battle of Islam and Capitalism 63
Battle of Stalingrad 76
Battle of Tell al-Kabir 147
Battle of the Auxiliary Police *(Bulūk al-Niẓām)* 141
biographical reconstruction 48
Black Book scandal 38–9, 43, 50, 69, 76
Black Saturday 5, 151–2
blasphemy 20–1, 183 n.11
blessed movement 118–24, 155–8
Blue Shirts (paramilitary group) 48–9, 61
Boddice, Rob 8
Bolshevik Revolution 86
Bourdieu, Pierre 92
The Boy and the Dog (short story) 110–11
Breuer, Josef 23
British occupation 2, 4–5, 19, 35–6, 85, 110, 126, 134, 147, 171
Buthayna 97–8

Cairo 1
- demonstration 134
- happy 148
- under occupation 33–7
- population 24

Cairo Fire 1, 5, 15, 139, 147, 151–3, 156–7

Certeau, Michel de 169, 181 n.61
Churchill, Winston 123–4, 134, 140, 142–3, 163, 172
Clancy-Smith, Julia A. 59
code-switching 13, 164
Cold War 4–6, 9–11, 15, 63, 73, 119, 128–9, 160–1
  communism during 77–81
colonization 7, 29, 85, 108, 129, 162
commandos 140–5
Commonwealth troops 3–4, 34
communism 6, 9, 46, 48, 63, 79–80, 83, 86–7, 91, 93, 110, 160, 167
communist morality tales 107–11
Communist Pasha 87–92
conceptual metaphor theory 26
conversion story 14, 47–8
Craggs, Ruth 7
Curiel, Henri 75–7, 79, 85–6, 89–91, 168

dangerous mob 3
Darwin, John 159
Darwish, Yusuf 75, 85, 90, 108, 208 n.58
Dawh, Hasan 58, 146
al-Da'wa 67, 96, 114, 136, 145–6, 154
decolonization 6–7, 11, 115, 137, 159–60, 162
Democratic Movement for National Liberation (DMNL) 81, 83, 89, 91, 117, 136, 156, 158
Democratic Union 75–6
Denison, J. H. 7
al-Din, Salah 55
Dinshaway massacre 20, 37, 128–30
al-Din, Siraj 154
The Dog's Birthday Party (short story) 111–15
Downes, Stephanie 12
Dulles, Allan 157
Durkheim, Émile 22, 181 n.64
Duwayk, Raymond 75

Eden, Anthony 163
effendiyya 56
Egypt
  blessed movement 118–24
  emotions 98, 131–6
  General Mission schools 52
  higher education 21
  house of 42–4
  moral marketplace 29–30
  normative discourses in 1940s 24–9
  political parties 75
  politics of 137–8
  twentieth-century 19–24, 29
Egyptian Constitution of 1923 20
Egyptian Movement for National Liberation (EMNL) 9, 14, 43, 76–81, 83–7, 89, 92
Egyptian Penal Code of 1937 20
Emotional Communities (Rosenwein) 11
emotional economy 182 n.66
emotional labor 133, 138, 152, 165
emotional regulation repertoire 137
emotional turn 2, 7
Emotion as the Basis of Civilization (Denison) 7
emotions
  Egyptian 98, 131–6
  female 100
  history of 2, 7–8, 11–12
  importance of 60
  in modern Middle East 7–10
  moral 12, 14–15, 22, 96–103, 165
  production of 13, 22, 59, 165
  of revolution 164–8
  in revolution and protest 10–14
Erskine, George 124, 141–2
ethics 24, 78

facial expressions 14, 25, 30, 98, 165
faḍīl (good, virtuous) 26
al-Fajr al-Jadid 43–4, 67, 77, 81–2, 84, 103, 107–8, 110–13
fanatics 6–7, 137, 164
Fanon, Frantz 162
Farghali, Shaykh Muhammad 68
Farkhani 153–4
Faruq, King 34, 37, 39–42, 131, 152, 157–8, 161
Fawzi, Jamal 41, 166
February 4 Incident 36–40, 43, 62, 156
female emotion 100
Festinger, Leon 74
fezzed shaykh (lay activist) 53
fidā'īyīn 1–2, 117, 121, 141–2, 147, 173
First World War 3–4, 19, 42
fitna (civil war) 20, 56, 66, 195 n.53
Free Officers 5–6, 14, 35, 38, 42, 65–6, 129, 139, 152, 156–7, 161–4

French Penal Code of 1810 20
French Revolution 81–2, 128, 131
Freud, Sigmund 22–3
fuṣḥa (literary Arabic) 13
Fu'ad University (Cairo University) 32, 61–4, 97, 106, 110, 144, 146–7, 150
Fyfe, Hamilton 2, 176 n.11

Gandhi 125–7
Gessler, Albrecht 127
Gibb, H.A.R. 5
Goldilocks principle 4
Goldstone, Jack A. 5
Gordon, Joel 5–6
gossip 40–1, 152
Great Communist Plot of 1946 64
Great Depression 23
Green Shirts (paramilitary group) 49, 61
guerrilla warfare 122, 124, 128–9, 132, 140, 143–4, 147

Habbashi, Fauzi 93
Hahn, Peter 163
al-Hakim, Tawfiq 22, 24
Hall, Todd 154
hand gestures 14, 25, 30, 98
"happy Cairo" 148
Harb, Muhammad Salih 121
Hasan, Turkiyya 52
Hasan, ʿAbd al-Majid 64, 68–70
Hassafiyya Society for Charity 51
Hatata, Sharif 79, 167
hayā' 99–100
Haykal, Muṣṭafā 38, 86–7
Hazan, Yusuf 44, 79, 91
Henderson, Hamish 34, 188 n.16
ḥishma 100
Hopkins, Phil 24–5
al-Hudaybi, Hasan 145–6, 148, 153–4, 164
Humphreys, R. Stephen 55
Husayn, Ahmad 41, 47–50, 67, 123, 131, 134, 148, 153–5, 157
Husayn, Taha 24
hysteria 3, 5, 22–3, 117, 138
hysterics 1, 164

iftiqād 33, 187 n.7
iḥsās 12
Ikhwan. *See* Muslim Brotherhood (Ikhwan al-Muslimin)
al-Ikhwan al-Muslimun 64, 87, 114
Imani (My Faith) 47–8
Ioanide, Paula 170, 182 n.66
Iran 6, 41, 117, 119, 125
Iskra 43, 77, 79–81, 83, 87–9, 110, 156
Islam 51–3, 55–7, 83–7
Islamic activism 9, 50
Islamic Freedom Institute 52
Islamic modern 53
Islamic National Party 49–50
Islamic socialism 86, 161
Islamism 6, 63, 160
Ismaʿiliyya 43, 52, 62, 117, 122, 128, 132, 140–1, 146–7, 149–50
Israel, Marcel 83
istiʿāra (metaphor) 26
al-Ithnayn 22, 25, 118–21, 124, 127, 132–5, 140, 142

Jabir, Mustafa 1–2, 10, 164
jāhiliyya 174
al-Jamahir 80
Jankowski, James P. 9, 50
Jasper, James 8, 10–11, 165
Jeep Case 46, 68, 70–2, 146
jihad 56, 90, 120, 123, 125, 127, 153, 160
Joan of Arc 125, 127
Juha's Nail *(Mismār Juḥā)* 14, 125–6, 129–30

Kafr ʿAbduh 142–4
Kamal, Ahmad ʿAdil 32–3, 35, 45, 54, 57, 59, 64, 70–1, 146, 168
khajal 99–100, 104
khaṭīb (mosque preacher) 72
al-Khudari, Muhammad 33
al-Khuli, Bahi 63, 163
Kifah al-Shaʿb 82–3
Kifāḥ al-Umma 84, 111
Krämer, Gudrun 53

Labib, Fakhri 92–3
Lampson, Sir Miles 36–7
Law of July 19–22, 1791 20
Laylat al-Qadr (Night of Power/Destiny) 120
Lia, Brynjar 9
Liberation Battalions 123, 128, 135–6, 140, 143–4, 146–7, 155, 168
Liberation Rally 163–4
liberation struggle 117, 127

Mahfouz, Naguib 22, 63, 115
Majallat al-Azhar 105
Majallat al-Risala 1–2, 10, 24–6, 42, 95, 97, 128, 149
Majallat ʿIlm al-Nafs 22
majāz (metaphor) 26
al-Manara al-Misriyya 67
al-Maraghi, al-Azhar Shaykh Muhammad 39
al-Maraghi, Murtada 41
masculinity 47–8, 56, 61, 105, 134, 161
Masʿud, Muhammad 28
al-Maʿaddawi, Anwar 148–9
Maʿalim fi al-Tariq 174
metaphors 26, 28, 30, 43, 73, 96, 99, 101–3, 111–12, 155, 165, 170, 182 n.66
Middle East Defense Organization (MEDO) 161
military
  blessed movement 155–8
  failures 174
  myth 5
Ministry of Education 106, 111
al-Minshawi, Bahija 148
al-Minyawi, Muhammad Hilmi 63
Misr al-Fatah. *See* Young Egypt (Misr al-Fatah)
al-Misri 136
al-Misri, ʿAziz 36, 124
Mitchell, Richard P. 9
modern Middle East 7–11
Morack, Ellinor 175 n.6
morality *(akhlāq)* 14, 25–6, 28–30
  moral economy 19–24, 167, 182 n.66
  moral emotions 12, 14–15, 22, 96–103, 165
  moral maps 103–6
  moral Marxist 76, 81–3, 90
  moral regimes 15, 18–19, 29
  moral socialization 19, 204 n.10
  moral talk 14, 18–19, 25, 30, 112
  moral totems 114
  moral vocabulary 25, 112, 164
  tales 13–15, 48, 55, 72, 74, 96, 100, 105–13, 126, 129–31, 152, 161
moralpolitik 42–4
Mossadegh, Mohammed 6, 125, 157, 171
Mossallam, Alia 173
Mubarak, Zaki 42, 96–8, 101
al-Mudarrik, Yusuf 90
Muhammad (The Prophet) 40, 62
Muhammad, Sayyid 28
Muhammad, Shabab Sayyidna 106
Muhammad's Youth (Society of Our Master Muhammad's Youth/ Jamaʿat Shabab Sayyidna Muhammad) 9, 14, 62, 67, 75, 104–7, 114, 152, 170
Muharram 120
Muhyi al-Din, Khalid 37, 42, 65–6, 156, 194 n.38
munḥarif 26
Munshaf, Bakhur Minahim 93
Al-Muqawama al-Shaʿbiyya 153, 202 n.33
al-Musawwar 39, 118, 120, 123–4, 128, 133, 135, 210 n.5, 144, 146, 168
Muslim Brotherhood (*Ikhwan al-Muslimin*) 5–6, 9, 14, 32–3, 35–6, 38, 43, 45–7, 49–60, 62–4, 67–75
  affective and moral world 53–60
  Fifth Conference 61
  role in the Canal Struggle 145
  third way doctrine 63
Muslim revolt 9
Muslim Women's Society 148
Muʾnis, Husayn 124
myths 5, 8–9, 14, 20, 37, 45, 47–8, 53, 55–6, 71–4, 76, 81–2, 127–9, 168–70

al-Nadhir 53, 62
Naguib, Muhammad 5, 35, 37, 158, 163
al-Nahhas, Mustafa 20, 37–40, 62, 117, 119, 121–2, 124, 128, 148, 152, 154
Nahum, David 76
Naḥwa al-Nūr 195 n.56
al-Najjar, Husayn Muhammad 40
Nasser's Blessed Movement (Gordon) 5
National Party (1907) 2
naẓāfa 61
Nightingale, Florence 2
1923 Constitution 20
1948 Palestine War 50, 67–8, 72, 81, 91
1919 Revolution 3, 19–20, 37, 43, 47, 90, 120, 122, 127–8, 132, 135
1951 Revolution 5–6, 15, 74, 96, 117–20, 122, 126, 128–31, 137–8, 140, 155, 159–60, 167
1952 Revolution 5–6, 161
al-Nuqrashi, Mahmud 63–4, 67–70

Operation Eagle 15, 149–50
Operation Flatten 142–3
Ottomans 11, 55

People's Liberation 77, 81, 83, 85
Pharaonism 47, 54
Pollard, Lisa 42–3, 190 n.52
Port Sa'id 122, 127, 134, 140, 147, 172–3
The Progress of Nations (1861) 2
prosody 13, 165
pundits 4–5, 29, 155, 161, 164

Qasr al-Nil barracks 33, 64, 119
Qumayhah, Jabir 53–4, 57, 166
Qur'an 8, 51, 53–6, 79–80, 92, 102
Qutb, Sayyid 14, 22, 28, 37–8, 59, 63, 73, 101–2, 104, 115, 118, 136, 149, 154, 162–3, 165, 174, 217 n.37

Rabitat al-Shabab 66
Radwan, Fathi 47, 131
al-Rahmi, Khalil 128
Red Dinshaway 128–30
Reddy, William M. 11
religious neutrality 85
Revere, Paul 14, 124, 129
revolutionary hubs 19
Reynolds, Nancy, Y. 139
Ricoeur, Paul 26
al-Rifa'i, Sulayman 80
Rif'at, Mustafa 150
al-Risala. See Majallat al-Risala
Robertson, Brian 124, 143
Rommel, Erwin 1
Roosevelt, Kermit 157
Rose, Jacqueline 169
Rosenwein, Barbara H. 11
Rossano, Diane 31, 33, 35, 75, 79, 90
rumors 41, 87, 131
Russell, Thomas 3
Ruz al-Yusuf 136

Šabasevičiute, Giedre 115
al-Sadat, Muhammad Anwar 38, 58–9, 156
Salah, 'Ali Mutawalli 129–30
ṣāliḥ (pious, righteous) 25
Sarukhan, Alexander 122
Sayyid, Ahmad Lutfi 21
al-Sayyid, 'Afaf Lutfi 114
al-Sa'dawi, Nawal 80, 110, 147
Sa'dist Party 18, 63, 67–8, 123, 136
Sa'id, Rif'at 38, 58
Sa'id, 'Abd al-Mughni 83, 86
School for Mothers of the Believers 52
Schwartz, Hillel 90
Second Battle of Isma'iliyya 141
Second World War 1, 4, 14, 32–3, 35, 43, 49, 62
Shabab Sayyidna Muhammad 10, 106, 170, 206 n.33
shahīd 90
Shakir, Thuraya 79–80, 88
Shalabi, 'Ali 49
sharīf (honorable) 26
Shaybub, Siddiq 23
Shaykh in a Dance Club 99–100, 104, 111
Shaykh Rasputin 60–7
shu'ūr 12
Sidarus, Geneviève 87–8
Sidqi, Isma'il 64, 84, 102–3
Siraj al-Din Pasha, Fu'ad 140, 149–50, 152, 154
Sirri, Husayn 41, 157
slogans 42, 45, 93, 122, 142, 165
Social Justice in Islam 63
social movements 8, 11–13
  stories and 168–71
Society for Morality and Ethics (Jama'at al-Akhlaq al-Adabiyya) 51
Society for the Prevention of the Forbidden (Jama'at Mana' al-Muharramat) 51
sociospiritual services 59
Soviet Union 4
Special Section *(Niẓām al-Khāṣṣ)* 62, 64, 66, 69, 146, 154
Stadlbauer, Susanne 13, 164
Stambouli, Raymond 91–2
Stevenson, Ralph 139
storytelling 9, 13–15, 124, 131
Suez Canal 2, 4–6, 14, 52, 64, 117–19, 121–4, 126, 128–9, 132–7, 140–2, 146–9, 163, 168, 171–4
Suez Crisis 171–4
Suez Emergency 5–6, 117
Suez Massacre 140–7
al-Sukkari, Ahmad 51–2, 61, 66

al-Tantawi, Shaykh ʿAli 95–6
al-Tatawwur 86, 165
Tell, William 127
third-worldism/third-way doctrines 6, 163
three-legged stool approach 36–7
Tulaymat, Zaki 128
23 July Revolution (1952 Revolution). *See* 1952 Revolution

ʿUbayd, Makram 38, 43, 132, 192 n.23
Union of Peace Partisans 75
the United States 125, 128–9, 157, 171
ʿUrabi Revolution of 1879 127
ʿUthman, Taha Saʿd 57–8, 66, 86

vocalizations 25, 165
Vongsathorn, Kathleen 11

Wafd Party 18–20, 37–8, 45–6, 49–50, 62
Walzer, Michael 160
Wilaya, Muhammad 1–2, 10, 164–5, 168
Wilson, Woodrow 3
Wings of Wax 108–10
Winkelried, Arnold von 127
Wintle, Claire 7
The Workers' Vanguard (Taliʿat al-ʿUmmal) 9, 14, 44, 76–7, 82–3, 85, 87, 89–90, 92, 96, 102, 107, 110, 112, 164, 166
The Worst of Enemies (article) 96–7

Yassin, Hilmi 87, 89
Yassin, Ismaʿil 40
Young Egypt (Misr al-Fatah) 5, 9, 14, 36, 38, 41, 45–51, 54–5, 61–3, 67, 72, 74–5, 90, 96, 104, 117, 123, 131, 136, 141, 147, 153–6, 158, 161, 165, 167, 173
Young Men's Muslim Association (YMMA) 52–3, 87, 121, 123
Yusuf, Abu Sayf 93
Yusuf, Husayn 62

Zaki, Salim 63–4, 68
zakiy (pure, blameless) 26
Zayd, Mahmud Abu 62
al-Zayyat, Ahmad Hasan 42, 103
al-Zayyat, Latifa 38, 78, 89

www.ingramcontent.com/pod-product-compliance
Lightning Source LLC
Chambersburg PA
CBHW071820300426
44116CB00009B/1381
9781350383791